Gilles Deleuze and Metaphysics

Gilles Deleuze and Metaphysics

Edited by
Alain Beaulieu, Edward Kazarian,
and Julia Sushytska

LEXINGTON BOOKS
Lanham • Boulder • New York • London

Published by Lexington Books
An imprint of The Rowman & Littlefield Publishing Group, Inc.
4501 Forbes Boulevard, Suite 200, Lanham, Maryland 20706
www.rowman.com

Unit A, Whitacre Mews, 26-34 Stannery Street, London SE11 4AB

British Library Cataloguing in Publication Information Available

Library of Congress Cataloging-in-Publication Data
Gilles Deleuze and metaphysics / edited by Alain Beaulieu, Edward Kazarian, and Julia
Sushytska.
    pages cm
  Includes index.
  ISBN 978-0-7391-7475-3 (cloth : alk. paper) -- ISBN 978-0-7391-7476-0 (electronic)
1. Deleuze, Gilles, 1925-1995. 2. Metaphysics. I. Beaulieu, Alain, 1940- editor.
  B2430.D454G535 2014
  110--dc23
                        2014037493
ISBN 978-1-4985-0867-4 (pbk : alk. paper)

Printed in the United States of America

Contents

The Problem of an Immanent Metaphysics

Arnaud Villani

There is undoubtedly something twisted in the classical history of philosophy. Indeed, subject to the request, which I gladly accepted, to write a preface for a collection of texts about Deleuze and his immanent metaphysics, my immediate reflex as professional philosopher was to try to justify this last form of metaphysics, as if it were some fantastic figure in the contemporary landscape. On reflection, what I mean to show is entirely the opposite, that *transcendent* metaphysics, far from being a pleonasm, constitutes a monstrous requirement that is primarily in need of justification.

We can feel this in the 1981 interview where Deleuze, on draft paper and with a green ballpoint pen, answers my question about the "end of metaphysics" and its "overcoming" in a few words: "I feel I am a pure metaphysician."[1] This could be understood as: "I feel that I belong to a line of thinkers that has, with Nietzsche and Whitehead, its great texts and titles. No need to argue, there is metaphysics. The 'end of metaphysics' only signifies 'the end of the metaphysics that believes itself to be or pretends to be transcendent.' But in reality, there has never been any other kind of metaphysics than an immanent metaphysics."

So if the burden of proof is to be inverted, what title could transcendent metaphysics produce to certify and grant it, if not a completely contingent facticity of "turning" in history—the strategies and benefits of which need to be analyzed—then at least a simple right to exist? Indeed, one can think that what comes "after the books on physics" and, oddly enough, after the "First Philosophy" that implied no "beyond," takes the name *metaphysics*; it is symptomatic of what happened, namely an extension of Pythagorism that nevertheless modifies its essence. Indeed, the acroamatic teaching of Pythagoras, even though it was grounded on Number, did not intend to eliminate the sensible, but rather, in the manner of all the Pre-Socratics, to deliver its Rule or Principle. The sovereign abstraction that Plato believed he saw there transfers the "world to be put in order" to an abstract world composed of what escapes the sensible and time! As if a mathematical abstraction, even a "spermatic" one, could replace the living-concrete real! As if the real world becomes mute in an outgrowth of the Rule! One finds there, as Nietzsche would say, a "knack," a sleight of hand. Eternal and unchanging as a mathematical symbol, the Idea takes the place of the real that it was supposed to put in order. But this science of the Idea never concerns the world; it is not a position regarding the world, but the world's denial.

Conversely, to feel like a pure metaphysician, to want at any price a metaphysics for our time and for all times, is to search in a more appropriate way for the principle that would allow the world to endure in its composition of the multiple and to remain immanent instead of being submitted to the edict of inexistence. Metaphysics is linked to the immanence of a world that continues to exist despite the forces that are pulling it in opposite directions and tending to make it explode (*polyplangtôn*, says Parmenides, fragment XVI). Since the first Greek thinkers, the principle that allows the world to persist within immanence—whether it is a matter, after the Elements that are too elementary, of Number, Logos, Being, Love/Hate, or *Noûs*—is a balanced principle of organization, and never a principle of choice between the elements of the world, never a principle of exclusive judgment in the name of the Best that would permit, in all innocence, the rejection or crossing out of the real. Let us suppose, moreover, that we did not have in Plato the arguments in the *Phaedo* (67) against the body, or in the *Republic* on the exact line of exclusions desirable for trimming the fat from the City. The Ideas would then be the control points of the sensible, and not fortresses which supervise its exile or extermination. The Idea would be like a sketch, a model for improving the sensible: the prelude to an algebra of the sensible. Metaphysics would once again take up with a heuristic of the treasures of the sensible, with their ideal combinatory.

Plato was preoccupied by presence in person: one can feel it in his defense of orality against writing. In fact, this is a crucial point. What is important is not the emergence of the individual, for which Hegel was hoping and which Plato would hinder. What is important is the *irreplaceability* of beings. The member of a traditional community is not an individual, and yet he is irreplaceable. He can be neither displaced nor replaced, because he has a place assigned in society and in the nature-universe. He is absolutely resistant to abstraction. Now, what is an idea or a theory if not what can constantly be displaced?

One could draw upon an etymology of the word "immanent": "what remains within, remains there, holds on firmly to its location." This comes closer to the animal which is unable to leave the unity that its body forms with what models it and is modeled on it (*Umwelt*). The transcendent, in a general sense, is what detaches and unbinds itself (see the importance of the chain for Parmenides), as the supposed soul does in relation to the body. The gesture of transcendence, in its simplest and most foundational meaning, is the tearing-away, the annulment, so comparable to the conceptual, of adhesion to concrete situations. The "primitive" is in its place, it has the sense of the "earth," because it is held in the diverse and confrontational concreteness of narrative, of dances and songs, of the clan, of the community, of nature, of the universe, of the Forces present everywhere and of the dead. How can one live the concreteness of situations (by definition a situation is always concrete) if one is displaceable and replaceable? The respect for concreteness—which needs to be substituted (in terms of philosophical importance) for finitude—consists in remaining tied to a body, to a port, to the dead. Ulysses comes back to Ithaca. Being is the opposite of floating, in empty liberty, nowhere.

There are thus two reasons to assert that metaphysics is immanent: respect for the real understood as "this world," and respect for the chance to enjoy a place and an irreplaceable. Conversely, we see that the transcendent respects neither this world nor irreplaceability.

If one asks, with good reason, whether this concept of place is not too essentialist to suit Deleuze's philosophy, one would have to answer without hesitation, in short, that the "place" of each difference is simultaneously constitutive of the fold and submitted to a thousand cuttings and buildings-up of waves that re-determine it while making it travel. In this way, these places, by creating a block while remaining nomadic, differ radically from any *assigned location*. In other words, they are relational and correspond to what Kant speaks of as the difference between *Grenz*, the boundary, and *Schranke*, the limit.

But this world and irreplaceability carry difference along with them. This world is only well-balanced dosage of differences, and irreplaceability is the uniqueness of what has no equivalent and cannot be reproduced. Strangely enough, with the Myth of Thoth and the eviction of the imitators, we could say that Plato shares this conviction, except that number is a concept and the Idea is also a concept generalized to its higher level. Nothing distinguishes the concept from the Idea except height. A concept is only a resemblance, reality is only difference, "what cannot divide itself without changing its nature." Immanent metaphysics is suitable to irreplaceability and to difference. And the living cannot escape, not even for a second, the situation that is a *situs*. Hence the necessity of a topology of metaphysics, reproducing the a-topical and anomalous character of situations. The earth, the here or there, the universal *situs* could then constitute a *physis*, could be the other name of different and irreplaceable occurrences, the "always new." This is what immanence is all about, the courage to endure in its place and in its role and its task. Stoicism, with its universal breath, its corporeality, its tactility.

The non-transcendence, the irreplaceability, the difference, the situations, the enduring courage of finitude culminate in an "everything connects with everything, elsewhere just as here" of reciprocal fittings. Leibniz, in Deleuze, is the logic of Deleuzianism. The discovery of the infinite rhizome. Language as order-word is a mere translation of the concept that tears away, de-localizes, and maintains in the abstract. Leibniz is the good fortune of a mathematician who wards off abstraction and reshapes it towards life. Parmenides was already referring to the unity of what is, of the *synechès,* the *synechesthai*, the *desmoi* and *peirata*, the *sunistamenon*, of all these ways of making one on the unassailable basis of the multiple.

But if all these characters obviously correspond to an immanence, can we say that they also correspond to a metaphysics? Metaphysics is above all a First

Philosophy, the highest science, that of principles and first causes. Yet we see that one mistake about metaphysics makes the world literally un-livable. Because differences are not considered for what they are, genetic differences, as functions of a myriad of other differences with which their agreement lets a form appear, but in order "to make difference," to appear differently than any other, to accumulate, to be eminent and to dominate, "to make a name for oneself." While difference is there to nestle and fit itself into the tight network of differences, to "find its place," metaphysics, understood as a system of Ideas, "places itself," "takes place," "removes" the other and takes its place. Into the place where, following an ancestral thought, a cosmic ethics was presenting itself, there comes a daughter of war who puts everything into an order of victors and vanquished. And yet, how could one not see that *rhizomatic metaphysics*, as metaphysics is recast in the Deleuzian interpretation of immanence, gave an account of all the characters needed to make a world: topology, anti-eminence, the unceasing bifurcation of difference, the irreplaceability of the always new, courage in remaining in one's place, like Socrates at Potidaea. Like anyone, in his debate with death, like grass, un-dislodgeable under our arrogant feet.

Translated by Alain Beaulieu, Edward Kazarian, and Julia Sushytska

Note

1. See Gilles Deleuze, 'Responses to a Series of Questions,' interview by Arnaud Villani, *Collapse III*, edited by R. Mackay (Falmouth: Urbanomic, 2007), 39–43. The response Villani cites appears on page 42 [Translators' Note].

Gilles Deleuze and Metaphysics?

Alain Beaulieu, Edward Kazarian, and Julia Sushytska

Why Ask Whether Deleuze is a Metaphysician?

Why raise the question of Deleuze's relationship to metaphysics? The twentieth century opened new directions for and even dimensions of thinking, but simultaneously it cast some of the most well-established philosophical discourses and ways of inquiry into doubt—at times extreme doubt. Philosophy was challenged on what was considered for millennia its highest calling, its innermost task: "the theory of first principles [*archē*] and reasons [*aitia*],"[1] the science that is "the most appropriate kind for god to have."[2] This search for answers to the most basic "Why?" came to be known as metaphysics, literally "beyond the things of *phusis*." Such a name was originally meant to indicate the order in which Aristotle's works were arranged by his commentators: this particular treatise, or, what is much more likely, a compilation of student notes, came after the one on nature or *phusis*, hence "beyond the things of *phusis*." Aristotle considered metaphysical inquiry to be after what is most intelligible, and perhaps for just this reason the twentieth century pronounced this quest undesirable and even impossible. The claim to intelligibility of the world is suspect in a culture that used and continues to use reason to justify the irrationality of its prejudices and acts of violence.

The science of the first principles and reasons is more excellent than any other, although all others are more necessary, Aristotle famously claimed.[3] The book in which he wrote this, although far from being as intelligible as its subject of inquiry, set the tone for centuries to come for those who wished to pursue such thinking. In 1940, R. G. Collingwood wrote, "A great deal of work has been done in metaphysics since Aristotle created it; but this work has never involved a radical reconsideration of the question of what metaphysics is."[4] From our vantage point, we can see that such a radical critique of this most excellent science is precisely what the past century undertook, frequently not leaving a

1

stone unturned in the effort to expose the many delusions and shortcomings of
the "first philosophy."

Does the critical work accomplished by many of our renowned contemporaries in fact prove that metaphysical questions and the attempts to answer them
are a result of confusion, perhaps even linguistic confusion, as some of Ludwig
Wittgenstein's remarks seem to suggest? Is metaphysical inquiry a result of
breaking the rules of thinking, of trespassing into illegitimate territory, or into
the realm of nonsense? Can we have truth or even truths in the age that became
aware and weary of dogmatism, intolerance and oppression? Can we hope to
attain any positive knowledge of ourselves and those who are not like us?

A lot is at stake in determining answers to these questions, for they will
enable us to better articulate our position on many concrete social, political and
cultural issues, as well as reimagine and reconfigure the world in which we live.

Raising the problem of Deleuze's relationship to metaphysics can help us to
do just that. There are several reasons why this is the case.

Deleuze's voice is one of the strongest and most original voices of the twentieth century. So if we clarify where Deleuze stands on the question of metaphysics, we will be able to better understand philosophy's fate. If, for instance,
we determine that Deleuze is a metaphysician, and a successful one at that, since
his work gives us access to positive knowledge about the world—to use
Deleuze's own terminology, if he creates, and not only criticizes—then, indeed,
the first philosophy cannot be bankrupt, even if it in no way resembles what
Aristotle once imagined.

More importantly, however, raising the question of Deleuze's relationship
with metaphysics allows us to reveal the problematic nature of so-called post-
modernism and the critique it leveled at the first philosophy. This does not, of
course, entail that postmodern criticism is empty. To render something problematic, as Deleuze himself so well understood, is to allow the criticisms to be critically assessed, and thus to give them new life, as well as to open entirely new
possibilities for thought. To formulate a problem is to allow our thinking move
forward—toward new depths and surfaces.

By acknowledging that it is not self-evident that Deleuze is a "post-
metaphysical thinker," we open up a new trajectory for thinking. And even if we
are not able to determine once and for all in what sense Deleuze was a metaphysician, or agree on whether he was one to begin with, we will enrich our understanding through questioning what has not been sufficiently questioned. It is
possible that in the course of this inquiry we will even reconfigure and redirect
the current philosophical debates.

Deleuze famously struggled to unsettle our habits of thinking—these
crutches that, instead of helping us walk, foreclose the possibility for new kinds
of movement. This inquiry, therefore, is very much Deleuzian in spirit.

On a more "local" level, understanding in what sense Deleuze was or was
not a metaphysician would allow us to acknowledge a dimension of his thinking
that so far has not received much attention in the scholarly literature, yielding a
rather one-sided picture of his thought.

Yet another reason why Deleuze might be one of the best candidates for raising the question of metaphysics is that his involvement with first philosophy is so ambiguous. In his book *Deleuze: The Clamor of Being*, Alain Badiou makes a rather striking claim that both he and Deleuze never had much patience with the idea of the end of philosophy as metaphysics—both were, he says, "actively indifferent" to the "omnipresent theme of 'the end of philosophy.'"[5] Badiou's assertion is striking because Deleuze himself repeatedly suggests that his work is aimed at overturning what is often understood to be the core of traditional metaphysics: for instance, insofar as it reverses or brings about the destruction of Platonism.[6] Furthermore, discussing Alfred Jarry's notion of pataphysics, or the kind of thinking that extends "as far beyond metaphysics, as the latter extends beyond physics," Deleuze points out: "Metaphysics is and must be surpassed. In so far as its fate is conceived as metaphysics, philosophy makes room and must make room for other forms of thought, other forms of thinking."[7] In this context Deleuze even suggests "the death of philosophy properly speaking."[8]

Still, occasionally Deleuze asserts something that immediately sets him apart from his contemporaries and compatriots such as Michel Foucault, Philippe Lacoue-Labarthe, Jean-Luc Nancy, Jacques Derrida, and Jean-François Lyotard. Consider the statement that will resound time and again throughout this volume: "I feel like a pure metaphysician."[9]

Immersing ourselves into the tensions and folds of his work, we hope to not only address a question that so far has not been systematically raised in Deleuze scholarship, but also confront one of the major questions of our century.

Deleuze and Metaphysics in Europe

The panorama of contemporary thought is dominated by a desire to reverse, destroy, go beyond or deconstruct Western metaphysics, but it would be a mistake to consider that Deleuze is alone trying to keep metaphysics alive. Bergson[10] and Whitehead,[11] two major sources of inspiration for Deleuze, both remain faithful to the metaphysical tradition. Husserl also presents his phenomenology as a critical continuation of the metaphysical tradition: "phenomenology indeed *excludes every naïve metaphysics* that operates with absurd things in themselves, but *does not exclude metaphysics as such.*"[12] To be a metaphysician, according to Husserl, is to propose through phenomenological inquiry new answers to the old questions that animate the tradition (Who am I?, What can I know?, What is real?, What is the truth?, etc.). A similar view can be found in Heidegger, whose existential analysis presented in *Being and Time* remains a metaphysical task: *Dasein*'s capacity to take its distance from the ontical, and the destruction of the history of ontology are metaphysical endeavors.[13] The project of "overcoming metaphysics," for instance the rejection of metaphysics as onto-theology, comes at a later point in Heidegger's itinerary. For both Husserl and the early

Heidegger, it is not a matter of developing a post-metaphysical thinking, but of criticizing the dogmatic metaphysics, of reforming and replacing it with a new way of studying the relationship between the "two worlds": the physical world and its noetic-noematic correlates for Husserl, the ontical and the ontological worlds for Heidegger.

However, Deleuze considers phenomenology as another attempt to escape "this world," an undertaking that reintroduces transcendences within immanence. For Deleuze (and Guattari) the "plane of immanence" has to be immanent only to itself and cannot be something transcendent or ideal.[14]

Deleuze dedicated more time—even though he is still too succinct on this point—to explicating his position on the phenomenological reforms of metaphysics than on presenting his take on the so-called anti- or post-metaphysical thinking to which Heidegger's project of "overcoming metaphysics" or Derrida's "deconstruction of metaphysics" belong. It is a pity because their views are not radically distinct from Deleuze's: at the very least they all share a common critique of several basic features of modern philosophy (critiques of representation, reason, identity, consciousness, etc.), although it is true that the intellectualist views of Heidegger and Derrida are not compatible with Deleuze's vitalism. They could probably be considered, from a Deleuzian standpoint, as "assassins of philosophy," to borrow an expression used in the *Abécédaire* (letter W for "Wittgenstein"), or the ones who no longer believe in the concrete effectiveness of concepts. Deleuze's silence toward anti- or post-metaphysical thinking already indicates his characteristic way of doing philosophy: he avoids as much as possible speaking against the ones he dislikes, or criticizing without creating, as he puts it in *What Is Philosophy?*. Perhaps more importantly, several other crucial questions are left unanswered by Deleuze in relation to metaphysics: How can a plane of immanence be a metaphysical reality? How can one feel like a "pure metaphysician" while leaving no place for transcendences which were, after all, the core components of the traditional metaphysics? Spinoza and Nietzsche give us the tools to answer these questions, the two thinkers who form, as Deleuze states majestically, the "great Spinoza-Nietzsche equation"[15] (*la grande identité Spinoza-Nietzsche*), and perhaps even a "purely metaphysical equation" as one might say. For both Spinoza and Nietzsche, there is no supra level of reality that would be external and ontologically superior, there is no "real world" or "world beyond this one." One particularity of an immanent metaphysics is that it brings traditional distinctions together at the same axiological level of reality. Spinoza's parallelism between the mind and the body, Nietzsche's problematization of moral progress, and Deleuze's disjunctive synthesis between the virtual and the real are good examples of this feature of an immanent metaphysics. One other point that these thinkers have in common is that their conceptions of the body are always means of resistance strategically oriented toward a critique of dogmatic metaphysics.[16]

An immanent metaphysics is a system of thinking that de-hierarchizes the two "worlds" that characterized dogmatic metaphysics. Distinctions without hierarchies: that is one of immanence's secrets. Thinkers of the immanence are assuming the existence and interaction of entities with different natures that are delegated by dogmatic metaphysicians to hierarchized worlds. Deleuze called these dimensions of reality "states-of-affairs" and "chaosmic forces." This distinction between the "states-of-affairs" and "chaosmic forces" corresponds to a metaphysical division that is experienced and studied by Deleuze, but it does not lead to any metaphysical superiority or eminence of one entity over the other, since each is necessary and complete in itself. In other words, the value of one is not greater than the value of the other, and this is what Deleuzean metaphysical plane of immanence entails, as best as it can, knowing that perfection is itself a transcendence and that it is almost impossible not to have some illusions (transcendences, universals, eternity) holing the plane of immanence and weakening it for a variable period of time.

Reading, commenting, and loving Deleuze imply experiencing two interconnected sides of one reality: sensible states-of-affairs (whether figural arts, bodies without organs, moving/time-images, etc., as well as other states-of-affairs unexplored by Deleuze that can be experienced in a Deleuzian way), and impersonal forces that are a part of inorganic life, and that affect state-of-affairs. One cannot appreciate Deleuze without navigating this metaphysical landscape, even if the vast majority of the commentators do not take metaphysics as an entry point to Deleuze's philosophy. Similar to Molière's Mr. Jourdain who learned that he has been speaking "prose" all his life without knowing it, it is easy with Deleuze to do metaphysics without being aware of it. In fact, it is not even required of someone who intends to grasp and appreciate his work. The relative lack of concern in the secondary literature for Deleuze's metaphysics can be explained by the scarcity of Deleuze's own remarks on this subject, especially compared to what Carnap, Heidegger, or Derrida wrote about metaphysics. A goal of the present volume is to rectify the situation, making a contribution to the study of Deleuze's metaphysics.

Among the few who commented on Deleuze's relationship to metaphysics in the French world are Arnaud Villani and Alain Badiou.

Villani—a philosopher, poet, Hellenist, and translator (of Parmenides and Whitehead, among others)—honored us with the foreword to this volume. He was not a student of Deleuze, but, as he told us, the power of Deleuze's books led him to work intensively on his philosophy, including the metaphysical aspects of Deleuze's thinking.[17] Villani also had an enduring correspondence with Deleuze. In an exchange from November 1981, Deleuze restated his attachment to metaphysics. To the question: "Are you a non-metaphysical philosopher?," Deleuze answered simply and clearly: "No, I feel I am a pure metaphysician."[18] Villani stresses the importance of metaphysics for Deleuze's: "We must not take lightly Deleuze's affirmation of metaphysics. It concerns his whole philosophy."[19] For Villani, it is impossible to get anything from Deleuze's conceptions of sensibility, arts, nature, ethics, micropolitics, etc. without referring to his immanent metaphysics. It links everything together while reminding of an old, classical way of experiencing concrete life. This is a way exceedingly respectful of certain forgotten aspects of the Greek thought (especially of some of the

Presocratics) such as the inseparable character of intelligence and sensibility understood not only from an anthropological perspective, but that also finds a c(ha)osmological resonance. It might be that Villani "mediterranianised" Deleuze too much, but there can be no doubt that this refreshing metaphysical reading suggests an original, perhaps essential, point of entry in Deleuze's thinking.

The case of Alain Badiou is quite different, since he is a former colleague of Deleuze at *Université de Paris 8* and a well-known philosopher whose relationship with Deleuze evolved over the decades: in the 1970s he sent his Maoïst troops to disrupt Deleuze's classes, and in the 1990s dedicated some of his own seminars to a philosopher that he came to respect and admire despite some significant "ontological differences." Badiou's provocative book on Deleuze[20] truly polarized its readership. It created a shock wave among Deleuze scholars, some thanking Badiou for the clarity of the views expressed regarding the "true" Deleuze presented as "an ontologist of the One," while others denounced this reduction sometimes in a very virulent way by expressing their opposition to what they saw as nothing more than a polemical book of no use to those wishing to grasp Deleuze's concept of multiplicity and his vitalist philosophy.[21] Regarding the issue of metaphysics, Badiou is quite clear in the first chapter entitled "Which Deleuze?" about his view of Deleuze's "contribution to the ruin of metaphysics" described as an "overturning of Platonism" that promotes a "post-metaphysical" thinking. It is of course possible that a philosopher who is a self-proclaimed "pure metaphysician" would actually be "ruining metaphysics" instead. After all, Christopher Columbus believed himself to have achieved the passage to India while he was still on Hispaniola. . . . It might also be the case that Badiou simply does not have the necessary tools to grasp Deleuze's singular quest for an "immanent metaphysics of difference." This is what Deleuze (with Guattari) seems to suggest when he considers that Badiou's "event site" might "reintroduce the transcendent."[22]

Both Deleuze and Badiou explicitly declared themselves to be indifferent to the end of metaphysics, while trying to recreate a metaphysical tradition. "The death of metaphysics or the overcoming of philosophy has never been a problem for us," writes Deleuze (with Guattari), "[. . .] so long as there is a time and place for creating concepts, the operation that undertakes this will always be called philosophy."[23] In the *Logics of Worlds*, Badiou similarly asserts that he seeks, like Deleuze for that matter,[24] "to create the conditions for a contemporary metaphysics" and he admits practicing a "metaphysical mathematics."[25] Yet, Badiou considers Deleuze an anti-metaphysician who is joyfully experimenting with intensities without any "real" metaphysical conviction,[26] whereas Deleuze sees Badiou as a dogmatic metaphysician of a new kind fed by the illusion of transcendence. What is it to be a real non-dogmatic metaphysician? What kind of metaphysics is needed for today? Deleuze and Badiou offer distinct answers to these questions: for Deleuze a non-dogmatic metaphysician creates concepts while maintaining his distance as best as he can from all types of transcendences, whereas for Badiou a non-dogmatic metaphysician can still remain faithful to a specific type of transcendences, namely the universal mathematical transcendences. The intellectual relationship between Deleuze and Badiou is discussed at length in some of the chapters that follow.

Deleuze and Metaphysics in the English-Speaking World

Deleuze's entry into the Anglophone philosophical and theoretical scene has occurred in several phases: via his studies of Proust and Masoch; via his and Guattari's opposition to psychoanalysis; via his influence on Nietzsche scholarship; and only after all of this, via the appearance in English of his great works of the late 1960s—last among them the most important, *Difference and Repetition*, which was published within months of Deleuze's death.

In each of these phases before the last, Deleuze could easily be seen as a somewhat peripheral figure, one who made interesting contributions, but also somewhat puzzling and even perhaps injudicious ones—and not, on the whole, someone who called for the sort of sustained attention being given at the time to figures like Heidegger, Lacan, Foucault, and Derrida. As Elie During has noted, much of this reception was structured by the image of 'French theory,' within which Deleuze in fact sat uncomfortably, even if his work could be and was drawn upon to provide some of its key gestures with a philosophically sophisticated foundation.[27] Such an embrace, however, only went so far. "The truth is that the reception of Deleuze in America was prepared, and to a certain extent 'arranged' (as in 'arranged marriage'), by a very simple, yet very efficient machine. Its function is to sort out the available sources in order to produce the Deleuze that America is willing to use, a figure that is both user-friendly and sophisticated enough to retain its appeal."[28] Nor are the principles of this arrangement difficult to discern if one simply reviews sequence of translations to see which version of Deleuze was operative and connects it to the larger academic context operating at the time: *Masochism* in 1971 and *Proust and Signs* in 1972; *Anti-Oedipus* in 1977—preceded by the 'Schizo-Culture' conference organized by *Semiotext(e)* at Columbia University in November, 1975, at which Deleuze and Guattari both spoke,[29] and followed by two issues of that journal, one devoted to Deleuze and Guattari's book and the other devoted to themes arising from the conference[30]; *Nietzsche and Philosophy* in 1983; and *Dialogues* and *A Thousand Plateaus* in 1987. It is only after this that the project of translating Deleuze's corpus in a more comprehensive fashion got under way in earnest, and it was largely completed in the next decade. Looking back, this gives us the following sequence: a Deleuze for literary theorists; a politicized, anti-psychoanalytic Deleuze; a 'New Nietzschean' Deleuze[31]; and finally, Deleuze the philosopher, first presented as the author of a series of provocative monographs and finally as one who speaks in his own right.

If we linger over this history, it is in order to reinforce a point suggested above about the extent to which the project of the 'overcoming of metaphysics'—even if it were somewhat anachronistically read backward into Heidegger's early work—formed an almost unquestionable background assumption in light of which Deleuze's philosophy, as it first came to light for English-speaking audiences, would almost inevitably have been read. Indeed, this project exerted such force in the discursive and conceptual space of Anglophone 'Continental Philosophy' in the 1980s and 1990s that an affirmative approach to anything explicitly called 'metaphysics' would have been profoundly counter-intuitive. Which is not to say that some people did not recognize a 'metaphysical' dimension of Deleuze's thought. Only that such a recognition would have—and did—provoke real discomfort.[32] Not surprisingly, people avoided discussing it in print; and a survey of the literature in English on Deleuze will reveal precious few mentions of the term metaphysics prior to the appearance of Badiou's book in translation in 2000.

After that, and in the midst of all the other debates that Badiou's text provoked, our reluctance to speak of Deleuze as a metaphysician has diminished. Let us consider one or two cases in point.

By 2005, for instance, we can find Alexi Kukuljevic taking a cue from both Deleuze and Guattari's late declaration that the problem of the end of metaphysics was "idle chatter" and "Badiou's conviction that Deleuze's philosophy opposes the identification of the 'end of metaphysics' with the discovery of the transcendental" in order to argue that Deleuze's two most important philosophical strategies, constructivism and expressionism, entail not the end of metaphysics but precisely its continuation, pure thought being the only way to access the reality of the non-representational virtual transcendental field that is constructed and expressed in philosophy.[33]

Or again, in the first article in the inaugural issue of *Deleuze Studies*, Daniel W. Smith pointedly claims that "[f]or Deleuze, the conditions of the new can be found only in a principle of *difference*—or more strongly, in a *metaphysics* of difference."[34] For the most part, Smith remains happy to discuss Deleuze's ontology, and does not lay a heavy emphasis on the language of metaphysics; but in accounting for the specificity of Deleuze's problem of novelty and his claim that 'the principle of difference' constitutes the only philosophically adequate response to it, Smith offers what amounts to a sketch of the elements of that metaphysics. He begins by showing that posing the problem of novelty amounts to asking about the conditions of reality, rather than either logical or transcendental possibility. This means that philosophy will seek to account for conditions that are genetic (and future-oriented or productive of the new), non-resembling with respect to what they condition, and non-categorical (or no broader than what they condition); all of which, in turn, requires us to discover in the place of the unconditioned that determines both condition and conditioned not a totality or an identity, but a principle of difference that serves as the 'groundless ground'—an operation of grounding that proceeds statically, from virtual to actual, rather than through a dynamic, historical development between actual terms.[35] Smith then turns to the task of explaining the principle of difference that serves as the groundless ground, showing how Deleuze derives one of his methods for thinking such a principle by invoking a mathematical model—that of calculus—which supplies us with the notion of a "differential relation [that] is not only external to its terms (Bertrand Russell's empiricist dictum), but [. . .] also determines its terms."[36] This mathematical model is also shown to supply Deleuze with the material from which to deduce two more of his basic concepts, singularity (or event) and multiplicity, with which Deleuze replaces the traditional metaphysical concepts of essence and substance.[37] Smith goes on to exemplify Deleuze's use of these concepts in terms of a Leibnizian notion of unconscious perceptions, which constitute multiplicities that are "objects of Ideas in a modified Kantian sense, because even though they are not given directly in experience, they can nevertheless be *thought* as its conditions," being "as it were, the noumenon closest to the phenomenon."[38] And these virtual Ideas, like non-linear differential equations, are seen to be objectively problematic structures that can only be determined as they are actualized, that is, differentiated in ways that are not predicted or predictable by their virtual structure as such.[39]

And by this point, it should begin to be evident how Smith's article delivers on the promise of presenting Deleuze's *metaphysics* of difference, showing how, beginning from such a principle, Deleuze's thought exceeds the Kantian strictures that, to return to Kukuljevic for a moment, make any account of "the possibility of metaphysics [. . .] also a diagnosis."[40] Following mathematics and science as they have actually developed in the modern period, on the one hand, but also taking seriously philosophical criticisms of Kant's critical philosophy that began to be articulated during his lifetime by figures like Solomon Maimon, Deleuze orients philosophy toward thinking what can only be thought, a virtuality is truly noumenal, but which also follows the actual and which can only be thought as its differential condition. All of which, in turn, begins to evidently fulfill the goal that Deleuze set himself when he claimed, in his responses to Villani, that "when Bergson says that modern science as not found its metaphysics, the metaphysics it needs. It is that metaphysics that interests me."[41]

And if Anglophone scholarship on Deleuze has become more and more aware of the fundamentally metaphysical nature of Deleuze's project, that awareness has developed along two basic paths, one of which has been followed by those seeking to grasp Deleuze's relationship to science and mathematics and the other those seeking to understand his readings of historical figures in philosophy and his position in relation to the philosophical tradition more broadly.

The first of these paths has been represented perhaps most prominently by Manuel Delanda, but also by work like Keith Ansell Pearson's studies of Deleuze's relationship to the life sciences, John Protevi's attempts to grasp the range of Deleuze's engagements with the human, social and physical sciences, as well as Daniel W. Smith's and Simon Duffy's studies of Deleuze's relationship to the history of mathematics—to which Rocco Gangle's essay in the present volume also contributes.[42]

The second—which is not, in many cases, easily or cleanly separated from the first—is represented by the growing list of scholars who have recognized that, in rejecting the Kantian construction of metaphysics as a discourse about conditions of possibility and insisting instead on an account of the genesis of the real or of the new, Deleuze is both reviving important, though neglected, strands of post-Kantian thinking—especially, as Smith has long noted, that of Solomon Maimon, but also Bergson, Whitehead, and even Nietzsche—and insisting on the continued relevance after Kant of a number of earlier figures—not only Spinoza, but also Hume, Leibniz, and even Hegel.[43] And so, the careful work of unpacking Deleuze's rich and complex engagement with the history of philosophy appears to be more than simply exegesis as soon as we realize that this engagement was itself a work of recovery—"buggery," perhaps, but only if it is understood as a real form of love, or a genuine attempt to make these various bodies of thought bear fruit in the metaphysical project in which Deleuze finds himself engaged. Many of the essays in our volume will seek to advance this work.[44]

Beyond these two paths, it is also important to mention the work undertaken by Miguel de Beistegui, first in *Truth and Genesis* and more recently in *Immanence: Deleuze and Philosophy*.[45] In the first of these texts, Beistegui seeks to specify the place of a Deleuzian ontology—which he acknowledges will amount to a metaphysics, under a fundamentally new conception thereof—alongside Heidegger's ontology, even with its attendant critique of the metaphysics. On this reading, Deleuze is not wholly or even substantially at odds with Heidegger, taking as read the latter's critique of the metaphysics of presence and even his identification of the fundamental ontological project as being that of thinking the ontological difference between being and beings. But if this is so, Deleuze nevertheless inflects the ontological project in significantly different ways than Heidegger does, moving away from the poetics of human experience of being as a groundless ground and toward a scientific conception of difference serving the same function—but in a way that more radically exceeds the position of the human. Beistegui thus says that if philosophy can still be "'first' philosophy, it is no longer so as the science regarding the highest principles, the first causes, and the worthiest being: in other words, it is no longer so as onto-theology, but as ontogenesis *and* onto-epiphany."[46] He goes on to argue that these two 'sides' of the project are irreducible to one another, so that the latter, exemplified by Heidegger, cannot supplant or foreclose upon the former, which he assigns to Deleuze. In this respect, Deleuze's revival of the ontogenetic problem posed by Maimon and other post-Kantians also amounts to a departure from the anti-Naturalism that Beistegui takes to be characteristic of phenomenology generally, and which Heidegger certainly inherited from Husserl. Deleuze thus shows us how to locate the first philosophy's "ontological problematic within science itself," so that "nature could be unified under the concept of difference as designating processes of differentiation."[47] Such an ontology thus amounts to a metaphysics, a first philosophy, in a complex sense that never fully separates that thinking from the various processes of differentiation that give rise to all the beings which we seek to know and account for. If "[o]nly that which differs can be said *to be*,"[48] then metaphysics may be seen to lead us to many different forms of being, and different sciences in which the truth of being and beings happens.

In the chapters that follow, the stakes of the question of whether and how Deleuze's philosophy includes, endorses, develops, and proceeds from a metaphysics will be explored.

Chapter Summaries

In the first chapter, entitled "Leaving Metaphysics? Deleuze on the Event," Alberto Anelli recalls that one of the new and most insistent ideas of the 'postmetaphysical' thought is the category of 'event.' The event has become a recurrent theme in contemporary debates, yet it lacks clarity: there is neither consensus about its meaning nor about its theoretical origin. The event is obviously an important dimension of Deleuze's work, and the author argues that it cannot be adequately elucidated until Deleuze's relationship with metaphysics is clarified. In order to understand meaning and consequences of any theory of the event, one has to refer to Heidegger. After a discussion of Deleuze's conception of the event, through a careful reading of *Différence et répétition* and *Logique du sens*, Anelli compares it with Heidegger's *Ereignis* in order to answer the question of whether, and to what extent, Deleuze can be called a metaphysician.

In "Mathematics, Structure, Metaphysics: Deleuze and Category Theory," Rocco Gangle interrogates the possibilities which exist for modeling or expressing Deleuze's metaphysics of the virtual mathematically. He begins by noting that Deleuze's metaphysics of the virtual and his complex relation to structuralism pose a unique set of problems for any attempt to model his philosophy mathematically. Nonetheless, it is clear that mathematics plays an important role throughout Deleuze's work. Gangle's essay proposes that the mathematics of category theory—an important alternative to set theory in contemporary mathematical foundations—offers an adequate model of Deleuze's metaphysics insofar as the problem of the relation between formal models and real instantiations may itself be modeled within category theory itself. The influence of Lautman's dialectical conception of mathematics on Deleuze is emphasized in this regard.

Sjoerd van Tuinen's chapter, "Difference and Speculation: Heidegger, Meillassoux, and Deleuze on Sufficient Reason," uses Heidegger's reading of Leibniz's principle of sufficient reason as point of departure into a discussion on the end of metaphysics. Heidegger follows a path of thinking that takes us out of the Greek metaphysics and hence beyond Leibniz's principle of reason. In *Difference and Repetition* and *The Fold*, Deleuze shares many of Heidegger's intuitions as to Leibniz's use of the principle of sufficient reason and his concept of the ground as a folding movement. The author shows that Deleuze's reading of Leibniz, mediated by Nietzsche, takes its distance from Heidegger as it opens up the possibility for the plane of immanence to be populated by becomings instead of beings, and to relate it with Leibniz's metaphysical principles of reason (*Vernunft, raison*) and ground (*Grund, fond/fondement*).

In "The Physics of Sense: Bruno, Schelling, Deleuze," Joshua Ramey and Daniel Whistler contend that Deleuze's work exists in a 'minor' tradition of philosophy, alongside Giordano Bruno and F. W. J. Schelling, that entwines metaphysics with rhetoric and affect. Philosophy in this tradition is cast as a pragmatic art of choosing the most effective and affective means of concept-construction. The authors demonstrate these claims by situating Deleuze's assertion "I am a pure metaphysican" in a genealogy of metaphysical pragmatism leading from Bruno and through Schelling. At stake in all three thinkers' work, they argue, is metaphilosophical reflection on the specific deployments of sense necessary to make philosophy happen.

In her chapter "Obscure Metaphysics of Gilles Deleuze" Julia Sushytska argues that if metaphysics is an act of thinking being, as opposed to an articulated theory about beings or Being, then Deleuze is, indeed, a metaphysician. The vital place that the notion of univocity occupies in Deleuze's writings confirms the fact that Deleuze is engaged in thinking being. Deleuze, however, is an obscure metaphysician—his thinking takes the form of paradox, and thereby defies or postpones dogmatization of thought, as well as draws the reader into its movement. The key example is Deleuze's notion of univocity: univocity is difference, he claims. To understand this 'distinct yet obscure' thought we need to return to one of his early works, *Bergsonism*, where Deleuze insists on the existence of the difference in kind that is not *ontological* difference. Deleuze's obscurity inevitably opens him to misinterpretations, including a widespread opinion that he is an anti-metaphysician.

In "Deleuze and Badiou on Being and the Event," Alain Beaulieu presents the debate between Badiou and Deleuze as a true metaphysical duel over the status given to immanence and transcendence, to the multiple and the singularity, to the Cosmic Animal and the Number. After presenting the assessments and re-assessments of Deleuze by Badiou since the 1970s, the author discusses the incompatibility between the two thinkers regarding their conceptions of Being and the Event. One of the core questions that fuels this debate is: Is radical immanence determined by the axiomatic (Badiou) or is it conquered by vitalist experience (Deleuze)? It also infers the question: Is there one or many possible avenues to immanence? The study shows that the two thinkers provide different ways to remain faithful to metaphysics.

In his chapter "Disanalogous Being: Deleuze, Spinoza, and Univocal Metaphysics" Adrian Switzer proposes that the traditional texts of metaphysics need to be read in such a way as to allow the greatest difference to emerge. Metaphysics, he argues, is always active, and he specifies that for Deleuze this means that metaphysics is an immanent analogy of itself. Deleuze distills such a notion of analogy from the texts of Spinoza, for whom analogical thinking brings together incomparable beings. Switzer points out that in proposing such an understanding of analogy Spinoza uncovers a meaning hidden under the layers of standard interpretations of Aristotelian texts—a paradox at the heart of Aristotle's measured thinking. As in the story by Borges about the rewriting of *Don Quixote* that Switzer references at the end of his chapter, Deleuze's texts are analogous to those of Spinoza, and Spinoza's to Aristotle's—although, of course, analogous in an immanent way.

In "Crowned Anarchies, Substantial Attributes, and the Transcendental Problem of Stupidity" Gregory Kalyniuk shows that Antonin Artaud's problematization of stupidity and violence enables Deleuze and Guattari to subvert Spinoza's rationalist presuppositions about the origin of thought. The animality peculiar to thought enables thinking to adopt the attitude of 'active metaphysics.' Deleuze recognizes the full significance of Artaud's idea that metaphysical thought needs to be stimulated through most visceral experiences. The idea of active metaphysics, argues Kalyniuk, is taken up by Deleuze and developed into transcendental empiricism.

In "Revolution and the Return of Metaphysics," Thomas Nail draws parallels between the disenchantment of revolutionary politics and the metaphysical thinking's lack of truth in contemporary philosophy. However, as the author argues, Badiou and Deleuze attempt to give revolutionary politics and metaphysics a new legitimacy that remains independent from the traditional theories of representation. Despite the significant divergences between Badiou and Deleuze in view of their conceptions of politics and metaphysics, both give a fresh start in line with their conception of the event. Ultimately, the author shows that their revolutionary politics of the event is tied with their evental metaphysics. In that sense, Badiou and Deleuze value revolution and metaphysics while being philosophically committed to the non-representational reality of events.

Finally, Mary Beth Mader's chapter "Whence Intensity?: Deleuze and the Revival of a Concept" situates Deleuze's thinking within Western philosophical tradition by bringing to our attention the "obscure but genuine" sources for Deleuze's thought on intensity. The essay exposes the disruptive undercurrents within Western philosophy, thereby questioning and simultaneously transforming the standard notion of metaphysics. Mader reveals Deleuze as a veritable interlocutor of philosophical discussions that span millennia—discussions that are much more nuanced and multiplicitous than we are frequently lead to believe when labeling them as 'metaphysical.' Mader helps us realize by tracing out the early philosophical history of the concept of intensity that we need to look to Western metaphysical tradition with an eye for intensities, as opposed to simply quantifying it as either bankrupt or opulent.

Acknowledgments

We would like to thank all the authors for their dedicated work and patience as we completed the process of putting this volume together. Our thanks also go to Jana Hodges-Kluck and her team at Lexington Books for the support and direction they provided through the editing process. Finally, we would like to thank NASA for the imagery we have used on the cover.

Notes

1. Aristotle. *Metaphysics*, 982b10. Here and in what follows translation by Richard Hope (Ann Arbor: University of Michigan Press, 1960).

2. Aristotle. *Metaphysics*, 983a10, translation modified by JS.

3. Aristotle. *Metaphysics*, 983a10.

4. R. G. Collingwood. *An Essay on Metaphysics* (Oxford: Clarendon Press, 2002), 5.

5. Alain Badiou, *Deleuze: The Clamor of Being*, translated by Louise Burchill (Minneapolis: University of Minnesota Press, 1999), 5.

6. Gilles Deleuze, *Difference and Repetition*, translated by Paul Patton (New York: Columbia University Press, 1990), 66.

7. Quoted in Gilles Deleuze, "An Unrecognized Precursor to Heidegger: Alfred Jarry," in *Essays Critical and Clinical*, trans. Daniel W. Smith and Michael A. Greco (Minneapolis: University of Minnesota Press, 1997) 91. The second quotation is from Deleuze, "How Jarry's Pataphysics Opened the Way for Phenomenology" in *Desert Islands and Other Texts: 1953–1974*, ed. David Lapoujade, trans. Michael Taormina (New York: Semiotext(e), 2004), 74.

8. Gilles Deleuze, *Nietzsche and Philosophy*, trans. Hugh Tomlinson (New York: Columbia University Press, 1983), 195.

9. Gilles Deleuze, "Responses to a Series of Questions," *Collapse* III (November 2007): 42.

10. Henri Bergson, *An Introduction to Metaphysics* (Basingstoke/New York: Palgrave Macmillan, 2007).

11. Alfred North Whitehead, *Process and Reality: An Essay in Cosmology* (New York: Free Press, 1978).

12. Edmund Husserl, *Cartesian Meditations* (The Hague: Martinus Nijhoff, 1960), 156. See also *Husserliana VII: Erste Philosophie* (The Hague: Martinus Nijhoff, 1956), 188n, where phenomenology is presented as "a metaphysics with a new meaning" ("*Metaphysik in einem neuen Sinn*").

13. Martina Roesner, "Métaphysique," in *Abécédaire de Martin Heidegger*, ed. Alain Beaulieu (Paris: Vrin/Sils Maria, 2008), 139–141.

14. Gilles Deleuze and Félix Guattari, *What is Philosophy?*, trans. Hugh Tomlinson and Graham Burchell (New York: Columbia University Press, 1994), 148–150. See also Alain Beaulieu, "Edmund Husserl," in *Deleuze's Philosophical Lineage*, ed. Graham Jones and Jon Roffe (Edinburgh: Edinburgh University Press, 2009), 261–281.

15. Gilles Deleuze, *Negotiations*, trans. Margin Joughin (New York: Columbia University Press, 1995), 135.

16. It is also true of Husserl's conception of the living body (*Leib*). See Alain Beaulieu, "L'enchantement du corps chez Nietzsche et Husserl," in *Phenomenology of life: Meeting the Challenges of the Present-Day World*, ed. Anna-Teresa Tymieniecka (Dordrecht/Boston: Kluwer Academic Publishers, 2005), 339–355.

17. See for instance: Arnaud Villani, "'I feel I am a pure Metaphysician': The Consequences of Deleuze's Affirmation," *Collapse* III (November 2007): 45–62; Arnaud Villani, "Deleuze et l'anomalie métaphysique," in *Gilles Deleuze. Une vie philosophique*,

ed. Éric Alliez (Plessis-Robinson: Synthélabo, 1998), 43–53; Arnaud Villani, "Deleuze et le problème de la métaphysique," in *La Guêpe et l'orchidée* (Paris: Belin, 1999), 35–51.

18. Deleuze, "Responses to a Series of Questions," 42. The exchange originally appeared in Arnaud Villani, *La Guêpe et l'orchidée* (Paris: Belin, 1999), 129–31.

19. Villani, "'I feel I am a pure Metaphysician': The Consequences of Deleuze's Affirmation," 48.

20. Badiou, *Deleuze: The Clamor of Being*.

21. See for instance: Éric Alliez, Arnaud Villani and José Gil, "Dossier Badiou/Deleuze," *Futur antérieur* 43 (April 1998): 49–84; Clayton Crockett, *Deleuze Beyond Badiou: Ontology, Multiplicity and Event* (New York: Columbia University Press, 2013).

22. Deleuze and Guattari, *What Is Philosophy?*, 151.

23. Deleuze and Guattari, *What Is Philosophy?*, 9. See also Gilles Deleuze, *Negotiations*, translated by Martin Joughin (New York: Columbia University Press, 1995), 88: "I've never worried about going beyond metaphysics or the death of philosophy, and I never made a big thing about giving up Totality, Unity, the Subject."

24. "Bergson says that modern science has not found its metaphysics, the metaphysics it needs. It is that metaphysics that interests me" (Deleuze, "Responses to a Series of Questions," 41).

25. Alain Badiou, *Logics of Worlds: Being and Event II*, trans. Alberto Toscano (Continuum: New York, 2009), 7 and 544. See also Alain Badiou, "Metaphysics and the Critique of Metaphysics," *Pli* 10 (2000): 174–190.

26. Another critique, although more allusive, takes a different path by denouncing Deleuze's and Guattari's metaphysical convictions associated with a disembodied "metaphysics of energy." See Richard Beardsworth, "Nietzsche, Freud, and the Complexity of the Human: Towards a philosophy of failed Digestion," *Tekhnema. A Journal of Philosophy and Technology* 3 (Spring 1996): note 37.

27. See Elie During, "Blackboxing in Theory: Deleuze versus Deleuze," in *French Theory in America*, ed. Sylvère Lotringer and Sande Cohen (New York: Routledge, 2001), 163–189.

28. During, "Blackboxing in Theory," 167–168.

29. See Sylvère Lotringer and Sande Cohen, 'Introduction: A Few Theses on French Theory in America," in Lotringer and Cohen, *French Theory in America*, 1–9.

30. See *Semiotext(e)*, Vol. II, No. 3, 1977 ("*Anti-Oedipus*: From Psychoanalysis to Schizopolitics") and Vol. III, No. 2, 1978 ("Schizo-Culture").

31. See David B. Allison, ed., *The New Nietzsche: Contemporary Styles of Interpretation* (New York, Dell Press, 1977) and *Semiotext(e)*, Vol. 3, No. 1 ("Nietzsche's Return"). The former includes a translation of the second chapter of *Nietzsche et la philosophie*, and a selection entitled 'Nomad Thought,' which Deleuze presented at a conference on Nietzsche at Cerisy-La-Salle, the proceedings of which were published in 1973; the latter contains another, very different translation of this same text.

32. For instance, I can clearly recall a professor in graduate school telling me, in the Fall of 1994, that he was suspicious of Deleuze, on grounds that he seemed to be a "classical metaphysician" [EK].

33. Alexi Kukuljevic, "Deleuze's Metaphysics and the Reality of the Virtual," in *Philosophy Today*, 49 (2005): 145–151. The quoted text appears on p. 145.

34. Daniel W. Smith, 'The Conditions of the New,' in *Deleuze Studies*, Vol. 1, No. 1 (June 2007): 1–21, the quoted text appears on p. 1.

35. See Smith, "The Conditions of the New," 6–8.

36. Smith, "The Conditions of the New,' 11.

37. See Smith, "The Conditions of the New," 12.

38. Smith, "The Conditions of the New," 14.

39. See Smith, "The Conditions of the New," 15–17.

40. Kukuljevic, "Deleuze's Metaphysics and the Reality of the Virtual," 146.

41. Deleuze, "Responses to a Series of Questions," 41.

42. See Manuel Delanda, *Intensive Science and Virtual Philosophy* (New York: Continuum, 2002); Keith Ansell Pearson, *Germinal Life: The Difference and Repetition of Deleuze* (New York: Routledge, 1999); John Protevi, *Life, War, Earth: Deleuze and the Sciences* (Minneapolis, University of Minnesota Press, 2013); Daniel W. Smith, "Deleuze on Leibniz: Difference, Continuity and the Calculus," in *Essays on Deleuze* (Edinburgh: Edinburgh University Press, 2012), 43–58; and Simon Duffy, *Deleuze and the History of Mathematics: In Defense of the 'New'* (New York: Bloomsbury, 2013).

43. See for instance Daniel W. Smith, "Deleuze, Hegel, Hegel and the Post-Kantian Tradition," in *Essays on Deleuze*, 59–71 and "Logic and Existence: Deleuze on the Conditions of the Real," in *Essays on Deleuze*, 72–85; Jeffrey Bell, *Deleuze's Hume: Philosophy, Culture, and the Scottish Enlightenment* (Edinburgh, Edinburgh University Press, 2009) and "Between Realism and Anti-realism: Deleuze and the Spinozist Tradition in Philosophy," in *Deleuze Studies*, Vol. 5., No. 1 (2011): 1–17; and Henry Sommers-Hall, *Hegel, Deleuze and the Critique of Representation: Dialectics of Negation and Difference* (Albany, SUNY Press, 2012).

44. Deleuze, *Negotiations*, 6.

45. Miguel de Beistegui, *Truth and Genesis: Philosophy as Differential Ontology* (Indianapolis, Indiana University Press, 2004) and *Immanence—Deleuze and Philosophy* (Edinburgh, Edinburgh University Press, 2010).

46. Beistegui, *Truth and Genesis*, 336.

47. Beistegui, *Truth and Genesis*, 337.

48. Beistegui, *Truth and Genesis*, 339.

CHAPTER ONE

Leaving Metaphysics? Deleuze on the Event

Alberto Anelli

In the complex and hazy weave that makes up the varied responses to Deleuze's thought, one can recognize four interpretative lines that recur with a certain insistence. The first tends to assimilate Deleuze to the scope—though not thoroughly stated—of the poststructuralist area, whose most significant features are characterised in anarchism, in emphasising difference, intended as resistance to being fixed in an identity, in the Nietzschean love for chaos.[1] The second line, on the contrary, diametrically opposed to the previous one, sees in Deleuze's thought the risk of relapsing into metaphysics in a twofold way; in the first place, by revealing, through the notion of difference, the risk of proposing, surreptitiously, a strong category which would tend to slip back into the reestablishment of a metaphysical approach;[2] and secondly, by identifying, in the univocity of the being, the element that inevitably pushes Deleuzian philosophy towards the depths of metaphysics.[3] In the third type of interpretative response, the actuality of Deleuzian philosophy lies in its inherent vocation to establish relationships and comparisons with all that is not exactly philosophy, stressing the idea of non-self-sufficiency of the philosophical discourse, forcing it therefore to a natural opening to other discourses.[4] Lastly, the fourth interpretative line sees in Deleuze's reflection the formulation of a real ontology of events or an ontological theory on difference: in any case, he sees a proposal therein that aspires to place itself at the level of a metaphysical kind of discourse, which is obviously characterised by the abandonment of those aspects of traditional metaphysics considered "unacceptable" today.[5] On first consideration, one may be astonished to find an ontological interpretation of Deleuze in the period of "the end of metaphysics," but the real problem is the all but manageable variety of meanings which now characterises the idea of metaphysics and, in correlation, that of its end. This variety can be schematised by taking, as reference, the two poles represented by the categories of the ground and the subject respectively: thus, in relation to the first pole, the end of metaphysics implies the sacrifice of any ground; in relation to the second pole, such an end implies the drastic reassessment and weakening of human subjectivity. Such a reassessment is then generally developed in three directions which make up as many variants: the "epistemological" one, which sees a drastic limitation in the possibilities and actual capacity of conceptual rationality; the "historical-existential" one, which challenges the modern figure of subjectivity as the apotheosis of the universal and of the general, claiming the rights of the particular and the individual; lastly, the "post-modern" one, which reveals the impossibility, on behalf of the subject, to access the totality of the real and the existent. Regarding this panorama, Deleuze's thought seems difficult to place: in certain aspects it shows indisputable anti-metaphysical traits, like the abolition of the human subject or the preference for the individual; in other aspects, it engages in the direction of typical elements of metaphysical tradition, like the discourse on totality, the re-comprehension of the problem of the ground, the refusal to completely eliminate conceptual reason and the language it is associated with. In the reflections that follow, we wish to contribute as far as possible to the solution of this problem through an alternative interpretative proposal: the hypothesis we shall herein develop is actually based on the conviction that the ambiguity and the indecidable nature of the complex relation which Deleuze has with metaphysics and with the variegated proclamations of its end can only be solved by focusing on and analysing the category of "event" and the interesting theoretical consequences which result from it.

As regards this category, the unavoidable reference, at least within the continent, is Martin Heidegger's thought. Of course, the event and the correlating discourse on difference are characterised by completely different meanings in Heidegger and in Deleuze: the content of such categories is different, the theoretical context of reference in the two authors is different, and their course is different.[6] And yet, there is a deeper level that binds these two philosophies and that opens up as soon as one asks what problem they have intended to answer since the very beginning. Actually, it is only at this level that one understands how they make up two different and decisive phases, during the formulation of an ontology of the event, whose main prerogative is that of being structured as an alternative proposal to modernity, that is, that of developing and revealing its own deep meaning through close comparison with modern metaphysics.

1. From Modern Metaphysics to the Problem of the Event

The itinerary that led to modern metaphysics and to its progressive development is well known. Medieval metaphysics has remained in a problematic alternation between two lines starting a long and complex debate regarding the *subjectum* of metaphysics: on the one hand it seems that such a *subjectum* can only exist as the concept of being in general, on the other hand, it is identified in the discourse on supreme and eternal substances. It can be said that the problem originated as long ago as Aristotle's reception in the Arab-Islamic world, which was basically of Neo-Platonic influence.[7] Duns Scotus later referred back to Avicenna's ontological tradition while Thomas Aquinas sought a tendential balance between the two lines, giving prominence, as a philosopher, to ontology while regaining, as a theologian, the supremacy of God. Modern metaphysics manifests as already structured with Suarez, who severs the medieval alternation and gives origin to a separation between reflection on the being as such on the one hand, and on God on the other. This is how the typically modern structure, based on duality between *metaphysica generalis* and *metaphysica specialis*, is inaugurated. Throughout the eighteenth century, the German *Schulmetaphysik* enriched and stabilised special metaphysics, dividing it into the three parts dedicated to the ego (rational psychology), to the world (rational cosmology), and to God (rational theology).[8] It is precisely this division of metaphysics that Kant refers to in transcendental dialectics.

And it is still this division that gives origin to the turn that leads one out of metaphysics, inaugurating contemporary discourse on its end and inducing a new thought: that of event. Actually, we can say that the itinerary of Heideggerian thought begins, since its origins, from the problem of a reformulation of the relations that bind ego and world (the hermeneutics of facticity first, and the fundamental ontology of *Being and Time,* then), thus finding again the problem of being and placing again in it the problem of the sacred and the divine (the more mature thought, that of the history of being).[9] Though continental philosophy received the turn toward the event from Heidegger, it should be remembered that even Whitehead succeeded in formulating a new ontology of events, starting right from reassessment of the fundamental categories of modern metaphysics, particularly regarding the relation between the world and God, where he put subjectivity back into place. There is the risk of oversimplifying the importance of Whitehead's organic philosophy if one reduces it to "processualistic" ontology. Analytical philosophy seems attracted to such a reduction and this is due to its ontological premises: actually, the ontology that is implicitly professed by most of the analytical approaches, and often not expressed clearly, tends to identify entities with "things," thus revealing its theoretical origin from the ontology of Meinong and from its general theory of the object.[10] From this point of view, one can explain why analytical philosophy grasps the originality of Whitehead's theoretical move, simply in the fact that the latter replaced the notion of substance with that of actual entity, namely, process of concrescence.[11]

In this context and in this line of development, even Deleuze's theorization on the event is revealed precisely as an interesting and deep attempt to overcome modern metaphysics through the radical reassessment of the ego-world axis. But first of all, in order to grasp Deleuze's originality, it is necessary to understand in what way his philosophy of difference differs from the Heideggerian concept of difference.

2. Event and Ontological Difference

In the thought of difference, as in the thought of event, reference to Heidegger cannot be disregarded. In fact, the German philosopher brought about a gradual and inexorable exposure of western thought, as "metaphysical." Metaphysics is the thought that reduces the phenomenon to a purely present entity, believing it can grasp, precisely in this presence, the completeness of the phenomenon, which can be, exactly because of this, transparent to reason. But this power of reason turns out to be an illusion. Phenomenal reality is in fact structurally marked by a difference: that between the dimension of the entity, what simply appears, and the horizon or opening in which the entity becomes intelligible and which makes it possible for the entity itself to appear. This difference is some-how already present in the fundamental ontology of the early Heidegger; in par-ticular, it is announced in the new understanding of the notion of truth given in *Being and Time*.[12] Here, metaphysics is actually exposed as a thought that re-duces the phenomenon to its dimension of presence, forgetting that all that is, always already appears in the horizon of the radically temporal understanding of *Dasein*, the meaning, which establishes itself in the complex reference to the three temporal ecstasies of past, present, and future. In the Heidegger that fol-lows *Being and Time,* this opening is no longer bound to the temporal structure of the *Dasein*, but is action of the Being itself which poses this ontological dif-ference; it poses it as event, that is, as historical occurrence in which the Being gives itself (*es gibt*), in a different way, giving origin to the different figures of periods in history related to western thought.[13] In this difference, the Being—precisely because it represents the horizon in which everything can appear—is itself not visible. This means that there is an area that is impervious to the clari-fying activity of rationality; all the meanings we can understand, all the concep-tual and cultural facts, have their origins in preconditions that are bound to es-cape us. Event indicates this particular dynamic of the Being, which always gives itself even by escaping, exactly as a condition that makes every meaning possible. In modern ontology, the notion of being, re-examined this way, places in the foreground the relation between being on the one hand and man—always placed into a world—on the other. In the issues related to the sacred, which de-veloped Heidegger's more mature phase, the question of God is then recovered and, in turn, incorporated into the Being as event. In this way, while the end of metaphysics is announced, this end is pursued through the transformation of the ideas of the being and of the supreme entities, but also and especially through a different structure in the relation between what traditionally used to be the di-mensions of *metaphysica generalis* and of *metaphysica specialis*. The ontologi-cal difference does not actually attempt to reintroduce modern dualism but, on the contrary, intends to re-establish a relation of inseparability and mutual ne-cessity between Being and entity. This is precisely the second key aspect of the Heideggerian event: it is not only "difference"—that is, the impossibility to go back to a definable foundation like an entity, since the Being is the non-objectifying horizon which always vanishes—but rather, it is also, at the same time, inseparability, a necessary mutual involvement, of Being and entity.

3. Event and Difference in the French Philosophical-Cultural Debate

1. The progressive publication of Heidegger's *Gesamtausgabe,* starting from the mid-seventies, triggered a new interest in the German philosopher and in fact set the conditions for the development of a new debate, even in the French-speaking area which, starting from the nineties, was enriched through a real turn toward phenomenology. This is the context in which *Ereignis* and ontological difference became the object of renewed attention. Reception substantially shattered the complexity of ontological difference taking it back to its internal components: on the one hand focus was placed on the problem of the subject, on the other it was the Being that became the object of focus, through emphasis on the aspect of otherness and non-objectification.

The first line represents a quite inevitable comparison in the French circle, which is traditionally characterised by the Cartesian *Wirkungsgeschichte* and by the role the epistemological supremacy of self-consciousness plays in it. This first type of reception developed in two quite well-defined directions: firstly, observing Heidegger's persistence on a problem of subjectivity made the debate acknowledge the *Dasein* as an interesting opportunity with regard to that general re-assessment of the subject that typifies contemporary philosophy. In particular, Heidegger's suggestion on the matter turns out to be prescriptive, precisely in the invitation to dismiss subjectivity from its self-referential nature, from its self-establishing character so as to recover, instead, the qualifying aspect of a hetero-established phenomenon.[14] This is the result of Heidegger's post-metaphysical proposal basically consisting of the replacement of "subjectivity" with "ipseity" to reassess the traditional problem of personal identity. Secondly, however, this first interpretative line knows the critical variant according to which Heidegger's persistence on the subject is rather a limit and a theoretical defect; Heidegger's weakness consists precisely in staying entangled in the Cartesian tradition; his general theoretical attempt should therefore be ruled out in that it is stranded in metaphysics.[15] It is clear that, to such a globally critical judgement, a precise idea of metaphysics is preliminary, that is, the idea according to which it represents a type of knowledge bound to the modern age, namely, a way of approaching reality whose beginning correlates to the beginning of the modern category of subject.[16] In other words, metaphysics is that particular attitude in which the predominance of subjectivity is exposed as ineliminable in the whole of reality and in which, as a result, there is no real space for any authentic otherness.

The second line of the response dwells upon the problem of Being and considers it in its separation from entity and believes it could condense the project of the last Heidegger in the aporetic characteristic of the "phenomenology of the inapparent." This second line, too, presents a double orientation within itself. In the first one, there is very strong scepticism toward the possibility of gaining access to the Being without the entity, that is, to construct a phenomenology without a phenomenal basis: the Heideggerian approach seems to lead inexorably to a dead end, as there cannot be phenomenology without phenomena.[17] Even the second orientation is strongly critical toward Heidegger, but for exactly the opposite reason: that is, Heidegger's reformulation of the Being does not seem to be sufficiently radical. Even though he had descried the goal he was to pursue, and the way to reach it, Heidegger was not able to reach his own objective; it is therefore a matter of accomplishing his project.[18]

In any case, the French response to Heidegger, in both his lines, developed according to an undisputed postulate: that of a dualistic understanding of ontological difference, and therefore of event.

2. Deleuze does not, however, belong to this phase of the debate, in which the ontological difference becomes acquainted with a structured response, but belongs culturally and historically to the previous period of French philosophy, the one that was formed in the fifties under the structuralist hegemony and developed in the sixties. Here, too, "difference" lies in the centre, but the theoretical referent for thinking and looking into this category is not Heidegger,[19] but rather structuralism. It actually refers to that heterogeneous period which is commonly defined as post-structuralism,[20] whose common characteristics are not easy to indicate, but which appears as a number of positions that progressively establish themselves through a sort of self-criticism within structuralism itself. There are two theoretical lines that meet in the authors of this debate and that contribute to the establishment of a particular conception of difference and event.

The first, as previously mentioned, starts from structuralism and from its qualifying ideas, but brings about a progressive deconstruction of it. In the structuralist approach, which originally started as linguistic theory, it is the difference between signified and signifier that generates the sense, but this difference can only be triggered within a system—the structure—in which the internal elements are arranged according to a network of already-defined relations: every time sense is generated from such differences, it is somehow the structure itself that—at the occurrence of such differences—occurs and is involved. Now, this also exactly constitutes the point that is gradually made into a problem. What one perceives as aporetic is not so much the fact that sense is generated from the difference between signs, but rather the fact that these differentiations find their condition of possibility only in the closed system of the structure. It is therefore a question of dissolving the rigidity of the structure, making it mobile, indefinitely open to infinite and new transformations, or of dissolving the structure itself abolishing its existence, so as to keep the differences from remaining constrained in the tightness of predefined and static systems of relations. Thus, one understands why post-structuralism coincided with abandonment of the Hegelian paradigm, which had been a reference point in the French-speaking area up to that moment: crisis of dialectical reasoning—which had been brought back to the fore thanks to the combined efforts of Kojève, Hyppolite, Sartre, and Merleau-Ponty—means refusal of a rationality that is still functional for the creation of identity and stable systems.

The second line of the post-structuralist debate, which, in its own way, also contributed to accelerating the dissolution of the structure, consists in the massive response to Nietzsche's thought, which involved almost all these authors and started a real *Nietzsche-Renaissance* in France in the seventies. Thanks to the debate on Nietzsche, two new acquisitions became necessary: firstly, the identification between Being and being, that is a monistic ontology and an ontology of immanence; secondly, the idea that the reality of things does not originate from one great difference alone, conceived as a kind of primordial element, but, on the contrary, that reality is the result of an infinite number of differences. That is plural rather than "unique" difference. In this sense, the adoption of Nietzsche as a theoretical reference point, made this period of French philosophy immune to any possible influence by Heidegger.[21] However, the authors who were most influenced by structuralism exercised a certain resistance toward a plural difference and preferred to reassert the supremacy of a great and unique difference, considered as the origin of all the single existing differences.[22] Thus, the achievement of a "unique" rather than plural difference was still present in Derrida and Lacan, unlike what occurred in Foucault and Deleuze, and inspired some significant interpretations of Nietzsche in the seventies;[23] but a pluralistic conception of difference prevails in Klossowski, Bataille and Blanchot. As stated, comparison with Nietzsche makes it possible to gain univocity of the being—with the prospect of immanence that it is connected to—and plural difference. The most significant consequence of this original combination is the fundamental change in paradigm in the thinking of difference: in fact one goes from the still too Heideggerian otherness to the most immanent multiplicity. The most visible consequence of such a shift concerning the difference is coexistence of two contrasting meanings of "event." In the first meaning, difference is understood as unique and refers to the interplay between the condition intended as absence and the particular dynamism that this absence triggers, setting into motion a set of sublimations (the symbolic-imaginary dyad in Lacan)[24] or of endless references (the *différance* in Derrida).[25] In the second meaning, outcome of Nietzsche's reception, difference is pluralised and event takes on the significance of multiplicity and chaos as qualifying aspects of the slippery and fluid origin of reality, of the arrangements we perceive in it and which make up ever provisional identities, as a result of processes that are inexorably bound to escape us because of their intrinsic chaoticity. It is in this second line that Deleuze's reflection on the event is placed.

4. Event and Difference in Deleuze

Deleuze continuously refers to the concept of event in his works. Besides the numerous explicit recurrences of the term,[26] he actually speaks about them on many occasions, in the most diverse contexts, giving the impression of elaborating, each time, proposals that do not lend immediately to an organic recovery and that do not seem easily referable to an overall vision. Besides, the author's particular literary style, deliberately chaotic and opposed to rigid or consistent terminological choices, does not favour attempts at reconstruction or even at the specification of the theoretical categories he elaborated. This explains why the reflections dedicated to this theme hesitate to go beyond a lexicographical recognition of the problem and to attempt interpretations with a broader scope.[27] Abandoning fidelity to the Deleuzian style, which imposes reproduction of the chaotic and unsystematic pattern, and accepting his suggestions,[28] it is perhaps necessary to isolate and carve out logic in the chaos if one wishes to try to obtain an initial explanation of the relations between this original philosophy of difference and metaphysics.

If one considers the whole of Deleuze's work, one can notice how he assigns a double set of characterizations to the category of event, that have a key role not just in the explanation of such a category, but also in the complete thought of Deleuze. This double characterization is revealed starting from his early historical-philosophical works, and is substantially accomplished in the theoretical works at the end of the sixties. Deleuze continuously returns to them even in the following years, giving different accentuations and looking for theme variations, without modifying the reference chart to any considerable degree. Event is above all "origin" and secondly "effect."

4.1 The Event as Origin

As origin, the event is, in turn, characterized by two fundamental characteristics: relationism and processuality. They are already present and operating, though only implicitly, in his early studies on Bergson, where they correspond to the three fundamental notions that qualify the philosophy of the author of *Matière et mémoire*: *durée* and *mémoire,* they correspond to relation, whereas *élan vital* is linked to process.[29]

1. First of all, the event is relation. It is generated as singularity or a combination of pre-individual singularities at that original level of the reality that forms the impersonal transcendental field. Each singularity is in turn the result of pure difference, to be understood as differential relation, relation among forces in which the relation is original compared to the elements it is composed of, and which are formed following the occurrence of the relation itself. According to Deleuze, the original character of the relation should be one of the qualifying points and theoretical advantages of Hume's empiricism, whose most significant

contribution may be condensed in the following result: relations are exterior to their terms.[30]

In other words, the fact that relation is the pure difference, the difference-in-itself, means that it establishes itself in the scope of an inflexible multiplicity, a plurality of heterogeneous elements. In multiplicity every reference point disappears, there is no privileged orientation: it is a question of deconstructing the metaphysical mechanism of *analogia attributionis*, denying the existence of any *analogatum princeps*. This is the theoretical operation which Deleuze claims to be necessary in order to demolish the uncontested supremacy in western history, starting from Plato, of a thought of representation or of identity: the copy, still bound to the idea of an ideal model of reference, must be replaced with the simulacrum. The differential relation does not apply among states of things that are pre-established and existing in themselves, it is not a comparison depending on resemblance and to identity. Deleuze's reversal of Platonism is concentrated on the destruction of the devices put into effect by representational thought in order to remove the original nature of difference and subordinate it to a perspective that can always unite different elements: resemblance, identity, opposition, analogy.[31] The relation forming the event is therefore characterized by oneness: each singularity is unique, to the same extent that the forces from which it originates are. Things in general do not exist, but there is only and always something here and at this moment. And since the concept does not give the essence, but the event, the most obvious epistemological consequence is that the precise concept must not answer the question "what is it?," but rather a set of questions that try to establish the combination of circumstances: "where? when? how?"[32] From the point of view of history of the philosophical thought, Leibniz is the one who is said to have inaugurated a theory of the event based on relation, the one who thought nothing else but relation,[33] establishing a turnaround in the way of conceiving substance: from essentialism to mannerism.[34] As theorist of relation meant as compossibility, Leibniz does not however go as far as thinking of relation among heterogeneous elements, the disjunctive synthesis, where there is no room for exclusion:[35] by introducing the notion of incompossibility, he again subordinates difference to identity because of a theological residue in his procedure, that is, reference to a God that calculates and plans and imposes a very precise arrangement for reality.[36] It is with the coming of Whitehead that divergence will contribute legitimately to the forming of the world.

2. Event is also and especially bound to the process. Within the differentiating becoming that forms the chaotic dynamism of reality, the event has a quite particular role. On the one hand, it is the unique and unpredictable effect of a chaotic interaction of forces, an original production of novelties, without models behind it and without a purpose in front of it, a haecceity.[37] On the other hand, though, such a singularity is not concretized into a state of things, but stays in an incorporeal state, it stays at a virtual level where it encloses and embodies all the potential contained in the interaction of forces that generated it. Such a potential actually reveals itself as the event in the never-exhaustible capacity of actualiz-

ing itself in the state of things, without allowing such infinite actualizations to consume or diminish the potential that is active, starting from the virtual level.

In Deleuze's terms, in the first case the event represents the result of a differentiation process, while in the second case, it sets into motion the differenciation process. This particular amphibological role of the event in the dynamism of becoming always places it "in the middle," never at the beginning, nor at the end as, for that matter, it never has a beginning or an end, it being, as it were, always "in progress": this much is noticed also by the fact that its linguistic expression is given by the verb form in the infinitive mode. The event is not an occurrence, but it is what becomes involved in the occurrence, it is the passage from virtual to actual.

As regards the processual component of the event, Whitehead, who is considered the author of the third great theory of the event in western thought, is the historical-philosophical referent of Deleuze. Whitehead's credit consists, above all, in the universal extension of the notion of event, in the definitive abandonment of any substantialistic ontology through characterization of the ultimate constituent of reality as a process of concrescence of actual entities. However, while Whitehead was able to grasp the processual component of the event, and actually thought of the event as a process, he lacks a satisfactory reflection on the conditions of the event, on the problem of its genesis, he lacks the "differentiation." In fact, process philosophy starts from events that have already been given as a relation of prehensions, but does not problematize the datum, does not say how, in the world, one reaches these conjunctions, whose existence is not obvious to Deleuze.[38]

4.2 The Event as Effect

Characterization of the event as an effect is elaborated by Deleuze in close relation to the third great historical-philosophical referent which he acknowledges in western thought, which forms, in chronological order, the first great theory of the event: the stoic doctrine of the *lekton*. It is well known that Deleuze based himself on Bréhier's research[39] which had, at the time, two important general works on stoic logic: those by Brochard and Hamelin.[40] Bréhier studies the idea of incorporeal in stoicism, in the conviction that there is an evolution from the time of Plato and Aristotle to that of the Epicureans and the Stoics: actually, while the former seems to have identified the principles of reality in incorporeal entities, according to the latter it is the corporeal nature of things which has a leading role. Interaction and the mutual action of things produces events, namely, modifications that do not form new realities, properties or real qualities, but rather ways of being, attributes that can be expressed linguistically through verbs, never with nouns, and lack a real being.[41] Deleuze accepts the basic ideas from Bréhier's studies. Events have an incorporeal character and the Stoics introduced, in the being, the distinction between two levels: one real and deep level of bodies and forces, the other, a superficial and incorporeal level of events.[42] Yet, the accentuation that Deleuze introduces in his critique is quite different, especially because the connotation "unreal" of the incorporeal[43] is attenuated by attributing a sort of quasi-being, an "extra-being" to it, not an existence but inherence.[44] Moreover, throughout the same work, which starts with the critique of the stoic doctrine of the *lekton*, Deleuze himself progressively deconstructs and contradicts the stoic idea according to which the events, unlike all that is of corporeal nature, can only and exclusively be effects, without the prerogative of acting, or of causing anything, and have the role of being totally inactive.[45]

5. Event and the Univocity of Being

Since the years of his philosophical education, which was completed in the context of history of modern philosophy,[46] Deleuze was certainly familiar with one of the main problems of modernity, that is with the gnoseologistic feature, perception of the relationship between the ego and the world as no longer obvious but rather in need of demonstration and foundation. Having distanced this theoretical context early, steering toward the formulation of transcendental empiricism, Deleuze definitively conquers the level of his original proposal when he finds the need to deconstruct the modern system, based on the triad God-world-ego, in favor of the fluidization of reality in an endless diversity of variable relations. This is the exact aim of the project to overturn Platonism, to destroy the metaphysical period structured on representational thinking; and again, this is what is aimed at with the claiming of a thought that places in the heart of the matter the "real" conditions of experience, rather than the "possible" ones of Kant. Such conditions only concern the case under examination, taking one case at a time, without these conditions imposing themselves as laws carrying necessities, and without the possibility of applying to portions of reality that are more extended than it, the case, is presumably affected by or based on. One would be guilty of oversimplification if one just saw in Deleuze another form of post-Kantianism: what he wishes to cast light on, through the cancellation of the ego, world and God is not so much the unbearability of Kant's transcendental dialectics, but rather, the whole modern metaphysical project.[47]

Yet, this is exactly where the main obstacle appears: the continuous recurrence of the "repressed." Actually, it is as if the being—a term that Deleuze tends to avoid and views with suspicion, as chaos cannot be totalized—resisted any attempt to reduce it to pure univocity. In Deleuze's work, this resistance is represented by numerous phases. Just to limit ourselves to recalling the key moments, we can think of the duality between being and language, of structuralist origin, that deeply influenced his theoretical works at the end of the sixties (*Différence et Répétition*; *Logique du Sens*); then the one between images and words prepared by the autonomization of the image, as opposed to language, in his second study on the cinema (*Cinéma II: L'Image-temps*); and again to the duality between the "outside" and "inside" that characterises his production in the eighties (*Foucault*) and which also generates the variant of the quadruple fold: body, knowledge or truth, social forces, outside itself or the ultimate.[48]

To this we must add the disturbing constant represented by the distinction between the two planes, the virtual and the actual, that complicates the problem considerably by casting an unsettling shadow of ambiguity on the actual success of a project which, in the intent, has always been thought of as ontologically univocist.

Now, Deleuze relies on the event for success of his own project, giving it an ambitious theoretical role: it consists in maintaining constant ontological resistance, that is, the continuous reviving of otherness in the universe, in a fundamentally univocal system of the being. Univocity of the being must be protected and, from this point of view, the responsibility that rests on the event is enormous. How does the event accomplish its role? It puts into effect three theoretical operations and—although philosophical reception and the critical literature on Deleuze stigmatized them as fundamental aporia of thought—they are actually three theoretical moves whose extremely interesting consequences were not appreciated, even by Deleuze himself, and with which he put an end to modern metaphysics, laying however the basis of a new ontology. At this point the destinies of Deleuze and Heidegger meet again.

5.1 The Event as Originated Origin: The Anomaly

In *Logique du sens* (1969) the event plays a strategic role in the chaos, that is, its position within chaos is such that event constitutes a sort of crossroads. Here Deleuze inaugurates an operation that is also found subsequently in his works with different terms and that he never rejected: the event becomes contemporarily the bond that structures the various arrangements of difference and of multiplicity each time Deleuze raises them. The first theoretical move, with which he attributes a resolving role to the event, in his ontology, is that of assigning an abnormal statute to it, in reality, an amphibological function in a way that it becomes the connection between the virtual and the actual dimension.

As a primordial result of the chaotic differential relations that reside in the virtual, the event is not really the origin, but an originated origin, that is, something that is, in turn, already an effect. It is differentiation that produces the event as the result of interaction among forces, in that no unity or convergence of forces exists before it, it being the first to be such a unity. It is creative unit, a convergence that can never be brought forward, the production of novelty lacking any determined finality. It is, however, an abnormal unit, in that it continues to belong to the virtual field: therefore it lacks the identity and determination typical of the actual level. It actually presents the prerogative of neutrality or eternity, a state of fundamental opening to indefinite and infinite effects to which it is indifferent and from which it is never exhaustible; it encloses an infinite potentiality of actuations. This is why it is expressed, linguistically, with a verb in the infinitive form and its quite peculiar temporality is that of *aion* and not of *chronos*, pure becoming that continuously escapes the present.[49] As pure casuality, the event destroys the possibility of a world intended as cosmic order, but allows one to catch a glimpse of the existence of chaos as inflexible to any rule and yet casual producer of regularity. Even this production, however, escapes every possible rule, so as to avoid slipping back into the totalization of chaos, which would make it a substitute for being or the metaphysical One. That of Deleuze is not the mathematics or physics of chaos, where the universe continues to be intended in a deterministic manner and in principle, measurable, but the metaphysics of chaos: his is chaosmos.

The two-faced role of the event also holds epistemological implications that Deleuze covered several times in his last works. As a casual and local production of order and regularity, the event can be expressed in the concept,[50] allowing philosophy to continue to exist without necessarily and inevitably having to "end" and allowing Deleuze himself to avoid any discourse on the end of philosophy or metaphysics. Through the event, philosophy can work as creative production precisely because chaosmos is production of novelty and singularities that form the events. The problem of philosophy is that of being able to produce concepts without diminishing the chaotic complexity of the plane of immanence, which means that it is part of the anphibological anomaly of the event.[51]

The event is the fundamental expression of multiplicity that exists and teems in the chaosmos: on the one hand, it is the only doorway to chaos, which is by definition absolute, unthinkable and elusive and, on the other hand, it is a form of singularity, but structurally undetermined, so that when it lends to linguistic expressibility and understanding, it withdraws, at the same time, from any fixation of an identity, that could block its intrinsic dynamism and eliminate its characteristic of being a combination of infinite potentialities of realization. And this is the first theoretical operation with which Deleuze entrusts the event with the success of his ontological project: the event as anomaly in the existent, and anomaly as articulation of the virtual and actual dimensions.

5.2 The Event as Originating Origin: Static Genesis

The event is also, however, the point of expression of the duality being-language or things-words that seems problematically inflexible within the dimension of the actual; namely, it has to lead back to univocity the inflexible differences and multiplicities that inhabit the empiric level.

Static genesis is the procedure through which Deleuze carries out a real "inference" of ordinary reality, in its complexity, from the event; it is accomplished in three actuations of the virtual, the first two are ontological,[52] while the last one is logical:[53] it concerns the individual, the knowing subject, the language, or a being that appears as subdivided into the fundamental contexts of objectuality, of subjectivity and of language.

The first phase of static genesis (ontological) leads to the effectuation of the individual. The pre-individual singularities are distributed through the rules of convergence and divergence: now, following the selection of an infinite set of converging singularities, a world is generated, and individuals are formed within it, through a further selection of a finite number of singularities in such a set. The effectuation of individuals and the world is therefore simultaneous and is characterized by a set of selections that occur according to rules of convergence. In a set of singularities, convergence around one that serves as a particular condensation point (the "singular point" compared to the "ordinary points") forms the individual: thus, the individual "tree" is generated from convergence around the singularity point or event "to green," and the proposition "the tree is green," traditionally based on the structure of a subject with a predicate, is interpreted in this new sense only.[54]

Only when there is a synthesis among diverging series and therefore among incompossible worlds of the first level, is an Ego generated; it is a knowing subject that is formed by correlatively constituting a world before it (*Welt*) that thus transcends the previously identified worlds of the precedent level (*Umwelt*). Deleuze's referent for considering the appearance of the subject is not Husserl of the fifth Cartesian meditation, but once again Leibniz. Despite their divergence, however, the incompossible worlds have something in common, which consists in the ambiguity of a genetic element, that is, of a problem in relation to which the incompossible worlds are like the possible and different solutions. In this regard, the Leibnizian mathematical example of the equation of the conic sections is particularly illuminating.[55]

Strictly speaking, while the first level of the *Umwelt* and of the individuals is the result of sense, the level of the *Welt,* which is common to the previous identified worlds and defined by people, is the result of ambiguity open to several solutions. This is what Deleuze defines as "non-sense," which always becomes involved with sense, and which he also calls aleatory point or ambiguous sign.

The event, as sense and open genetic element, eventually generates the logical proposition that expresses one of the possible answers to the problematic field of sense. Such a generation is possible because between events and language there is an essential relation: being expressible and enunciable in propositions is actually a prerogative of events. It is as if the virtual dimension of reality benefitted from the intrinsic property of being linguistically assertable.[56] It is not casual that this idea of Deleuze's is so much like that of some contemporary ontological projects that try to get through the modern hiatus between subject and world, to attempt a universal theory of the being, precisely by resorting to the medium of the expressibility of what exists, considering the logical-linguistic scope a little as having its own consistency, that is, not immediately bound to the subject.[57] The most interesting theoretical advantage in logical and ontological static genesis consists in confirming that sense or the event, whose own position is the virtual surface that forms the transcendental field, acts as boundary and never as separation, that is, such a subdivision is based on it so that sense-event is at the same time what happens to bodies and what insists in propositions: propositions and states of things are thus the two sides in which sense-event is structurally induced.[58]

5.3 The Event as Effect: Dynamic Genesis

At the end of the seventeenth series of *Logic of Sense*, the idea of dynamical genesis,[59] through which the stoic theory of *lekton* is resumed, had already appeared, but this time not to emphasize the incorporeal character of the event, its particular status suspended between being and not being, but rather to qualify it as the product of bodies and of their mutual actions. At first, it seems that—while in the case of static genesis one goes from events to states of things and to bodies—in dynamical genesis the vector is inverted, going from bodies and states of things to events. But this impression proves misleading in the course of Deleuzian argumentation. First of all, states of things and bodies are here intended not as already formed individualities, that is, as magnitudes in static balance, but are considered bearing in mind pre-individual components and the primitive forces that form them, that is, as magnitudes with an internal dynamism. If the first case is that of the tertiary arrangement, the second one constitutes the primary order, while, between the two, the secondary organization of sense plays a strategic role. Thus, in the two different geneses, "bodies" and "states of things," according to an equivocal predication of the same term, intend two different things.

In the field of dynamic genesis, Deleuze only discusses and analyzes the case of genesis of language. How does one reach language, the proposition, and the reign of the tertiary arrangement? One reaches them through the event; it is thanks to the event that the proposition is made possible. But in order to make all this possible, it is necessary to go back, from the primary order to the event. Here are found the bodies, which produce noises through their mutual actions and only when these sounds, thanks to the event, separate from the bodies—ceasing to be their qualities—can there be language.[60]

It is from the sounds produced by the action of bodies that the atomistic process leading to the formation of language begins. The first phase goes from sounds to the voice of those surrounding the child, the sound being perceived as familiar but still impossible to understand as language.[61] In the second phase, the child puts into effect three operations: to select the phonemes within the homogeneous flow of language, both because each one is a mass of differential relations, and because they are, in turn, members of those differential relations which represent phonemic relations. Such phonemes are then strung together again, according to the criterion of conjunctive syntheses of converging heterogeneous series, creating more complex entities, the construction of esoteric words that act as morphemes. Lastly, disjunctive syntheses of diverging series form portmanteau words that act as semantemes.[62] But the word is still at a pre-linguistic level, on a physical surface.

Passage to the metaphysical surface of the sense-event, described as an enigma, occurs like a leap;[63] phonemes, morphemes, and semantemes are brought to a new level in which the sense-event makes them linguistic propositions that can create denotations, manifestations, and significations, in relation to which sense is the expression that founds them all, but never reduces to them.

Here the dynamic genesis reveals all its ambiguity. On the one hand, one does not go from the event to its actualization in states of affairs and to its expression in propositions, like in static genesis, but one goes the opposite, from states of affairs to events, from the depth to the surfaces, so that the surface is produced and the incorporeal event results from the bodily states.[64] On the other hand, however, the model of production is abandoned in favor of a sort of transcendental schematism without a subject, where it is still the events, which, at a certain point, intervene, in giving expression to words, initiating a language and filling the gap that separates them from the words. In this second case, bodies, sounds, words, the primary order do not seem to have any power to generate the event, but are, in any case, necessary for triggering the potentiality, that is, "having it begin."[65]

But it is this very ambiguity of structures, this duality of models that hides the most interesting result that Deleuze reaches.

6. Deleuze and Metaphysics: Toward an Ontology of the Event

The ambiguity of this dualism of models did not escape criticism from those who saw the inelegant inconsistency, the radical indecision recurring continuously in *Logic of Sense*, namely, oscillation between a fundamentally materialistic ontological model—from the bodies to the incorporeal event—and a genuinely idealistic one that comes from the incorporeal event towards the states of things. In other words, it is a matter of problematic fluctuation between two incompatible meanings of "sense," at times intended as the effect of material causes, at other times as causal principle of the production of things.[66] The arguments of Žižek see a necessary tension in this juxtaposition of ontologies, but their objective seems to be more historical than theoretical and it seems apologetically oriented towards bringing Deleuze back into Lacan's orbit, where Badiou, too, seems destined to go back because of his dualism of Being and Event, to which continuity of the real dimension and the production of novelties that emerges from it at its breaking correspond respectively.[67] By formulating the question this way, the most significant theoretical contribution that can be attributed to Deleuze and to his theory on the event, is simply resolved by having confirmed a sort of emergentist ontological theory, where the most signifi-cant advantage is reduced to an explanation on the appearance of the novelty in the dimension of reality.

But what would happen if one interpreted the ontological ambiguity of Deleuze with a more radical theoretic finality, instead of with the usual histori-cal-philosophical perspective, and if one considered it as joined to the other the-oretical operations that have just been analysed and were put forward by Deleuze to allow the event to fully carry out its difficult role in the chaosmos?

Now, reassessment of Deleuze's ontological operations, that can finally allow exit from the usual "post-structuralist" constellation and open new ways and reveal new horizons, consists precisely in a synoptic interpretation of Heidegger's and Deleuze's theories on the event: to reach Deleuze through Heidegger—or vice versa—helps us to see something that deserves reflection.

6.1 Heidegger and Transcendence in Immanence

Both Heidegger and Deleuze have an ambitious operation in common: they have both transformed modern metaphysics into ontology of the event, but with dia-metrically opposed and symmetrical results.

The Heideggerian project constitutes a reformulation of modern *metaphysi-ca generalis* through radical transformation of the concept of Being, followed by deconstruction of the *metaphysica specialis*, where ego and world, and subse-quently God, are reinterpreted in the light of the new physiognomy of the Being.

In Heidegger, the ontological difference between Being and being also es-tablishes the inseparable relationship between the two and this creates the *Ereignis*. The event is the interplay that governs the intrinsic relation between transcendence (*Sein*) and immanence (*Seiendes*), where the latter finds its own conditions of possibility in the former, compared to which it is always late, and which it can never employ.

Though transcendent, the Being needs the *Dasein*, the two establish a rela-tionship of mutual necessity. And though non-objectifiable, the event is not un-known to man: of course he cannot employ it, he cannot know about it other than through an inevitable delay, other than from its effects. But the task of thought, putting an end to metaphysics, is precisely that of preserving this acqui-sition:[68] starting to listen to the *Ereignis* implies that one at least knows that the ultimate dimension of the Being consists in this occurrence, in the occurrence of this relation between transcendence and immanence. This is a sort of revenge of Thomas Aquinas: a creeping presence of Thomist epistemology, because of which it is not possible to know who and what the originary is, but it is possible to understand that it is there, starting precisely from the effects. Lastly, there is one last anomaly in the Heideggerian event: *Ereignis*, the interplay between transcendence and immanence, does not refer to anything mysterious and inex-pressible but to itself, its own contingency. All reality is in this occurrence, in this intrinsic relation between what is and the opening that precedes it and makes it possible: if the immanence of the being is contained in the transcendental opening of the Being, it is as if the *Ereignis* contained both of them enveloping them in the radical contingency of its own second degree immanence. Therefore, that of the Heideggerian Being is transcendence in immanence; and its thought is not the thought of otherness, as is all too often misunderstood. Heidegger's thought is something subtler: it introduces transcendence but only to immediately reorganise otherness. Here, the event represents a radical resistance to transcendence.

6.2 Deleuze and Immanence in Transcendence

Even Deleuze's project arises from modern metaphysics. The traditional *metaphysica specialis* is liquefied as artificial structure and without any foundation: there is no longer an ego, as it is a question of a derived phenomenon, of a "molar" quantity which turns into the microscopic components that form it: God no longer exists; it was a theoretical stratagem that had the function of preventing legitimacy of the disjunctive syntheses among heterogeneous elements, and the preserving task of founding the tripartite structure of modern metaphysics, which completed itself with the ego and the world.[69] As for the world, it merges with the being reassessed as chaosmos, coming to liquefy even *metaphysica generalis*.

Once the triadic structure of ego, world and God is dissolved, the whole theoretical system of analogy that was based on it disappears and a univocist understanding of reality moves in.[70]

But has Deleuze really managed to construct a consistent vision of univocity of the being, and therefore of immanence?

On closer inspection, there is something in the Deleuzian chaosmos that seems to offer resistance to the reduction of reality to pure univocity: the role and function of the event testify this very anomaly, this strangeness. In fact, as the effect of the singularities that form it, the event represents the connection point and link between the realm of pure chaos, inexpressible, and that of empiric reality, carrying out, at the same time, the function of gateway to chaos itself. In this way, introducing two fundamental levels into the universe seems inevitable: the virtual dimension and the actual one. But this doubleness seems to be too strong in a universe that should be characterized by radical univocity of the being. The spectre of the reappearance of a type of dualism is outlined; here, too, it is a question of vengeance: that of Plato. According to Deleuze, it is possible to gain access to the transcendental field, even if it is just through an experience that violates the ordinary one related to habitual perceptions of the empirical world. And yet the event differs in nature from the corporeal causes from which it derives: The event results from the bodies but, by nature, differs from them (dynamic genesis).[71] In the same way, the event, as a sense, differs in nature from the proposition and from its three dimensions,[72] precisely when it forms them and gives them value as their condition and foundation (static genesis).[73] But there is also more reasoning through which Deleuze tends to separate the virtual level from the actual one. In fact, according to Deleuze, modern metaphysics and transcendental philosophy—and, throughout all western tradition, representative thought—are actually based on an unauthorised or unauthorizable reversal: the fact of having traced the transcendental onto the empirical, of having structured the first using the second as a model, of having considered the condition by imitating the conditioned.[74] But the founded element never resembles the founding one, the virtual never resembles the actual: the virtual does not coincide with the possible in modern metaphysics.

Even in the field of static genesis, Deleuze mentions the danger in the non-recognition of the heterogeneity of the transcendental compared to the empirical. Through passive genesis, sense produces the individual and his individualized world (*Umwelt*), while non-sense produces the person with their *Welt* common to several individualized worlds. Now, starting from the individual, the principle of "good sense" is formed; on the strength of this principle, the formation of a certain order in things appears as original, to the detriment of differences; in the same way, starting from the person, the principle of "common sense" is formed and this principle appears as original in identifying, that is, individualizing and guaranteeing identity within difference. Such principles are then projected onto the transcendental level, that is, they are mistaken for original when, instead, original are the sense for individuality, which is formed starting from a pre-individual transcendental field, and non-sense for the person, which is formed starting from an impersonal transcendental field.[75] In both cases, the product does not resemble what it generates, unless the derived is mistaken for the original, a bit like what occurs in the case of fallacy of the misplaced concreteness in Whitehead[76] where such a mistake is simply the tendency to consider as primary data elements that are in fact already the result of an elevated degree of abstraction, as substance and quality, essence and matter.[77] Even in logical genesis, the proposition never resembles the problem that generates it, and the condition must never be conceived as the image of the conditioned.[78]

In Deleuze, immanence runs the risk of recreating in its inner self a problematic double that takes on the functions of traditional transcendence. Therefore, that of Deleuze is immanence that finds again transcendence; and his thought cannot be completely reduced to a thought of univocity. Something subtler occurs even in Deleuze: immanence and univocity seem to demand and postulate their insufficiency. Here the event represents a radical resistance to immanence.

7. Beyond Metaphysics?

We have stated and looked into what the event was to Deleuze (4) and what strategic role it played within the Deleuzian universe (5). At this point, we can finally resume the hypothesis expounded earlier that has led up to here. This hypothesis was based on two principles, expressed in order to understand what relation there was between Deleuze and metaphysics.

First principle: just by considering the figure of the event, it is possible to qualify the relation between Deleuze and metaphysics. Now, why does the event allow us to explain this problem, that is, the position of Deleuze towards metaphysical thought? Because the event is the key to understanding what type of ontology Deleuze suggested.

The philosophy of Deleuze is metaphysics if, by "metaphysics," we mean a thought that aspires to give a complete description of the wholeness of what exists. This remains true, even if Deleuze believes it is not possible to have direct access to or direct knowledge of the dimension that is at the origin of reality. It is however always possible to know that such a dimension exists and that it works.

The philosophy of Deleuze is not metaphysics if, on the other hand, by "metaphysics" we mean that which is represented by modern metaphysics. Deleuze, in fact, develops an ontology that tries to go beyond modern metaphysics, at least as regards two fundamental points: firstly, the language and basic concepts of modern metaphysics (God-world-ego) are laid aside in view of new formulations, often by resorting to real linguistic experimentation (which has drawn terrible criticism towards Deleuze: for putting into practice superficial eclecticism). Secondly, the surpassing that Deleuze pursues regards the basic structure of modern metaphysical thought. In fact, this was structured in two broad versions: one dualist (in which the foundation of reality is introduced in a postulating way and remains extrinsic to reality itself), the other monist (in which the foundation coincides and identifies with immediate reality). Now, it is precisely in this structural aspect that Deleuze's ontology is original: in fact, this ontology is neither dualist nor monist.[79] And the event is precisely what allows the revealing, in the clearest of ways, of the peculiarity of this ontology, which is structured in two dimensions—virtual and actual—which are neither radically separated nor identical.

Naturally, even Deleuze's ontology is not free from problems: there are some points in which the French philosopher did not provide a definitive solution or did not reach satisfactory clarity. In fact, one in particular could be mentioned, perhaps one of the most significant: the relation between forces, differential relations on the one hand, and bodies, material realities, on the other. Deleuze certainly wanted to abandon the ontology underlying modern science whose mechanist direction only admitted two components in the universe: matter and force. But how matter can be reduced to the forces that make it up remains a problem.[80]

Second principle: to better understand what the event is to Deleuze—and thus what the relation between the French philosopher and metaphysics is— comparison with reflection on the event, suggested by Heidegger, is useful, or better decisive. Such a comparison helps to reveal a similarity of intents between the two authors and their respective thoughts, helping us to discover another interesting aspect of Deleuzian ontology, which is specified even better in this way: reality is structured in two dimensions. One represents the level of the original (the Being in Heidegger, the transcendental in Deleuze), the other, the level of the immediate or of originated reality (*Dasein* in Heidegger, the empiric in Deleuze). Now, the most original aspect consists in precisely this: the two dimensions—the original and the immediate—are related to each other in an "asymmetrical correlation." In other words: while maintaining its own role of original reality, the original dimension is inseparable from the originated reality. Without the originated and immediate reality, the original could not exist or be what it is.

Interpreting Deleuze through Heidegger and taking as reference the problem of the event, is something that Deleuze himself induced by comparing the Heideggerian concept of *Zwiefalt* to his own idea of *Fold*.[81] Ontic and ontological on the one hand, empirical and transcendental, actual and virtual on the other, they are subdivided by the event, which, while differentiating them, connects them at the same time.[82] Therefore, once the two principles that formed the initial working hypothesis are verified, they allow us to reach two progressive explanations as regards the question we started with. Determining the figure of the event in Deleuze helps us to understand the originality of his ontology only by negative definition (what it is not: that is, it is neither monist nor dualist). Comparison with Heidegger allows us to qualify the originality of Deleuzian ontology by positive definition (what it is: namely, asymmetrical correlation of two dimensions). Both explanations provided by the two principles therefore allow us to better understand the relation of Deleuze with metaphysics and, above all, to understand why such a relation is a complex and structured question.

This asymmetric correlation must be maintained without suppressing either of the two options at stake: it is necessary to resist the temptation to abolish immanence, because in such a case there would only be asymmetry, with no correlation (and one would slip back into dualistic ontology). But it is also necessary to resist the temptation to abolish transcendence, because in that case, there would only be correlation among the equal, the identical, without asymmetry (and one would slip back into monistic ontology).

Deleuze always comes back to this enigmatic average form, which also works in its idea of "sign": things do not exist, only signs do. These are not the clear and distinct objects of representation, they are not the things we have already given an autonomous identity to, they do not possess pre-defined contents, and yet they are not "nothing." They are not something defined, and yet one can encounter them. This is the ontology of event that the comparison between Heidegger and Deleuze allows us to see and which goes beyond both Heidegger and Deleuze, leaving us with the feeling that both these thoughts simply represent some ideal stages which converge toward a new ontology. This new ontology of course is yet to be specified and formulated, but is already outlined in its basic theoretical requirement: to keep asymmetry, to keep correlation. These two philosophers and their reflections are points, which moving along the same line, thus approach an ideal centre, despite starting from two opposite directions. The strange figure called event which is thus outlined, is not a materialistic ontology, nor a thought of radical otherness, and it poses a totally new challenge which, in the past, in different contexts, and through different courses, could perhaps only be spotted, for a moment, in all its dramatic force, by the particular Neo-Platonic metaphysics of Proclus: how can the transcendence of the One remain secure if this event causes the world? And paraphrasing Foucault one may wonder: perhaps the next century will be that of the event?

Notes

1. See Jürgen Mümken, *Freiheit, Individualität und Subjektivität. Staat und Subjekt in der Postmoderne aus anarchistischer Perspektive* (Frankfurt a. M.: Verlag Edition AV, 2003); Jürgen Mümken, ed., *Anarchismus in der Postmoderne* (Frankfurt a. M.: Verlag Edition AV, 2005); Todd May, *The Political Philosophy of Poststructuralist Anarchism* (University Park: Pennsylvania State University Press, 1994); May, *Gilles Deleuze: An Introduction* (Cambridge: Cambridge University Press, 2005).

2. See Gianni Vattimo, *The Adventure of Difference: Philosophy after Nietzsche and Heidegger*, trans. Cyprian Blamires (Baltimore: The John Hopkins University Press, 1993).

3. See Alain Badiou, *The Clamor of Being*, trans. Louise Burchill (Minneapolis: University of Minnesota Press, 1999).

4. See for example Brian Massumi, *A User's Guide to Capitalism and Schizophrenia: Deviations from Deleuze and Guattari* (Cambridge: MIT Press, 1992); *Paul Patton, Deleuze and the Political* (London: Routledge, 2000); Brian Massumi, ed., *A Shock to Thought. Expression after Deleuze and Guattari* (London: Routledge, 2002); Friedrich Balke and Marc Rölli, eds., *Philosophie und Nicht-Philosophie: Gilles Deleuze—Aktuelle Diskussionen* (Bielefeld: Transcript, 2011). More cautious During: "It may well be that Deleuze pushes philosophy out of itself in order to find philosophy everywhere at work (bringing out the philosophy folded into cinema, for example). Yet in another sense this movement entirely takes place within philosophy itself, so that one may argue that if nomad thought cannot be confined to philosophy, it is not because philosophy is too narrow, but on the contrary because it encompasses much more. Hence Deleuze can say, in the series of interviews with Claire Parnet entitled *Abécédaire*, that one only gets beyond philosophy through philosophy, by means of philosophy [. . .]." Elie During, "Blackboxing in Theory: Deleuze versus Deleuze," in *French Theory in America*, ed. Sylvère Lotringer and Sande Cohen (London: Routledge, 2001), 176.

5. See Michael Hardt, *Gilles Deleuze: An Apprenticeship in Philosophy* (Minneapolis: University of Minnesota Press, 1993); Constantin V. Boundas, "An Ontology of Intensities," *Epoché* 7, no. 1 (2002): 15–37; Véronique Bergen, *L'ontologie de Gilles Deleuze* (Paris: L'Harmattan, 2001). Those readings of Deleuze for which his thought is a kind of process philosophy or that identify Being with creative power belong to this onto-

logical interpretation: Cf. Catherine Keller and Anne Daniell, eds., *Process and Difference: Between Cosmological and Poststructuralist Postmodernism* (Albany: SUNY, 2002); André Cloots and Keith A. Robinson, eds., *Deleuze, Whitehead and the Transformations of Metaphysics* (Brussel: Flemish Academy of Sciences, 2005); Peter Hallward, *Out of this World: Deleuze and the Philosophy of Creation* (London: Verso, 2006); Keith A. Robinson, ed., *Deleuze, Whitehead, Bergson: Rhizomatic Connections* (Basingstoke: Palgrave Macmillan, 2009); Roland Faber, "Organic or Orgiastic Metaphysics? Reflections on Whitehead's Reception in Contemporary Poststructuralism," *Japanese Journal of Process Thought* 14 (2010): 203–222; Roland Faber, H. Krips and D. Pettus, eds., *Event and Decision: Ontology and Politics in Badiou, Deleuze, and Whitehead* (Newcastle upon Tyne: Cambridge Scholars Publishing, 2010); Roland Faber, "Surrationality and Chaosmos: For a More Deleuzian Whitehead (with a Butlerian Intervention)," in *Secrets of Becoming: Negotiating Whitehead, Deleuze, and Butler*, ed. Roland Faber and Andrea M. Stephenson (New York: Fordham University Press, 2011), 157–77.

6. As known, Zourabichvili denies any possibility of connection between Deleuze and Heidegger, unlike Badiou and de Beistegui: cf. François Zourabichvili, *Le vocabulaire de Deleuze* (Paris: Ellipses, 2003), 38–39; Zourabichvili, "Introduction Inédite: L'ontologique et le Transcendental," in *La philosophie de Deleuze*, ed. François Zourabichvili, A. Sauvagnargues and P. Marrati-Guénoun (Paris: PUF, 2004), 6–10; Badiou, *Deleuze: The Clamor of Being*, 19–20; Badiou, *Briefings on Existence: A Short Treatise on Transitory Ontology*, trans. Norman Madarasz (Albany: SUNY Press, 2006); Miguel de Beistegui, *Truth and Genesis: Philosophy as Differential Ontology* (Bloomington: Indiana University Press, 2004), 16–17 and 21.

7. Whereas for Avicenna the question of being *qua* being incorporates that of God, Averroes thinks that metaphysics must deal first of all with God and the other eternal things.

8. See Christian Wolff, *Vernünfftige Gedancken von Gott, der Welt und der Seele des Menschen, auch allen Dingen überhaupt* (Halle: Renger, 1720); Alexander Gottlieb Baumgarten, *Metaphysica* (Halae Magdeburgicae: Hemmerde, 1739).

9. For a reading in this sense see Alberto Anelli, *Heidegger e la teologia* [Heidegger and Theology] (Brescia: Morcelliana, 2011), 15–56.

10. See Alexius Meinong, *Abhandlungen zur Erkenntnistheorie und Gegenstandstheorie*, ed. Rudolf Haller, vol. 2 (Graz: Akademische Druck- u. Verlagsanstalt, 1971).

11. For an in-depth analysis of this problem see Alberto Anelli, *Processualità e definitività. La teologia a confronto con Whitehead* [Process and Finality. Theology compared with Whitehead] (Assisi: Cittadella, 2004).

12. See par. 44 in Martin Heidegger, *Being and Time*, trans. J. Stambaugh (Albany: SUNY Press, 1996), 196–211.

13. We should not forget that *Ereignis* has not always the same meaning in Heidegger's works: a comparison between the works of the 1930s and the works of the early 1960s shows a quite significant difference. For an overview of this problem see Rudolf Wansing, "Im Denken erfahren: Ereignis und Geschichte bei Heidegger," in *Ereignis auf Französisch. Von Bergson bis Deleuze*, ed. Marc Rölli (Münich: Fink, 2004), 81–102; Alberto Anelli, *Heidegger und die Theologie. Prolegomena zur zukünftigen theologischen Nutzung des Denkens Martin Heideggers* (Würzburg: Ergon Verlag, 2008), 137–151; Anelli, *Heidegger e la teologia*, 45–56.

14. Cf. Jean Greisch, "Descartes selon l'ordre de la raison herméneutique," in *Revue des Sciences Philosophiques et Théologiques* 73, no. 4 (1989): 529–548; Jacques Colléony, "Heidegger et Lévinas: La question du Dasein," in *Les Études Philosophiques 45*,

no. 3 (1990): 313–331; Jocelyn Benoist, "Être soi-même: Heidegger et l'obsession de l'identité," in *Revue Philosophique de Louvain* 94, no. 1 (1996): 69–91.

15. Jean-Luc Marion, *Reduction and Givenness: Investigations of Husserl, Heidegger and Phenomenology*, trans. Thomas A. Carlson (Evanston: Northwestern University Press, 1998), 77–107; Jacques Taminiaux, *Lectures de l'ontologie fondamentale* (Grenoble: Millon, 1995).

16. See Jean-Luc Marion, "La science toujours recherchée et toujours manquante," in *La métaphysique. Son histoire, sa critique, ses enjeux*, ed. Jean-Marc Narbonne and Luc Langlois (Paris: Vrin, 1999), 13–36.

17. See Jean-François Courtine, *Heidegger et la phénoménologie* (Paris: PUF, 1990); Dominique Janicaud, *Le tournant théologique de la phénoménologie française* (Combas: L'Éclat, 1991); Emmanuel Gabellieri, "De la métaphysique à la phénoménologie: une relève?," in *Revue Philosophique de Louvain* 94, no. 4 (1996): 625–645; Marc Richir, "Commentaire de la phénoménologie de la conscience esthétique de Husserl," in *Revue d'Esthétique* 36 (1999): 15–27.

18. See for example Jean-Luc Marion, *Reduction and Givenness*, 40–76; Serge Champeau, *Ontologie et poésie: Trois études sur les limites du langage* (Paris: Vrin, 1995).

19. Derrida can be considered an exception to this: his concept of difference is influenced both by Heidegger and Structuralism.

20. As known, in the 1980s the German philosopher Manfred Frank introduced the alternative definition of "Neostructuralism." See Manfred Frank, *What is Neostructuralism?*, trans. Sabine Wilke and Richard Gray (Minneapolis: University of Minnesota Press, 1989).

21. In fact, in the sixties and seventies, people became aware of the turn which, at a certain point, had arrived in Heidegger's path. Those same years—however questionable that may seem today—Heidegger's late philosophy was perceived as a thought of the Being, where the Being appeared as something transcendent: therefore, the exact opposite of a thought of immanence, like Nietzsche's. But there is also another reason that made French culture hostile to Heidegger that period. Structuralism first, then Nietzsche, removed any possible privileged position of man in the universe: man had become the result of relationships and forces, from which he was formed as a derived phenomenon. In Heidegger, instead, man loses any supremacy or power with respect to reality, but continues to maintain a unique role, which makes him essentially different from the other non-human living beings and things: only the Dasein in the universe is the interlocutor of the Being. In the French philosophical conscience of those years, Heidegger's ontological difference combined per se exactly these two unacceptable postulates: transcendence (in a metaphysical sense) and persistence of the subject.

22. Pluralisation of the difference was however already in progress in the fluidization of the structure operated by the metamorphosis within structuralism.

23. See Bernard Pautrat, *Versions du soleil: Figures et système de Nietzsche* (Paris: Seuil, 1971); Bernard Pautrat and Maurice de Gandillac, eds., *Nietzsche aujourd'hui?* (Paris: Union générale d'éditions, 1973); Jean-Michel Rey, *L'enjeu des signes: Lecture de Nietzsche* (Paris: Seuil, 1971); Sarah Kofman, *Nietzsche and metaphor*, trans. Duncan Large (London: The Athlone Press, 1993); Kofman, *Nietzsche et la scène philosophique* (Paris: Union générale d'éditions, 1979).

24. See Jacques Lacan, *The Four Fundamental Concepts of Psycho-Analysis*, trans. Alan Sheridan (New York: Norton, 1978).

25. See Jacques Derrida, *Margins of Philosophy*, trans. Alan Bass (Chicago: University of Chicago Press, 1982).

26. For the recurrence and different usages of the term *événement* in Deleuze's writings see Robert Sasso, "Événement," in *Le vocabulaire de Gilles Deleuze*, ed. Robert Sasso and Arnaud Villani (Paris: Vrin, 2003), 138–140.

27. See for example Robert Sasso, Événement, 138–153; Cliff Stagoll, "Event," in *The Deleuze Dictionary*, ed. Adrian Parr (Edinburgh: Edinburgh University Press, 2005), 87–89; Maël Le Garrec, "Événement," in *Apprendre à philosopher avec Deleuze* (Paris: Ellipses, 2010), 69–85. Zourabichvili's book is a more comprehensive attempt, but despite its title it focuses not as much on event as on a general understanding of Deleuze's philosophy: cf. François Zourabichvili, *Deleuze: Une philosophie de l'événement* (Paris: PUF, 1994).

28. Gilles Deleuze and Félix Guattari, *What is Philosophy?*, trans. Hugh Tomlinson and Graham Burchell (New York: Columbia University Press, 1994), 42–43, 118, 197, 202.

29. Gilles Deleuze, *Desert Islands and Other Texts 1953–1974*, trans. Michael Taormina (Los Angeles: Semiotext(e), 2004), 44.

30. Deleuze, *Desert Islands*, 163.

31. Gilles Deleuze, *Difference and Repetition*, trans. Paul Patton (New York: Columbia University Press, 1994), 265–272.

32. Deleuze, *What is Philosophy?*, 21.

33. Gilles Deleuze, *The Fold: Leibniz and the Baroque*, trans. Tom Conley (Minneapolis: University of Minnesota Press, 1993), 53.

34. Deleuze, *The Fold*, 56–57.

35. Gilles Deleuze, *The Logic of Sense*, trans. Mark Lester with Charles Stivale (New York: Columbia University Press, 1990), 113–114.

36. Deleuze, *The Logic of Sense*, 172.

37. Gilles Deleuze, *Two Regimes of Madness: Texts and Interviews 1975–1995*, trans. Ames Hodges and Mike Taormina (New York: Semiotext(e), 2006), 351.

38. See Gilles Deleuze, "Cours Vincennes—St. Denis, L'événement, Whitehead: 10/03/1987," last modified May 13, 2010, http://www.webdeleuze.com/php/texte.php?cle=140&groupe=Leibniz&langue=1.

39. Émile Bréhier, *La théorie des incorporels dans l'ancien stoïcisme* (Paris: Vrin, 1928).

40. Victor Brochard, "Sur la Logique des Stoïciens," *Archiv für Geschichte der Philosophie* 4, no. 5 (1892): 449–468; Octave Hamelin, "Sur la logique des Stoïciens," *Année philosophique* 12 (1902): 13–26.

41. Bréhier, *La théorie des incorporels*, 11–13.

42. Bréhier, *La théorie des incorporels*, 13.

43. Bréhier, *La théorie des incorporels*, 21.

44. Deleuze, *The Logic of Sense*, 7.

45. Bréhier, *La théorie des incorporels*, 35. See also Bergen, *L'ontologie de Gilles Deleuze*, 109–117; Alain Beaulieu, "Gilles Deleuze et les Stoïciens," in *Gilles Deleuze. Héritage philosophique*, ed. Alain Beaulieu (Paris: PUF, 2005), 45–72.

46. Cf. Stéfan Leclercq, ed., *Aux sources de la pensée de Gilles Deleuze* (Mons: Sils Maria, 2005).

47. "Thus the personal self requires God and the world in general. But when substantives and adjectives begin to dissolve, when the names of pause and rest are carried away by the verbs of pure becomings and slide into the language of events, all identity disappears from the self, the world and God." Deleuze, *The Logic of Sense*, 3.

48. Gilles Deleuze, *Foucault*, trans. Seán Hand (Minneapolis: University of Minnesota Press, 1988), 104.

49. Deleuze, *The Logic of Sense*, 1–2 and 164–165.

50. Deleuze, *What is Philosophy?*, 33–34.

51. "Chaos makes chaotic and undoes every consistency in the infinite. The problem of philosophy is to acquire a consistency without losing the infinite into which thought plunges. . . ." Deleuze, *What is Philosophy?*, 42.

52. See the sixteenth series in Deleuze, *The Logic of Sense*, 109–117.

53. See the seventeenth series in Deleuze, *The Logic of Sense*, 118–126.

54. Deleuze, *The Logic of Sense*, 112.

55. Deleuze, *The Logic of Sense*, 114.

56. Deleuze, *The Logic of Sense*, 12.

57. See Puntel's ontological project: Lorenz B. Puntel, *Structure and Being: A Theoretical Framework for a Systematic Philosophy*, trans. Alan White (University Park: Pennsylvania State University Press, 2008.

58. Deleuze, *The Logic of Sense*, 125.

59. Deleuze, *The Logic of Sense*, 124–126.

60. Deleuze, *The Logic of Sense*, 181–182.

61. Deleuze, *The Logic of Sense*, 193–194 and 229.

62. Deleuze, *The Logic of Sense*, 229–232.

63. Deleuze, *The Logic of Sense*, 238.

64. Deleuze, *The Logic of Sense*, 186.

65. Deleuze, *The Logic of Sense*, 181.

66. Slavoj Žižek, *Organs Without Bodies: Deleuze and Consequences* (New York: Routledge, 2004), 20–21; Slavoj Žižek and Glyn Daly, *Conversations with Žižek* (Cambridge: Polity Press, 2004), 81–84.

67. See Alain Badiou, *Being and Event*, trans. Oliver Feltham (London: Continuum, 2007).

68. See Martin Heidegger, *Elucidations of Holderlin's Poetry*, trans. Keith Hoeller (Amherst: Humanity Books, 2000), 101–173; Heidegger, *What is Called Thinking?*, trans. J. Glenn Gray (New York: Perennial, 2004); Heidegger, *The Principle of Reason*, trans. Reginald Lilly (Bloomington: Indiana University Press, 1996); Heidegger, "The End of Philosophy and the Task of Thinking," in *Basic Writings*, ed. David F. Krell, trans. John Stambaugh (New York: Harper & Row, 1977), 369–392.

69. Deleuze, *The Logic of Sense*, 175–176.

70. Deleuze, *The Logic of Sense*, 179.

71. Deleuze, *The Logic of Sense*, 182.

72. Deleuze, *The Logic of Sense*, 145.

73. Deleuze, *The Logic of Sense*, 181.

74. Deleuze, *The Logic of Sense*, 105.

75. "But it would be an error to conceive of these produced principles as if they were transcendentals. That is, it would be an error to conceive of, in their image, the sense and nonsense from which they are derived." and "The individual and the person, good sense and common sense, are produced by the passive genesis, on the basis of sense and nonsense which do not resemble them, and whose pre-individual and impersonal transcendental play we have seen." Deleuze, *The Logic of Sense*, 116–117.

76. "There is an error; but it is merely the accidental error of mistaking the abstract for the concrete. It is an example of what I will call the 'Fallacy of Misplaced Concreteness.'" Alfred North Whitehead, *Science and the Modern World, Lowell Lectures 1926* (New York: The Free Press, 1967), 51. And "This conception of the universe is surely framed in terms of high abstractions, and the paradox only arises because we have mistaken our abstraction for concrete realities." Whitehead, *Science and the Modern World*,

54–55. Cf. also Alfred North Whitehead, *Process and Reality. An Essay in Cosmology. Gifford Lectures Delivered in the University of Edinburgh During the Session 1927–28,* Corrected Edition, ed. David Ray Griffin and Donald W. Sherburne (New York: The Free Press, 1978), 7, 18, 93 and 94.

77. "Of course, substance and quality, . . . are the most natural ideas for the human mind. It is the way in which we think of things, and without these ways of thinking we could not get our ideas straight for daily use. . . . The only question is, How concretely are we thinking when we consider nature under these conceptions? . . . When we examine the primary elements of these simplified editions, we shall find that they are in truth only to be justified as being elaborate logical constructions of a high degree of abstraction." Whitehead, *Science and the Modern World,* 52.

78. Deleuze, *The Logic of Sense,* 121–122.

79. It is no accident that the two main pieces of criticism on Deleuze's ontology are opposing: to Žižek, the ontology of Deleuze is a form of dualism, while to Badiou, instead, it is monism. Cf. Žižek, *Conversations with Žižek,* 81–84; Badiou, *Deleuze: The Clamor of Being;* Badiou, "The Event in Deleuze," in *Parrhesia,* no. 2 (2007): 37–44.

80. It is true that reducibility of matter to energy is a basic fact in contemporary physics. However, physical explanations do not exclude or replace a philosophical and ontological approach to the same problem.

81. Deleuze, *The Fold,* 10, 30 and 120.

82. Deleuze, *The Fold,* 30. Therefore it seems to be a simplification to consider on the one hand Heidegger's position a sort of Platonism, on the other hand Deleuze's thought a radicalization of ontological immanence: cf. Marc Rölli, "Begriffe für das Ereignis: Aktualität und Virtualität. Oder wie der radikale Empirist Gilles Deleuze Heidegger verabschiedet," in *Ereignis auf Französisch,* (Münich: Fink, 2004), 337–361.

References

Anelli, Alberto. *Heidegger e la teologia.* Brescia: Morcelliana, 2011.

———. *Processualità e definitività. La teologia a confronto con Whitehead.* Assisi: Cittadella, 2004.

———. *Heidegger und die Theologie. Prolegomena zur zukünftigen theologischen Nutzung des Denkens Martin Heideggers.* Würzburg: Ergon Verlag, 2008.

Badiou, Alain. *Deleuze: The Clamor of Being.* Minneapolis: University of Minnesota Press, 1999.

Balke, Friedrich, and Marc Rölli, eds. *Philosophie und Nicht-Philosophie: Gilles Deleuze - Aktuelle Diskussionen.* Bielefeld: Transcript, 2011.

Bergen, Véronique. *L'ontologie de Gilles Deleuze.* L'Harmattan: Paris, 2001.

Bréhier, Emile. *La théorie des incorporels dans l'ancien stoïcisme.* Paris: Vrin, 1928.

Deleuze, Gilles. "Cours Vincennes – St. Denis, L'événement, Whitehead: 10/03/1987." Last modified May 13, 2010. http://www.webdeleuze.com/php/texte.php?cle=140&groupe=Leibniz&langue=1.

———. *Difference and Repetition.* Translated by Paul Patton. New York: Columbia University Press, 1994.

———. *Desert Islands and Other Texts 1953–1974.* Translated by Michael Taormina. Los Angeles: Semiotext(e), 2004.

———. *The Fold: Leibniz and the Baroque.* Translated by Tom Conley. Minneapolis: University of Minnesota Press, 1993.

————. *Foucault*. Translated by Seán Hand. Minneapolis: University of Minnesota Press, 1988.

————. *The Logic of Sense*. Translated by Mark Lester with Charles Stivale. New York: Columbia University Press, 1990.

————. *Two Regimes of Madness: Texts and Interviews 1975–1995*. Translated by Ames Hodges and Mike Taormina. New York: Semiotext(e), 2006.

Deleuze, Gilles and Félix Guattari. *What is Philosophy?* Translated by Hugh Tomlinson and Graham Burchell (New York, NY: Columbia University Press, 1994).

Derrida, Jacques. *Margins of Philosophy*. Translated by Alan Bass. Chicago: University of Chicago Press, 1982.

Faber, Roland, H. Krips and D. Pettus, eds. *Event and Decision: Ontology and Politics in Badiou, Deleuze, and Whitehead*. Newcastle upon Tyne: Cambridge Scholars Publishing, 2010.

Faber, Roland, and Andrea M. Stephenson, eds. *Secrets of Becoming: Negotiating Whitehead, Deleuze, and Butler*. New York: Fordham University Press, 2011.

Frank, Manfred. *What is Neostructuralism?* Translated by Sabine Wilke and Richard Gray. Minneapolis: University of Minnesota Press, 1989.

Heidegger, Martin. *Being and Time*. Translated by John Stambaugh. Albany: SUNY Press, 1996.

Lotringer, Sylvère and Sande Cohen, eds. *French Theory in America*. London: Routledge, 2001.

Rölli, Marc, ed. *Ereignis auf Französisch: Von Bergson bis Deleuze*. Münich: Fink, 2004.

Whitehead, Alfred North. *Process and Reality. An Essay in Cosmology. Gifford Lectures Delivered in the University of Edinburgh During the Session 1927–28*. Corrected Edition. Edited by David Ray Griffin and Donald W. Sherburne. New York: The Free Press, 1978.

————. *Science and the Modern World, Lowell Lectures 1926*. New York: The Free Press, 1967.

CHAPTER TWO

Mathematics, Structure, Metaphysics: Deleuze and Category Theory

Rocco Gangle

Against a broadly Heideggerean "post-metaphysical" tendency in much recent French thought, Deleuze is unashamed to declare himself a "pure metaphysician."[1] We wish to understand the sense of this claim by pushing it further in asking to what extent Deleuze the metaphysician might also be described as a "pure mathematician." In what sense and to what extent, if at all, may Deleuze's metaphysics be modeled by or expressed within mathematics? In particular, is there a kind of mathematics—either already in existence or possibly to be constructed—that would be adequate to the full range and power of Deleuze's key metaphysical concept of the virtual?

The importance of mathematics for Deleuze's philosophy in one form or another is evident throughout his work. In some of his earliest writings, Deleuze emphasizes the concept of a generalized mathematical practice understood in terms of Hermetic *mathesis*.[2] Yet by the late 1960s with the publication of *Difference and Repetition* and *The Logic of Sense*, Deleuze comes to organize his thought on the basis of a comprehensive metaphysics of the virtual. He correspondingly shifts his mathematical focus toward the dynamics of differential calculus on the one hand as a model for the different/ciation of virtuality and actuality and, on the other, in the direction of a subsumption of mathematical ideality into a transcendental field of virtual infinitives, or sense-events.[3] Mathematics thus comes to serve as a privileged theoretical model for the virtual and yet remains only a relatively restricted instance of it. In the later collaborations with Guattari, especially *A Thousand Plateaus*, the coordination of mathematics and virtuality is reconfigured in various ways, perhaps most interestingly in terms of an abstract machinic and diagrammatic conception of metaphysics drawing on Hjelmslevian and Peircean semiotics.[4] Can we locate a mathematics general enough, supple enough and powerful enough to express the unity of the metaphysics that cuts across these diverse stages? We will suggest that *category theory*—a fundamental branch of contemporary mathematics with deep connections to algebra, topology, and logic, as well as quantum physics, computer science, and linguistics—offers precisely this as both an adequate theory and a faithful model of the virtual.

The relation (at once actual and potential) between mathematics and philosophy in Deleuze's metaphysics involves various problems concerning the essence of thought itself—in particular those of its abstractness, ideality, and immanence. In regard to each of these, we must attend especially to the term "pure" in the formulation "pure metaphysician." A *pure* metaphysician is one who rejects any relation of similitude or mirroring between the ideal and the real or between thought and experience, whether that be to the benefit of the ideal as the abstract essentialization of the real (dogmatism) or to that of experience as the merely accidental instigation of ideality (empiricism). In *The Idea of Pure Critique*, Iain Mackenzie has shown along such lines how the Deleuzian philosophical project may be understood as a radicalization or purification of Kant's transcendental turn and how Kant's own critical outflanking of the effect of "indifference" elicited by the simple and abstract opposition of dogmatic and skeptical thought returns in an intensified way in Deleuze's work.[5] This perhaps surprising link between Deleuze and Kant, however, only serves to sharpen a longstanding paradox determining much of Western metaphysics since Plato, namely the apparent contradiction that the ideal universality of thought is understood on the one hand as attainable only by means of an act of abstraction from concrete experience and yet on the other hand as already fully realized within a pure and indivisible immanence-to-itself. In short, ideality must be both transcendent and immanent with respect to the mixtures of experience—hence the Kantian (and Deleuzian) recourse to the transcendental as a subtle finessing of this very distinction.

The question of how mathematical thought might model or fail to model metaphysics finds itself everywhere overdetermined by this paradox, which is at once that of the unity and difference of abstraction and concretion, ideality and reality, and immanence and transcendence. It is worth recalling in this context the canonical structure of Platonic metaphysics as expressed diagrammatically in the *Republic*'s "divided line":[6]

	VISIBLE	:	INTELLIGIBLE	
eikasia :	*pistis*		*dianoia*	:	*noēsis*

The divided line is organized into four sections, which are produced through the reiteration of a distinction (and, thus, a relation) made once and then made again within each of the terms thus distinguished. The unequal (and thus ordered) relation between the visible (*to horāton*) and the intelligible (*to noēton*) is in this manner reproduced within the visible itself as the relation between illusion (*eikasia*) and faith (*pistis*) and within the intelligible as the relation of deductive reasoning (*dianoia*) to intellectual intuition (*noēsis*). In this way, the three relations indicated in the diagram above are in fact conceived as equal—although *what* they relate is different in each case: (visible : intelligible) = (*eikasia* : *pistis*) = (*dianoia* : *noēsis*). The target of the philosophical ascent for Plato is of course the fourth region, the intelligible pole reiterated and intensified: *noēsis*, or intellectual intuition.

This fourth and in an important sense final section of the line represents the fullest intensification or purification of the intelligible and is expressed in the dialogue in terms of an immanent axiomatics that is at once mathematical and meta-mathematical. As distinguished from the mixed, deductive thinking of *dianoia* in which mathematical and logical axioms are taken for granted and simply applied or reproduced (the visible part of the intelligible), *noēsis* involves a purely intuitive form of thought (the intelligible part of the intelligible) in which—in Plato/Socrates's words—"argument itself grasps with the power of dialectic, making the hypotheses not beginnings but really hypotheses—that is, steppingstones and springboards—in order to reach what is free from hypothesis at the beginning of the whole."[7] The mathematical relation between axioms and deductions as understood and applied at the level of *dianoia* is here both fulfilled and transcended: in *noēsis* the constructive power of the axioms is conceived entirely through and within the forms themselves. Socrates describes the immanence of this "beginning of the whole" as in some sense including its opposite and relational term (*dianoia*) while nonetheless excluding the entire region opposed and related to this conjoined pair taken together (the visible): "When it has grasped this, argument now depends on that which depends on this beginning and in such fashion goes back down again to an end; making no use of anything sensed in any way, but using forms themselves, going through forms to forms, it ends in forms too."[8]

Often overlooked in well-worn readings of Platonic "transcendence" and "dualism" is the thoroughgoing and explicit *immanence* that characterizes the theoretical aim of Platonic philosophy. From forms through forms to forms without "making [. . .] use of anything sensed in any way"—clearly it is the precise characterization of the forms themselves that must bear the weight of any clear analysis of the Socratic/Platonic account. What is noticeable at any rate in the present context is how the very act of noetic intuition attains *with respect to* the forms a surprisingly Deleuzian cast. What Deleuze seems here to share with Plato (at least as restricted to the level of Platonic *noēsis*) and which would seem to preclude any formal axiomatization in the modern mathematical sense of *either* philosopher's thought is the definite rejection of any external mediating apparatus that would structure or represent—no matter how abstractly—the immanent power of thought itself. As a metaphysician of the virtual, Deleuze thus appears to intensify a drive to immanence that is already implicit in Plato's divided line; in intensifying this, however, he aims to purify it, much as he radicalizes and aims to purify the Kantian notion of the transcendental on MacKenzie's reading.

Deleuze casts Kant and Plato as among his foremost philosophical adversaries. Yet in his explicit opposition to Platonic and Kantian philosophy, Deleuze rejects what he understands to be an illegitimate dualism within the infrastructure of their respective metaphysics while yet intensifying and radicalizing a drive toward pure immanence at work in each of them. This practice of rejecting conceptual dualisms while nonetheless strategically making use of them serves as more or less a general method for Deleuzian thought. In *A Thousand Plateaus*, he and Guattari write:

> We invoke one dualism only in order to challenge another. We employ a dualism of models only in order to arrive at a process that challenges all models. Each time, mental correctives are necessary to undo the dualisms we had no wish to construct but through which we pass. Arrive at the magic formula we all seek—PLURALISM = MONISM—via all the dualisms that are the enemy, an entirely necessary enemy, the furniture we are forever rearranging.[9]

Any search for a mathematics adequate to Deleuze's metaphysics finds itself standing here before a significant challenge. Any particular system or method of mathematics would appear to fix a given abstract and formal "model" in such a way that the philosophical "challenging of all models" would thereby become impossible. This would seem to be the crux of the difference whereby philosophy is able to define itself as irreducible to any mathematics: philosophy must engage not only the purity of ideal abstraction but, equally, this latter's difference from the reality of what resists abstraction—not to mention the complexes of relation holding (and failing to hold) across these two domains.[10] So if a mathematics adequate to Deleuzian metaphysics is to be found, it will be a matter of locating—or of constructing—a mathematical milieu for thought in which the invocation of mediating dualisms (including those of mathematics) is, in the service of the challenging of dualisms more generally, conceived immanently, that is, without reference to any exterior domain or domains in which such a movement of thought would be either grounded *a priori* or applied *a posteriori*. In other words, the requisite mathematics must be capable of both theorizing its real processes of abstraction and transcendentally generating the events or sequences of its modelization. A mathematics must thus be identified which is sufficiently "dialectical" to include—that is, to model adequately—its own *open relation* to the non-mathematical fields and domains from which it may emerge and to which it may be applied. Clearly, this task itself represents a challenge to the way the inherited problem of ideality and reality has in the Western tradition largely determined the relation between metaphysics and mathematics. It is in light of this challenge that any aiming at a mathematical model of the Deleuzian virtual must take its bearings.

From Deleuze's Virtual to Lautman's Mathematics

When Deleuze explains his terminology of the "virtual" in *Difference and Repetition* he invokes a distinction between the in-itself "complete" reality of the virtual and the "whole" of the actual object of which the virtual constitutes one part.[11] Before making this clarification, however, in defining the virtual as such Deleuze specifies how its difference from the actual undercuts the traditional distinction of the ideal from the real:

> The virtual is opposed not to the real but to the actual. *The virtual is fully real in so far as it is virtual.* Exactly what Proust said of states of resonance must be said of the virtual: 'Real without being actual, ideal without being abstract'; and symbolic without being fictional. Indeed, the virtual must be defined as strictly a part of the real object—as though the object had one part of itself in the virtual into which it plunged as though into an objective dimension.[12]

Of what exactly, then, does the virtual "part" of an object consist? To address this question, Deleuze alludes to the extended interpretation of differential calculus that takes up much of the first part of chapter 4 of *Difference and Repetition*.[13] Consolidating the results of that earlier analysis, he writes, "The reality of the virtual consists of the differential elements and relations along with the singular points which correspond to them. *The reality of the virtual is structure*."[14] The specific reality of the virtual is thus clearly determined, and in one sense our question of how precisely to conceive the virtual (and *a fortiori* any mathematicization of the virtual) is answered. But we must take great care to ensure that Deleuze's statement is not misinterpreted, since "structure" is generally understood to signify a set of merely abstract relations that may be indifferently satisfied by any possible objects. And in this light, Deleuze explicitly warns us: "The only danger in all this is that the virtual could be confused with the possible."[15]

Rather than subsisting as simple, abstract possibilities, virtualities—including mathematical virtualities—must be conceived in terms of transcendental events of becoming. Thus, to grasp the full scope of the problem of mathematicizing the virtual, the interpretation of differential calculus in *Difference and Repetition* must be coordinated with the analysis of the Stoic sense-event in *The Logic of Sense*. The key link for our purposes takes place between the Eighth Series of Structure and the Tenth Series of the Ideal Game in *The Logic of Sense*, where Deleuze situates the Ninth Series of the Problematic. He begins with the straightforward question "What is an ideal event?," and answers immediately: "It is a singularity—or rather a set of singularities or of singular points characterizing a mathematical curve, a physical state of affairs, a psychological and moral person."[16] With this identification of ideal events and singular points—indifferently mathematical, physical, psychological, moral—Deleuze sets up the conjugation of the virtual as structure with a concept of transcendental becoming that will ensure that the virtual cannot be misconstrued as merely abstract or formal possibility. Virtual structure must consist of dynamic production and not merely static representation. In *The Logic of Sense*, the concept of the *problematic* links the corresponding discussion of problems and solutions in *Difference and Repetition* to a theory of the constitution of sense itself as an expressive field of ideal, transcendentally generative events. Deleuze will oppose these directly to Plato's ideas as in a kind of reversal: "To reverse Platonism is first and foremost to remove essences and to substitute events in their place, as jets of singularities."[17] As Deleuze describes it, this reversal fights—with undeniable Kantian echoes—a "double" or "twofold" battle against dogmatism on the one hand and empiricism on the other: "A double battle has the objective to thwart all dogmatic confusion between event and essence, and also every empiricist confusion between event and accident."[18]

Interestingly, in *Logics of Worlds* Badiou chooses this very passage to epitomize his critique of Deleuze's notion of the sense-event and to distinguish his own concept of the event from Deleuze's. Badiou first cites the "double battle" claim just quoted and then writes:

> There's nothing to add. Except that, when he thinks the event as the intensified and continuous result of becoming, Deleuze is an empiricist (which after all he always claimed to be). And that, when he reabsorbs the event into the One of the 'unlimited *Aion*, of the Infinitive in which it subsists and insists,' in the always-there of the Virtual, he has a tendency to dogmatism.[19]

In effect, Badiou is accusing Deleuze of succumbing to *both* of the forms of confusion over the event that Deleuze himself identifies. Deleuze's philosophy, in Badiou's view, remains both empiricist and dogmatic at once. And in a repetition of Deleuze's own purifying Kantian gesture, Badiou concludes his discussion of Deleuze with a summary of his own strategy for breaking with empiricism and dogmatism in thinking the event:

> To break with empiricism is to think the event as the advent of what subtracts itself from all experience: the ontologically un-founded and the transcendentally discontinuous. To break with dogmatism is to remove the event from the ascendancy of the One. It is to subtract it from Life in order to deliver it to the stars.[20]

The complex debate between Deleuze and Badiou has been analyzed at length elsewhere.[21] It is generally agreed at any rate that one major point of difference between them remains the philosophical status of mathematics as an index of metaphysical being. Is the mathematics of set theory fully adequate to ontology (Badiou) or must every mathematical model ultimately be subordinated to an irreducible dynamism between the virtual and the actual (Deleuze)? To understand more precisely how this dispute ties in to our present line of questioning, let us turn to an important philosophical and mathematical source common to both Deleuze and Badiou, a "common factor" of sorts that may help us to move past the simple dichotomization of these two thinkers and the *agon* of their respective approaches to philosophy toward a standpoint from which their separate contributions to contemporary thought may perhaps be consolidated and mutually reinforced. This source is the Platonically-inspired reflections on mathematical method carried out by Albert Lautman in the 1930s.

Let us examine a particular thesis set forth by Lautman in his 1937 article "The Axiomatic and the Method of Division." This thesis concerns the role and process of abstraction in mathematical method. Lautman first works through a series of general concepts drawn from various domains of mathematics—equality, multiplication, unity, measure and integral, absolute value—and then in reflection upon these he suggests the conclusion that the mathematical abstraction of concepts works otherwise than by identifying general types or abstract kinds: "The passage from notions said to be 'elementary' to abstract notions doesn't present itself as a subsumption of the particular under the general but as the division or analysis of a 'mix' which tends to release the simple notions with which this mix participates."[22] The Platonic language of "participation" here is not accidental. Lautman goes on to distinguish this method of abstraction explicitly as a Platonic division or *diaeresis* opposed to the Aristotelian categorization through genus and species: "It is therefore not Aristotelian logic, that of genera and species, that plays a part here, but the Platonic method of division, as taught in the *Sophist* and *Philebus*, for which the unity of Being is a unit of composition and a starting point for the search for principles that are united in the Ideas."[23]

Importantly, Lautman conceives this Platonic interpretation of abstraction as a way to understand mathematical axiomatics in a purely dynamic or "structural" way, relative to the mathematical material to which they are applied, and he finds in this dialectical relationship between axiomatic abstraction and mathematical material a kinship with the *Sophist*'s intertwining of Same, Other and Being:

> The axiomatic definitions "by abstraction" of equivalence, measure, operators, evaluation, etc., thus characterize not a "type" in extension but the possibilities of structuration, integration, operations, of closure conceived in a dynamic and organizational way. The distinction that is thereby established within a same notion between the intrinsic properties of an entity or notion and its possibilities of action seems to be similar to the Platonic distinction between the Same and the Other that is found in the unity of Being. The Same would be that by which a notion is intrinsic, the Other that by which it can enter in relation with other notions and act on them.[24]

What Lautman proposes is a concept of the inner dynamism that necessarily characterizes the development of mathematics itself, a structural dialectic of problematization and axiomatization.

A somewhat detailed analysis based on an example offered by Lautman himself helps to clarify the point at issue.[25] We pose the general conceptual question: what is unity, or oneness? More determinately and formally, we ask:

what is 1 in the context of an algebraic formula such as $1X = X$ or $X1 = X$? As Lautman says, in such formulations "the term 1 plays a dual role: it is the unit element of the domain of operators acting on the domain of X, and it is also the identity operator that transforms the elements X of the base domain."[26] Despite its apparent simplicity, to fully grasp the conceptual stakes of this dual role of a single operator, here "1" as "unit element" and/or "identity operator," in fact provides a key to understanding Lautman's entire philosophy of mathematics as well as his remarkable prescience with respect to the mathematics of category theory that emerges in the decades after his early death.

What exactly are the two roles as distinguished here? For simplicity of exposition, we translate "unit element" to "unity" and "identity operator" to "identity." On the one hand, then, as *unity* the operator "1" is conceived as functioning in a special relation to all the other possible operators on the domain X. In other words, "1" is conceived not insofar as it interacts with X itself, but with the many possible ways X may be transformed. In the space of possible relations among all such transformations, this unique transformation plays a particular and privileged role, that of inert reproduction. For instance, if we consider the set F of endofunctions $f: X \rightarrow X$, any one of these (say, f_a) may be composed with any other (say, f_b) to form a new function: $f_b(f_a)$. Yet exactly one function, namely the function $f_u(x) = x$, composes commutatively with any other endofunction in this way to output precisely that other function itself. Formally, $f_u(f_n) = f_n = f_n(f_u)$ for all f_n belonging to F. Indeed, this cancelling operation applies not only to endofunctions on X, but to *any* function into or out of X for which $f_u(f_n)$ or $f_n(f_u)$ is defined. Thus, this particular function f_u serves as the uniquely non-transforming, non-distorting relay of any and every other transformative function on X. In short, "1" conceived as *unity* is a certain *relation defined and understood with respect to its interactions with other relations.*

On the other hand, as *identity* the operator "1" is understood in a more straightforward manner as acting directly upon the object-domain X itself, or rather in a single, formally identical way upon each of that domain's unique elements. It is clear that there exists exactly one function, f_i, such that for every element x of X, that function returns in every case the very same value that it takes as argument. Formally, $f_i(x) = x$. Without considering the relational, or immanently structured space of all possible transformations of X (i.e., functions into and out of X), the identity function is conceived in this way "absolutely" with respect to X itself as simply returning, for any given element of X, that same element itself. This, then, is not a function understood in terms of its possible interactions with other functions (as is the case with "unity" as analyzed above), but solely in terms of its own specific character, its unique "direct functioning" of identical repetition or self-identity. In short, "1" is conceived here as a *relation determined only with respect to its given elements, or terms.*

The key dialectical point here is that Lautman is not speaking of two distinct functions in this regard, but of precisely *one and the same* function (unity = identity) considered in two distinct but interrelated roles ("unity" ≠ "identity"), the one conceived as effectively "immanent" to the relative space of possible transformative operators on the base domain and the other as essentially "transcendent" with respect to the base domain on which it operates in an absolute manner. Mathematically and formally the two functions are the same, $f_u = f_i$, although conceptually they are quite different. Here we see Lautman's Platonic dialectic of Same and Other as manifest within a given mathematical instance, yet the more general point that Lautman aims to illustrate is that mathematics as a whole advances always through such a dialectic being played out by all its key concepts. Mathematics is always already in itself characterized by a formal-conceptual dialectic of transcendence and immanence that constitutes an open mathematical-philosophical *problem*, indeed mathematics *as* (philosophical) problem. Every act of abstract transcendence in mathematical thought, that is, every theoretical abstraction away from the given determinacies of some mathematical or extra-mathematical object or domain, necessarily calls upon and simultaneously produces a paradoxically higher-order immanence, a new domain of reciprocrally-determined structural transformations into which the simple act of transcendence is thereby subsumed and differentiated. The simple abstraction of a target "form" that is intended only to reproduce the essential Same of its concrete source necessarily induces a variability and relationality— an irreducible Other—which relativizes and "de-simplifies" the abstract target itself.

In this way, Lautman defines the proper dialectic of mathematical thought: an insistently recurring continuous structuration (relational immanence) following upon punctual acts of abstract objectivation (simple transcendence). In the present context, we must ask: can Lautman's essentially philosophical insight into the immanent/transcendent movement of mathematical concepts be brought into the fold of mathematics itself? Can there be a proper *mathematics* of Lautman's dialectical philosophy of mathematics? Such a mathematics, if it exists, would answer the need for a model of Deleuze's metaphysics that would not reduce the real distinction between the virtual and the actual to the merely formal distinction of the abstract and concrete. It would, in addition, give us grounds—among other things—for the rigorous comparison and communication of Deleuze's metaphysics with Badiou's set-theoretical ontology.[27]

From Lautman to Category Theory

Lautman died in 1944. Yet what is startling in retrospect when reading the writings primarily from the 1930s collected in *Mathematics, Ideas and the Physical Real* is how much Lautman's dialectical conception of mathematical thinking anticipates the subsequent development of the mathematics of category theory.[28] The emergence of this branch of mathematics from its relatively obscure origins in algebraic topology into a universal, quasi-foundational mathematical discipline today with applications not only in other branches of mathematics but also in many extra-mathematical domains ranging from cognitive science and physics to computer programming is perhaps the most striking event in the mathematics of the past half-century. Coming out of the work of Eilenberg and MacLane in the 1940s and taking shape in its current form with the developments initiated by Grothendieck, Kan, Lawvere, and others in the 1950s and 1960s, category theory has become in recent decades the most promising avenue for keeping the diverse branches of mathematics in productive communication without merely reducing them to the common axiomatics of a sterile and unwieldy "foundation."[29] Unlike the foundational usage of set theory, for instance, category theory unifies mathematics not by positing that all mathematics really amounts to one and the same kind of thing, sets, but by establishing an open terrain of inter-translatability across disparate object-domains: sets, groups, topoi, logical languages, programming algorithms, etc. Category theory does not simply convert the objects of these various domains into categories, but rather accepts their relative autonomy while nevertheless showing how categories naturally arise within them, allowing their native insights and results to be generalized and translated into other mathematical and extra-mathematical contexts.

Category theory may thus be conceived as a kind of "universal translator" for mathematics. Yet part of its power results from the fact that while translating structure from one domain to another, it does not serve as a transcendent mathematical meta-language but is itself rather one more relatively autonomous mathematical domain. Category theory is thus able rigorously to investigate all domains of mathematics *including itself*. How is this possible without inducing the well-known paradoxes of set theory? By way of shifting the terrain of investigation from objects to relations, or—what amounts to the same thing—from entities to structures. This shift, however, does not invoke a transcendence but rather takes place within the immanence of the theory itself. In this way, category theory is able to be both a "science of itself and of its object" without thereby restricting its field of application to some set of transcendentally deduced models.[30] It is this dialectical aspect of category-theoretical mathematics that suggests its relevance for Deleuze's metaphysics in particular.

Now, the language of "structures" is likely to raise immediate suspicions among Deleuzian-minded philosophers. Deleuze is often held up as one of the paradigmatic "post-structuralists," and even if this term resists easy definition, surely—it is thought—it implies a rejection of thought that works by way of "structures." However, just as the received notion of Deleuze as a philosopher who simply breaks with Plato and Kant dissolves under critical scrutiny, so the conception of Deleuze the "post-structuralist" must be suitably reconsidered. It is clear at any rate that the concept of structure is an important one for Deleuze, as evidenced by the depth and detail of his essay "How Do We Recognize Structuralism?" and his review of the French Spinoza scholar, Martial Guéroult.[31] An examination of Deleuze's condensed analysis of Guéroult in particular shows that what is at stake in this kind of structuralism is *not* just the more familiar notion that seeps into many fields of the humanities and social sciences in the 1960s and 1970s largely through the influence of de Saussure and Lévi-Strauss. Instead, Guéroult's structuralism represents a unique interpretative framework for research in the history of philosophical concepts in particular. It is meant to provide a rigorous critical tool for examining how philosophical concepts and systems develop and transform with respect to one another without importing irrelevant concerns of merely cultural or historical interest. In this regard, Guéroult aims at a relatively independent analytical framework in which philosophy from diverse historical epochs involving disparate conceptual vocabularies and grammars may be studied comparatively without presuming a single meta-vocabulary or an already-established philosophy of (philosophical) history. This structuralism thus provides a way to examine the conceptual transformations and innovations in philosophy that is at once historical, critical, and philosophical.

Deleuze's own philosophical practice participates in this broader aim. Much of the importance of Deleuze's work, especially in its early phases, may be understood at this quasi-formal interpretative level, whereby he shows us how philosophers of the past and present (Spinoza, Leibniz, Hume, Kant, Nietzsche, Bergson, Foucault) may be lifted from their historical and textual contexts and examined primarily in terms of the disembedded conceptual relations that may be extracted and constructed from their work. To be sure, it is precisely the constructive aspect of this project that appears to resist the "structuralist" label, and a scholar such as Guéroult does seem to take the conceptual elements of the structures themselves as a kind of ultimate given to be catalogued, whereas Deleuze *mobilizes* the structures implicit in the philosophers he treats in such a way that their concepts no longer function, even transcendentally, as static structures. This would constitute his broadly "Nietzschean" reaction against structuralism. But note that this creative (and no longer merely critical) usage of structuralist methods corresponds closely to Deleuze's rejection of ideality as mere abstraction in favor of his conception of virtuality as fully real—though not concrete or actual.

Category theory provides a mathematics that supports both "structuralist" and "post-structuralist" practices in the senses just outlined. A category is in itself nothing more nor less than a collection of objects in principle denuded of their intrinsic properties and conceived solely in terms of the system of external relations or transformative mappings holding *between* these objects themselves. The axioms of category theory guarantee that the relations thus specified hold together in a determinate, intelligible way so that the relevant internal information about the category's objects (from the standpoint of the given category) is recoverable solely from examining the relations among these relations themselves. In other words, a category effectively abstracts away from properties understood as adhering to distinct individuals and translates instead a certain *kind* of property—a category—into a determinate relational system structuring a collection of any such individuals. The individuals themselves thereby come to be regarded as mere placeholders (categorical "objects") for specifying how the (meta-)relations among the relations themselves in the given system (categorical "arrows" and their compositions) in fact represent all the relevant information pertaining to any such individuals *with respect to* the determined kind of property at issue (precisely, the "category" itself). At this level, we are thus able to characterize in a fully general way the determination of a structure that may be conceived independently of its constituent elements. Only the relations between the elements are determined, and these are themselves determined only via their mutual interactions. In other words, categories are in this sense realized unities of structures-of-relation *as such*.

Yet this is only one half of the story. Category theory reveals its full potential not in the specification of abstract structures of particular categories, however important these may be (e.g., those of sets and functions, groups and homomorphisms, topological spaces and continuous functions, etc.). The real power of category theory becomes evident when categories themselves are considered as objects related to one another by means of *functors*, which may be understood roughly as generalizations of set-theoretical functions (from the relations of functions between sets, we move up to a level at once more abstract and more richly structured: that of functors between categories, and indeed from there to the next level up of *natural transformations* between functors themselves). All the relevant internal structure of particular categories may then be recovered at the level of functors by way of the system of external relations that link all categories to one another through all the possible functors translating one into another. This system itself constitutes **Cat**, the *category of categories* first posited and investigated as a possible universal foundation or milieu for mathematics by William Lawvere in the late 1960s.[32] At this level, structured categories themselves may be investigated and understood solely on the basis of their external relations with one another via functors, their translations-within-the-relevant-kind of categories as such. Seen from this perspective, the structures-of-relation that characterize particular categories become absolved from any interpretation in terms of a simple and abstract transcendence with respect to their elements or objects. Instead, the structures themselves are determined immanently on the basis of their potential variations or translations through and into other structures. Structures thus become objects in the sense unique to category theory, that is, nodes or placeholders within a system of immanent transformations of arrows, or morphisms. Structures as such thus become subject to the same determinations via external relational and transformational operations generally characterizing the objects or elements of structures themselves.

The most important point is that these two different aspects, the specific double-articulation of which constitutes category theory in all its expressive range and power, are one and the same from the perspective internal to category theory itself. When one specifies a category abstractly, one simultaneously determines the internal system of relations holding among its objects *and* the external relations that hold between that category itself and any and all other categories. These determinations—like those dear to Deleuze of the "order and connection" of ideal and extensional causal series in Spinoza's *Ethics*—may be distinguished (rationally) as two and yet remain perfectly identical (formally).[33] Understood in this way, every category essentially *is* the translation or translatability of its internal into its external relations. One could say that in general category theory uses the difference between internal and external relational determinations to demonstrate the objective *in*-difference of this distinction itself from the relative perspective of some appropriate level of conceptualization. Like Deleuze's philosophical distinction between the virtual and the actual, one is concerned here with a structural difference that does not divide a common genus into two separate classes, but rather unfolds a progressive, genetic determination immanent to the relation of ideality and objectivity at work in the object itself.

From a Deleuzian perspective, this means that the category-theoretical "image of thought"—or, rather, the image of thought whose "logic" is at once formalized and materialized in category theory—is that of *realized immanence*. Because categories are determined structurally and thus remain essentially indifferent to their various actualizations (up to isomorphism), the entire field of mathematics is itself generalized in principle by category theory across any system of objects and relations at whatever level of abstraction or concretion. The category **2**, for instance, is equivalently realized in a function between two sets, a homomorphism between a pair of groups, or any single, unilateral relation—unrequited love, say—between two people.[34] Nevertheless, **2** is not thereby determined as a genus or equivalence class (although such generalities may in various ways be derived from it). In this way, the mathematics of category theory is as much in direct contact with concrete, worldly actuality as with the most formal theories and meta-theories. What Lautman saw in a glass darkly—an immanent dialectic between mathematical abstraction and real modelization—category theory sets before our (indifferently perceptual and conceptual) eyes and allows us to see (at once visibly and intelligibly) face to face.

Conclusion

We answer our question, then, concerning the possibility of a mathematical model of Deleuze's virtual with a speculative hypothesis: V = C. This formula is meant to represent the claim that the internal structure of Deleuze's metaphysics of the virtual (V) is identical to the mathematical theory of categories (C) as conceptualized within the post-Lawvere tradition of a universal mathematics modeled within **Cat**, the category of categories. If this hypothesis is correct, we then possess an infinitely rich and yet non-arbitrary and definite field of rigorous experimentation in which the relation of the actual and the virtual in Deleuze's philosophy may be investigated in its own right as well as translated into diverse contexts. At any rate, it provides a clear path for advancing such investigations and translations.

Philosophical and mathematical experimentation within the framework of the hypothesis V = C promises, among other things, the possibility of a rigorous formalization of the notion of pre-individual singularities and of the passage from the pre-individual field of events to that of actualized individuals that is the act or process of individuation itself as different/ciation. It is clear that this key aspect of Deleuze's metaphysics resists formalization along the lines of standard first-order logic. Because variables ("dark precursors") in Deleuze's thought do not quantify over a pre-specified domain of individuals, but rather organize virtual problems the solutions to which necessarily invoke a moment of creative construction, it would seem that any mathematical or logical formalization of this aspect of Deleuze's metaphysics remains impossible. Unfortunately, this resistance to formalization easily slides into commentary and critical reception of Deleuze's work that is less than thoroughly rigorous. But if the diverse processes of Deleuzian individuation may be formalized within category theory without losing their creative and relatively indeterminate character, this would be because category theory itself is able to preserve in a rigorous fashion— performatively, as it were, in its own functioning—the problematic relation of continuity between the virtual and the actual themselves, which Lautman identified as the essential structural dialectic of mathematics as a whole. In this way, the problematic conceptualization of the relation between the actual and the virtual finds a solution adequate to the problem itself through its modeling by category theory; it thereby preserves the creative and constructive power of the problem without loss of rigor. This same flexibility and power provides a definite, rigorous framework as well for investigating such later concepts as diagrammaticization in *A Thousand Plateaus* and the distinction of the movement-image from the time-image in *Cinema 1* and *2* as continuous and translatable with Deleuze's earlier work.[35] Seen in the light of category theory and the V = C hypothesis, such concepts become understandable as grounded in the metaphysics of the virtual and thus explicable on its basis. The unity of Deleuze's wide-ranging philosophical project becomes visible and operative.

The hypothesis V = C also opens a way to clarify in a non-partisan manner the differends and convergences of Deleuze and Badiou and, more importantly, to put their respective philosophies into productive communication despite their obvious antagonisms. Badiou himself has turned in a very limited way to the mathematics of category theory in his *Logics of Worlds* in order to patch up what he must now admit is the incomplete set-theoretical picture proffered in *Being and Event*. This somewhat disappointing maneuver, however, which makes of the otherwise insightful and useful formal apparatus of *Logics of Worlds* a restrictive and fundamentally conservative metaphysics of relation, may be taken up and revitalized in a Deleuzian vein by "turning Badiou on his head" and inverting the priority Badiou maintains of set theory over category theory and of objects over relations. Where Badiou (like the Neo-Platonist Porphyry) refuses the full "descent of the One" into real, material immanence (and thus ultimately finds a sufficient mathematical metaphysics in the binary logic of set theory), Deleuze requires the immanence of the virtual One within material actuality (like Porphyry's opponent Iamblichus) and is thereby pushed in the direction of a more supple mathematics of continuity and purely relational difference—category theory. In general, by working from within category theory directly as the mathematical expression of the Deleuzian virtual, Deleuze's philosophy may be brought to a higher level of theoretical rigor without thereby excluding the anti-formalist, minoritarian, and deterritorializing impulses that make it so essential to our contemporary philosophical and political conjuncture. Rather than cancelling out these "model-challenging" tendencies, their investment in category-theoretical mathematics promises a much wider field for the deployment of Deleuzian thinking than has previously been possible, particularly into such mathematically-based disciplines as economics, computer science, physics, and bio-technology.[36] Much work waits to be done along these lines.

In the same 1981 interview with Arnauld Villani in which Deleuze identifies himself as a "pure metaphysician," Deleuze explains that he shares with Bergson a desire to produce a philosophy equal to the scientific breakthroughs of modern physics and biology. Alongside Bergson, he laments in this regard that "modern science has not found its metaphysics, the metaphysics it needs." With respect to the possibility of satisfying this need, Deleuze remarks, "It is that metaphysics that interests me."[37] Perhaps in the mathematics of category theory, philosophers in the wake of Deleuze have at last found a formal apparatus adequate to the abstract machinic creativity of the virtual. It is at any rate a hypothesis worth being put to the test.

Notes

1. Gilles Deleuze, "Responses to a Series of Questions," *Collapse: Philosophical Research and Development* III (2007): 42.

2. Gilles Deleuze, "Mathesis, Science and Philosophy," *Collapse: Philosophical Research and Development* III (2007): 141–55. See also Joshua Ramey, *The Hermetic Deleuze: Philosophy and Spiritual Ordeal* (Durham: Duke University Press, 2012).

3. See Gilles Deleuze, *Difference and Repetition*, trans. Paul Patton (New York: Columbia University Press, 1994) and Gilles Deleuze, *The Logic of Sense*, trans. Mark Lester and Charles Stivale (New York: Columbia University Press, 1990). In this way, as defined across this pair of works, the virtual comes to be conceived in a particular formal relation to mathematics while still remaining irreducible to any mathematics in principle.

4. Gilles Deleuze and Félix Guattari, *A Thousand Plateaus: Capitalism and Schizophrenia*, trans. Brian Massumi (Minneapolis: University of Minnesota Press, 1987), 111–48. The new elements drawn from Hjelmslev and Peirce appear to have been largely Guattari's contribution in the partnership. See Felix Guattari, *The Machinic Unconscious: Essays in Schizoanalysis*, trans. Taylor Adkins (Los Angeles: Semiotext(e), 2011).

5. Iain Mackenzie, *The Idea of Pure Critique* (New York: Continuum, 2004), 1–14. In similar fashion, Deleuze scholars such as Christian Kerslake, *Immanence and the Vertigo of Philosophy: From Kant to Deleuze* (Edinburgh: Edinburgh University Press, 2009) and Beth Lord, *Kant and Spinozism: Transcendental Idealism and Immanence from Jacobi to Deleuze* (New York: Palgrave Macmillan, 2011) have demonstrated how despite Deleuze's explicit repudiations of Kant, the turn to the transcendental remains essential to Deleuze's own thought. François Laruelle makes the same point in a more general way, showing how this Kantian element remains a common milieu for all contemporary, allegedly "post-Kantian" philosophy, in particular the philosophies of Deleuze, Heidegger and Derrida. See François Laruelle, *Philosophies of Difference: A*

Critical Introduction to Non-Philosophy, trans. Rocco Gangle (New York: Continuum, 2010).

6. Plato, *Republic* 509d–511e, trans. A. Bloom (New York: Basic Books, 1991).

7. Plato, *Republic* 511b.

8. Plato, *Republic* 511b.

9. Deleuze and Guattari, *A Thousand Plateaus*, 20–21.

10. Cf. the differentiation of philosophical concepts from scientific functions in Gilles Deleuze and Félix Guattari, *What is Philosophy?*, trans. Hugh Tomlinson and Graham Burchell (New York: Columbia University Press, 1994), 117–35.

11. Deleuze, *Difference and Repetition*, 209.

12. Deleuze, *Difference and Repetition*, 208–9.

13. Deleuze, *Difference and Repetition*, 170–82.

14. Deleuze, *Difference and Repetition*, 209, emphasis added.

15. Deleuze, *Difference and Repetition*, 211.

16. Deleuze, *The Logic of Sense*, 52.

17. Deleuze, *The Logic of Sense*, 53.

18. Deleuze, *The Logic of Sense*, 53.

19. Alain Badiou, *Logics of Worlds*, trans. Alberto Toscano (New York: Continuum, 2009), 387.

20. Badiou, *Logics of Worlds*, 387.

21. See in particular Daniel W. Smith, "Mathematics and the Theory of Multiplicities: Badiou and Deleuze Revisited," *The Southern Journal of Philosophy* 41 (2003): 411–49.

22. Albert Lautman, *Mathematics, Ideas and the Physical Real*, trans. Simon Duffy (New York: Continuum, 2011), 41.

23. Lautman, *Mathematics*, 41.

24. Lautman, *Mathematics*, 41.

25. The formalism has been slightly modified in what follows ("x" becomes "X") and the argument itself considerably expanded. In addition, we shift Lautman's own discussion in terms of mathematical rings to the generally more familiar terrain of sets and functions. The essential point remains the same.

26. Lautman, *Mathematics*, 37 (translation slightly modified and notation regularized with what follows).

27. Indeed, Lautman's dialectic seems to include both Deleuzian and Badiousian elements as moments of its own movement. In a sense, this dialectic simultaneously distinguishes and unites the immanence of a Deleuzian virtual One and the transcendence of the Badiousian count-as-One as dual aspects immanent to the unity of mathematics as a whole.

28. Cf. Fernando Zalamea, "Albert Lautman and the Creative Dialectic of Modern Mathematics," in Albert Lautman, *Mathematics*, xxxiv–xxxvii.

29. For a historical analysis of the development of category theory, see Ralf Krömer, *Tool and Object: A History and Philosophy of Category Theory* (Basel: Birkhäuser, 2007). The standard reference for basic category theory remains Saunders Mac Lane, *Categories for the Working Mathematician*, 2nd ed. (New York: Springer-Verlag, 2010). The best elementary introduction to category theory is F. William Lawvere and Stephen Schanuel, *Conceptual Mathematics: A first introduction to categories*, 2nd ed. (Cambridge: Cambridge University Press, 2009).

30. The phrase "science of itself and of its object" is taken from the work of Laruelle and his distinction notion of non-philosophy. See, for instance, Francois Laruelle, *Théorie des Identités* (Paris: PUF, 1992).

31. Gilles Deleuze, "Guéroult's General Method for Spinoza" and "How Do We Recognize Structuralism?," *Desert Islands and Other Texts: 1953–1974*, multiple translators (Los Angeles: Semiotext(e), 2004), 146–55 and 170–92.

32. Today, this initial work by Lawvere has developed in a more differentiated fashion through the diverse technical specializations of higher-order category theory and its relatives. See J. Lambek and P.J. Scott, *Introduction to Higher Order Categorical Logic* (Cambridge: Cambridge University Press, 1986).

33. Formally, this insight is expressed by the fact that any category C is isomorphic to the category of functors and natural transformations from the (unique up to isomorphism) terminal category (called 1) into C.

34. Here, 2 is simply the unique-up-to-isomorphism category consisting of two objects and exactly one non-identity arrow between them.

35. Gilles Deleuze, *Cinema 1: The Movement-Image*, trans. Hugh Tomlinson and Barbara Habberjam (Minneapolis: University of Minnesota Press, 2001) and Gilles Deleuze, *Cinema 2: The Time-Image*, trans. Hugh Tomlinson and Robert Galeta (Minneapolis: University of Minnesota Press, 2001). For a study of how the diagrammatic expression of category theory may inform a Deleuzian pedagogy of mathematics, see Rocco Gangle, "From Brackets to Arrows: Sets, Categories and the Deleuzian Pedagogy of Mathematics," *Deleuze and Education*, ed. Inna Semetsky and Diana Masny (London: Edinburgh University Press, 2013).

36. In this regard, the V = C hypothesis should be especially amenable to those following in the tradition of Manuel DeLanda, *Intensive Science and Virtual Philosophy* (New York: Continuum, 2002).

37. Gilles Deleuze, "Responses to a Series of Questions," 41.

References

Badiou, Alain. *Logics of Worlds*. Translated by Alberto Toscano. New York: Continuum, 2009.

DeLanda, Manuel. *Intensive Science and Virtual Philosophy*. New York: Continuum, 2002.

Deleuze, Gilles. *Cinema 1: The Movement-Image*. Translated by Hugh Tomlinson and Barbara Habberjam. Minneapolis: University of Minnesota Press, 2001.

———. *Cinema 2: The Time-Image*. Translated by Hugh Tomlinson and Robert Galeta. Minneapolis: University of Minnesota Press, 2001.

———. *Desert Islands and Other Texts: 1953–1974*. Multiple translators. Los Angeles: Semiotext(e), 2004.

———. *Difference and Repetition*. Translated by Paul Patton. New York: Columbia University Press, 1994.

———. *The Logic of Sense*. Translated by Mark Lester and Charles Stivale. New York: Columbia University Press, 1990.

———. "Mathesis, Science and Philosophy." *Collapse: Philosophical Research and Development* III (2007): 141–55.

———. "Responses to a Series of Questions." *Collapse: Philosophical Research and Development* III (2007): 39–43.

Deleuze, Gilles and Félix Guattari. *A Thousand Plateaus: Capitalism and Schizophrenia*. Translated by Brian Massumi. Minneapolis: University of Minnesota Press, 1987.

————. *What is Philosophy?* Translated by Hugh Tomlinson and Graham Burchell. New York: Columbia University Press, 1994.

Gangle, Rocco. "From Brackets to Arrows: Sets, Categories and the Deleuzian Pedagogy of Mathematics." Edited by Inna Semetsky and Diana Masny. *Deleuze and Education.* London: Edinburgh University Press, 2013.

Guattari, Félix. *The Machinic Unconscious: Essays in Schizoanalysis.* Translated by Taylor Adkins. Los Angeles: Semiotext(e), 2011.

Kerslake, Christian. *Immanence and the Vertigo of Philosophy: From Kant to Deleuze.* Edinburgh: Edinburgh University Press, 2009.

Krömer, Ralf. *Tool and Object: A History and Philosophy of Category Theory.* Basel: Birkhäuser, 2007.

Lambek, J. and P.J. Scott. *Introduction to Higher Order Categorical Logic.* Cambridge: Cambridge University Press, 1986.

Laruelle, François. *Philosophies of Difference: A Critical Introduction to Non-Philosophy.* Translated by Rocco Gangle. New York: Continuum, 2010.

————. *Théorie des Identités.* Paris: PUF, 1992.

Lautman, Albert. *Mathematics, Ideas and the Physical Real.* Translated by Simon Duffy. New York: Continuum, 2011.

Lawvere, F. William and Stephen Schanuel. *Conceptual Mathematics: A first introduction to categories.* Second edition. Cambridge: Cambridge University Press, 2009.

Lord, Beth. *Kant and Spinozism: Transcendental Idealism and Immanence from Jacobi to Deleuze.* New York: Palgrave Macmillan, 2011.

Mackenzie, Iain. *The Idea of Pure Critique.* New York: Continuum, 2004.

Mac Lane, Saunders. *Categories for the Working Mathematician.* Second edition. New York: Springer-Verlag, 2010.

Plato. *Republic.* Translated by A. Bloom. New York: Basic Books, 1991.

Ramey, Joshua. *The Hermetic Deleuze: Philosophy and Spiritual Ordeal.* Durham: Duke University Press, 2012.

Smith, Daniel W. "Mathematics and the Theory of Multiplicities: Badiou and Deleuze Revisited." *The Southern Journal of Philosophy* XLI (2003): 411–49.

CHAPTER THREE

Difference and Speculation: Heidegger, Meillassoux, and Deleuze on Sufficient Reason

Sjoerd van Tuinen

Those who seek a contemporary return to philosophy as a speculative enterprise, thereby going against the grain of self-critical and self-reflexive postmodern thought, make abundant use of first principles. Not because they ignore the Kantian crusade against the contradictions to which every attempt to find ulti-mate reasons necessarily falls victim, but because we need them in order to es-cape from ourselves and reach for the Outside. In particular, contemporary speculative philosophy is in defiance of the Heideggerian interpretation of the Principle of Sufficient Reason (PSR) as the original sin of Western philosophy. On the one hand, it agrees with Heidegger's rejection of metaphysics as onto-theology. As Quentin Meillassoux, whose work is exemplary in this respect, writes: "metaphysics culminates in the ontological argument, viz., in the claim that this or that entity must absolutely be *because* it is the way it is," which in turn culminates in the PSR.[1] On the other hand, speculation implies a non-dogmatic return to metaphysics precisely to the extent that it does not accept the hermeneutical twist that Heidegger gives to this principle. While the *principium reddendae rationis* literally means that beings must be sufficiently well-founded and representable as such for us, Heidegger demonstrates how it can also be read as a principle of Being according to which reason and ground or thinking and Being co-belong in the element of "the Same," even though this ontological el-ement cannot but remain unfounded or without principle in itself. The conse-quence of this second interpretation would be that nothing positive can be thought of what lies outside of the "co-propriating event" (*Ereignis*) of man and Being. Meillassoux has aptly called this position "strong correlationism": whereas a weak correlationist such as Kant argues for the thinkability of the absolute in itself, even if it cannot be known, strong correlationists like Heidegger or Wittgenstein deny that we can conceive of anything that lies out-side the realm of human access. Yet precisely insofar as they continue to rely on the necessary existence of human thought, they cannot distinguish themselves from the dogmatic metaphysics they so vehemently criticize. Speculative phi-

losophers, by contrast, seek to uncover "an absolute necessity that does not rein-
state any form of absolutely necessary entity."[2] The nature of this absolute necessity and the principles according to which it can be thought form the bifurcation points between the various, often mutually excluding speculative trajecto-
ries.

Within the emerging field of speculative philosophy, Deleuze's place is
somewhat contested. For many, Deleuze is an inveterate metaphysician who, in
the tradition of Leibniz, Hegel, Schelling, Nietzsche and Bergson, hypostatizes
the correlation between Being and thought. Alain Badiou thus famously refers to
Deleuze as an "involuntary Platonist,"[3] whereas Ray Brassier speaks of
Deleuze's "noocentrism."[4] Unlike Heidegger, Deleuze is clearly not a correlationist thinker in the strong sense, since the finitude of human experience is no
longer the touchstone for the thinkable. But neither does he break entirely with
the "correlationist circle," since he agrees with Kant and Heidegger that anything that is totally a-subjective cannot be thought.[5] After all, transcendental
empiricism aims for the "Being of the sensible," that is, Life in *and* for itself. It
is the "complex unity" of difference and repetition or being and thought that
leads Deleuze and Guattari to postulate a "material vitalism,"[6] in which a nonorganic life stretches out to all of nature such that molecules are capable of feeling
whereas human apperception is only one material image among others. Deleuze
thus still seeks access to the absolute by reinstating a form of absolutely necessary entity ("a consciousness by right"),[7] which implies that he must also uphold
some version of the PSR. Does it follow that Deleuze is some aberrant species
of "speculative idealist" whose speculations are not only "absolutizing," but also
"absolutist?"[8] Or is the tripartite division of contemporary philosophy into metaphysics, correlationism and speculative materialism simply inadequate, that is,
too epistemological for describing Deleuze's empiricist and pragmatist revision
of the PSR? Does the PSR still play a role today or must the first principle of
contemporary speculative thinking be the absence of reason altogether (e.g.,
Meillassoux's "principle of unreason," i.e., "the necessity of contingency")?

Transformations of Sufficient Reason

In order to answer these questions, let us begin with Mogens Laerke's observation that Deleuze's work contains nothing less than an attempt at what Leibniz
called a "New System of Nature."[9] Not only is it teeming with references to
Spinoza and Leibniz, Deleuze sees himself as a "pure metaphysician" in the
rationalist tradition, whose concepts form a system that seeks to be true to what
is given in experience. Yet his concept of reason is both complex and recalci-
trant. Just as Marx wanted to put the Hegelian dialectic with its feet back on the
ground, Deleuze pursues a "reconstruction of reason"[10] that is simultaneously a
"new critique of reason."[11] For often "[i]t is not the slumber of reason that engenders monsters, but vigilant and insomniac rationality,"[12] such that we "rave

with reason (*insanire cum ratione*)"[13] no less than without. Moreover, we will never be able to understand Deleuze as long as we read him as a critical philosopher in the tradition of Kant or Foucault, that is, as someone who fails to observe the limits he has set up for himself. Instead, the Deleuzian system maintains a non-religious alliance with theology, insofar as "God or Nature" returns as infinite thinking subject. Hence Deleuze's self-characterizations as "innocent"[14] and "naive,"[15] or his definition of philosophy as the challenge "to acquire a consistency without losing the infinite in which thought plunges."[16] And what is this infinite if not the element of reason: a ground or *milieu* which inheres in the finite although remaining infinite and unfinished in itself?

This is the thesis of *Expressionism in Philosophy: Spinoza*. Whereas Descartes is regarded as the father of modern philosophy who gave human reason its central place, Deleuze discovers in Spinoza and Leibniz a radically anti-Cartesian program in which everything revolves around thought as immanent expression of the world as created by God in its totality and necessity. For how can thought represent the world or God if it is ontologically distinct from it? Whether it concerns God, extension, or individuals, in each case Descartes deduces existence from abstract properties relative to finite human consciousness—infinite perfection, clarity and distinctness, or the composition of body and soul respectively—instead of demonstrating how these properties are founded in Being itself. By contrast, as soon as we shift from correspondence to adequacy as the criterion for truth, the nominalist gap between logic and being is closed. To know a thing or to give a real definition is to express all the "existentifying" (Leibniz) causes that are analytically included in it, even if these extend to infinity. In their quest for sufficient reason—reason in German meaning both reason (*Vernunft*) and ground (*Grund*)—Spinoza and Leibniz thus shift the focus of thought from the representational givenness of a thing to its genesis. They look for "the foundation from which flow all the [Cartesian, abstract] properties" in order to reach "an absolute that measures up to Cartesian 'relativism.'"[17]

Yet even if this element of the "absolute" reappears under the Bergsonian name of the "virtual" in most of Deleuze's other works, he emphasizes time and again that today "the conditions of the problem itself have changed."[18] We no longer live in the classical "age of sufficient reason,"[19] because it is no longer theological reason that is at stake, but "human reason."[20] In other words, we cannot pretend that Kant's Copernican revolution has not taken place. Instead of infinite analysis, the PSR has become the principle of finite synthesis. As such it appears as the principle of differential reason in *Difference and Repetition*, while in *What is Philosophy?* it metamorphoses into that of geophilosophy. Moreover, it is exposed to several unexpected influences, of which Hume, Bergson and Nietzsche are the most important.

Historically speaking, a first break with classical representational thinking, in which the order of thought was deemed to be the same as that of nature, appears with Hume, who radically disconnected reason from what it grounds. Not because he was a proto-critical thinker who rejected the presuppositions of a systematic order in nature, Deleuze teaches us, but because he investigated how such a system comes about. According to Kant, we have universally valid knowledge of the world because the transcendental subject's imagination schematizes sensation such that the categories of the understanding become applicable to it. By contrast, Deleuze stresses that Hume's "schematism"[21] could never be a subjective system rendering possible empirical knowledge, as the subject is not an a priori ground, but itself an experimental and provisory actualization of a virtual schema rooted in the impersonal and pre-individual intensity of experience. The schematism—or as Deleuze later calls it, the "diagram" or "abstract machine"—is a system or "image of thought" that emerges in and through experience in the form of spontaneous syntheses of which the unity of apperception is only one integrated "habit" or "manner" among a myriad of other "larval subjects."[22] As a consequence, sufficient reason doesn't stand on its own awaiting to be discovered, but neither is it the form of which we impose upon the world. Rather, it does not belong to an order of knowledge, but, as with post-Kantians such as Maïmon, Fichte and Schelling or later empiricists such as James and Whitehead, to an order of production, such that the genesis of the system or image of thought also implies the material genesis of the world "in and through the system."[23] Hence Deleuze's complex identity of being and thought or ground and reason, where the two meet in the intensive aspect of thought and not in its representational aspect: *Physis* or the pure power of being (intensity) becomes a determinate system through *Nous* or the power of thinking (virtuality), at the same time as *Nous* or the image of thought is actualized by nature or *Physis*, one folding over the other.[24] Due to this mutual immanence, the system of nature is something that is "experienced" or "lived"[25] while systematic thought or reason becomes an "inquiry" into the conditions or grounds of legitimacy of actual, material practices.[26] "Life will no longer be made to appear before the categories of thought; thought will be thrown into the categories of life."[27] In this way, Deleuze reconciles empiricism with rationalism in reciprocal reinvention while Hume appears as the continuation of the classical paradigm of the system of nature as an immanent way of life: *Ethica*.

If the system of nature is no longer a system of Being, but a system of becoming—a "system of the future"[28]—this transforms the PSR into the principle of a transcendental empiricism that experiments with the conditions of real instead of possible experience.[29] From his earliest essays on Bergson onwards, Deleuze holds against Kant and Hegel that a contemporary philosophy of sufficient reason should not seek a foundation for what already is, but rather schematize the consolidation of becomings. As Bergson argues, the question "Why is there something rather than nothing?" is a badly posed problem, since it begins from an abstract generality, being, which can only mean anything in relation to its equally abstract negation, nothingness, just as order is an abstraction that derives its meaning solely from its opposition to chaos.[30] The real, or concrete, problem was already formulated by Leibniz in his *Confessio Philosophi*: *dic cur hic*, why this here and now rather than something else?[31] Whereas oppositions are always based on "external differences," sufficient reason can only be found in the "internal difference" that makes something *become what it is*.[32] Bergson calls this difference the "living nature," "intensity," or "pure duration" of an actual thing, that is, the singular manner in which it varies from itself and continues to express the multiplicity of virtual tendencies ("memory") that traverse it. Since duration is not representable or quantifiable in extension, Bergson dismisses logic and science as methods of philosophy. Only metaphysical intuition, by staying immanent to "the things themselves" (i.e., by stubbornly repeating the qualitative difference they make in concrete experience), immediately participates in the becoming of the multiple as an Open Whole of nature differentiated by intensities alone.[33] This intuition is far from an un-systematical or even "anti-intellectual"[34] method, Deleuze emphasizes, since Bergson "does not invite us to abandon reason but to reconnect with the true reason of the thing in the process of being made, the philosophical reason that is not determination but difference."[35] Intuition is precisely the ability to contract and select the infinite reserve of creative potential that is the past as it is virtually present to each passing moment into a precise concept, thus enabling the mind to recapitulate the constitutive elements of the cosmic whole in new and unforeseeable ways.[36]

With difference or intensity instead of identity as the ultimate philosophical reason we have arrived at the crux of Deleuze's use of the PSR in *Difference and Repetition*. At the beginning of the first chapter, he defines the "quadruple yoke" of conceptual representation—identity, analogy, opposition, resemblance—in correspondence with "the four principle aspects" of the PSR: the form of the undetermined concept, the relation between ultimate determinable concepts, the relation between determinations within concepts, and the determined object of the concept itself. In other words, sufficient reason according to Deleuze is the very "medium of representation," the element in which identity is conceptually determined.[37] In itself, however, this medium or element remains "different" or "unformed" (albeit not "formless"):[38] "Difference is the state in which one can speak of determination *as such*,"[39] that is, determination in its occurrent quality of a difference being made, or rather making itself in the sense of a unilateral distinction. It is with the event of difference that what appears to be a breakdown of representational reason is also a breakthrough of the rumbling ground as differential element of determination (or individuation). Deleuze illustrates this with an example borrowed from Nietzsche:

> Instead of something distinguished from something else, imagine something which distinguishes itself—and yet that from which it distinguishes itself, does not distinguish itself from it. Lightning, for example, distinguishes itself from the black sky but must also trail behind it . . . . It is as if the ground rose to the surface without ceasing to be the ground.[40]

Between the abyss of the indeterminate and the superficiality of the determined, there thus appears an intermediate element, a field potential or intensive "depth, which perhaps in a way exceeds sufficient reason itself. . . ."[41] This is a depth which Deleuze finds prefigured in Schelling's and Schopenhauer's "differend"[42] conceptualization of the ground (*Grund*) as both ground (*fond*) and grounding (*fondement*). The ground attains an autonomous power that exceeds classical sufficient reason by including the grounding moment of sufficient reason *for itself*. Because this self-grounding ground remains "groundless" (*sans-fond*) *in itself*, however, Hegel famously ridiculed Schelling's ground as the indeterminate night in which all cows are black. He opposed it to the surface of determined identities that are only negatively correlated to each other. By contrast, Deleuze interprets the self-grounding ground through Nietzsche's eternal return of the same. Whereas the passive syntheses of habit (the present as foundation of connective series) and memory (the past as ground of conjunctions of connective series) are the processes by which representational reason grounds itself in time, the eternal return (the future as disjunctive synthesis of series) "ungrounds" (*effonde*, a contraction of *fondement* and *effondrement*) this ground by introducing the necessity of future becomings, that is, of difference as ongoing differentiation. Far from being a denial of the PSR, this threefold process of self-(un)grounding constitutes the positive, relational system that "brings difference out of the night of the Identical, and with finer, more varied and more terrifying flashes of lightning than those of contradiction: *progressivity*."[43]

The breakthrough of the ground in the process of ungrounding itself in sheer distinction-production of the multiple against the indistinguishable is what Deleuze calls "violence" or "cruelty," as it determines being or nature in a necessary system of asymmetric relations of intensity by the acausal action of chance, like an ontological game in which the throw of the dice is the only rule or principle.[44] But it is also "the vigil, the insomnia of thought,"[45] since it is here that reason or thought achieves its highest power of determination. It becomes a pure creativity or virtuality in which no well-founded identity (God, World, Self) remains: "[T]hought is that moment in which determination makes itself one, by virtue of maintaining a unilateral and precise relation to the indeterminate."[46] Since it produces differential events without subjective or objective remainder, however, Deleuze argues that thought belongs to the "pure and empty firm of time,"[47] a time that is no longer subordinate to (cosmological, psychological, eternal) movement in space. Time qua form of transcendental synthesis is the ultimate ground of everything that is, reasons and acts. It is the formal element of multiple becoming, no longer in the sense of finite *a priori* conditioning, but in the sense of a transfinite *a posteriori* "synthesizer":[48] an empty interiority in ongoing formation and materialization. Let us now see how this new understanding of the PSR offers an alternative to the criticisms of Heidegger and Meillassoux.

Heidegger and Deleuze: Univocity and Ground

How much Deleuze is tributary to Heidegger's reading of the PSR can be learned from the title of his first transcribed course, *Qu'est-ce que fonder?* This course includes a long section on Heidegger's essays on the abyssality of the

PSR, that is, its insufficiency to discover its own ground (i.e., the Being of reason/ground). In his last hermeneutical *Erörterung* of Leibniz, *The Principle of Ground*, Heidegger traces back metaphysics to its epochal destiny in the "twifold" or "dupicity"[49] (*Zwiefalt*) of Being and thought and thus follows the ground in its self-ungrounding (*zugrundegehen*). Since the foundation of thought is also the foundation of Being, reason and ground are not equal but belong together (*zusammenhören*) in the Same as the ungrounded yet historical horizon of the metaphysical destiny of Being: "On the one hand we say: Being and ground: the Same. On the other hand we say: Being: the abyss (*Ab-Grund*). What is important is to think the univocity (*Einsinnigkeit*) of both 'Sätze,' those *Sätze* that are no longer '*Sätze.*'"[50] In *Difference and Repetition*, similarly, Deleuze tells us that sufficient reason is "twisted" into the groundless. He confirms that the "Fold" (*Pli*) is the "differenciator of difference"[51] (engulfed in groundlessness, always folding, unfolding, refolding: "to ground is always to bend, to curve and recurve."[52] He thus concludes: "Sufficient reason or ground is strangely bent: on the one hand, it leans towards what it grounds, towards the forms of representation; on the other hand, it turns and plunges into a groundless beyond the ground which resists all forms and cannot be represented."[53]

Despite the fundamental similarity of their conclusions, however, our short overview of Deleuze's transformation of the PSR has already indicated that his argumentation is very different from Heideggerian hermeneutics. "To ground," Deleuze agrees, "is always to ground representation."[54] But we should distinguish between two kinds of representation: organic or finite representation and orgiastic or infinite representation. What unites the classicisms of Kant, Descartes and Aristotle is that representation retains organic form as its principle and the finite as its element. Here the logical principle of identity always precedes ontology, such that the ground as element of difference remains undetermined and "in itself." It is only with Hegel and Leibniz that representation discovers the ground as its principle and the infinite as its element. It is precisely the PSR that enables thought to determine difference in itself. The ground is "like a single and unique "total" moment, simultaneously the moment of the evanescence and production of difference, of disappearance and appearance."[55] What the attempts at rendering representation infinite reveal, therefore, is that the ground has not only an Apollinian, orderly side, but also a hidden Dionysian, orgiastic side. Representation "discovers within itself the limits of the organized; tumult, restlessness and passion underneath apparent calm. It rediscovers monstrosity."[56]

The question then is how we evaluate this ambiguity that is essential to the ground. For Heidegger, the *Zwiefalt* is either naively interpreted from the perspective of its concave side, following the path of the history of Western thought as the belonging together of Being and thought in a common ground; or it is meditated from its convex side, excavating it from the history of the forgetting of Being—the decline of the Fold (*Wegfall der Zwiefalt, Vorenthalt der Zwiefalt*) as the pivotal point of the Open in its unfolding[57]—and following the path that leads from the ground to the abyss. Instead of this all or nothing approach,

Deleuze takes up the question in a Nietzschean, that is, genealogical fashion. The attempt to represent difference in itself cannot be disconnected from its malediction, that is, the moral representation of groundlessness as "a completely undifferentiated abyss."[58] As Bergson already observed, representational reason poses the problem of the ground in terms of the alternative between order and chaos. This goes in particular for the kind of representational reason that seeks to represent the irrepresentable: "Representation, especially when it becomes infinite, is imbued with a presentiment of groundlessness. Because it has become infinite in order to include difference within itself, however, it represents groundlessness as a completely undifferentiated abyss, a universal lack of difference, an indifferent black nothingness."[59] Indeed, if Deleuze is so hostile to Hegel, it is because the latter embodies like no other the "ultimate illusion" inseparable from the PSR insofar as it grounds representation, namely "that groundlessness should lack differences, when in fact it swarms with them."[60]

Does Heidegger's leap into the abyss in order to arrive at the essence of the ground hiding the Open protect him from the ultimate illusion of sufficient reason, the moral alternative of order versus chaos or rationalism versus irrationalism? Does he really go further than Leibniz and Hegel, when he retains the identity of Being? Or do not all three lack precisely what is most crucial, a genetic account of representation itself? Do they not miss the differential power of the ground/abyss in their attempts to claim it for poetic human residing or divine or human reasoning respectively?

In *Difference and Repetition* the answers to these questions are framed in terms of a choice between Nietzsche or Heidegger, depending on who goes furthest in upholding the univocity of Being as reason/ground. "But does he [Heidegger] effectuate the conversion after which univocal Being belongs only to difference and, in this sense, revolves around being? Does he conceive of *being* in such a manner that it will be truly disengaged from any subordination in relation to the identity of representation? It would seem not, given his critique of the Nietzschean eternal return."[61] In the third volume of his *Nietzsche*, Heidegger opposes his concept of "the Same" (*das Selbe*) to Nietzsche's concept of the eternal return of "the same" or "equal" (*des Gleichen*). Whereas Heidegger's Same consists of the *Zwiefalt* of the deep (*hintergründig*) identity in difference of reason and ground, Nietzsche's same is taken superficially (*vordergründig*) as the identity of what is self-identical.[62] Deleuze, by contrast, seeks an affirmation of Nietzsche's eternal return precisely by replacing the same/equal (*das Gleiche*) for the Heideggerian Same (*das Selbe*). It is eternally the same throw of the dice that returns and thus produces the continuity of becoming.[63] The eternal return is the eternal return of time itself and in this way it becomes "the effective realization" of the univocity of being. For even if Heidegger thinks and affirms the univocity of Being, he does not extend it all the way to difference in itself, that is, from the Being of difference to the differentiality of being qua becoming. Instead of the Being of the ground as an abyss that gives difference while withholding itself, in order to bring univocity to effect Being must be affirmed "*of* all its individuating differences or intrinsic modalities," precisely because all these differences are not yet individuated "beings" but intensive becomings by which the given is given as diverse.[64] By realizing the immanence of the ground (the elastic will to power as "the principle of the synthesis of forces"[65]) in its synthetic effects or modes, Nietzsche effectively reverses the relation between ground and surface in "nomadic distributions" and "crowned anarchy."[66] Each individuating difference, each "intensity," is a fold expressive of the same Being yet only grounded in it insofar as it constitutes a "path" of becoming that is fully singular in itself. "The return is the being of becoming itself, the being which is affirmed in becoming."[67] In other words: if, according to Heidegger, the great metaphysical systems of representation are unable to incorporate that which grounds them and the abyss always has to remain concealed, inimical to systematic thought, with Nietzsche and Deleuze the ground itself rises to the surface in a "universal ungrounding" teaming with differences and germinal becomings that give food for further speculative and practical thought.

The most obvious illustration of this "Copernican revolution"[68] of the eternal return that transforms the returning of Being as reason/ground into the repetition of a myriad of becomings is Deleuze's treatment of the history of philosophy and his resistance to the so-called end of metaphysics. Heidegger seeks to give back to modern philosophy its supposedly lost origin in Greek thought by "folding" (*verwinden, umlegen*) its history back upon its inaugural unfolding and thus by continuing the meditation of the *Zwiefalt* as unity of the veiling-unveiling. For Deleuze, by contrast, to keep posing the problem in terms of the sameness of Being means that philosophy can only ever be a reprise of the Ancient Greek identity of thought.[69] Under the spell of a transcending "illusion of the eternal" that arises from it "like a vapor from a pond,"[70] philosophy restricts itself to a repetition of an image of thought from the past and thus remains indebted to an original and authentic understanding of Being instead of unfolding new problems and constructing new concepts. In reality, there is no *a priori* affinity of thought with that which is to be thought, no *philia* or homology.[71] Even if there could be no reason without ground that forces it to think, the ground is always also the enemy of thought, its radical Outside, as it is nature itself in all its groundless cruelty: pure momentaneous conjugation, disjunctive synthesis. This is why Deleuze and Guattari frame the questioning of the conditions of thinking in the a-historical terms of a geophilosophy—in interference with geology and geophysics as the sciences of the chaotic and unformed intensities or forces that traverse the surface of the earth. Accordingly, the time of philosophy should be thought of as "a grandiose time of coexistence that does not exclude the before and after but *superimposes* them in a stratigraphic order."[72] Philosophy is neither intrinsically bound to a determined place or ground nor develops according to a linear genealogy. Rather, like all speculative thought it arises out of an encounter with what is not yet thinking: "What the Greeks did is not to reveal Being or unfold the Open in a world-historical gesture. . . . This is what the Greeks did: they folded force."[73] If thought never sets out from a "beautiful interiority," this is because any beginning of thought is forced to conceal itself at

its beginning, to wrap itself up in that which is exterior to it. To think is precisely to produce a different kind of interiority, related not to the time of historical
formations but to time as infinite variability, an "absolute memory" as opposed
to "the forgetting of forgetting,"[74] or time as Outside, "an outside more distant
than any external world because it is an inside deeper that any internal world"[75]
such that "[t]o think is to double the outside with a coextensive inside."[76] It follows that even if philosophy indeed appears for the first time with the Greeks,
this happens only as a chance encounter between the relative deterritorialization
of Greek territory and the absolute deterritorialization of a plane of immanence
of thought, like a lightning flash or a throw of the dice:

> In short, philosophy does have a principle, but it is a synthetic and contingent
> principle—an encounter, a conjunction. It is not insufficient by itself but con-
> tingent in itself. . . . The principle of reason such as it appears in philosophy is a
> principle of contingent reason and is put like this: there is no good reason but
> contingent reason; there is no universal history except of contingency.[77]

Because for Heidegger the destiny of the *Zwiefalt* contains an internal (analytic)
necessity to philosophy, there must be a ground or territory to which philosophy
belongs as the sufficient reason from which it derives its historical identity.[78]
This explains why, even in Leibniz's principle of sufficient reason, Heidegger
can still hear resound its Greek origin. By contrast, Deleuze and Guattari point
out that any synthesis of ground (intensity) and reason (virtuality) remains contingent and is not valid for every age: "The plane [of immanence—author's
note] is certainly not the same in the time of the Greeks, in the seventeenth century, and today (and these are still vague and general terms): there is neither the
same image of thought nor the same substance of being."[79]

Consequentially, *What is Philosophy?* is written from the standpoint not of
philosophy's twilight demise, but of its eventual, programmed assassination.[80]
Nothing guarantees that in the future there will exist something like philosophy.
Indeed, in order to kill philosophy it suffices to endow the present with the power to judge the past and to dismiss metaphysics as something outmoded. After
all, the complex unity of being and thought or of difference and repetition—
indeed, of being and time—implies that no image of thought is simply a representation of something that it does not at the same time condition or ground.
Hence, the crucial importance of the Nietzschean hammer of the eternal return
as that which ungrounds and differentiates between the increase and decrease in
power of modes of living and thinking, including philosophy as a material
force:[81] "Eternal philosophy, but also the history of philosophy, gives way to a
becoming-philosophical. What becomings pass through us today, which sink
back into history but do not arise from it, or rather that arise from it only to leave
it?"[82]

Meillassoux and Deleuze: Time and Materiality

"The principle of reason such as it appears in philosophy is a principle of con-tingent reason": not only have we seen in what sense philosophical reason con-cerns difference instead of identity, we have also seen why the PSR can no longer be understood in terms of absolute necessity. In other words, Deleuze disconnects the PSR from the onto-theological tradition no less than from its Heideggerian deconstruction. What remains then of Meillassoux's criticism in *After Finitude. An Essay on the Necessity of Contigency* that Deleuze no less than Hegel "hypostatizes" or "absolutizes" the correlation between thinking and being and thus brings back a vitalist version of speculative idealism through the back door?[83]

At stake in Meillassoux's criticism of the PSR is a double problem: the conditions of possibility of thinking and knowing an absolute and subsequently the conditions of possibility of rational ideology critique. The first problem is primarily epistemological: how can philosophy justify scientific knowledge claims about a reality that is anterior to our relation to it and that is hence not given in the transcendental object of possible experience (the "arche-fossil")? This is a problem for all post-Kantian epistemologies that hold that we can only ever know the correlate of being and thought. Instead of confronting this "weak correlationist" position head on, however, Meillassoux seeks a solution in the even stronger correlationist position that denies not only the knowability of the in itself, but also its very thinkability or imaginability. Simplified: if strong cor-relationists such as Heidegger or Wittgenstein insist on the historicity or fac-ticity (non-necessity) of the correlation of reason and ground in order to demon-strate the impossibility of thought's self-absolutization (metaphysics or specula-tion is incapable of grounding itself in reason, let alone science), then the very force of their argument, if it is not to contradict itself, implies more than they are willing to accept: the *necessity* of the contingency of the transcendental structure of the for itself. As a consequence, correlationism is incapable of demonstrating itself to be necessary. This is what Meillassoux calls the "principle of factiality" or the "principle of unreason." It says that it is possible to think of two things that exist independently of thought's relation to it: contingency as such and the principle of non-contradiction. The principle of unreason thus enables the "intel-lectual intuition" of something that is absolutely in itself, namely "the absolute impossibility of a necessary being."[84] And this in turn implies the real possibility of the completely random and unpredictable transformation of all things from one moment to the next. Logically speaking, the absolute is thus a "hyper-chaos" or "something akin to Time" in which nothing is impossible, except it be necessary beings or necessary temporal experiences such as the laws of phys-ics.[85] There is, moreover, nothing mysterious about this chaos. Contingency, and Meillassoux consistently refers to this as "Hume's discovery," is a purely logical and rational necessity, since without the principle of non-contradiction not even the principle of factiality would be absolute. It is thus a *rational* necessity that puts the PSR out of action, since it would be irrational to claim that it is a *real* necessity as everything that is is devoid of any reason to be as it is. This leads Meillassoux to the surprising conclusion that "[t]he Principle of Sufficient Reason is thus another name for the irrational. . . . The refusal of the Principle of Sufficient Reason is not the refusal of reason, but the discovery of the power of chaos harboured by its fundamental principle (non-contradiction)."[86] The principle of factiality thus legitimates or founds the rationalist requirement that reality be perfectly amenable to conceptual comprehension at the same time that it opens up "[a] world emancipated from the Principle of Sufficient Reason"[87] but founded only on that of non-contradiction.

This "emancipation" brings us to the practical problem Meillassoux tries to solve, namely the possibility of ideology critique. Correlationism is essentially a discourse on the limits of thought for which the deabsolutization of the PSR marks "reason's discovery of its own essential inability to uncover an absolute."[88] Thus, if the Galilean-Copernican revolution of modern science meant the paradoxical unveiling of thought's capacity to think what there is regardless of whether thought exists or not, then Kant's correlationist version of the Copernican revolution was in fact a "Ptolemaic counter-revolution."[89] Since Kant and even more since Heidegger, philosophy has been adverse precisely to the speculative import of modern science as a formal, mathematical knowledge of nature. Its unintended consequence is therefore that questions of ultimate reasons have been dislocated from the domain of metaphysics into that of non-rational, fideist discourse. Philosophy has thus made the contemporary end of metaphysics complicit with the religious belief in the PSR beyond its very thinkability ("There must be something . . .").[90] Whence Meillassoux's counter-intuitive conclusion that the refusal of the PSR "furnishes the minimal condition for every critique of ideology, insofar as ideology cannot be identified with just any variety of deceptive representation, but is rather any form of pseudo-rationality whose aim is to establish that what exists as a matter of fact exists necessarily."[91] In this way a speculative critique pushes skeptical rationalism's relinquishment of the PSR to the point where it affirms that "there is nothing beneath or beyond the manifest gratuitousness of the given—nothing but the limitless and lawless power of its destruction, emergence, or persistence."[92] Such an absolutizing—even though no longer absolutist—approach would be the minimal condition for every critique of ideology: "to reject dogmatic metaphysics means to reject *all* real necessity, and *a fortiori* to reject the principle of sufficient reason, as well as the ontological argument."[93]

On the one hand, Deleuze's criticism of Heidegger bears many similarities to that of Meillassoux when he redefines the PSR in terms of contingent reason—or with Nietzsche and Mallarmé: "nothing rather than something"[94]—such that whatever exists is a *fiat* in itself.[95] His PSR is the "plastic, anarchic and nomadic principle"[96] of a "superior" or "transcendental" empiricism that "teaches us a strange "reason," that of the multiple, chaos and difference."[97] On the other hand, however, the fact that Deleuze still speaks of reason should make us wary. For whereas Deleuze seeks to reunite chaotic being with systematic thought,

Meillassoux revives the classical opposition between empiricism and rationalism precisely in order to attack the pre-Kantian, "absolute validity" of the PSR.[98] His argument implies a return to a non-correlationist version of Kantianism insofar as it relies on the gap between being and thought and thus upon a logic of representation that renders Deleuze's PSR unrecognizable. There are at least two points on which the consequences of this difference spring to the fore. One concerns the concept of time, the other that of materialism.

As Heidegger demonstrates in *Kant and the Problem of Metaphysics*, Kant limits the metaphysical hypostatization of the logical possibility of the absolute by subordinating the latter to a domain of real possibility circumscribed by reason's relation to sensibility. In this way he turns the necessary temporal becoming of sensible intuition into the sufficient reason of the possible.[99] Instead, the anti-Heideggerian thrust of Meillassoux's intellectual intuition is that it absolutizes the *a priori* realm of pure logical possibility and disconnects the domain of mathematical intelligibility from sensibility.[100] Hence, the chaotic structure of his absolute time: "Anything is possible." Whereas real possibility is bound to correlation and temporal becoming, logical possibility is bound only by noncontradiction. It is a "pure" or "absolute" possibility that points to a radical "diachronicity" of thinking and being: we can think of being without thought, but not of thought without being.

As we have already seen, Deleuze clearly situates himself in the first camp when he argues with Kant and Heidegger that time as pure auto-affection (folding) is the transcendental structure of thought. Whatever exists, in all its contingency, is grounded by the first two syntheses of time and ungrounded by the third, disjunctive synthesis in the implacable difference between past and future. For Deleuze, it is precisely the eternal return of the ordinal relation between what exists and what may exist that destroys necessity and guarantees contingency. As a transcendental empiricist, he thus agrees with the limitation of logical possibility to real possibility. On the one hand, he thus also agrees with Hume and Meillassoux that "[r]eality is not the result of the laws which govern it."[101] The law of entropy or degradation in thermodynamics, for example, is unveiled as nihilistic by Nietzsche's eternal return, since it is based on a "transcendental illusion" in which "difference [of temperature] is the sufficient reason of change only to the extent that the change tends to negate difference."[102] On the other hand, Meillassoux's "absolute capacity-to-be-other relative to the given"[103] falls away in the face of what is actual here and now. This is because although Meillassoux's hyper-chaos may be temporal, it also contains a tendency to undermine or even reject the significance of time. Thus, one may wonder with Jon Roffe how time, as the sheer possibility of any future or different state of affairs, can provide the (non-)ground for the realization of this state of affairs in actuality.[104] The problem is less that Meillassoux's contingency is highly improbable than that his ontology includes no account of actual processes of transformation or development. As Peter Hallward has noted, the abstract logical possibility of change is an "empty and indeterminate postulate," completely abstracted from all experience and worldly or material affairs.[105] For this reason, the difference between Deleuze and Meillassoux seems to come down to what is more important (rather than what is more originary): the ordinal sequences of sensible intuition or the logical lack of reason.

But for Deleuze time as the *creatio ex nihilo* of pure possibility is not just irrelevant in relation to real processes of "chaosmosis," which are both chaotic *and* probabilistic, molecular *and* molar. Rather, because it puts the PSR as principle of difference out of real action it is either meaningless with respecting to the real or it can only have a negative or limitative function. This is why Deleuze replaces the possible/real opposition with that of virtual/actual. Whereas conditions of possibility always relate asymmetrically and hierarchically to any real situation, the virtual as sufficient reason is no less real than the actual since it is first of all its unconditioned or unformed potential of becoming-other.

From a Deleuzian perspective, the problem with Meillassoux's argument seems to be that it still treats the logical and material domains interchangeably and thus revives instead of overcomes the classical ontological argument. According to Meillassoux, the ontological argument is the cornerstone that allows metaphysics as a system of real necessity to close in upon itself. To overcome metaphysics is to maintain that there is no legitimate demonstration that a determinate entity exists unconditionally.[106] So far, Deleuze couldn't agree more. Rather than discarding the PSR *tout court*, however, Deleuze merely disconnects it from the realization of the possible. For what enables the ontological argument to conclude existence from the abstract identity of the concept is the sheer possibility of the existence of God, part of whose concept is precisely necessary existence. And even with God subtracted, what remains of the ontological argument is precisely the ideal of mathematical representation, which establishes the correlation between thought and abstract being—or as Deleuze defines this correlation, the "resemblance' between what conditions or grounds and what is conditioned or grounded—in an *a priori* fashion. Because of this very formality, however, it could be argued that the ontological argument has always been wrongly referred to as such.[107] For what is ontological about it, if it relies entirely on a depotentialized being, a possibility emptied out of any materialization? But then what to think of Meillassoux's "speculative realism" or "speculative materialism,"[108] based on the attempt to fuse absolute mathematical necessity with an equally absolute contingency of being? Even if it succeeds in avoiding the pitfall of correlation and resemblance, are we not stuck again in the logic of all or nothing, denying ourselves all means of accounting for the real genesis of what is already given conceptually?

This was of course precisely the critique of the category of the possible as put forward by Bergson, namely that it homogenizes both Being and thought, enabling the subject of representation to see the real object as corresponding to the identity of the concept as its essence. Instead of a mathematical formalism, Deleuze therefore follows Bergson in proposing an onto-biological materialism. As a consequence, rather than simply giving up on the ontological argument, the complex unity of intensive being and virtual thought rather seems to reverse it such that "the conditions of the true genesis become apparent."[109] For what lies between the sensible intuition of the emergent and the intellectual analysis of what has already appeared is *life* as a *real*, intensively differentiated transcendental field of "problems." Being or the groundless ground, Deleuze tells us, presents itself only as problematic, differential and temporal. It always takes the form of a problem or a series of problematic ideas that are of an intelligible or reasonable nature (they are the "ideal syntheses of difference"), although they are inseparable from the intensive relations in which they are given to us (hence from the "asymmetrical syntheses of the sensible").[110] What matters is the full reality of the virtual on which its actualization through different/ciation depends and without which it would lack all reason or necessity. Or as we should say with Deleuze, "without which the famous Copernican Revolution amounts to nothing."[111] But then shouldn't we also call this vitalist transformation of the PSR leading to a reversal of the ontological argument a truly "speculative materialism."[112]

Difference and Speculation

The PSR is Deleuze's speculative principle par excellence. It is no longer a principle of identity, nor is it subordinate to, or in conflict with, the latter's inverse, the principle of non-contradiction. Rather, the PSR is the principle of difference to the extent that the differential element or intensive ground is the only "truly sufficient reason."[113] But is it really a principle? Isn't Deleuzian empiricist speculativism rather "a vital protest against principles?"[114]

The problem of the principle of reason/ground is architectonic. As such it is the great theme of modern philosophy: how and where to begin? The two classical answers are provided by romanticism and enlightenment thinking. If there is a "romantic side" to Heidegger,[115] as Deleuze says, then Meillassoux inherits and continues a long-standing tradition of enlightenment.[116] Whereas the first always looks for a foundation or ground, even if it turns out be an abyss, the critical reason of the latter rabidly dismantles all grounds. Alternatively, Deleuze calls for a third answer which he calls "modernism" or "constructivism" and which always begins "by the milieu (*par le milieu*)." Instead of rising out of first principles like a tree from its roots, his metaphysics proliferates like a rhizome, never straying far from the events at the surface in a groping experimentation with the conditions of real experience. For Deleuze, the milieu is not the solid ground on which we stand, but neither is it an abyss or a void. Rather it is the fluctuating ground in which we must "learn to swim."[117] It is the element of the "problematic" as such, an element that "matters" and calls for an ethics of life. To think by the milieu means to think both without reference to a fixed ground yet also without separating thought from the forces it requires to exist.[118] Whereas Meillassoux reinstalls the Kantian tribunal of reason and the generality of its judgments, Deleuze always emphasizes his own conditions of enunciation, that is, the matters of concern that enable him to learn. While the anticorrelationist position is one of right, Deleuze's own position is always one of fact.

In this sense of a necessarily existing milieu, the PSR is less a metaphysical principle than a practical principle. Yet the very bifurcation between metaphysical and practical reason is Kantian: Ideas have uses that can be practical, religious or aesthetic, but no longer metaphysical. Deleuze, by contrast, is a classical rationalist who doesn't accept the nominalist illusion that the "is" and the "ought" must or even can be separated.[119] Even where he adopts the distinctions from Schopenhauer's fourfold "root" of the PSR[120]—representation relies on four classes of reasons: reasons of being, reasons of knowing, reasons of willing, and reasons of becoming, even though these reasons are not capable of explaining themselves or the will "in itself"—what matters is less the critical distinction of reasons than what they do or effectuate. Again conforming to the complex identity of being and thought, the "speculative and practical object"[121] of Deleuze's philosophy is not the representation of being, truth, or the just, but the multiple becomings that are present within them. Indeed, if the milieu is the truly transcendental element of the Copernican Revolution,[122] then even truth is a matter of construction, an eventual becoming by which a form is given to the unformed ground. "Truth [is] solely the creation of thought . . . thought is creation, not will-to-truth."[123] As Isabelle Stengers describes the problem of "speculative constructivism": "The problem is not to ground, to define conditions for valid knowledge, but to care for the consequences of the event."[124] Or put yet differently, whereas both Heidegger and Meillassoux interpret the PSR as the speculative principle that says that all that exists must be logically accounted for, Deleuze treats it not as a principle of accountability but as a principle of prudence or active responsibility for the effects of our reasoning no matter whether these concern being, truth or the good. The PSR is the principle of an ethics of our present becomings. In the ethical vision of the world, speculative affirmation and practical joy join hands.[125]

At the outset of this chapter, we have noted that Deleuze sees himself as the most naïve of his generation, as he "who most lacked the feeling of guilt about 'doing philosophy.'"[126] Naivety, however, doesn't imply the lack of a critical stance. It is rather the name for a trust and belief in the very activity of philosophy. In this sense it is indeed the speculative attitude par excellence. While his milieu is poisoned by the criticist image of thought of the end of metaphysics, Deleuze speculates that it can be reclaimed for "a people to come and a new earth."[127] The milieu is thus no longer a limiting condition (most certainly not a "postmodern" one), but rather an enabling constraint. To phrase it in Leibnizian terms, "reasons for contingent truths incline, rather than necessitate"[128] and although these inclinations are indeed "needed, they are not required by necessity."[129] To speculate with the PSR is to speculate on a dispositional basis for future existence, thought and action. It is to speculate on the virtual becoming of what is actual, that is, on the "genitally innate" ideas[130] inherent to any actual situation.

In this sense, Deleuze's version of speculative philosophy is already well-known as the procedure of "counter-effectuation" or "counter-actualization." In defiance of the causal laws of an actual situation, speculation experiments with the quasi-causal intensities capable of bringing about effects that have their own retro-active power. This is its political import. Leibniz already argued that all things are effects or consequences, even though they do not necessarily have a cause, since the sufficient reason of what exists always lies outside of any actual series and remains "virtual."[131] With the PSR he thus reinvented the Stoic disjunction between the series of corporeal causes and the series of incorporeal effects. Not because he anticipated the modern bifurcation of given necessary causes (How?) and metaphysically constructed reasons (Why?), but because for him the virtuality of effects is no less real than the interaction of causes. The effect always "includes" its own cause, since divergent series of events (incompossible worlds) enter into relation with any particular event (in this world), while these interpenetrating series are prior to, and not limited by, actual relations of causality per se. In terms of Deleuze, cause and effect do not share the same temporality. Whereas causes relate to one another in an eternal present ("Chronos"), effects relate to one another in a past-future purified of the present ("Aion"). Taken together, these temporalities form the "double structure of every event."[132] When the night is lit up by a sudden flash of lightning, this is the effect of an intensive, metaphysical becoming that contains its own "destiny," integrating a differential potentiality that is irreducible to the physical series of "necessary" efficient causes that nonetheless participate in it.[133] In order for such a contingent conjugation of events to be actualized (i.e., for effects to influence causes and become individuated in a materially extended state of affairs), however, its impersonal and pre-individual presence must be trusted upon. This takes a will to speculate or *amor fati* that forms its precursive reason/ground.[134] Indeed, if speculative thought cannot be detached from a practical concern, Deleuze at the same time states that "[t]here is no other ethic than the *amor fati* of philosophy."[135] Speculative reasoning is thus an art of pure expression or efficacy, an art of precipitating events: an art that detects and affirms the possibility of other reasons insisting as so many virtual forces that have not yet had the chance to emerge but whose presence can be trusted upon to make a difference.

In Deleuze's own terms, there is no such thing as 'pure' reason, only heterogeneous processes of rationalization, of actualizing an irrational potential: "There is no metaphysics, but rather a politics of being."[136] For this reason, the method of speculative philosophy is the "method of dramatization." It is a method that distributes events according to a logic that conditions the order of their intelligibility. As such it belongs to what in *Difference and Repetition* is referred to as the proper "order of reasons": "differentiation-individuation-dramatisation-differenciation."[137] "A book of philosophy," Deleuze famously writes in the preface, "should be in part a very particular species of detective novel, in part a kind of science fiction."[138] On the one hand, the creation of concepts cannot be separated from a problematic milieu or stage that "matters" practically; on the other hand, it seeks to deterritorialize this milieu by speculating on the quasi-causal intensity of its becoming-other. Let us conclude with an example of such practical speculation, the mathematico-philosophical concept of infinitesimal difference.

If difference is the ground of being qua becoming, it is not difference as contradiction (Hegel), but as infinitesimal difference (Leibniz). Accordingly, the world is an ideal continuum or "transfinite totality"[139] of compossibilities and incompossibilities analyzable into an infinity of differential relations.[140] As the physical world is merely composed of contiguous parts that actually divide until infinity, it finds its sufficient reason in the reciprocal determination of evanescent differences (dy/dx, i.e., the perfectly determinable *ratio* or intensive magnitude between indeterminate and unassignable differences that relate virtually but never actually). But what is an evanescent difference if not a speculation or fiction? As Leibniz writes to Johann Bernouilli on 7 June 1698: "Maybe the infinite and the infinitely small that we conceive of are imaginary, although they are suitable for determining real things, as do imaginary roots. They are to be located in the infinite reasons that govern things like laws, although we do not find them in the parts of matter."[141] In other words, Leibniz refuses to make a distinction between the ontological nature and the practical effectiveness of infinitesimals. For even if they have no actuality of their own, they are nonetheless the genetic "requisites" of actual things.

Moreover, infinitesimals are precisely those paradoxical means through which the finite understanding is capable of probing into the infinite. They are the elements of a logic of sense, that "great logical dream of a combinatory or calculus of problems."[142] On the one hand, intensive magnitudes are entities that cannot be determined logically, that is, in extension, even if they appear—or are determined in sensation—only in connection with already extended physical bodies. This is because in themselves they are determined at "infinite speed."[143] Just as Alice becomes larger than she is now and by the same token, becomes smaller than she is now, infinitesimals possess the paradoxical identity of two simultaneous directions of sense: "the simultaneity of a becoming whose characteristic is to elude the present."[144] On the other hand, we should wonder whether thought is still bound by the principle of non-contradiction once we leave aside the sensible. Is not the differential precisely this problematic entity at the limit of sensibility that exists only virtually, formally, in the realm of thought? Isn't the differential precisely "a minimum of time" which refers only to the swiftness ("as quickly as possible"[145]) of its fictional apprehension in thought, since it is synthesized in Aion, that is, "in a time smaller than the minimum of continuous [chronological, empirical] time"[146] and hence in the interstitial realm where "time takes thought"[147] instead of thought taking time?

Contrary to the Kantian critique that seeks to eliminate the duality between finite understanding and infinite understanding in order to avoid the contradictions of reason, Deleuze thus agrees with Maïmon that we shouldn't speak of differentials as "mere fictions unless they require the status of a fully actual reality in that infinite understanding."[148] The alternative between mere fictions and actual reality is a false problem that hides the paradoxical reality of the virtual as such: "real but not actual, ideal but not abstract."[149] If Deleuze is interested in the "esoteric history of differential philosophy,"[150] this is as a speculative alternative to the exoteric history of the extensional science of actual differences and to Kantian critical philosophy.[151] It is precisely through conceptualizing intensive, differential relations that finite thought is capable of acquiring consistency without losing the infinite in which it plunges. This brings us back to Leibniz and Spinoza. As Deleuze writes about the former: "no one has gone further than Leibniz in the exploration of sufficient reason . . . [and] the element of difference"[152] and therefore "[o]nly Leibniz approached the conditions of a logic of thought."[153] Or as he argues of the latter, fictional abstractions are only a preliminary stage for thought to become 'more real,' that is, to produce an expressive or 'progressive' synthesis: "The introduction of a fiction may indeed help us to reach the idea of God as quickly as possible without falling into the traps of infinite regression."[154] In Maïmon's reinvention of the Kantian schematism as well as in the Deleuzian system of nature, the differentials are the immanent noumena that are dramatized by reciprocal determination in the complete determination of the phenomenal. Even the Kantian concept of the straight line, Deleuze emphasizes, is a dramatic synthesis or integration of an infinity of differential relations.[155] In this way, infinitesimals constitute the distinct but obscure grounds enveloped by clear but confused effects. They are not empirical objects but objects of thought. Even if they are only known as already developed within the extensional becomings of the sensible and covered over by representational qualities, as differences they are problems that do not resemble their solutions and as such continue to insist in an enveloped, quasi-causal state.[156] They thus constitute the genetic milieu of speculative thought, the intensive stage of our current becomings, or, indeed, "the bond of a profound complicity between nature and mind."[157] As forces that do not act, they are the sufficient reasons that are never brought to rest in their effects. They are exemplary of the Deleuzian method of counter-effectuation in which the breakdown of the form of the true (judgment over being) implies the breakthrough of the speculative powers of the false (eventual becoming as metamorphosis).

Notes

1. Quentin Meillassoux, *After Finitude. An Essay on the Necessity of Contingency*, trans. Ray Brassier (London: Continuum, 2008), 22–23.

2. Meillassoux, *After Finitude*, 34.

3. Alain Badiou, *Deleuze. The Clamor of Being*, trans. Louise Burchill (Minneapolis: University of Minnesota Press, 2010), 87.

4. Ray Brassier, *Nihil Unbound. Enlightenment and Extinction* (Basingstoke: Palgrave Macmillan, 2007), 200.

5. Meillassoux, *After Finitude*, 10–11 and 37–38.

6. Gilles Deleuze and Félix Guattari, *A Thousand Plateaus*, trans. Brian Massumi (Minneapolis: University of Minnesota Press, 1987), 411.

7. Gilles Deleuze, *Cinema 1: The Movement-Image*, trans. Hugh Tomlinson and Barbara Habberjam (Minneapolis: University of Minnesota Press, 1986), 61.

8. Meillassoux, *After Finitude*, 34.

9. Mogens Laerke, "Gilles Deleuze and the System of Nature and Philosophy," *Alegrar* 2 (2005), http://www.alegrar.com.br/02/mogensing.pdf.

10. Christian Kerslake, "Deleuze's 'Reconstruction of Reason.' From Leibniz and Kant to *Difference and Repetition*," in *Thinking Between Deleuze and Kant*, ed. E. Willat (New York: Continuum, 2009), 101–27.

11. Gilles Deleuze, *The Logic of Sense*, trans. Mark Lester with Charles Stivale (London: Continuum, 1990), 296.

12. Gilles Deleuze and Félix Guattari, *Anti-Oedipus*, trans. Robert Hurley, Mark Seem, and Helen R. Lane (London: Continuum, 2003), 112.

13. Baruch Spinoza, *Complete Works*, trans. Samuel Shirley (Indianapolis: Hackett, 2002), 520–526.

14. Gilles Deleuze, *Expressionism in Philosophy: Spinoza*, trans. Martin Joughin (New York: Zone Books, 1997), 28.

15. Gilles Deleuze, *Negotiations. 1972–1990*, trans. Martin Joughin (New York: Columbia University Press, 1995), 88–89.

16. Gilles Deleuze and Félix Guattari, *What is Philosophy?*, trans. H. Tomlinson and G. Burchill (London: Verso, 1994), 42.

17. Deleuze, *Expressionism in Philosophy*, 325.

18. Gilles Deleuze, *The Fold: Leibniz and the Baroque*, trans. Tom Conley (Minneapolis: University of Minnesota Press, 1993), 136.

19. Deleuze, *Expressionism in Philosophy*, 321.

20. Deleuze, *The Fold*, 67.

21. Gilles Deleuze, *Empiricism and Subjectivity: An Essay on Hume's Theory of Human Nature*, trans. Constantin V. Boundas (New York: Columbia University Press, 1991), 65.

22. Gilles Deleuze, *Difference and Repetition*, trans. Paul Patton (New York: Continuum, 2001), 73–79.

23. Gilles Deleuze, *Desert Islands and Other Texts 1953–1974*, ed. D. Lapoujade, trans. M. Taormina (New York: Semiotext(e), 2004), 146.

24. Deleuze and Guattari, *What is Philosophy?*, 38.

25. Deleuze, *Desert Islands and Other Texts*, 36.

26. Deleuze paraphrases Hume's examples of typically empiricist questioning: "Why is the ground more important than the surface in a juridical system, whereas in painting, the paint is more important than the canvas." (Deleuze, *Desert Islands and Other Texts*, 162, 169 and Gilles Deleuze and Claire Parnet, *Dialogues*, trans. Hugh Tomlinson and Barbara Habberjam (New York: Columbia Unviersity Press, 1987), 56.

27. Deleuze, *Cinema 2: The Time-Image*, trans. Hugh Tomlinson and Barbara Habberjam (Minneapolis: University of Minnesota Press, 1989), 189.

28. Deleuze, *Difference and Repetition*, 116.

29. Deleuze, *Difference and Repetition*, 154.

30. Henri Bergson, *The Creative Mind. An Introduction to Metaphysics*, trans. Mabelle L. Andison (New York: The Philosophical Library, 1946), 78–80.

31. Deleuze draws a direct parallel between Leibniz and Bergson, when he writes, "a kind of principle of sufficient reason, as well as indiscernibles, can be found in Bergson's work. What he rejects is a distribution that locates cause and reason in the genus and the category and abandons the individual to contingency, stranding him in space. Reason must reach all the way to the individual, the genuine concept all the way to the thing, and

comprehension all the way to 'this.' Bergson always asks of difference: why 'this' rather than 'that'" (Deleuze, *Desert Islands and Other Texts*, 36)?

32. Deleuze, *Desert Islands and Other Texts*, 32.

33. The intuitive thinker is not distinguished from the things he thinks about because he relates to his objects in a subjective manner (an external difference between thinker and thing), but because the difference between things and thinker is itself a difference in nature (an internal difference). To have an intuition of something implies the self-cancellation of the thinker as human subject and a metamorphosis of thought. It involves a continual effort to develop and sustain an intuition; it is a matter of cultivation and risk rather than method. In the same way, Deleuze and Guattari write that whilst a biologist knows a particular animal by classifying it according to objective characteristics and a grown-up human knows his pets on the basis of subjective empathy and identification, in both cases this knowledge stays representational. To create a philosophical concept of an animal, by contrast, always goes accompanied by an absolute and singular "becoming-animal": "one does not think without becoming something else, something that does not think—an animal, a molecule, a particle—and that comes back to thought and revives it" (Deleuze and Guattari, *What is Philosophy?*, 42).

34. Alfred North Whitehead, *Process and Reality. An Essay in Cosmology* (New York: The Free Press, 1985), xii.

35. Deleuze, *Desert Islands and Other Texts*, 31.

36. Gilles Deleuze, *Bergsonism*, trans. Hugh Tomlinson and Barbera Habberjam (New York: Zone Books, 1990), 106.

37. Deleuze, *Difference and Repetition*, 29.

38. Deleuze, *The Logic of Sense*, 107.

39. Deleuze, *Difference and Repetition*, 28.

40. Deleuze, *Difference and Repetition*, 28.

41. Deleuze, *Desert Islands and Other Texts*, 109.

42. Deleuze, *Difference and Repetition*, 230.

43. Deleuze, *Difference and Repetition*, 191.

44. Deleuze, *Difference and Repetition*, 198.

45. Deleuze, *Difference and Repetition*, 29.

46. Deleuze, *Difference and Repetition*, 29.

47. Deleuze, *Difference and Repetition*, 86.

48. "The synthesizer, with its operation of consistency, has taken the place of the ground in a priori synthetic judgment: its synthesis is of the molecular and the cosmic, material and force, not form and matter, *Grund* and territory" (Deleuze and Guattari, *A Thousand Plateaus*, 343).

49. Besides Being and the Fourfold, the only concept of Heidegger that Deleuze adopts is the *Zwiefalt* between thinking and Being. Notwithstanding the fact that the concept of *Zwiefalt* is used by Heidegger only in a late and ephemeral stage, between 1947 and 1953, Deleuze claims that the notions of the *Zwiefalt* and *Vierfalt* are "arguably the key to the whole of Heidegger's philosophy," because the fold is "the condition for any visibility of phenomena" (Deleuze, *Negotiations*, 112). In the English edition of *The Fold*, the neologism *Zwiefalt* has been erroneously reduced to *Zweifalt*, since it is a compound of two ambiguous conjunctions that bears witness to its original doubleness as opposed to the trivial "duality" or "twofold (*zwiefältig*)"-edness, such as it has also been translated in the English translation of Heidegger's essay "Moira." In Deleuze's words, it is "not a fold in two—since every fold can only be thus—but a "fold-of-two," an *entre-deux*, something "between" in the sense that a difference is being differentiated" (Deleuze, *The Fold*, 10). In *Foucault*, Deleuze translates it as a "between-two (*entre-*

deux)," marked by a hyphen that joins and separates in differentiating. See Gilles Deleuze, *Foucault*, trans. Seán Hand (University of Minnesota Press, 1988), 112. In *The Fold*, he proposes "Fold (*Pli*)." The suffix *-falt* corresponds to -fold; the prefix *zwie-* is etymologically related to *Zweifel* (doubt, dilemma) and occurs in combinations such as *Zwielicht* (twilight, cf. Deleuze and Guattari, *A Thousand Plateaus*, 314) and *Zwielaut* (diphthong), words that express an intrinsic dividedness, ambiguity and instability. The best English translation would therefore be "twifold," second best but less forced is "duplicity."

50. Martin Heidegger, *Kant and the Problem of Metaphysics*, trans. Richard Taft (Bloomington: Indiana University Press, 1997), 93.

51. Deleuze, *Difference and Repetition*, 65, 117.

52. Deleuze, *Difference and Repetition*, 273.

53. Deleuze, *Difference and Repetition*, 274–275.

54. Deleuze, *Difference and Repetition*, 274.

55. Deleuze, *Difference and Repetition*, 42.

56. Deleuze, *Difference and Repetition*, 42.

57. Martin Heidegger, *Early Greek Thinking: The Dawn of Western Philosophy*, trans. D. F. Krell and F. A. Capuzzi (San Francisco: Harper and Row, 1984), 86–101.

58. Deleuze, *Difference and Repetition*, 276.

59. Deleuze, *Difference and Repetition*, 276.

60. Deleuze, *Difference and Repetition*, 277.

61. Deleuze, *Difference and Repetition*, 66.

62. Martin Heidegger, *Nietzsche. Volume III: The Will to Power as Knowledge and as Metaphysics*, trans. Joan Stambaugh, David Ferrell Krell, Frank A. Capuzzi (New York: Harper and Row, 1991), 164–65.

63. Deleuze, *Difference and Repetition*, 41, 126, 243.

64. "The point is that he [Heidegger] retains the primacy of the Same, even if this is supposed to include and comprehend difference as such—whence the metaphors of gift which are substituted for those of violence" (Deleuze, *Difference and Repetition*, 212, note 11). Deleuze's concern seems justified insofar as in the destiny of the *Zwiefalt* that which gives does not give itself and thus remains the Same. As Heidegger writes in *Zur Sache des Denkens*: "A giving which gives only its gift, but in the giving holds itself back and withdraws, such a giving we call sending [destiny—author's note]" (Martin Heidegger, *On Time and Being*, trans. Joan Stambaugh (New York: Harper and Row, 1972), 8).

65. Gilles Deleuze, *Nietzsche and Philosophy*, trans. H. Tomlinson (New York: Columbia University Press, 1997), 50.

66. Deleuze, *Difference and Repetition*, 40–42.

67. Deleuze, *Nietzsche and Philosophy*, 24.

68. Deleuze, *Difference and Repetition*, 40–41.

69. Deleuze, *Difference and Repetition*, 129.

70. Deleuze and Guattari, *What is Philosophy?*, 49.

71. Deleuze, *Difference and Repetition*, 321n.

72. Deleuze and Guattari, *What is Philosophy?*, 59.

73. Deleuze, *Foucault*, 100–101.

74. Deleuze, *Foucault*, 107–108, 99.

75. Deleuze and Guattari, *What is Philosophy?*, 59.

76. Deleuze, *Foucault*, 118.

77. Deleuze and Guattari, *What is Philosophy?*, 93.

78. Historical identity, Michel Serres writes in *Genesis*, is nothing if not a "great chain of reason." But as such it is always covered up and torn apart by a "chain of contingency" (Michel Serres, *Genesis*, trans. Genevieve James and James Nielson (Ann Arbor: University of Michigan Press, 1995), 71–72.

79. Deleuze and Guattari, *What is Philosophy?*, 39.

80. Isabelle Stengers, "Deleuze and Guattari's Last Enigmatic Message," *Angelaki: Journal of Theoretical Humanities* 10, no. 2 (2005): 151–67.

81. Foucault's warning in *Theatrum Philosophicum* is instructive in this respect: "We must avoid thinking that the return is the form of a content that is difference; rather, from an always-nomadic and anarchic difference to the unavoidable excessive and displaced sign of recurrence, a lightning storm is produced which will bear the name of Deleuze: new thought is possible; thought is again possible" (Michel Foucault, "Theatrum Philosophicum," in *Aesthetics, Method, and Epistemology*, ed. J. D. Faubion (New York: The New Press, 1998), 367).

82. Deleuze and Guattari, *What is Philosophy?*, 59.

83. Meillassoux, *After Finitude*, 37–38.

84. Meillassoux, *After Finitude*, 60.

85. Meillassoux, *After Finitude*, 64.

86. Meillassoux, *After Finitude*, 61.

87. Quentin Meillassoux, "Potentiality and Virtuality," *Collapse* II (March 2007): 60.

88. Meillassoux, *After Finitude*, 48.

89. Meillassoux, *After Finitude*, 115–121.

90. Meillassoux, *After Finitude*, 46–109.

91. Meillassoux, *After Finitude*, 33–34.

92. Meillassoux, *After Finitude*, 63.

93. Meillassoux, *After Finitude*, 33.

94. Deleuze, *The Fold*, 67.

95. Deleuze, *Difference and Repetition*, 199.

96. Deleuze, *Difference and Repetition*, 56–57.

97. Deleuze, *Difference and Repetition*, 193.

98. Meillassoux, *After Finitude*, 124–125, 71.

99. Heidegger, *Kant and the Problem of Metaphysics*, 120–141.

100. Ray Brassier, "The Enigma of Realism: On Quentin Meillassoux's *After Finitude*," *Collapse* II (March 2007): 41.

101. Deleuze, *Difference and Repetition*, 227.

102. Deleuze, *Difference and Repetition*, 223.

103. Meillassoux, *After Finitude*, 58–59.

104. Roffe frames the problem as follows: "if what exists now cannot be a contradictory entity, and can be neither *solely* supported by the modal status of possibility nor protected by the modal status of necessity, then in order that another situation, whether identical to this one or different, exists, it would have to do so in a time other than this one." (Jon Roffe, "Time and Ground. A Critique of Meillassoux's Speculative Realism," *Angelaki. Journal of the Theoretical Humanities* 17, no. 1 (2012): 65.)

105. As Hallward observes: "Although Meillassoux insists that contingency applies to every event and every process, it may well be that the only event that might qualify as contingent and without reason in his absolute sense of the term is the emergence of the universe itself" (Peter Hallward, "Anything is Possible: A Reading of Quentin Meillassoux's *After Finitude*,' in *The Speculative Turn*, ed. Levy Bryant, Nick Smicek and Graham Harman (New York: re.press, 2011), 138–39).

106. Meillassoux, *After Finitude*, 33.

107. Éric Alliez, "Deleuze, Bergson und das Virtuelle," in *Telenoia. Kritik der virtuellen Bilder*, ed. Elisabeth von Samsonow and Éric Alliez, (Vienna: Turia+Kant, 1999), 68.

108. Meillassoux, *After Finitude*, 38.

109. Deleuze, *Difference and Repetition*, 144.

110. Deleuze, *Difference and Repetition*, 244.

111. Deleuze, *Difference and Repetition*, 162.

112. Éric Alliez, "Deleuze, Bergson und das Virtuelle," in *Telenoia. Kritik der virtuellen Bilder*, ed. Elisabeth von Samsonow and Éric Alliez, (Vienna: Turia+Kant, 1999), 74.

113. Deleuze, *Nietzsche and Philosophy*, 49; Deleuze, *Difference and Repetition*, 222.

114. Deleuze, *Difference and Repetition*, 55.

115. Deleuze, *Foucault*, 113.

116. Whilst Meillassoux sees a solidarity between critical philosophy and the return of the religious, we could point with Whitehead to the solidarity of the critical philosopher with the speculative realist insofar as philosophy has replaced the question "What do we know?" by the question "What can we know?" As Isabelle Stengers argues, in this way speculative realism remains stuck in the ritualized war between experimental science and philosophers who have proposed correlationism as a means to critically restrict the scope and meaning of supposedly objective scientific claims. From a Whiteheadian perspective, then, there is nothing new about Meillassoux's position: "It could be said that philosophical correlationism was invented "against" scientists." (Isabelle Stengers, "Speculative Philosophy and the Art of Dramatization," paper presented at a research seminar of the Centre for Art and Philosophy at Erasmus University Rotterdam, 31 May 2012.)

117. Deleuze, *Difference and Repetition*, 165.

118. A more nuanced criticism of Deleuze than that of Meillassoux, i.e. one that includes the ethical or practical import of his PSR, is put forward by Reza Negarestani, who agrees with Deleuze that ontology is the "science of cruelty" whilst adding that the univocity of being should be abandoned in favor of a universal void on which any intensive course of unilateral distinction remains dependent ("equivocal inexistence"): "Philosophy of cruelty explains ontological determinations in terms of sadistic (imperative) and masochistic (contractual) bondages to that which does not belong to being, i.e., the problematic chains to the void. In order for the ethics of justice to confront the problems and conditions associated with ontological determinations—ourselves and our world—it must tread through such problematical fields which are equivocally determined by the void and the ontological medium. The philosophy of cruelty, in this sense, inaugurates the opportunities of grounding ethics on a new definition of being unshackled from the priority of its ontological necessity and mobilized by its chains to that which is exterior to it—the universal" (Reza Negarestani, "Differential Cruelty. A Critique of Ontological Reason in Light of the Philosophy of Cruelty," *Angelaki. Journal of the Theoretical Humanities* 14, no. 3 (2009): 82).

119. Laerke, "Gilles Deleuze and the System of Nature and Philosophy."

120. Deleuze, *Expressionism in Philosophy*, 321–322.

121. Deleuze, *The Logic of Sense*, 266.

122. Deleuze, *Difference and Repetition*, 86.

123. Deleuze and Guattari, *What is Philosophy?*, 54; Deleuze, *Difference and Repetition*, 152–54.

124. Isabelle Stengers, "William James. An ethics of thought?," *Radical Philosophy* 157 (2009): 9–17.

125. Deleuze, *Expressionism in Philosophy*, 272.

126. Deleuze, *Negotiations*, 89.

127. Deleuze and Guattari, *What is Philosophy?*, 109.

128. Leibniz, *Philosophical Essays*, 76.

129. Leibniz, *Philosophical Essays*, 204.

130. Deleuze, *Difference and Repetition*, 148.

131. Leibniz, *Philosophical Essays*, 41, 45, 58.

132. Deleuze, *The Logic of Sense*, 151.

133. Deleuze, *The Logic of Sense*, 6.

134. In *Difference and Repetition*, Deleuze refers to such a speculative will as the "dark precursor" which determines the path of a thunderbolt "in advance but in reverse, as though intagliated" by setting up a communication of difference with difference. It is therefore the "differenciator of these differences" or "in-itself of difference" (Deleuze, *Difference and Repetition*, 119–20). We find a paradigmatic example of this will to make a difference in William James' *The Will to Believe* when he writes: "We can and we may, as it were, jump with both feet off the ground into a world of which we trust the other parts to meet our jump—and only so can the making of a perfected world of the pluralistic pattern ever take place. Only through our precursive trust in it can it come into being" (William James, *Some Problems of Philosophy. A Beginning of an Introduction to Philosophy* (Lincoln: University of Nebraska Press, 1996), 230). As Stengers explains, we can and do speculate each time we precursively trust in the possibility of connecting, of entering into a (partial) *rapport* that cannot be derived from the ground of our current, dominant premises. Or as Deleuze writes: "the dark precursor is not the friend" (Deleuze, *Difference and Repetition*, 2001), 145) but rather the bad will of a traitor or enemy, since the will does not precede the presubjective cruelty of the event in its involuntariness. At the same time, however, we never jump into a vacuum. We always speculate by the milieu, since a jump in general could never be trusted: "If a jump is always situated, it is because its aim is not to escape the ground in order to get access to a higher realm. The jump, connecting this ground, always this ground, with what it was alien to, has the necessity of a response. In other words, the ground must have been given the power to make itself felt as calling for new dimensions" (Stengers, "Speculative Philosophy and the Art of Dramatization").

135. Deleuze and Guattari, *What is Philosophy?*, 159.

136. Gilles Deleuze, "Pericles and Verdi: The Philosophy of François Châtelet," trans. Charles T. Wolfe, *The Opera Quarterly* 21/4 (2006): 717.

137. Deleuze, *Difference and Repetition*, 251.

138. Deleuze, *Difference and Repetition*, xx.

139. Deleuze, *The Fold*, 51.

140. Deleuze, *Desert Islands and Other Texts*, 101.

141. Gottfried Wilhelm Leibniz, *Philosophical Papers and Letters*, ed. and trans. Leroy E. Loemker (Dordrecht: Kluwer, 1989), 511.

142. Deleuze, *Difference and Repetition*, 157.

143. Deleuze and Guattari, *What is Philosophy?*, 42.

144. Deleuze, *The Logic of Sense*, 1; Marc Rölli, "Deleuze on Intensity Differentials and the Being of the Sensible," *Deleuze Studies* 3, no. 1 (2009): 26–53.

145. Deleuze and Guattari, *What is Philosophy?*, 207.

146. Deleuze, *The Logic of Sense*, 269.

147. Deleuze, *Difference and Repetition*, 166.

148. Deleuze, *Difference and Repetition*, 193, 176; Deleuze, *The Fold*, 96; Daniel W. Smith, "Genesis and Difference: Deleuze, Maïmon, and the Post-Kantian Reading of Leibniz," in *Deleuze and the Fold. A Critical Reader*, ed. Sjoerd van Tuinen and Niamh McDonnell (Basingstoke: Palgrave Macmillan, 2010), 132–54.

149. Deleuze, *Difference and Repetition*, 208.

150. Deleuze, *Difference and Repetition*, 170.

151. Corresponding to the distinction between science and philosophy in *What is Philosophy?*, in *The Fold* Deleuze argues that the Newtonian and Leibnizian versions of differential calculus account for the "two aspects of the calculus that, even if they are inseparable, must be distinguished" (Deleuze, *The Fold*, 97–8). Accordingly, Leibniz's calculus applies only to the ideal actualization of perceptions in the soul whilst Newton's calculus applies only to the realization of empirical phenomena in material flux. Newton referred to a varying or flowing quantity as a "fluent" (i.e., a function) and to its instantaneous rate of change as a "fluxion" (i.e., its derivative), a quantity flowing from one magnitude to another by infinitesimally small increments that are determined by the relative speed of movements that form them. By contrast, Leibnizian calculus isn't based on physical fluxions but on the reciprocal determination of differentials that appear and disappear at infinite or absolute speed and thus also has a logical and metaphysical purport: "[W]hile considering that these fluxions disappear in the growing magnitude of which they are a part, Newton leaves aside the problem of knowing where the different parts remain. To the contrary, Leibniz's calculus, based on the reciprocal determination of "differentials," is strictly inseparable from a Soul, insofar as the soul alone conserves and distinguishes the small components" (Deleuze, *The Fold*, 98).

152. Deleuze, *Difference and Repetition*, 213.

153. Deleuze, *Difference and Repetition*, 253.

154. Deleuze, *Expressionism in Philosophy*, 137.

155. Deleuze, *Desert Islands and Other Texts*, 143–144.

156. Deleuze, *The Logic of Sense*, 268–269.

157. Deleuze, *Difference and Repetition*, 165.

References

Alliez, Éric. "Deleuze, Bergson und das Virtuelle." In *Telenoia. Kritik der virtuellen Bilder*, edited by Samsonow, Elisabeth von and Alliez, Éric, 67–78. Vienna: Turia+Kant, 1999.

Badiou, Alain. *Deleuze. The Clamor of Being*. Translated by Louise Burchill. Minneapolis: University of Minnesota Press, 2000.

Bergson, Henri. *The Creative Mind. An Introduction to Metaphysics*. Translated by Mabelle L. Andison. New York: The Philosophical Library, 1946.

Brassier, Ray. *Nihil Unbound. Enlightenment and Extinction*. Basingstoke: Palgrave Macmillan, 2007.

Brassier, Ray. "The Enigma of Realism: On Quentin Meillassoux's *After Finitude*." *Collapse* II (2007): 15–54.

Bryant, Levi R. "The Ontic Principle: Outline of an Object-Oriented Ontology." In *The Speculative Turn*, edited by Levy Bryant, Nick Smicek and Graham Harman, 261–278. New York: re.press, 2011.

Deleuze, Gilles. *Empiricism and Subjectivity. An Essay on Hume's Theory of Human Nature*. Translated by Constantin V. Boundas. New York: Columbia University Press, 1991.

———. *Nietzsche & Philosophy*. Translated by H. Tomlinson. New York: Columbia University Press, 1997.

———. *Bergsonism*. Translated by Hugh Tomlinson and Barbara Habberjam. New York: Zone Books, 1991.

———. *Expressionism in Philosophy: Spinoza*. Translated by Martin Joughin. New York: Zone Books, 1997.

———. *Difference and Repetition*. Translated by Paul Patton. New York: Continuum, 2001.

———. *The Logic of Sense*. Translated by Mark Lester and Charles Stivale. London: Continuum, 1990.

———. *Cinema 1: The Movement-Image*. Translated by Hugh Tomlinson and Barbara Habberjam. Minneapolis: University of Minnesota Press, 1986.

———. *Cinema 2: The Time-Image*. Translated by Hugh Tomlinson and Barbara Habberjam. Minneapolis: University of Minnesota Press, 1989.

———. *Foucault*. Translated by Seán Hand. Minneapolis: University of Minnesota Press, 1988.

———. *The Fold: Leibniz and the Baroque*. Translated by Tom Conley. Minneapolis: University of Minnesota Press, 1993.

———. *Negotiations: 1972–1990*. Translated by Martin Joughin. New York: Columbia University Press, 1995.

———. *Desert Islands and Other Texts 1953–1974*. Edited by D. Lapoujade. Translated by M. Taormina. New York: Semiotext(e), 2004.

———. "Pericles and Verdi: The Philosophy of François Châtelet." Translated by Charles T. Wolfe. *The Opera Quarterly* 21, no. 4 (2006): 713–24.

Deleuze, Gilles & Guattari, Félix. *Anti-Oedipus: Capitalism and Schizophrenia*. Translated by Robert Hurley, Mark Seem, and Helen R. Lane. London: Continuum, 2003.

———. *A Thousand Plateaus*. Translated by Brian Massumi. Minneapolis: University of Minnesota Press, 1987.

———. *What is Philosophy?* Translated by H. Tomlinson and G. Burchill. London: Verso, 1994.

Deleuze, Gilles & Parnet, Claire. *Dialogues*. Translated by Hugh Tomlinson and Barbara Habberjam. New York: Columbia University Press, 1987.

Foucault, Michel. "Theatrum Philosophicum." In *Aesthetics, Method, and Epistemology*, edited by J. D. Faubion, 343–68. New York: The New Press, 1998.

Hallward, Peter. "Anything is Possible: A Reading of Quentin Meillassoux's *After Finitude*." In *The Speculative Turn*, edited by Levy Bryant, Nick Smicek and Graham Harman, 130–41. (New York: re.press, 2011).

Heidegger, Martin. *Kant and the Problem of Metaphysics*. Translated by Richard Taft. Bloomington: Indiana University Press, 1997.

———. *Early Greek Thinking: The Dawn of Western Philosophy*. Translated by D. F. Krell and F. A. Capuzzi. San Francisco: Harper & Row, 1984.

———. *Der Satz vom Grund*. Stuttgart: Neske, 1997.

———. *Nietzsche. Volume III: The Will to Power as Knowledge and as Metaphysics*, Translated by Joan Stambaugh, David Ferrell Krell, and Frank A. Capuzzi, New York: Harper & Row, 1991.

———. *On Time and Being*. Translated by Joan Stambaugh. New York: Harper & Row, 1972.

James, William. *Some Problems of Philosophy: A Beginning of an Introduction to Philosophy.* Lincoln: University of Nebraska Press, 1996.

Kerslake, Christian. "Deleuze's 'Reconstruction of Reason'. From Leibniz and Kant to *Difference and Repetition.*" In *Thinking Between Deleuze and Kant,* edited by E. Willat, 101–27. New York: Continuum, 2009.

Laerke, Mogens. "Gilles Deleuze and the System of Nature and Philosophy." *Alegrar* 2 (2005). http://www.alegrar.com.br/02/mogensing.pdf.

Leibniz, Gottfried Wilhelm. *Philosophical Essays.* Edited and translated by R. Ariew and D. Garber. Indianapolis: Hackett, 1989.

———. *Philosophical Papers and Letters.* Edited and translated by Leroy E. Loemker. Dordrecht: Kluwer, 1989.

Meillassoux, Quentin, "Potentiality and Virtuality." *Collapse,* II (2007): 55–82.

———. *After Finitude: An Essay on the Necessity of Contingency.* Translated by Ray Brassier. London: Continuum, 2008.

Negarestani, Reza. "Differential Cruelty. A Critique of Ontological Reason in Light of the Philosophy of Cruelty." *Angelaki: Journal of the Theoretical Humanities* 14, no. 3 (2009): 69–84.

Roffe, Jon, 2012, "Time and Ground. A Critique of Meillassoux's Speculative Realism." *Angelaki: Journal of the Theoretical Humanities* 17, no.1 (2012): 57–67.

Rölli, Marc. "Deleuze on Intensity Differentials and the Being of the Sensible." *Deleuze Studies* 3, no. 1 (2009): 26–53.

Serres, Michel. *Genesis.* Translated by Genevieve James and James Nielson. Ann Arbor: University of Michigan Press, 1995.

Smith, Daniel W. "Genesis and Difference: Deleuze, Maïmon, and the Post-Kantian Reading of Leibniz." In *Deleuze and the Fold. A Critical Reader,* edited by Sjoerd van Tuinen and Niamh McDonnell, 132–54. Basingstoke: Palgrave Macmillan, 2010.

Spinoza, Baruch. *Complete Works.* Translated by Samuel Shirley. Indianapolis: Hackett, 2002.

Stengers, Isabelle. "Deleuze and Guattari's Last Enigmatic Message." *Angelaki: Journal of Theoretical Humanities* 10, no. 2 (2005), 151–67.

———. "William James. An ethics of thought?" *Radical Philosophy* 157 (2009): 9–17.

———. "Speculative Philosophy and the Art of Dramatization." Paper discussed at a research seminar of the Centre for Art and Philosophy at Erasmus University Rotterdam, 31 May 2012.

Whitehead, Alfred North. *Process and Reality: An Essay in Cosmology.* New York: The Free Press, 1985.

CHAPTER FOUR

The Physics of Sense: Bruno, Schelling, Deleuze

Joshua Ramey and Daniel Whistler

Introduction: The Becoming-Archaic of Metaphysics

In his monumental, yet perpetually neglected account of the origins of human thought, Giambattista Vico makes a claim about the nature of metaphysics that can serve as a surprising cipher for the tradition in which Deleuze, F. W. J. Schelling, and Giordano Bruno must all be situated. Vico writes that "the Queen of the Sciences, metaphysics, began when men began to think in human fashion, and not when philosophers began to reflect on human ideas."[1] Metaphysics and becoming-human are here fatefully interlinked, such that the role of the meta-physician (no matter in what era she lives) is identified with a continual process of anthropogenesis—traversing and retraversing the human-inhuman divide in a conceptual rhythm. The metaphysician must situate herself on the boundary of the very becoming-human of thought—and it is precisely here that metaphysics is synonymous with (and not opposed to) critique. Thought searches out its grounds, the conditions of possibility which first constituted it. Speculation is critique at the moment that philosophy becomes archaic.[2]

How does thought achieve this? How, that is, does the philosopher descend into these archaic depths to re-inhabit the inhuman/human boundary? And, what is more, how can one assess how successfully she does so? The answer that not only Vico but also Bruno, Schelling and Deleuze give is that thought must trans-form and mutate itself into that archaic condition. It is a case of a rhythmic in-tensification and de-intensification of thinking. We will consider Bruno, Schel-ling and Deleuze's reflections on this problem shortly; however, Vico puts it thus,

> Now rational metaphysics teaches us that man becomes all things through un-derstanding. . . . But with perhaps greater truth, this imaginative metaphysics [of the first humans] shows that man becomes all things by not understanding. . . .

When he does not understand [all things], he makes them out of himself and, by transforming himself, becomes them.[3]

Construction, self-transformation, and metaphysics are intertwined—and this intertwining (along with the added complications that the concepts of affect and rhetoric bring) forms the topic for what follows. What is at stake is the art of the metaphysician: the strategies, skills, and practices that allows her to think the becoming-thought of thought.

On Vico's account, then, metaphysics began not in rational reflection, but when the gigantic, feral creatures who were our ancestors began to *imagine* themselves in relation to the powerful forces of the awful nature around them. Vico writes,

> For providence ordained that the people with gigantic proportions and the greatest strength would wander the mountain heights like beasts with natural strength. Then, on hearing the first thunder after the universal flood, they entered the earth in its mountain caves, and subjected themselves to the superior force which they imagined as Jupiter. All their pride and ferocity was converted to astonishment, and they humbled themselves before this divinity.[4]

Metaphysics begins not reflectively, but poetically. It also begins in a kind of *piety*. Taking the awesome power of the lightening as an omen, our pagan ancestors crudely construe or "divine" its meaning and import as an auspice, a sign of an obscure and yet invested authority. Insofar as this piety issues immediately in a metaphorical conjecture, such conjecture is the first and last metaphysical gesture: metaphysics begins as an imaginative conjecture as to the ultimate nature of power (and power of nature). Vico simultaneously links divination (along with marriages and burial rites) to the essence of humanity: to be human is to construe, and to conjecture, from the known to the unknown. To be human, contemporary prejudices notwithstanding, is to be metaphysical.

But paradoxically, to be or become-metaphysical is not precisely to become rational, and humanity for Vico is not defined as a rational animal. In the concluding pages of the *New Science*, Vico avers that the ultimate ground of all human conjecture lies in the *affects*—specifically in affects of *wonder, veneration*, and *desire*.[5] Because initial (and final) conjecture emerges from these affects, without the affects, we do not have metaphysics. And without such a metaphysics, conversely, we do not have humanity as we know it. There is thus an immediately ethical dimension to poetic and primordial metaphysics:

> In their fear and reverence for such divine gods, [our ancestors] found themselves torn between the powerful restraints of fearful superstitions and the sharp goading of bestial lust, passions which must have been extremely violent in such people. Terrified by the aspect of the heavens, they checked their urge to sexual intercourse, and instead subjected their lustful impulses to a conscious effort. In this way, they began to enjoy human liberty, which consists in restraining the impulses of physical desire, and giving them a new direction.[6]

Affect is central to the emergence of metaphysics, and so a genuinely critical philosophy—one attuned to its own conditions of possibility—will therefore recover, repeat and redeploy affect, as such. This is, of course, a trope as old as the *Symposium*, but notice how Vico perverts the ascent which the desirous are meant to follow. It is no longer the case that desire withdraws us from bodily lusts in the name of intellectual visions; rather, desire (and affect generally) oscillates unstably between "the sharp goading of bestial lust" and abasement before the "fearful superstitions" of divine law. Desire deranges, fractures and degrades. And metaphysics is born out of such tension—not only for Vico, but also for Bruno, Schelling, and Deleuze.

This linking of metaphysics to the affects (and thus to ethics) is a particularly important theme in Deleuze's thought. In his book on Nietzsche, Deleuze avers that we have the truths we deserve based on the hour we watch over and the element we frequent.[7] In *Difference and Repetition*, Nietzsche's conception of eternal return is read as a *test* of whether one has the strength (viz. affective capacity) to endure the world as it is.[8] Metaphysics begins not in an emendation of the intellect, but an emendation of the affects. The potential of *sense* (that is, meaning and value) derives from alterations and transformations at the affective level. Metaphysics is, for Deleuze, grounded in the possibility of a "physics of sense," a genealogical and topological account of affective difference. Following Bergson, Whitehead, and Spinoza, Deleuze insists on understanding metaphysical capacity on the same plane of immanence as all other affective-based capacities (such as those of the tic or those of a war machine). But this is not the only tradition of affective immanence Deleuze inhabits: both Schelling and Bruno before him took up something like this position, and we must situate Deleuze in this line in order to broaden the scope of some of the most difficult questions about Deleuze's system. Such is the task of this paper. What emerges from it is a "minor" tradition that invites us to ask an extremely difficult metaphilosophical question: what criteria can be used to evaluate metaphysical positions, given that such positions have an ultimate ground (or unground) not in reason but in the affects?

We bring Deleuze together with Bruno and Schelling, first of all, because they engage, cite and repeat each other. Deleuze refers implicitly but approvingly to Bruno in *Expressionism in Philosophy*[9]; he speaks in hints and riddles of Schelling's importance to him in *Difference and Repetition*.[10] Schelling likewise makes Bruno "the patron saint of his philosophy."[11] However, beyond such citation (and neither Deleuze nor Schelling were particularly fulsome in their acknowledgement of sources) there is more significantly a conceptual structure which binds these three thinkers together in one minor tradition. They all foreground the role of the philosopher in constituting metaphysics; they all enumerate a series of practices and transformations for the philosopher to be initiated into metaphysics; in sum, they all (despite the many divergences and disagreements that exist between them) chart a physics of the sense of metaphysics.

Part One: The Figure of the Pure Metaphysician

In 1981, Deleuze confessed to Arnaud Villani, "I feel I am a pure metaphysician."[12] One way of characterizing our task over the next few pages is a commentary on this affirmation—to explicate and unfold what a "pure metaphysics" consists in. However, from the beginning we must be clear that this is *a* commentary and not *the* commentary. For Villani, Deleuze's outing of himself as a pure metaphysician is intended as a judgment on "the difficulty of doing justice to complexity, to multiplicity, to singularity," a judgment on the fundamental "decision" that gives rise to "certain modes of thinking" (for with such decision comes "loss").[13] Indeed, we must acknowledge that at the same time as Deleuze's comments on pure metaphysics gives rise to our analysis of the becoming-archaic of philosophy, they also put it into question. This is, of course, implicit in our labeling the Bruno-Schelling-Deleuze trajectory a *minor* tradition.[14]

However, with that qualification in mind, we pose the question: in what does pure metaphysics consist? It consists above all, as Vico made clear, in an affective metaphysics—a thinking in which affects are liberated from regulation. Where Kant imposes the discipline of pure reason, Deleuze insists on the indiscipline of reason—a reason that is no longer pure, but mutates and contaminates itself in adventure. The purity of metaphysics is guaranteed by the impurity of reason. In short, pure metaphysics is attained once we stop predetermining in advance what reason can do (and to this extent, of course, the very question, "in what does pure metaphysics consist?" is inaccurate): once reason is no longer essentially X or essentially Y, once there is no longer even a felt need to describe what reason is (as if it were something given), then it can become what it wants. This liberation—an emancipatory feeling of constructive power—is the vector along which pure metaphysics is generated.

Evidence for such a description of Deleuzian metaphysics emerges in his "Letter to a Harsh Critic," which (as Deleuze insists in the same Villani interview[15]) is to be taken as the definitive account of his development. One of Deleuze's critics had accused him of merely fawning over the intense experiences and experimental voyages of others—"vaguely savouring their transports," as Deleuze restates the charge.[16] Deleuze's response is profound. Rather than forswear his appreciation for the adventures of others, he points rather to his own experience, an experience he insists can only be spoken of indirectly, even *falsely.*

> But what do you know about me, given that I believe in secrecy, that is, in the power of falsity, rather than in representing things in a way that manifests a lamentable faith in accuracy and truth? If I stick where I am, if I don't travel around, like anyone else I make my inner journeys that I can only measure by my emotions, and express very obliquely and circuitously in what I write.[17]

We know that Deleuze, like Kant and like Proust, was no great traveller. Apparently his journey to the United States with Guattari was a miserable one (even the picture of Deleuze on the beach in Big Sur figures him playing morosely with the sand).[18] And yet Deleuze explicitly says here that his writing is a testament to emotional journeys, to affective states and experiences that cannot be the subject of direct representation. Given that Deleuze calls himself a "pure metaphysician," what can be made of a metaphysician who disavows the representational power of concepts in favor of an indirect discourse on his experiences? Is the disavowal itself ironic? False?

In the first place, Deleuze disavows that he is speaking from a position of "privileged" experience. In fact, he explicitly says there is something "bad and reactionary" about making arguments from such a position. He continues,

> The question's nothing to do with the character of this or that exclusive group, it's to do with the transversal relations that ensure that any effects produced in some particular way (through homosexuality, drugs, and so on) *can always be produced by other means. . . .* It's not a question of being this or that sort of human, but of becoming inhuman, of a universal animal becoming—not seeing yourself as some dumb animal, but unraveling your body's human organization, exploring this or that zone of bodily intensity, with everyone discovering their own particular zones, and the groups, populations, species that inhabit them.[19]

Presumably what one discovers in such experiments is a properly *universal*, rather than exclusive, domain of experience: the "Planomenon," the Unknown Natures that traverse individual organisms, species, groups, even societies.[20] We might risk the proposition that what Deleuze means by metaphysical language is the language of what, at the most abstract level, "*can always be produced by other means.*"

One of the most important things to notice in the above passage is the conjunction of zones and lines. On the one hand, everyone has her "zone," but on the other hand, there are transversal lines that cross the zones. Presumably the language of metaphysics, for Deleuze, is the language of those lines. But the criterion for the adequacy of the names of the lines is not whether they accurately or correctly represent what the lines are, but the degree to which they encourage, relay, or continue what the lines *may be*. That is to say, the critical question becomes, how do names such as "rhizome," "becoming-animal," "fold," "difference-in-itself," "metaphysical surface," bear witness to the specific singularity of zones *and* provoke more of the zones, groups, and populations that may yet become? What do such names *do*? It is this constructivism, or even pragmatism, in Deleuze's use of metaphysical language to which we return in the second half of the paper: words make metaphysics for Deleuze. And, to this extent, the "physics of sense" denotes the mapping of the specific rhetorical strategies that generate metaphysical entities.

Somehow metaphysical language, to be both referential and pragmatic, must have an irreducibly *rhetorical* dimension. There is a rhetoric specific to metaphysics. Since being is becoming, and since for Deleuze the becoming of language and concepts is not different in kind from the becoming of events, metaphysical language does not so much identify as *provoke* or continue events. At stake in metaphysics, therefore, is a knot between three terms: event, rhetoric and affect. The conscious manipulation of this knot and so the perpetual reconfiguration of metaphysics in relation to events, affects, and rhetoric is, above all, what marks out this minor tradition of metaphysics, the one in which Bruno, Schelling and Deleuze participate.

Part Two: Philosophical Frenzies

If, then, the above provides a broad account of the framework of pure metaphysics, what is required, in addition, is an enumeration of the various, specific practices of mutation by which it is constituted. One such practice is, as we have just delineated, rhetorical—and we return to it later in the paper. However, even more fundamental is a practice which (in divergent forms) governs all metaphysics undertaken in this tradition. Deleuze's version of it is presented in the closing pages of *Bergsonism*:

> It could be said that man is capable of rediscovering all the levels, all the degrees of expansion and contraction that coexist in the virtual Whole. As if he were capable of all the frenzies and brought about in himself successively everything that, elsewhere, can only be embodied in different species.[21]

Deleuze here repeats an old image: what exists *explicate* in humanity exists *complicate* in nature, or man is a microcosm of the All. It is an image that has been redeployed for metaphilosophical purposes in modernity, where it is the metaphysician above all who is able to rediscover the All, to express every frenzy in herself. According to Bruno, for example, this is the ideal of the *omniformis*: a philosopher who transforms herself perpetually into minerals, animals and gods. It is an ideal of the metaphysician as a sage who, by continually becoming-other, attains a knowledge of the whole.[22] This ideal continues into German Idealism, where Schelling too idealizes the philosopher as a figure able to repeat nature within herself. The above passage from *Bergsonism* situates Deleuze in a specific tradition of philosophy that passes through Bruno and Schelling. It is a tradition of pure metaphysics which cultivates and constructs frenzies (affective reason become productive) in order to repeat nature's own frenzies.

Bruno was perhaps the first modern philosopher to be explicit about the connection between the cultivation of frenzies and metaphysical insight. Whereas there had been a long Neo-Platonic tradition of *ecstasy*, Bruno's notion of *frenzy* hints at a to-ing and fro-ing within the world, an incessant alternation that is not quite the same as Neo-Platonic notions of *elevation* toward the One. Given Deleuze's cryptic but admiring mentions of Bruno, and his somewhat more substantial if equally cryptic nods to Bruno's ancestor Nicholas of Cusa,[23] it is worth more than simply mentioning Bruno as a kind of dark precursor to Deleuze (as well as to Schelling) in terms of such a metaphysics of affects.

Heroic Frenzies establishes the centrality of frenzy to Nolan metaphysics most firmly. The metaphysician becomes "a furious lover"[24] who is urged on to wilder deliberations by desire "decked in divers forms."[25] Affect and cognition become indistinguishable to the extent that the guiding imperative to metaphysical practice becomes: "Render your affect so fervent!"[26] The key to Bruno's metaphysical reconstitution of frenzy is his theory of bonding. Relationships (whether physical, mental, metaphysical, or affective) are all collapsed into a theory of different types of bonds or "different kinds of knots."[27] The subject of knowing is knotted in a specific way to the object of knowing, just as the lover is knotted in a very similar way to the beloved—and such similarity is precisely what the image of the metaphysician as "furious lover" represents. Philosophical bonds are creations of love: they are attractive or "heroic bonds"[28] which draw the object to the subject. The task of the philosopher, according to Bruno, is therefore to, first, understand and enumerate all the particular forms of bonding in existence (and this is what Bruno himself does in *A General Account of Bonding* and *On Magic*) and, second, to exploit this knowledge in order to manipulate bonds in the name of knowledge—in other words, to turn bonds that repel or keep the object at a distance into attractive bonds. The task of the metaphysician, here, is to make the world fall in love.

Thus, as Bruno writes, "The inclinations of all bonds can be actuated by a skilful effort."[29] Metaphysics is an art: it is the art of knowing what is the appropriate form of the attractive bond to be deployed in a certain situation. What will become increasingly crucial as our exposition of Bruno continues is his Aristotelian contention that "what is appropriate" is context-sensitive. One cannot predict in advance the type of bond which will reap knowledge: a good metaphysician is not she who continues to repeat the same method no matter what, but she who responds to the specific, concrete circumstances in which knowledge is to be gained.[30] The cultivation of bonds of attraction between the metaphysician and the object of knowledge is subject to finesse, a kind of pragmatism that we will see more clearly in Bruno's account of metaphysical language.

What is more, this metaphysical practice is the very definition of magic for Bruno. The magician "manipulat[es] active and passive powers,"[31] maintaining bonds between objects and also creating new ones. In particular, the magician, like the metaphysician, relies on "the use of words, chants, calculations of numbers and times, images, figures, symbols, characters or letters"[32] to achieve this. Indeed, the minor tradition of Bruno, Schelling and Deleuze we identify in this paper could be helpfully characterized as a tradition of magical metaphysics, to the extent that the role of the metaphysician is to produce new relations between objects and, indeed, to do so (as we shall see) by transforming her own self-relation to the world. For Bruno, Schelling and Deleuze, the metaphysician is also a magician.

Bruno's writings, one must conclude, emphasize the role of the philosopher. In opposition to a formalist current of metaphysical thought which erases the role of the subject of knowing in favor of a pure, subject-less inscription of reality, Bruno envisages the behavior of the philosopher as a key ingredient in the constitution of metaphysical reality. No longer, therefore, is the Platonic text a book on which reality writes itself, instead, Bruno writes, "Plato went twisting and turning and tearing to pieces and placing embankments so that the volatile and fugacious species should be as it were caught in a net."[33] The philosopher is the active ingredient in the creation of attractive bonds: through twisting, turning, ripping to shreds and erecting obstacles, Plato manages to cultivate precisely those bonds of love which bring reality to knowledge, like iron filings to a magnet. Indeed, in the final dialogue of *Heroic Frenzies*, Bruno idealizes the philosopher under the figure of Circe, the magician who transformed humans into pigs, who created her own transitions between the human and the inhuman. Circe is the conceptual persona of a heroic philosopher able to reconstitute bonds at will. Bruno writes, "Oh might it please heaven that in these days, as in the past more happy ages, some wise Circe might make herself present who, with plants and minerals working her incantations, would be able to curb nature."[34]

The heroic metaphysician thus turns humans into pigs and pigs into humans; she affirms weird, inhuman becomings in the name of knowledge. Humans become gods, minerals, and animals—there is no hierarchy here, only assemblages.[35] What is more, in contrast to Circe, the metaphysician does not merely transform others but primarily *herself*. The metaphysician must in some sense derange herself. The opening to *The Ash Wednesday Supper* insists upon this need for perpetual becomings:

> Become heroic and humble; master and disciple; believer and unbeliever; cheerful and sad; saturnine and jovial; light and ponderous; miserly and liberal; simian and consular; sophist with Aristotle, philosopher with Pythagoras; laugher with Democritus and weeper with Heraclitus.[36]

The Nolan universe is one of subjects in motion, transitioning repeatedly from one form to another; there is no stability, but "continuous mutation"[37]; no central *archē* around which motion is anchored.[38] All that exists is hybrid, destabilized and deranged becoming.

And such conscious derangement is done for the sake of the ideal of an omniform metaphysics. By means of such successive formations and reformations, "man in all his powers displays every species of being"[39] and so envelops in herself all of reality. The universe is internalized through the power of self-transformation. Therefore, Bruno (as a philosopher) himself attempts to cultivate this dynamic heterogeneity. He deranges himself and his texts in order to capture the whole. As he puts it in *Heroic Frenzies*, perfectly capturing the knotting together of affect and transformation in his work, "At once I tremble, sparkle, freeze and burn; am mute and fill the air with clamorous plaints."[40] These are the "exercises" Bruno refers to in *Heroic Frenzies*[41]: exercises which include inducing visions, trances, occult experiences and also, we contend, rhetoric. Such exercises are necessary to transform the self and envelop reality. Metaphysicians must be "artificers,"[42] Bruno writes a few pages later—and with that sentiment we are back with Deleuze's *Letter to a Harsh Critic*.

Part Three: What Lurks Beneath

Early in his agenda-setting *Freiheitsschrift*, Schelling spells out a basic epistemological presupposition:

> Whoever takes the theory of physics as his point of departure and knows that the doctrine of "like is recognised by like" is a very ancient one . . . such a one will understand that the philosopher . . . alone comprehends the god outside him through the god within himself by keeping his mind pure and unclouded by evil.[43]

The subject of knowing must resemble the object of knowing. To remain faithful to this injunction is, Schelling adds, "training in philosophy." Such training is enjoined (both explicitly and implicitly) throughout Schelling's philosophical trajectory: the necessary identity of subject and object produces the absolute I of *Vom Ich*, it makes possible the whole metaphysical apparatus of the *Identitätssystem* and even undergirds the later lectures. What is of interest to us here, however, is its metaphilosophical implications: *the philosopher must become what she would know*. Metaphysics is governed by the affect of sympathy—an attractive bond, in Bruno's terminology, which draws the philosopher and her subject matter together.

What is more, the above passage insists that the metaphysician who engages in such practices of identity-formation has a mind "unclouded by evil." This is certainly true of the Platonic metaphysician ascending towards the good; yet, it must be asked, does it ring true of the Schellingian philosopher? Indeed, does it ring true of Schelling's own philosophical practices in a treatise explicitly orientated towards knowing the possibility and actuality of *evil*? If like is known by like, evil is known by evil—or at least (and this qualification is essential) by those who resemble evil. And so it seems incumbent upon Schelling and Schellingian philosophers to cultivate a mind *clouded* by evil (or what resembles evil), rather than the reverse. Sympathy with evil is a prerequisite for embarking on the metaphysical project of the *Freiheitsschrift*.

The contrast with two-world Platonic metaphysics is worth pursuing.[44] Schellingian metaphysics consists in "the solicitation of the depths,"[45] rather than a flight into the heights. It is, moreover, not that such depths should be identified with evil in the way that the heights are often equated with the good;

rather, for Schelling, to neglect the depths is to impoverish reality: it is to fail to comprehend what reality can do, the extent of its productivity. Such is the reason Schelling berates all philosophers who have failed to appropriate nature, the unruly and all less potentiated phenomena into their systems. A guiding methodological principle throughout Schelling's oeuvre can be reconstructed as: what is foreclosed from philosophy necessarily weakens it. Such is what Grant dubs "the extensity test"[46] and it motivates Schelling's violent criticisms of idealizing metaphysics:

> Where the ideal principle really operates to a high degree but cannot discover a reconciling and mediating basis, it gives birth to a dreary and fanatic enthusiasm which breaks forth in self-mutilation or—as in the case of the priests of the Phrygian goddess—in self-emasculation, which in philosophy is accomplished by the renunciation of reason and science.[47]

At stake therefore in the Schellingian ideal of "reason and science" is an absolute metaphysical system in which everything from the unruly depths to the ideal heights is enfolded. And, as has already become clear, the cultivation of an affective bond with evil is a prerequisite for such absolutization.

In consequence, Schelling positions himself in the same tradition of omniform metaphysics as Bruno and Deleuze: the philosophical text must embrace every modality of power, every modification of what is. It must repeat reality in all its potencies. Schelling's metaphysical practice is therefore one of repetition and the basis of his *modus operandi* can be discerned in the following,

> The potencies pass through all the positions and relations to each other which they had in the process of nature. . . . The process that repeats itself . . . is the universal and absolute process, and thus the true science of mythology is accordingly the one that presents the absolute process in it.[48]

The philosopher is she who repeats, she in whom all the potencies of reality reoccur. The art of the metaphysician is the art of total repetition. To construct a system enveloping everything, the metaphysician must become like everything. She must cultivate resemblances and carry on repeating.

The philosopher must follow reality into depths as well as heights.[49] Schelling's fidelity to this principle is most clearly visible in the natural history sketched towards the end of the *Freiheitsschrift*, where he describes the continual potentiation of reality into ever higher and more rarefied regions of being (spirit emerges, then love). However, reality does not merely potentiate itself; it also periodically plunges down into the depths—and to think otherwise is to be tempted by precisely the ascetic idealism Schelling so violently criticizes. Thus, the *Freiheitsschrift* not only narrates the becoming rational of reality, but also its diseases, crises and absurdities:

Because the principle of the depths can never give birth for itself to true and complete unity, the time comes in which all this glory decays as through horrible disease, and finally chaos again ensues.[50]

Such is the significance to Schelling of these concepts of "disease," "crisis," "cission," and "flood"[51]: they designate an essential moment of reality. Absolute metaphysics must make manifest such essential moments of return to the depths.

Part Four: Schelling's Geological Etymology

One of the problems to which Schelling returns repeatedly is the following: if absolute metaphysics must speak of the depths as well as the heights, how does it do so? That is, the depths are precisely that which do not make themselves manifest, but remain hidden beneath phenomena. The problem is a geological one: strata of reality lie hidden below phenomena and the task of the philosopher is to dig them up. The philosopher becomes a geologist.[52]

It is within this problematic that Schelling's philosophy of language is to be situated. Schelling's later writing often turns to philology, precisely because language is one of the ways in which the depths become manifest as depths. The unruly appears through language—and so study of language is absolutely key for the formation of an absolute metaphysics. Indeed, one of the basic theses of the *Introduction to the Philosophy of Mythology* runs: the crises and floods that throw the earth into turmoil are repeated in the formation of language. Poetry, above all, embodies such disruption: "The crisis through which the world of the gods unfolds . . . is not external to the poets. It takes place in the poets themselves, forms their poems."[53] Texts are central to Schelling's work, because they manifest traces of the depths.[54]

Hence, a philosophy that truly intends to include the depths in its system—an absolute metaphysics—must pursue (at least some of the time) a geological etymology. As Schelling himself puts it, "In the formation of the oldest languages a wealth of philosophy can be discovered."[55] Schelling's clearest statement of this project of geological etymology occurs in his 1811 *Report on Schmid's Attempt at Pasigraphy*:

One may ask whether there are not homologous language formations, like there are mountain formations that can recur in quite different places in the world independently of each other. . . . When one cognises the physical in language, and pursues and arranges the facts of the history of peoples and language in connection with or at least in analogy to the geological, what wondrous and (at present) unbelievable regularity and lawfulness will then appear before our eyes![56]

"Cognising the physical in language" is not merely a matter of recognizing the materiality of the signifier, but also of thinking the linguistic "in connection with" the geological. Schelling establishes a geological model for linguistics based on language's capacity to make present the depths.

The significance of this insight for his philosophical project can be discerned from the very procedure of *The Deities of Samothrace*. *Deities* takes the names of the gods from the Samothracian mystery-cult as sediment to be stripped down, so as to reveal "a primordial system older than all written documents, which is the common source of all religious doctrines and representations."[57] The unruly depths of reality are, in fact, what is made present through this geological-philological operation; for example, the name *Axiokersus* contains the Hebrew root *hrs* which, in turn, is connected to fire, and, in this way, it manifests the Heraclitean truth that "the world is an eternal living fire."[58] The catastrophic unruliness of nature is implicitly contained in these names, and to etymologically analyze the names is also simultaneously to reveal the workings of reality itself.

As *Deities* shows in practice and the 1811 *Report* teaches in theory, to become an absolute metaphysician requires a focus on language; it requires learning philological practices of excavation. An absolute metaphysical text must oscillate perpetually between a language of the depths and a language of the heights. To become a metaphysician, one thus requires the appropriate rhetorical strategies. Schelling refers to such strategies in *The Deities of Samothrace*:

> Through the consecrations received, the initiate himself became a link of that magical chain, himself a Kabir, taken up into the unbreakable relation and *joined* to the army of the higher gods, as the old inscription expresses it. In *this* sense the Cabiri or their servants might well be called inventors of magical singing, as Socrates says the child in us must continually be exorcised and must be healed with magical singing until it is free of the fear of death.[59]

Both magic and metaphysics[60] consist in a form of singing that transforms the singer into that about which she sings (in this case, a god). To know the gods, one must sing like the gods; likewise, to know evil, one must sing "deeply." Moreover, the key to such linguistic imitation is (in part) the practice of magical and occult exercises—as it is for Bruno. Hence, the 1811 *Report* describes in detail occult practices by which the true nature of language is revealed. The following is an extract from this discussion:

> We know of a quantity of cases where people in a somnambulant condition have produced poetry which they were never again able to produce in a wakeful state. . . . In the *Actis Naturae Curiosum* there is the story of a woman who in the condition of pregnancy fell into an ecstasy in which she sang unknown songs and talked in foreign tongues. . . . All this is surely sufficient to prove that the source of language lies in man and, like so much else which hides in him, emerges more freely under certain circumstances and is developed into a higher, more universal sense of language.[61]

The extreme affects brought on by illness, frenzy, and ecstasy engender the extreme affects of language, its heights and its depths.[62] Once more, metaphysics, affect, and rhetoric are knotted together.

Part Five: Bruno's Affective Pragmatism

Giordano Bruno's philosophy of language consists for the most part in a critique of grammar. Just as Schelling polemicizes against idealists for neglecting the depths and thereby emasculating themselves, so, too, Bruno vehemently criticizes grammarians along the same lines:

> Having grown old . . . in anatomising phrases and words, [they] have sought to rouse the mind to the formation of new logic and metaphysics, judging and sentencing those which they had never studied nor understood. . . . They fast, they become thin and emaciated, they scourge the skin, and lengthen the beard, they rot. . . . [With] vile thoughts they think to mount to the stars, to be equal to gods, and to understand the good and the beautiful which philosophy promises.[63]

Linguistic attitudes have physical, ethical, and even metaphysical symptoms. What the grammarians do wrong, of course, is erect normative models for good language use; they regulate and discipline the way words are employed, prohibiting a deranged use of language. "Slaves of definite and determinate sounds and words,"[64] they establish *a priori* forms which are not context-specific. In contrast, Bruno insists on linguistic pragmatism: a pragmatism which does away with all forms of regulation (including linguistic good sense) in the name of radical experimentation with rhetorical strategies. He cultivates linguistic disorder.

One of the basic differences between the grammarians and Bruno concerns signification; in short, Bruno marginalizes it. While the grammarians judge language according to internal meanings, Bruno places stress on the external effect of words. To concentrate on the meaning of words is to limit their potential. Bruno is profoundly suspicious of such a move: when one does not determine in advance what language can do, language becomes capable of much more—and it is precisely what language does (the effect it has in the world) which is at issue. *What matters is effect.* And the possible effects of language are, of course, affective. At this juncture we return once more to the affect-rhetoric-metaphysics knot: what words do is "cause various effects and passions."[65] This is perhaps best exhibited in the very first stanza of the *Heroic Frenzies* which invokes the Muses as those deities who occasion "verses, rhymes and exaltation"[66]: rhetoric and frenzy are assembled into the same list. The Muses inspire a form of language which elevates the subject into frenzy, which creates and maintains attractive bonds of love. Hence, Bruno concludes a few pages later by explicitly bringing together the linguistic practice of poetry and the manipulation of affects: "Enthusiasm is born, by ploughing the field of the Muses and scattering the seed of his thoughts and waiting for the fruitful harvest, discovering in himself the fervour of the affections."[67] Rhetoric is an optimal strategy for the creation of those bonds by which the world is disclosed to the subject; it is therefore a crucial tool for both the magician and (what is almost the same thing) the metaphysician.

There is no rhetoric which is *a priori* effective (or affective); rather, language must be experimented with; it must be deranged, upended, and reconstructed. Hence, Bruno's own rhetorical project consists in the pragmatic reconfiguration of philosophical discourse: it is why his texts are such unique assemblages of satire, dialogue, doctrine, and nonsense. The pedant, Prudenzio, might cry out, "It seems to me you take little account of words,"[68] but Bruno revels in his eclecticism:

> [*The Ash Wednesday Supper* does] not appear to constitute a single topic, but appear[s] here like a dialogue, here a comedy, here a tragedy, here poetry and here rhetoric, here praise, here vituperation, here demonstration and teaching; here we have now natural philosophy, now mathematics, now morals, now logic; in conclusion, there is no sort of knowledge of which there is not here some fragment.[69]

Bruno is as innovative rhetorically as he is metaphysically—and for exactly the same reasons. The philosophical text is a site of pragmatic experimentation, just as the subject is the site of myriad becomings. Bruno's metaphysical language is just as subject to the practice of "pantomorphosis"[70] and the ideal of omniformis as is his universe.

Part Six: Deploying the Physics of Sense

For Deleuze (if for a moment we just concentrate on *The Logic of Sense*), the primary goal of the metaphysician has now become the capacity to "stretch our skin like a drum"[71]—the capacity to create spaces in which multiplicities of meanings can be re-engendered. The problem is not, as with Schelling, how to plumb depths, or, with Bruno, how to contain worlds in oneself, but rather how to create diagrammatic lines of flight. Proliferation becomes the act of piety and, in turn, piety becomes attention to how to allow as many hybrids and mutations as possible to proliferate. But the "as possible" has no measure; the virtual is infinitely fecund.

Nevertheless, continuities with Bruno and Schelling are legion. Bruno's stress on pragmatics is of course repeated in *A Thousand Plateaus*, in which Deleuze and Guattari repeatedly flag up "the necessity of a return to pragmatics."[72] Indeed, pragmatics must be, they claim, the central, orienting plank of any theory of language; it is "the presupposition behind all of the other dimensions and insinuates itself into everything."[73] Moreover, pragmatics is closely linked—as in Bruno—to the idea of becoming-animal and magic. In

"Becoming-Intense,   Becoming-Animal,   Becoming-Imperceptible,"   which
Kerslake has dubbed "a late modern occult treatise,"[74] Deleuze and Guattari
write that the pragmatic utilization of multiplicities is, in fact, the very definition
of sorcery.[75] Magic, the occult, and a pragmatic linguistics once again form a
nodal point around which the thought of Deleuze, like that of Bruno and Schelling, revolves.

Moreover, it is not just in *A Thousand Plateaus* that such a pragmatic rhetoric is espoused. *Anti-Oedipus* is equally committed to it. Here, too, language
works, rather than means: what matters is what it does and the effects it has,
rather than what it represents.[76] Language, Deleuze and Guattari write, "should
not be conceived of in terms of representation; it refers instead to the class of
'effects': effects that are not a mere dependence on causes, but the occupation of
a domain, and the operation of a system of signs."[77] In order to realize this ideal,
Deleuze and Guattari write about (and, importantly for our purposes, also produce) "a stream of words that do not let themselves be coded, a libido that is too
fluid, too viscous: non-sense erected as a flow, polyvocity that returns to haunt
all relations."[78] Language takes place on a plane of immanence alongside all
other forces—and because it is the force most proximate to both the philosopher
and the psychoanalyst it takes up a privileged position in their work.

The metaphilosophical significance of this conception of language is what
is key to the argument of this paper—and perhaps the best way to bring it out is
through a reading of the Eighteenth Series of *The Logic of Sense*, "The Three
Images of the Philosopher." Deleuze here distinguishes between Platonic
heights, Nietzschean depths, and Stoic surfaces in a way that repeats much of
the rhythm of a magical metaphysics, ascending and descending across that
threshold by which thought becomes human.

Thus, on the one hand, in Platonism, "the philosopher is a being of ascents;
he is the one who leaves the cave and rises up,"[79] whilst, on the other hand, "the
pre-Socratics placed thought inside the caverns and life in the deep . . . [and so
recognised] the absolute depth dug out in bodies and in thought."[80] To return to
an earlier argument, such is the duality by which *Schelling* measures the extensity of his metaphysics: to be able to be both Platonist and pre-Socratic. However,
Deleuze adds a third orientation which appears in Stoic and Cynic thought:

> This is a reorientation of all thought and of what it means to think: *there is no
> longer depth or height.* The Cynical and Stoic sneers against Plato are many. It
> is always a matter of unseating the Ideas, of showing that the incorporeal is not
> high above, but is rather at the surface.[81]

He continues,

> The autonomy of the surface, independent of, and against depth and height; the
> discovery of incorporeal events, meanings, or effects, which are irreducible to
> "deep" bodies and to "lofty" ideas—these are the important Stoic discoveries
> against the pre-Socratics and Plato.[82]

This surface is that on which sense occurs as an effect. Meanings "frolic on the surface of being, and constitute an endless multiplicity of incorporeal beings."[83] Such is what the Stoics found. In consequence, each philosophical text is envisaged as a surface on which sense is produced—"a machine for the production of incorporeal sense."[84] As Deleuze makes clear, different texts chart different surface effects: each philosophical singularity is generated from specific operations on the textual surface. Hence, *The Logic of Sense* is devoted to the description of a specific set of surface operations employed by certain philosophers which he dubs, the "Carroll effect":

> Sense is always an *effect* . . . or, even better, a surface effect, a position effect and a language effect. . . . It is a product which spreads out over, or extends itself the length of, the surface. . . . Such effects, or such a product, have usually been designated by a proper and singular name. . . . Thus physics speaks of the "Kelvin effect," of the "Seebeck effect," of the "Zeerman effect," etc.[85]

The specific set of operations of the Carroll effect consists in paradoxes which give rise to heterogeneous series.

What are we to make of the Eighteenth Series in this regard? Were Plato and the pre-Socratics *wrong* to affirm the heights and depths, respectively? This surely cannot be Deleuze's point: not only because the *Capitalism and Schizophrenia* project takes up once more the Nietzschean project of sounding out the depths, but also because the "final task" of *The Logic of Sense* itself consists in "the history of depths."[86] It would therefore be odd to read philosophies of depth (and philosophies of height) as falsifications of the surface on which sense occurs. Rather, they are *perversions* in the very technical sense Deleuze gives this term at the end of the Eighteenth Series: "Perversion implies an extraordinary art of surfaces."[87] A footnote to an earlier passage provides a gloss on this definition: for Nietzsche, Deleuze insists, "Height is but a mystification, a surface effect."[88] In other words, height and (presumably) depth are effects produced on the surface of sense; they are perversions and, as such, specific ways in which philosophers have configured surface effects. The innovative art of each new philosopher gives rise to a new idea of sense, to a new effect (the Plato-effect, the Empedocles-effect in analogy to the Kelvin-effect and the Seebeck-effect). The conjunctions and disjunctions that litter the surface of sense are rearranged. When Bruno speaks of Plato "twisting and turning and tearing to pieces and placing embankments so that the volatile and fugacious species should be as it were caught in a net," Deleuze similarly speaks of the Plato-event as a redeployment of sense.

In short, to trace each of these deployments of sense which give rise to images of philosophy is to embark on a "physics of sense." It is to understand philosophy in terms of its rhetorical productivity: to explicate the Plato-effect and the Nietzsche-effect alongside the Carroll-effect. And this is precisely what we have been embarking on in this chapter: not just a redescription of the theory of a physics of sense, but a performance of such a physics itself. What has been at issue is the genealogy of the Deleuze-effect.[89]

What, then, does this mean for the philosopher? What is at stake—affectively, ethically, physically—in the perversion of sense? In a strange and unexpected way, we return here to Vico's giants: for Deleuze in *The Logic of Sense*, what is at stake in the polymorphous production of sense is a question of *divination*—divination as the art of the metaphysician. In *The Logic of Sense*, the moral problem of the Stoic sage is how to become the quasi-cause of the incorporeal event.[90] To oversimplify, this is a matter of selective interpretation: one selects the *most limited possible present* within which to entertain a maximum of sense (and nonsense). The inclusion of nonsense is highly precise, and theatrical: Deleuze indicates that it is the *mime* that gives us the clearest image of what to do. The mime does not imitate a specific gesture (walking, climbing, eating) as performed by someone in particular, but selectively presents Walking, Climbing, Eating as if they were a pure, "incorporeal" medium in which the body operates. What the mime does, effectively, is allow the mind to *focus*. This is no small achievement, since in principle there is an infinity of sense, or at least an unlimited dimension of sense (and nonsense) within every event. Metaphysics is immediately ethical, from this perspective, in the sense that metaphysical discourse is not an attempt to comprehensively describe being as such, but to *limit* the potential overflow or superabundance of sense and nonsense in a particular way—namely, in a way that is productive of a specific configuration of surface effects. The metaphysician thereby *identifies* with sense or, more accurately, with the aleatory aspect of sense:

> The Stoic sage "identifies" with the quasi-cause, sets up shop at the surface, on the straight line which traverses it, or at the aleatory point which traces or travels this line. The sage is like the [Zen] archer . . . the bowman must reach the point where the aim is not the aim, that is to say, the bowman himself; where the arrow flies over its straight line while creating its own target; where the surface of the target is also the line and the point, the bowman, the shooting of the arrow, and what is shot at.[91]

The problem from this point of view, of course, is that it can appear as if the sage is in fact completely determined by physical causes—not actively identifying with the "quasi-cause" of sense itself, but rather wholly determined by physical causation, in the depths of bodies. But there is for Deleuze, as for the Stoics, a freedom proper to a certain usage of representation itself: "representation and its usage intervene at this point."[92] At what point? At the point of the "most limited possible present."[93] Here, one somehow is incorporeally incorporated (Deleuze speaks of the birth of the sage as a kind of "immaculate conception") by the very *difference* between two kinds of time, Aiôn and Chronos.[94] What one does once one achieves this state is literally beside the point, since the whole point, ethically speaking, is to *occupy* the instant and prevent it from overflowing. Divination is not a matter of selecting among possible meanings, possible senses, but *grasping sense itself* as the possibility of any continuity, any survival, any sustainable surface that can escape the warring determinations of the depths.

Here, we attain to a version of absolute knowledge, and metaphysics becomes ethics as divination. The physics of sense names the selective and transforming power of a word that has become adequate to a present moment, an instant which that word alone can grasp. We can now appreciate Deleuze's question, "How could the event be grasped and willed without its being referred to the corporeal cause from which it results, and through this cause, to the unity of causes as *Physics*?"[95]—and, as we have argued in this section, this is a question about the status of metaphysics as much as of ethics.

> Here divination grounds ethics. In fact, the divinatory interpretation consists of the relation between the pure event (not yet actualized) and the depth of bodies, the corporeal action and passions whence it results. We can state precisely how this interpretation proceeds: it is always a question of cutting into the thickness, of carving out surfaces, of orienting them, of increasing and multiplying them in order to follow out the tracing of lines and incisions inscribed on them. Thus, the sky is divided into sections and a bird's line of light is distributed according to them; we follow on the ground the letter traced by a pig's snout; the liver is drawn up to the surface where its lines and fissures are observed. Divination is, in the most general sense, the art of surfaces, lines and singular points appearing at the surface. This is why two fortune-tellers cannot regard one another without laughing, a laughter which is humorous.[96]

Can two metaphysicians regard one another without laughter? Let alone our three—Bruno, Schelling, and Deleuze? We would hope so! If laughter is humor, and humor is the essence of health, then Vico was right to discern the becoming-human of the giants in a poetic metaphysics of divination. Vico was right again, in the face of looming catastrophe during the nadir of civilizations, to continuously remind humanity of its initial divinatory emergence, its becoming-pious. This re-emergence is simultaneously poetic, metaphysical, and religious, such that it binds heaven and earth—sense and nonsense?—to avoid being overwhelmed by chaos. In this sense metaphysics has nothing to do with an afterthought of life, but names human survival, as such.

Notes

1. Giambattista Vico, *The New Science*, trans. David Marsh (New York: Penguin, 2001), 128.

2. To our mind, this is precisely one of the most striking outcomes of Philip Goodchild's *Capitalism and Religion* (inspired in part by Deleuze and Schelling). Goodchild's discovery of the metaphilosophical criterion of piety to account for the sub-rational or super-rational differences between metaphysical perspectives (in terms of how they direct

attention and the singular experiences to which they bear witness) can serve as a framework in which to understand our own explorations of Bruno, Schelling and Deleuze's rhetorics of affect. See especially Philip Goodchild, *Capitalism and Religion: The Price of Piety* (London: Routledge, 2002), 193–6.

3. Vico, *The New Science*, 160.

4. Vico, *The New Science*, 483. The specific relation between the crisis of "the universal flood" and the genesis of philosophy is equally central to Schelling's work, as we shall see.

5. Vico, *The New Science*, 491.

6. Vico, *The New Science*, 483.

7. Gilles Deleuze, *Nietzsche and Philosophy*, trans. Hugh Tomlinson (London: Continuum, 1983), 110.

8. Gilles Deleuze, *Difference and Repetition*, trans. Paul Patton (London: Continuum, 1994), 41.

9. Gilles Deleuze, *Expressionism in Philosophy: Spinoza*, trans. Martin Joughin (New York: Zone, 1990), 176. See further Joshua Ramey, *The Hermetic Deleuze: Philosophy and Spiritual Ordeal* (Durham: Duke University Press, 2012), 61–81.

10. See especially Deleuze, *Difference and Repetition*, 240, 289, 346. On Deleuze's use of Schelling more generally, see Alberto Toscano, "Philosophy and the Experience of Construction," in *The New Schelling*, ed. Jane Norman and Alistair Welchman (London: Continuum, 2004), 106–27 and Christopher Groves, "Ecstasy of Reason, Crisis of Reason: Schelling and Absolute Difference," *Pli* 8 (1999): 25–45.

11. Georg Lukács, *The Destruction of Reason*, trans. Peter Palmer (London: Merlin, 1980), 137. Schelling, of course, names an 1802 dialogue after Bruno, the protagonist of which, himself called Bruno, espouses Schellingian views. On the Schelling-Bruno connection, see further Jean-Louis Vieillard-Baron, "De la connaissance de Giordano Bruno à l'époque de l'idéalisme allemande," *Revue de métaphysique et de morale* 76, no. 4 (1971): 416–9 and Michaela Boenke, "Giordano Bruno dans la philosophie de l'identité de Schelling," trans. Tristan Dagron in *Mondes, formes et société selon Giordano Bruno*, ed. Dagron and Hélène Védrine (Paris: Vrin, 2003), 197–208.

12. Gilles Deleuze, "Responses to a Series of Questions," *Collapse* III (2007), 42.

13. Arnaud Villani, "'I Feel I Am a Pure Metaphysician': The Consequences of Deleuze's Affirmation," *Collapse* III (2007), 52–3.

14. See, of course, Gilles Deleuze and Félix Guattari, *Kafka: Toward a Minor Literature*, trans. Dana Polan (Minneapolis: University of Minnesota Press, 1986), 16–27.

15. Deleuze, "Responses to a Series of Questions," 40.

16. Gilles Deleuze, "Letter to a Harsh Critic," *Negotiations*, trans. Martin Jauphin (New York: Columbia, 1995), 11.

17. Deleuze, "Letter to a Harsh Critic," 11.

18. See François Dosse, *Gilles Deleuze et Félix Guattari: Biographie Croisée* (Paris: La Decouverte, 2007), 554–555.

19. Deleuze, "Letter to a Harsh Critic," 11.

20. Deleuze and Guattari, *A Thousand Plateaus*, 252.

21. Gilles Deleuze, *Bergsonism*, trans. Hugh Tomlinson and Barbara Habberjam (New York: Zone, 1988), 106. See also Christian Kerslake's discussion of this passage in his *Deleuze and the Unconscious* (London: Continuum, 2007), chapter six.

22. For an analysis of the *omniformis* ideal in Bruno's work, see Alfonso Ingegno's "Introduction" to Giordano Bruno, *Cause, Principle and Unity*, ed. and trans. Robert de Lucca (Cambridge: Cambridge University Press, 1988). Note Deleuze's explicit invocation of "frenzy" in the above passage; this concept will soon play a central role in this

paper. Bergson's use of frenzy should also be borne in mind, see Kerslake, *Deleuze and the Unconscious*, 165–9.

23. On Cusa, see Deleuze, *Expressionism in Philosophy*, 175–9. See further Ramey, *The Hermetic Deleuze*, 44–7.

24. Giordano Bruno, *The Heroic Enthusiasts*, trans. L. Williams (London: Norman and Son, 1889), 133. We follow a more literal translation in rendering this work, *Heroic Frenzies*.

25. Bruno, *The Heroic Enthusiasts*, 134.

26. Giordano Bruno, *The Expulsion of the Triumphant Beast*, trans. Arthur D. Imerti (Lincoln: University of Nebraska Press, 1992), 190.

27. Giordano Bruno, *A General Account of Bonding* in *Cause, Principle and Unity and Essays on Magic*, trans. Richard J. Blackwell (Cambridge: Cambridge University Press, 1998), 145.

28. Bruno, *Account of Bonding*, 157.

29. Bruno, *Account of Bonding*, 172.

30. For a pertinent linguistic example, see Bruno, *Account of Bonding*, 167.

31. Giordano Bruno, *On Magic* in *Cause, Principle and Unity and Essays on Magic*, trans. Richard J. Blackwell (Cambridge: Cambridge University Press, 1998), 105.

32. Bruno, *On Magic*, 105.

33. Bruno, *The Heroic Enthusiasts*, 176.

34. Bruno, *The Heroic Enthusiasts*, 210.

35. See (for example) Bruno, *The Expulsion of the Triumphant Beast*, 78.

36. Giordano Bruno, *The Ash Wednesday Supper*, trans. Edward A. Gosselin and Lawrence S. Lerner (Toronto: University of Toronto Press, 1977), 67–8. As Deleuze puts in "Letter to a Harsh Critic," "We have to counter people who think 'I'm this, I'm that,' . . . by thinking in strange, fluid, unusual terms: I don't know what I am—I'd have to investigate and experiment with so many things" (Deleuze, "Letter to a Harsh Critic," 11).

37. Bruno, *The Ash Wednesday Supper*, 214.

38. Hence, the importance of the Cusan maxim: "the centre is the circumference." See Giordano Bruno, *Cause, Principle, Unity* in *Cause, Principle and Unity and Essays on Magic*, trans. Richard J. Blackwell (Cambridge: Cambridge University Press, 1998), 89.

39. Bruno, *The Heroic Enthusiasts*, 86.

40. Bruno, *The Heroic Enthusiasts*, 40.

41. Bruno, *The Heroic Enthusiasts*, 49.

42. Bruno, *The Heroic Enthusiasts*, 51.

43. F. W. J. Schelling, *Philosophical Inquiries into the Nature of Human Freedom*, trans. James Gutmann (La Salle: Open Court, 1936), 8.

44. The qualification "two-world" Platonic metaphysics is necessary so as to not obscure Schelling's affirmation of a one-world Platonic physics derived from the *Timaeus*. See Iain Hamilton Grant, *Philosophies of Nature after Schelling* (London: Continuum, 2006), 26–58.

45. Schelling, *Inquiries*, 79.

46. Grant, *Philosophies of Nature*, 19–21.

47. Schelling, *Inquiries*, 31.

48. F.W.J. Schelling, *Historical-Critical Introduction to the Philosophy of Mythology*, trans. Mason Richey and Markus Zisselsberger (Albany: SUNY, 2007), 150–1.

49. The journeying of the philosopher above and below is insisted upon in a 1799 poem (often misdated to 1809) in which the philosopher's heart enjoins her thus, "[You]

must try to overleap many rungs / Thereby coveting the impossible, / Attain heaven, fired by thirst for the sun, / Then descend and let loose eternal night. / Dissolving the force of unknown magic... / Can be achieved by him who loves these words: / 'The first ground of everlasting evil / Is known by him who joins to the abyss. / The ground of good can only be attained / By him who dares climb to the source of light.'" F. W. J. Schelling, *Werke*, vol. 10, ed. K.F.A. Schelling (Stuttgart: Cotta, 1856–61), 447–9; translated by Judith Kahl and Daniel Whistler.

50. Schelling, *Inquiries*, 56.

51. On the latter three terms, see Schelling, *Inquiries*, 57–8.

52. See Grant, *Philosophies of Nature*, 201–4 and Daniel Whistler, "Language after Philosophy of Nature: Schelling's Geology of Divine Names" in *After the Postsecular and the Postmodern: New Essays in Continental Philosophy of Religion*, ed. Anthony Paul Smith and Daniel Whistler (Newcastle: Cambridge Scholars Press, 2010), 349–50.

53. Schelling, *Introduction to the Philosophy of Mythology*, 18.

54. See further Schelling, *Introduction to the Philosophy of Mythology*, 162.

55. Schelling, *Introduction to the Philosophy of Mythology*, 39.

56. Schelling, *Werke*, vol. 8, 452–3. On this passage (and the next couple of paragraphs in general), see Whistler, "Language after Philosophy of Nature."

57. F.W.J. Schelling, *The Deities of Samothrace*, ed. and trans. Robert F. Brown (Missoula: Scholars Press, 1977), 37.

58. Schelling, *The Deities of Samothrace*, 34.

59. Schelling, *The Deities of Samothrace*, 20.

60. And this is why Schelling is one more exponent, alongside Bruno and Deleuze, of a magical mode of philosophizing.

61. Schelling, *Werke*, vol. 8, 450–1.

62. On the role of the occult and, more generally, for an illustration of the metaphysics-rhetoric-affect knot in Schelling's work, see F. W. J. Schelling, *Clara or, On Nature's Connection to the Spirit World*, trans. Fiona Steinkamp (Albany: SUNY, 2002).

63. Bruno, *The Heroic Enthusiasts*, 170–1.

64. Bruno, *The Expulsion of the Triumphant Beast*, 72.

65. Bruno, *On Magic*, 119.

66. Bruno, *The Heroic Enthusiasts*, 25.

67. Bruno, *The Heroic Enthusiasts*, 33.

68. Bruno, *The Ash Wednesday Supper*, 83.

69. Bruno, *The Ash Wednesday Supper*, 72.

70. Bruno, *The Expulsion of the Triumphant Beast*, 166.

71. Gilles Deleuze, *The Logic of Sense*, trans. Mark Lester (London: Continuum, 1990), 72–73.

72. Gilles Deleuze and Félix Guattari, *A Thousand Plateaus*, trans. Brian Massumi (Minneapolis: University of Minnesota Press, 1987), 110.

73. Deleuze and Guattari, *A Thousand Plateaus*, 78. Jean-Jacques Lecercle's working through of a Deleuzian pragmatics is thus invaluable, see his *Deleuze and Language* (Basingstoke: Palgrave, 2002), 154–73.

74. Kerslake, *Deleuze and the Unconscious*, 169.

75. Deleuze and Guattari, *A Thousand Plateaus*, 506.

76. Gilles Deleuze and Félix Guattari, *Anti-Oedipus*, trans. Robert Hurley *et al* (London: Continuum, 1984), 109.

77. Deleuze and Guattari, *Anti-Oedipus*, 86.

78. Deleuze and Guattari, *Anti-Oedipus*, 133.

79. Deleuze, *The Logic of Sense*, 145.

80. Deleuze, *The Logic of Sense*, 146–7.
81. Deleuze, *The Logic of Sense*, 148.
82. Deleuze, *The Logic of Sense*, 150.
83. Bréhier, quoted in Deleuze, *The Logic of Sense*, 8.
84. Deleuze, *The Logic of Sense*, 82.
85. Deleuze, *The Logic of Sense*, 82.
86. Deleuze, *The Logic of Sense*, 214–5.
87. Deleuze, *The Logic of Sense*, 151.
88. Deleuze, *The Logic of Sense*, 152.
89. For a further example of this kind of analysis see Daniel Whistler, "Improper Names for God: Religious Language and the 'Spinoza Effect'," *Speculations 3* (2012), 99–134.
90. Deleuze, *The Logic of Sense*, 166–7.
91. Deleuze, *The Logic of Sense*, 166.
92. Deleuze, *The Logic of Sense*, 166.
93. Deleuze, *The Logic of Sense*, 166.
94. Deleuze, *The Logic of Sense*, 164.
95. Deleuze, *The Logic of Sense*, 163.
96. Deleuze, *The Logic of Sense*, 163.

References

Boenke, Michaela. "Giordano Bruno dans la philosophie de l'identité de Schelling." Translated by Tristan Dagron. In *Mondes, formes et société selon Giordano Bruno*, edited by Dagron and Hélène Védrine, 197–208. Paris: Vrin, 2003.
Bruno, Giordano. *The Heroic Enthusiasts*. Translated by L. Williams. London: Norman and Son, 1889.
———. *The Ash Wednesday Supper*. Translated by Edward A. Gosselin and Lawrence S. Lerner. Toronto: University of Toronto Press, 1977.
———. *The Expulsion of the Triumphant Beast*. Translated by Arthur D. Imerti. Lincoln: University of Nebraska Press, 1992.
———. *Cause, Principle, Unity*. In *Cause, Principle and Unity and Essays on Magic*. Translated by Richard J. Blackwell, 1–102. Cambridge: Cambridge University Press, 1998.
———. *On Magic*. In *Cause, Principle and Unity and Essays on Magic*. Translated by Richard J. Blackwell, 103–42. Cambridge: Cambridge University Press, 1998.
———. *A General Account of Bonding*. In *Cause, Principle and Unity and Essays on Magic*, 143–75. Translated by Richard J. Blackwell. Cambridge: Cambridge University Press, 1998.
Deleuze, Gilles. *Nietzsche and Philosophy*. Translated by Hugh Tomlinson. London: Continuum, 1983.
———. *Bergsonism*. Translated by Hugh Tomlinson and Barbara Habberjam. New York: Zone, 1988.
———. *The Logic of Sense*. Translated by Mark Lester. London: Continuum, 1990.
———. *Expressionism in Philosophy: Spinoza*. Translated by Martin Joughin. New York: Zone, 1990.
———. *Difference and Repetition*. Translated by Paul Patton. London: Continuum, 1994.

———. "Letter to a Harsh Critic." In *Negotiations*. Translated by Martin Joughin, 3–12. New York: Columbia University Press, 1995.

———. "Responses to a Series of Questions." *Collapse* III (2007): 39–44.

Deleuze, Gilles and Félix Guattari. *Anti-Oedipus*. Translated by Robert Hurley *et al.* London: Continuum, 1984.

———. *Kafka: Toward a Minor Literature*. Translated by Dana Polan. Minneapolis: University of Minnesota Press, 1986.

———. *A Thousand Plateaus*. Translated by Brian Massumi. Minneapolis: University of Minnesota Press, 1987.

Dosse, François. *Gilles Deleuze et Félix Guattari: Biographie Croisée*. Paris: La Decouverte, 1997.

Goodchild, Philip. *Capitalism and Religion: The Price of Piety*. London: Routledge, 2002.

Grant, Iain Hamilton. *Philosophies of Nature after Schelling*. London: Continuum, 2006.

Groves, Christopher. "Ecstasy of Reason, Crisis of Reason: Schelling and Absolute Difference." *Pli* 8 (1999): 25–45.

Ingegno, Alfonso. "Introduction." In Giordano Bruno, *Cause, Principle and Unity*, edited and translated by Robert de Lucca, vii–xxix. Cambridge: Cambridge University Press, 1988.

Kerslake, Christian. *Deleuze and the Unconscious*. London: Continuum, 2007.

Lecercle, Jean-Jacques. *Deleuze and Language*. Basingstoke: Palgrave, 2002.

Lukács, Georg. *The Destruction of Reason*. Translated by Peter Palmer. London: Merlin, 1980.

Ramey, Joshua. *The Hermetic Deleuze: Philosophy and Spiritual Ordeal*. Durham: Duke University Press, 2012.

Schelling, F. W. J. *Werke*. 12 volumes. Edited by K.F.A. Schelling. Stuttgart: Cotta, 1856–61.

———. *Philosophical Inquiries into the Nature of Human Freedom*. Translated by James Gutmann. La Salle: Open Court, 1936.

———. *The Deities of Samothrace*. Edited and translated Robert F. Brown. Missoula: Scholars Press, 1977.

——— *Clara or, On Nature's Connection to the Spirit World*. Translated by Fiona Steinkamp. Albany: SUNY, 2002.

———. *Historical-Critical Introduction to the Philosophy of Mythology*. Translated by Mason Richey and Markus Zisselsberger. Albany: SUNY, 2007.

Toscano, Alberto. "Philosophy and the Experience of Construction." In *The New Schelling*, edited by Jane Norman and Alistair Welchman, 106–27. London: Continuum, 2004.

Vico, Giambattista. *The New Science*. Translated by Anthony Grafton. New York: Penguin Classics, 2000.

Vieillard-Baron, Jean-Louis. "De la connaissance de Giordano Bruno à l'époque de l'idéalisme allemande." *Revue de métaphysique et de morale* 76, no. 4 (1971): 416–9.

Villani, Arnaud. "'I Feel I Am a Pure Metaphysician': The Consequences of Deleuze's Affirmation." *Collapse* III (2007): 45–62.

Whistler, Daniel. "Language after Philosophy of Nature: Schelling's Geology of Divine Names." In *After the Postsecular and the Postmodern: New Essays in Continental Philosophy of Religion*, edited by Anthony Paul Smith and Daniel Whistler, 335–59. Newcastle: Cambridge Scholars Press, 2010.

———. "Improper Names for God: Religious Language and the 'Spinoza Effect'." *Speculations* 3 (2012): 99–134.

CHAPTER FIVE

The Obscure Metaphysics of Gilles Deleuze

Julia Sushytska

> We call distinct the state of a fully differentiated Idea, and clear, the state of the actualized Idea, that is, differenciated. We must break with the rule of proportionality of the clear and the distinct: the Idea in itself is not clear and distinct, but on the contrary, distinct and obscure.
>
> —Gilles Deleuze, *L'Île déserte et autres texts*

> [I]t is being which is Difference.
>
> —Gilles Deleuze, *Difference and Repetition*

Deleuze is a metaphysician, but an obscure one. In the sense that Heraclitus is called obscure by Aristotle: *ho skoteinos* from *skotos*, or darkness, including that of death and womb.[1] This pre-Socratic does not quite contradict himself, but comes precariously close to denying the principle of non-contradiction, this foundation of rational thinking.[2] Deleuze, too, flirts with the dark side of reason—there is, of course, the dark precursor of chapters four and five of *Difference and Repetition*—but, as we shall see, his desire for obscurity reaches much further.[3] As a consequence, Deleuze is extremely difficult to catch, especially through such labels as "postmodern" or "opposed to tradition." His obscurity is further confirmed by the fact that in a late interview he calls himself a pure metaphysician,[4] for the "purity" of his thinking is intimately tied to its obscurity, and to the form his articulations favor—the form of paradox. From the beginning of his oeuvre (*Nietzsche and Philosophy, Bergsonism, Difference and Repetition, The Logic of Sense*) and all throughout his collaboration with Felix Guattari that culminates in *What Is Philosophy?* Deleuze relies on paradoxical form to convey his ideas. This is what places him in such proximity to the philosopher from another "end" of Western thinking—the end that, just as our own, is really a beginning. Deleuze, like Heraclitus, is a pure metaphysician because he allows the voice of being to resound and resonate throughout his writings, and this voice cannot be made any less forceful by numerous misinterpretations.

Just like in Heraclitus' case, Deleuze's fondness for paradox makes his writings both more and less accessible: they are simultaneously more and less susceptible to misinterpretation, and ultimately resist mastery or full understanding.

Most of Deleuze's commentators, at least until fairly recently, assumed that his attitude toward metaphysics was a negative one, placing him among those who endorse the idea of the end of metaphysics.[5] This is not entirely surprising, for his texts do sometimes lend themselves to such an interpretation, because they lend themselves to many different interpretations, even those that stray so far from Deleuze's own thinking as to copies: these take Deleuze's work as their model and try to mimic it, thus reinstating the dichotomy Deleuze tries so hard to surpass. A commentary trivializes Deleuze's carefully developed and formulated ideas when it portrays him positioning himself *against* the tradition because such a commentary relies on and reinforces the opposition between the old and the new, for instance, between the modernity and the postmodern. Only a reading inattentive to the nuances of Deleuze's thought, and especially to the paradoxical form of his writings can classify him as a postmodern thinker who altogether dismisses metaphysics. Such classification is particularly unfortunate, since, as I will argue, no thinker can belong to this category.

It is quite appropriate, of course, to stray from Deleuze's writings, but any such departure or transformation must begin with the actual texts, and requires close engagement with them. Deleuze's own image for his relationship to the philosophical predecessors is that of a sexual act during which a child is conceived, even if the child is a bastard, and the act is not heterosexual: "I saw myself as taking an author from behind and giving him a child that would be his own offspring, yet monstrous. It was really important for it to be his own child, because the author had to actually say all I had him saying."[6] Notice that the author—be it Duns Scotus, Henri Bergson, or Marcel Proust—is treated as a contemporary, and his authority or respectability is undermined by the carnal nature of thinking. The author, who, as a result, is no longer dead, says something right *now*, and she says it because I am saying it. We say it simultaneously, even if she died centuries or millennia ago. There is no contradiction at the heart of such an approach: to create something new or different—monstrous in Deleuze's terminology—we need to give voice to the "old," we must make it resound anew. There is no creation *ex nihilo*, yet to create is not to add another link to some historical chain of thinking; creation has its source in the event, and so is situated, although not determined by its situation.

To write about Deleuze, or to understand him is to make him say something that he actually says by stating it differently than he does. It is to say the same, or to *homologein* without repeating, and without producing a copy.[7] It is to say with difference. Here we are already approximating the key notion of this paper, that of the univocity of being.

This illegitimate, even indecent approach to understanding Deleuze is *the* philosophical approach: a philosopher reading another philosopher conceives a beautiful monstrosity without having any such intention, that is, while being a careful reader of the other's texts. The child born of this encounter will inevitably be different from either one of its parents, yet "of one blood" with them.[8] Deleuze is well aware of the paradox that lies at the heart of such an assertion.

Still, one might object that apart from the commentators who might be misrepresenting his thought, Deleuze himself indicates that his project is non- if not anti-metaphysical. For instance, in *The Logic of Sense* he tells us that both metaphysics and transcendental philosophy impose an alternative: "*either* an undifferenciated ground, a groundless, formless nonbeing. . . , *or* a supremely individuated Being and an intensely personalized Form. Without this Being or this Form you will have only chaos."[9] Deleuze, of course, refuses to submit to the dictatorial regime of this dichotomy, and thus, it seems, cannot possibly engage in metaphysics. Moreover, his frequent disparaging remarks about Platonism would seem to provide solid evidence for his anti-metaphysical attitude—after all, Plato is considered the first Western metaphysician. Consider a passage in which he tells us what he finds unacceptable for thinking:

> The whole of Platonism . . . is dominated by the idea of drawing a distinction between 'the thing itself' and the simulacra. Difference is not thought in itself but related to a ground, subordinated to the same and subject to mediation in mythic form. Overturning Platonism, then, means denying the primacy of the original over copy, of model over image; glorifying the reign of simulacra and reflections.[10]

How can Deleuze, who spends so much effort undermining this distinction between the original and the copy *not* be an anti-Platonist? How is he not taking a stance against the oppressive, misguided tradition?

Yet, there is evidence that he does not. Even though Alain Badiou's understanding of Deleuze is rather uneven,[11] he correctly points out that Deleuze, just like him, never had much patience for the "end of metaphysics" debates. Badiou speaks of the shared "active indifference" toward "the omnipresent theme of 'the end of philosophy.'"[12] Moreover, Deleuze himself maintained that he has "never worried about going beyond metaphysics or the death of philosophy," and called himself a "pure metaphysician."[13]

What are we to make of such dramatically different characterizations of Deleuze's thinking, and especially by Deleuze himself? Why is there a contradiction at the heart of his writings? Such inconsistency has pedagogical value: it is intended to confuse us, and therefore to make us think. Deleuze is well aware of the benefits of being perplexed, as is evident in *Difference and Repetition* where he calls back on Plato, of all philosophers: "The sign or point of departure for that which forces thought is thus the coexistence of contraries. . . ."[14] Still, if we carefully consider Deleuze's writings, or, better yet, listen to the voice that resounds in them, we will inevitably come to the conclusion that Deleuze is a metaphysician, even though such a claim requires us to reconsider what metaphysics is.

Metaphysics and Its Long Shadow

There are at least two different ways in which the term "metaphysics" can be used. On the one hand, metaphysics is a name of a theory, or a range of such theories—a narrative, we can even say—that presupposes and elaborates onto-logical hierarchies. Such a theory postulates ontological difference, or assumes the existence of at least two distinct kinds of being, one of which is necessarily better or more valuable than the other. This theoretical configuration requires an epistemological leap that turns out to be impossible without a third term—without something that would breach the abyss of radical difference between the two or more kinds of being. Mediation is supposed to reconcile or bring together what is completely and decisively apart. Metaphysics of this sort inquires about something independent from us, and from our ways of thinking—an impossible inquiry, and thus not an inquiry at all. It sets out to investigate that which lies beyond the limits of our "mortal" world, conceiving mortality in terms of a fun-damental lack or flaw. No wonder that metaphysics received so much criticism during this past century; it certainly deserved it. For not only did philosophy, especially with Kant, confirm that the distance between two radically different realms of being is unbreachable—I cannot get to know something that is alto-gether distinct from me—but also, as Nietzsche so eloquently shows, the desire to reach across the abyss to the other, greener, side inevitably results in *ressen-timent*: I refuse and try to devalue what surrounds me here and now, while, of course, secretly desiring it.

Erected around the assumption of ontological difference, such metaphysics aims to discern the austere order presumably inherent in being, and so produces theoretical constructions that arrest the movement of thinking. It aims toward completeness and attempts to say once and for all. It frequently falls back upon something that has been elaborated—feeding on the authority of the predeces-sors. No wonder that such metaphysics comes to name a stable theoretical con-struction, or something that has taken a precise shape. We say, for instance, "Plato's metaphysics," and have in mind something that can be studied, summa-rized, refuted, and that always belongs to the past. Metaphysics abounds in dogmatic claims: "Plato elaborated the theory of Forms. The Forms are the intel-lectual models for physical things that are their flawed copies." Yet, Plato qua philosopher never elaborates such a theory, and not only because he is always a step away from completing a theoretical edifice—after all, he writes in the dia-logue form, speaking only indirectly through his characters—but also because even these characters are in the end uncertain of the validity of their claims and undermine their own arguments and definitions. Consider, for instance, the *Phaedo* where some of the main arguments—or *logoi*—for the Forms are pre-sented: the dialogue begins with Socrates admitting that throughout his life he might have overemphasized *logos*, and now considers it necessary to turn to-ward *mythos*.[15] This, of course, might be interpreted as a joke on Plato's part, or even as a stab against *mythos*. Still, it would only corroborate my point: it *might* be interpreted as an ironic or even sarcastic remark, but it also *might not*, and such ambiguity inherent in all of Plato's dialogues prevents us from being justified in attributing a specific metaphysical theory to him.

Metaphysics in the second sense—the kind in which Deleuze is engaged—is nothing other than the movement, or the act of thinking. What I have been describing above is but a shadow of this movement, although a real and even necessary shadow; it is a caricature of metaphysics, a simplistic way in which thinking can be *represented*, and thus trivialized. Metaphysics in the second sense, however, is the act of thinking being. The absence of a proposition between "thinking" and "being" indicates the immediacy of this act, the lack of distance between thinking and the "thought-upon."[16]

A philosophical text is a record of such thinking, that is, something that has already began solidifying, yet its form could help the reader to recommence the movement that once created it. To that end a work of philosophy—however short or long—often takes the form of a paradox, and instead of telling us something dogmatically merely gives a sign.[17] "The lord whose oracle is in Delphi neither indicates clearly nor conceals but gives a sign," tells us Heraclitus, also commenting on his own, as well as Deleuze's philosophical style. Metaphysics enables us to formulate truths, yet these truths are always context-dependent—sensitive or responsive to the circumstances in which we think. When engaged in such thinking we create concepts that help us understand ourselves and the world, and these concepts are specific to our particular place and time without being their effects, as Deleuze frequently points out. This is why they can be reactivated or recut later or in a different context.

Metaphysics provides us with truths, although never with the Truth, as something formulated once and for all. As soon as metaphysical thinking solidifies into a theory with a definite, precise structure it has already became its own shadow. Although every movement of thought requires order and clarity, it is also never perfectly coherent and consistent. Metaphysics always involves mythical thinking, this other of *logos*, that does not render it contradictory or illogical.[18] As Deleuze writes in *The Logic of Sense*, "The force of paradoxes is that they are not contradictory; they rather allow us to be present at the genesis of the contradiction."[19] Truths can be best conveyed if they assume paradoxical form—the form that mythical thinking favors. Paradox defies or at least postpones dogmatization of truths by rendering them more supple, as well as creates space for our own thinking. Paradoxes, explains Deleuze, are not recreational. Instead they are the passion of thought "discovering what can only be thought, what can only be spoken, despite the fact that is it both ineffable and unthinkable. . . ."[20]

Paradoxical formulations steal us away from the well trodden paths of thinking, dispel the shadows of the past theoretical constructions that loom above us, threatening to topple over and bury our meager attempts to think. Paradox takes us from familiar turns of phrase, from that which everybody is supposed to know. It "is opposed to *doxa*, in both aspects of *doxa*, namely, good sense and common sense." Deleuze further explains: "Good sense affirms that in all things there is a determinable sense or direction (*sens*); but paradox is the affirmation of both senses or directions at the same time."[21] For instance, good sense tells us that Night and Day cannot be ever found together:

> Night and Day passing near greet one another as they cross the great bronze threshold. The one is about to go in and the other is going out the door, and never does the house hold them both inside, but always the one goes out from the house and passes over the earth, while the other in turn remaining inside the house waits for the time of her own departure, until it comes. The one holds much-seeing light for those on earth, but the other holds Sleep in her hands, the brother of Death—deadly Night, shrouded in murky cloud.[22]

Heraclitus criticizes this view of the world: "The teacher of most is Hesiod. It is him they know as knowing most, who did not recognize day and night: for there is one."[23] It is not even the case, as Kahn attempts to establish, that Heraclitus has in mind a twenty-four hour period.[24] Instead, in neither literal nor metaphorical way—to use another notion developed by Deleuze—Heraclitus establishes that Day and Night instead of being opposed are intimately connected with each other. Without denying or diminishing the difference between them Heraclitus asks us to stand on the threshold of the house of Day and Night, and notice something *new* about their relationship, something that exceeds our ordinary assumptions: for instance, their simultaneity, at least as they are crossing the threshold, or their co-belonging: after all, the one is impossible without the other. Yet he does not *tell* us anything. The way in which the last several words are usually translated—"*they* are one" or "for *they* are one" is not entirely accurate.[25] The Greek *esti gar hen* might also mean "for there is one." I find this translation more appropriate precisely because it is more far-reaching. Heraclitus certainly does not assert the identity of Night and Day; his approach converges with the principle and the operation that guides Deleuze's work, and that he calls crowned anarchy or disjunctive synthesis: "two things or two determinations are affirmed through their difference, that is to say, that they are the objects of simultaneous affirmation only insofar as their difference is itself affirmed."[26] Heraclitus, of course, does not explain even this much. His preferred method is of eloquent reticence. As a result, he asks much more of us than to re-evaluate the Night/Day dichotomy. "There is one," he writes, and so leaves no opposition undisturbed.

Apart from destroying or disorienting good sense, tells us Deleuze, paradoxical formulations dissolve fixed identities assigned by common sense. Paradox entails personal uncertainty.[27] "The paradox therefore is the simultaneous reversal of good sense and common sense: on the one hand, it appears in the guise of the two simultaneous senses or directions of the becoming-mad and the unforeseeable; on the other hand, it appears as the nonsense of the lost identity and the unrecognizable."[28]

It is possible, of course, to be oblivious to the paradoxical aspect of thinking, or to the paradoxical aspect of one's own articulations. Deleuze, however, consciously places his readers at the genesis of contradictions. This is precisely why his writings are frequently confusing or even bewildering, as well as why we find in them claims that are anti-metaphysical and anti-Platonist. He makes it difficult for us discern what exactly his relationship to metaphysics is. Yet, if we take a closer look, or tune in our ear we notice subtle distinctions that signal where exactly Deleuze stands. Consider, for instance, his relationship to Plato in light of the following statement: "Was it not inevitable that *Plato should be the first to overturn Platonism*, or at least to show the direction such an overturning should take?"[29] If Plato is the first anti-Platonist then there is no need to position oneself against him. Recognizing the difference between Plato-the-philosopher and trivializations of his thinking allows us to put aside the heavy armor of postmodernity. Plato "planted" deconstructive elements into his texts, and as a result, they are destabilizing themselves. Or, as Badiou astutely observes, Plato is in many respects a Deleuzian, and this observation is not at all anachronistic, but reveals an important truth: philosophy can only happen in the present.[30]

Paradoxes help resist or, at least, delay ossification of thinking. Of course, not even the paradoxical form of our articulations can prevent trivialization of thought—after all, the comfort we draw from dogmatic formulations is real, and we are never only philosophers, but also mortal beings who need food or sleep. This means that the two kinds of metaphysics do not form a dichotomy, and there is no ontological difference between them. In fact, in a strange, or, more exactly, paradoxical way the two are co-depended in much same way as absolute hospitality and the hospitality of the law turn out to be mutually dependent, even though the difference between them, as Derrida eloquently explains, cannot be greater.[31]

Deleuze's engagement with metaphysics is paradoxical because it defies common sense, sending us in both directions at once without therefore being contradictory or truthless. Deleuze is a metaphysician, but to assert this is to rethink what metaphysics is. He is a metaphysician because he is engaged in thinking being and does not endorse the idea of ontological difference, but instead proposes a notion of oneness that undercuts the oppressive hierarchical systems grounded in dualisms, as well as the relativistic refusal to name being— this rejection of truths.

Univocity of Being

To establish that Deleuze is engaged in metaphysical thinking in the sense elaborated above it is necessary to show that he relies on a specific notion of oneness. The evidence, I believe, is pervasive and abundant. It can be found in his early works, as well as those coauthored with Guattari: from *Nietzsche and Philosophy* through *Difference and Repetition* and *A Thousand Plateaus* to *What Is Philosophy?* a notion of oneness conceals itself on the surface of his books, protected from the superficial eye and ear by the paradoxical form. Consider merely several most vivid examples.

"Philosophy merges with ontology, but ontology merges with the univocity of Being. . . . The univocity of Being does not mean that there is one and the same Being; on the contrary, beings are multiple and different, they are always produced by a disjunctive synthesis, and they themselves are disjointed and divergent. . . ."[32] Note the jump from being to beings: being is not the same, rather beings are different.[33] Deleuze presents his thought in the form of paradox, encouraging us to pause and acknowledge that we don't quite understand. His formulations expose our habit of claiming mastery over the sentences that more or less quickly pass in front of our eyes, and of our reluctance to think, for thinking requires immense effort, and happens quite rarely. As Descartes noted, we think only several hours per year![34]

Univocity does not entail sameness. Still, being is also not different—if it were, it would be different *from* something else, and thus would no longer be univocal. Instead, being is *difference*, while beings are different. Moreover, asserting oneness of being is not equivalent to stating that being is one. The notion of oneness is not numerical, and being is not quantifiable. Deleuze's concept of the rhizome follows the same logic: "The rhizome is reducible neither to the One nor the multiple. It is not the One that becomes Two or even directly three, four, five, etc."[35] Numerical thinking is characteristic of hierarchical ontologies that emphasize order instead of movement; it feeds on dichotomies and multiplies them:

> The law of the book is the law of reflection, the One that becomes two. How could the law of the book reside in nature, when it is what presides over the very division between world and book, nature and art? One becomes two: whenever we encounter this formula . . . what we have before us is the most classical and well reflected, oldest, and weariest kind of thought. Nature doesn't work that way: in nature, roots are taproots with a more multiple, lateral, and circular system of ramification, rather than a dichotomous one.[36]

Articulations are natural—the notion appropriated by Deleuze from Plato via Bergson—and they don't follow the law of the book. Still, articulated thought is a kind of matter—it is actualized thought—and we have a tendency to count matter. To put it differently, the multiple does not have a number even if we frequently count it. After all, numerical thinking is not altogether avoidable, and Deleuze is well aware of this: even Plato is at times a Platonist, and even Deleuze makes use of dualistic thinking, although not in the sense attributed to him by Badiou—the point to which I will return in the final section. This means that there are no pure articulations, and taking on an anti-Platonic stance is just as dogmatic, as the position it opposes:

> If it is a question of showing that rhizomes have their own, even more rigid, despotism and hierarchy, then fine and good: for there is no dualism, no ontological dualism between here and there. . . . There are knots of arborescence in rhizomes, and rhizomatic offshoots in roots. Moreover, there are despotic formations of immanence and channelization specific to rhizomes, just as there are

anarchic deformations in the transcendent system of trees, aerial roots, and sub-terranean stems.[37]

The rhizomatic and the arborescent models are not opposed, even if frequently we present them as such to make a point. There is difference between the two, but even rhizomatic thinking "constitutes its own hierarchies" and "gives rise to a despotic channel."[38] This difference consists in the fact that the rhizome's hierarchy is fluid—it recognizes the porousness of its own categories.

"No doubt there is still hierarchy and distribution in univocal being, in relation to the individuating factors and their sense, but distribution and even hierarchy have two completely different, irreconcilable acceptations."[39] According to one of them, hierarchy proceeds by "fixed and proportional determinations."[40] However, the kind of hierarchy favored by Deleuze is likened by him to nomadic distribution: "It is not a matter of being which is distributed according to the requirements of representation, but of all things being divided up within being in the univocity of simple presence (the One—All)."[41] Deleuze recognizes indispensability of order, but only of the kind that acknowledges its own dispensability. Deleuze acknowledges that "mental correctives are necessary to undo the dualisms we had no wish to construct but through which we pass," and then discloses what is perhaps his key paradox, "the magic formula we all seek—PLURALISM=MONISM—via all the dualisms that are the enemy, an entirely necessary enemy, the furniture we are forever rearranging."[42] Deleuze calls the formula magic, and by this emphasizes its strange, apparently illogical form.

"Being is said in a single and same sense of everything of which it is said, but that of which it is said differs: it is said of difference itself."[43] There is indeed no ontological hierarchy: the differences abound without differing in kind. Still, such differences are not chaotic, or not entirely chaotic. Deleuze is famous for the concept of nomadic difference, but nomadic life is also an organized kind of life. In fact, it is a more developed form of life than the sedentary: "the sort of pastoralism practiced on the steppes by great moving nations like the Scythians or the Golden Horde was a specialised way of life which had long ago emerged from even earlier Neolithic farming societies."[44] Anarchy is always crowned, as Deleuze himself recognizes, and nomadism proceeds according to rigorous, even if non-hierarchical rules.[45] Structure is absolutely necessary for differences to flourish, although this structure will always be porous. Even the most chaotic of rhizomes are organized according to certain, however flexible; for instance, the law of desiring the new.

Univocity does not entail sameness or identity; it cannot, for being is difference, or is said of difference. Yet, "*equal being* is immediately present in *everything*, without the mediation or intermediary, even though things reside unequally in this equal being."[46] It is especially important to note Deleuze's emphasis on *unmediated* oneness of being and beings. A little further he explains: "With univocity . . . it is being which is Difference, in the sense that it is said of difference. Moreover, it is not we who are univocal in a Being which is not; it is we and our individuality which remains equivocal in and for a univocal Being."[47]

Here, Deleuze comes especially close to Parmenides' idea that we can name
being in any way we wish, and this will not undermine its oneness. It comes as
no surprise that at this point Parmenides is mentioned: "There are not two
'paths,' as Parmenides' poem suggests, but a single 'voice' of Being, which includes all its modes, including the most diverse, the most varied, the most differenciated."[48] Here, Deleuze plays on the fact that in French the word for
"roads" (*voies*) and the word for "voice" (*voix*) are homonyms. As I argue elsewhere, the number of ways, indeed, is one, but this is perfectly consistent with
the idea that we can name this road or this voice—being itself—in any way we
wish. Everything and anything can be its name: "For this the name shall be everything which mortals posit convinced that it is true: becoming as well as perish-
ing, being as well as not, and alteration through place, and exchange of bright
colors."[49] Being is Voice, continues Deleuze, and is "said in one and the same
'sense' of everything about which it is said. That of which it is said is not at all
the same, but Being is the same for everything about which it is said."[50] The
claim that being is voice is not a metaphor. Deleuze warns us about dismissing
notions or ideas by labeling them metaphors: "There are no literal words, neither
are there metaphors. . . . There are only inexact words to designate something
exactly."[51] Here is yet another paradox: to pick out some object exactly we will
use inexact words, and we will use them because only inexact words are available to us. Once again, we notice a most astonishing convergence with Heraclitus' saying quoted above: "The lord whose oracle is in Delphi neither declares
nor conceals, but gives a sign." Deleuze is in perfect agreement with this theoretical attitude: "Let us create extraordinary words, on condition that they be put
to the most ordinary use and that the entity they designate be made to exist in the
same way as the most common object." Indeed, to say that being is voice is to
say something ordinary, for being occurs as "a unique event for everything that
happens. . . ."[52] The term "univocity" is the prime example of an extraordinary
term that designates something that is most commonplace—being.

We cannot but say being in a potentially infinite number of ways: not only
infinitely many articulations of it are possible, but also neither one nor any combination of them exhausts being: "there are indeed forms of being, but contrary
to what is suggested by the categories, these forms involve no division within
being or the plurality of ontological senses."[53] Still, it is one voice of being that
resounds in this heterogeneous, equivocal multitude. In maintaining this Deleuze
is consistent with Heraclitus' saying quoted earlier: "Not from me, but from the
logos hearing, it is wise to say-the-same [*homologein*] that all is one."[54] Here,
logos does not mean rationality.[55] Rather, it is *xunos* or shared thinking in the
sense elaborated by D. C. Schindler: "thought is something one *simultaneously*
generates and finds."[56] *Logos* is both *a priori* and *a posteriori*, as Schindler concludes, that is, both something that is more than a particular situation, and is
informed by that situation.[57] The term "univocity" also takes us back to the origins of Western thinking, and the oral culture, in which, for instance, the *Odys-
sey* is recited each time differently, reflecting a specific political situation, or a

set of concerns of a particular bard. Still, these "obstacles in matter" do not compromise the oneness of the poem.[58]

Being is voice, and that is why Deleuze can be a pure metaphysician, as well as why metaphysicians can only be pure: the metaphysical act consists of saying-the-same as being: "The event occurring in a state of affairs and the sense inhering in the proposition are the same entity."[59] When the philosopher homologizes she says the same, however differently, hence the multiplicity of ways in which being can be said, yet "being itself is univocal, while that of which it is said is equivocal. . . ."[60] Being is said, and it also occurs as "the unique event in which all events communicate with one another."[61] It is not the same as the proposition, yet also does not preexist it.[62]

The term "univocity" both challenges the tradition, especially the most recent tradition of postmodernism—this tradition of rejecting all tradition—and threads its way through the history of philosophy, leaving tangible traces. Being speaks in beings with one voice, and not only does it speak differently in each being, but its voice is also not monotonous. Deleuze who says-the-same as being cannot be monotonous either, regardless of Badiou's assertion that, I hope, is meant as a challenge to us rather than a claim about Deleuze.[63]

If there is still a shadow of doubt about the sense in which Deleuze can be considered a metaphysician then the following famous passage should be able to dispel it entirely:

> There has only ever been *one* ontological proposition: *Being is univocal*. There has only ever been one ontology, that of Duns Scotus, which gave being a single voice. We say Duns Scotus because he was the one who elevated univocal being to the highest point of subtlety, albeit at the price of abstraction. However, from Parmenides to Heidegger it is the *same voice* which is taken up, in an echo which itself forms the whole deployment of the univocal.[64]

In the span of these three sentences a far-reaching claim is made—a claim that is simultaneously old and new: distinctly Deleuzian, for nobody before him said it in quite this way, and yet so proximate to the roots of Western philosophy—the rhizomatic roots that are all too frequently mistaken for arborescent. We need not even agree that it was Duns Scotus who "elevated univocal being to the highest degree of subtlety" in order to recognize a truth that resounds in Deleuze's assertion. We can situate this idea in a different field or plane, for instance, by extending it, on the one hand, to Heraclitus, or even to the oral culture that predates him, and to Deleuze, on the other. Instead of undermining or impoverishing Deleuze's point we will only corroborate it.

Upon a closer consideration a striking convergence between Deleuze and Heraclitus comes to the fore. Even though the circumstances of their thinking are quite "differenciated," one voice of being is discernable in the writings of both. This only confirms that in an important sense there is no progress (or regress) in philosophy. Metaphysics has no history. Deleuze is a pure metaphysician, and this purity has to do with the univocity of being that enables us to *speak being*, and not merely speak *about* beings. There is no epistemological gap that would need to be filled through mediation.

Univocity as Difference

To show that univocity does not fall prey to the criticism leveled at the One of the One/many dichotomy I will draw on Deleuze's argument from *Bergsonism*. In this text that predates *Difference and Repetition* by two years Deleuze does not yet elaborate the notion of univocity. However, the argument that appears toward the end of the book is absolutely crucial for understanding this notion: Deleuze's claim that the existence of the difference in kind does not entail the existence of ontological difference renders his ontology non-dualistic. This paradoxical argument from an early work, and the way it is developed in the fifth chapter of *Difference and Repetition* also enables us to answer the main charge brought against Deleuze by Badiou: that Deleuze never succeeds in leaving behind dichotomous thinking, but submits it "to a renewed concept of the One."[65]

This criticism reveals the main weakness of Badiou's theory: the axiomatic decision that he makes in favor of the multiple. Setting his foot on the "road for thinking," as Parmenides would say, Badiou mistakenly assumes that he is at the crossroads, confronted, much like Hamlet, with a choice: to be or not to be. Yet, as the goddess of Parmenides' *Poem* tells us, it has been decided.[66] There is only one *voie*. Not recognizing this, Badiou prevents himself from getting a clear grasp of univocity.[67] In other words, Badiou refuses to think the univocity of being—to make this "enormous effort"[68] of going beyond both simple identity and radical difference. He ends up "sacrificing both the One and images,"[69] and considers such a sacrifice to be "a question of taste."[70] Deleuze's insistence on univocity he mistakenly attributes to the same kind of aesthetic preference.

As a result, Badiou's keen ear—after all, we are concerned with the voice—betrays him: on the one hand, he correctly recognizes that Deleuze's method "rejects all recourse to mediations; indeed, this is why it is essentially antidialectical."[71] The univocity of being and the equivocity of beings are to be thought without recourse to categories, but only through the method of intuition. Yet, on the other hand, Badiou criticizes Deleuze for making constant use of the categorical opposition between the active and the passive that is at work in, for instance, the virtual/actual distinction.[72] Even though shortly afterward Badiou himself suggests that such reliance on the sets of opposites is introductory: once we understand a theory at a more profound level, he writes, we realize that the two terms of a dichotomy only seem to be opposed—the difference between them is of degree, and not of kind.

In the penultimate chapter of *Bergsonism* Deleuze establishes just this point: the distinction between the actual and the virtual taken up from Bergson is firmly grounded in the idea that both are real. Badiou is well aware of this theoretical move, as is clear from another part of *Deleuze: The Clamor of Being*, but seems to ignore it when discussing the notion univocity.[73] He is unwilling to recognize that the distinction is not an opposition: virtuality and actuality can be asserted of the same thing in the same respect, without producing a contradiction.

To clarify Deleuze's notion of oneness let us consider the argument from *Bergsonism* in which he draws on the distinction between the virtual and the actual, as well as on the notion of time as duration to establish that the reality of the difference in kind does not entail ontological difference. Virtually there is only "a single time," points out Deleuze, yet this "one time" is a multiplicity.[74] Deleuze uses quantitative terminology—"a single time"—but this should not mislead us into thinking that time is one numerically. Neither should we suppose that, being a multiplicity, time is many. After all, we have at our disposal only imprecise terms. Rather, time *becomes* many by dividing into elements that differ in kind, or, more precisely, appear to differ in kind. Since appearances are real, they are *really* different in kind without being virtually different in kind.

This "becoming many" or differenciation occurs when the division is "effectively carried out," or actualized.[75] Time is actualized as specific quantifiable and qualifiable instances. When it is represented spatially as a timeline it is quantified, and qualified time can be conceived in terms of different epochs. One of the most vivid examples of qualified time is found in Hesiod, who conceives the universe in terms of six ages: the age of gold, of iron, of heroes, etc. Qualified time is not time itself because it belongs to the order of resemblance: "qualities have much more stability, immobility and generality than is often admitted."[76]

Beyond or beneath such actualizations of time there lies the "entire nature" of time—the virtual.[77]

This discussion of time is relevant for our purposes since, as Deleuze clarifies, what Bergson means by time is being: "Being, or Time, is a *multiplicity*. But it is precisely not 'multiple'; it is One, in conformity with *its* type of multiplicity."[78] As Deleuze explains in *Difference and Repetition*, there are two types of multiplicities: explicit and implicit, and that of being and time is the implicit one.[79] Several pages later Deleuze reminds us that: "this One has a number—but only potentially."[80] That is, oneness is countable only when actualized.

The reality of the difference in kind does not imply dualism: "it is not enough to say that the difference in kind is *between* two tendencies, between two directions, between space and duration. . . . For one of these two directions *takes all the differences in kind on itself* and all the difference in degree fall away into the other direction, the other tendency."[81] This is the core of Deleuze's argument, and to fully understand it we need to consider a longer passage from *Difference and Repetition*. Once again, we seem to be presented with a choice: difference in kind, or difference in degree. If we opt for the first one we inevitably run into dualisms and have to endorse ontological hierarchies. Going with the second option we suppress or erase real difference. What does Deleuze choose? "Neither."[82] He reveals this choice to be a false fork in the road for thinking.

Difference is a matter of degree only within the extensity in which it is explicated; it is a matter of kind only with regard to the quality which covers it within that extensity. Between the two are all the degrees of difference—beneath
the two lies the entire nature of difference—in other words, the intensive. Differences of degree are only the lowest degree of difference, and differences in
kind are the highest form of difference. What differences in kind or of degree
separate or differenciate, the degrees or nature of difference make the Same,
but the same which is said of the different.[83]

Between the qualitative difference, or the difference in kind and the quantitative
difference, or the difference in degree there is only difference in degree. Moreover, the source for both qualitative and quantitative differences is the different
itself. The intensive "lies beneath," implicit, but in the movement of explication
becomes different from itself—different in kind and in degree.

This is precisely why Deleuze jumps from Being to beings when he says
that univocity "does not mean that there is one and the same Being; on the contrary, beings are multiple and different. . . ." Being is difference, but is expressed
as quantitative and qualitative differences. In this process being or difference
itself is cancelled: "Difference of intensity is cancelled or tends to be cancelled
in this system, but it creates this system by explicating itself."[84] Several pages
later Deleuze says that "there would no more be qualitative differences or differences in kind than there would be quantitative differences or differences of degree, if intensity were not capable of constituting the former in qualities and the
latter in extensity, even at the risk of appearing to extinguish itself in both."[85] It
is clear, then, that Deleuze does not reintroduce dualism. There are real differences, as well as the differences in degree, but this does not entail ontological
difference, for the difference that underlies them, is different from either.

How exactly is virtual intensity developed or explained? Time or being "is
differenciated according to the obstacles it meets in matter,"[86] yet it is differenciated "within itself through an internal explosive force."[87] Material or factual
reality incites actualization of difference, constituting the conditions for it, but
the source of its movement is virtual, and it presupposes or requires oneness.[88]
"Differenciation is always the actualization of a virtuality that persists across its
actual divergent lines."[89] The movement of differenciation "explains" or develops what always already is. It is important to notice that nothing *more* comes
into being, even though what *is* becomes. More exactly, something that *is* becomes differenciated, yet not in the sense of actualizing a potential that *was*—if
it did, Badiou's charge of dualism would be correct.[90] The usual categories of
past, present, and future do not apply here: the virtual is simultaneous with the
actual, or being is simultaneous with beings. Badiou is unwilling to accept such
simultaneity.

We cannot reproach Deleuze for presenting us with a theory that erases difference, imposing the dominance of the one—there is no one/many dichotomy
in his thought. Beings differ in kind and in degree, but there is no radical difference between them, and even if ordered they do not form strict hierarchies.

Conclusion

Oneness, although not identity. Difference, but never radical or ontological. This is almost an inconsistency, nearly an impossibility, but truths frequently take such form. Deleuze is the first to admit it, as well as to make use of this paradoxical form. Given the importance of paradox in Deleuze's work we simply cannot take literally such labels as "anti-metaphysician" or "anti-Platonist" even when Deleuze himself makes use of them. Yet, we also need to be careful around the claim that Deleuze is a "pure metaphysician."

Deleuze tells us that he "liked writers who seemed to be part of the history of philosophy, but who escaped from it in one respect or altogether. . . ."[91] He lists Lucretius, Spinoza, Hume, Nietzsche, and Bergson, and in doing so, as well as in elucidating their writings he pulls them out of obscurity into the blinding sunlight of his own popularity, and simultaneously casts Plato or Aristotle into the shadows of philosophical borderlands—the shadows that help give birth to beautiful monsters. "When you work," continues Deleuze, "you are necessarily in absolute solitude. You cannot have disciples, or be a part of a school."[92] However, once Deleuze's disciples emerge, Plato and Aristotle acquire the kind of strangeness that draws Deleuze to Lucretius and Nietzsche; they begin accumulating, or, better, revealing "something which cannot be assimilated."[93]

Concepts are movements or becomings, and when they take a definite shape, especially by being committed to paper, they can easily become crutches or obstacles that hinder thinking. This is exactly what happened with Plato's concept of the Forms—his act of thinking solidified, taking a shape of a textbook definition, and now everybody "knows" what Plato meant by this term. If we treat Plato as a marginal figure, as an itinerant stranger who is as difficult to pinpoint as movement itself, we notice that for him the Forms are an open question. Traces of this can be found in *Parmenides* where Socrates is reminded that his understanding of the Forms is far from adequate or complete.[94]

Why does Deleuze at times claims to be an anti-Platonist, or speaks out against metaphysics? To confuse us, and, even more importantly, to confuse himself, for only when we are bewildered enough to admit our own ignorance as to what metaphysics or tradition is can we free ourselves to make yet another immense effort of thinking.

There are several ways of outwitting dogmatism that, like dust, accumulates around thinking. One is to find in the traditional works the remnants of the philosophical movement that created them—these almost imperceptible cracks in the shell that surrounds the turbulent waters of thought, or the clues that plant themselves with or without the author's consent to unsettle the unavoidable trivialization of ideas. Another way is to cast a concept away, and in the space that opens up create another, thus inadvertently enabling the now marginalized concept to receive a new impulse for life. The first approach overtly relies on the notion of oneness, but even the second one presupposes univocity without which it is impossible to think being. Thus even the second way of violent overturning does not entail the impossibility of metaphysics.

Metaphysics is the act of questioning; to be engaged in it is to formulate problems, and to create concepts that would constitute their answers in a given historical or political context, and that could be brought to life in a different situation, although only after being transformed. Since every answer is necessarily provisional or transitory, dogmatic claims are incompatible with metaphysical thinking. A "metaphysics" Deleuze sometimes criticizes is nothing but an ossified double, a shadow that metaphysical thinking casts, or merely one of the ways in which such thinking is differencaited as it encounters the mud and the hair of existence.

Although Deleuze's thoughts frequently assume paradoxical form this does not mean that any interpretation of his work is correct, just as it is in the case with Heraclitus. Paradox allows for greater flexibility of thinking, yet does not allow for dogmatism—be it traditional or anti-traditional, and the discourse of the end of philosophy as metaphysics is almost always dogmatic.

Even if in my attempt to engage with Deleuze's thought I did violence to it, even if I altered some of his concepts or reconfigured the plane of immanence that constitutes their horizon—that is, even if I created a monstrosity out of his thought—I only confirmed the idea that philosophy as metaphysics is far from being impossible. Provided, of course, that my creation is not itself dogmatic and relies on in-depth engagement with Deleuze's texts. Pointing out Heraclitean elements in Deleuze, as well as Deleuzianism of Heraclitus is consistent with Deleuze's method: "The history of philosophy ought not repeat what was said by a philosopher, but say what he was necessarily implying; what he was not saying, and yet, what is present in what he said."[95] To be true to Deleuze, but also to Heraclitus, it is essential to deviate from their singular paths, even though in the end the same voice of being will resound in this new and simultaneously old work.

Notes

1. From antiquity onward Aristotle is considered to be the author of this epithet even though the text in which it appears is by pseudo-Aristotle (*De Mundo* 396b20).

The obscure metaphysics is not opposed to a transparent or clear metaphysics. In fact, it has no opposite, although it has an other—the dogmatic thought. There is no such thing as transparent metaphysics because a metaphysical act is obscure "by nature:" when thinking is actualized or explicated it must conceal itself.

2. Aristotle is aware of this: "For no one can believe the same thing to be and not to be; though, as some hold, Heraclitus may have denied this, he did not necessarily believe it in the way in which he stated it." Aristotle, *Metaphysics* 4.3.1005b20, trans. Richard Hope (Ann Arbor: University of Michigan Press, 1960), 68.

3. See Parmenides, frag. 1 Diels-Kranz.

4. This is Deleuze's reply to the question whether he is a non-metaphysical philosopher. See an interview with Arnaud Villani "Responses to a Series of Questions," *Collapse: Philosophical Research and Development* III (2007): 39–43.

5. It is believed, writes Badiou, that Deleuze "participates in modern (postmodern?) 'deconstruction'" and "adds his contribution to the ruin of metaphysics" and "overturning of Platonism." Alain Badiou, *Deleuze: The Clamor of Being*, trans. Louise Burchill (Minneapolis: University of Minnesota Press, 1999), 9.

6. Deleuze, *Negotiations: 1972–1990*, trans. Martin Joughlin (New York: Columbia University Press, 1995), 6, and in the original French: "Que ce soit bien le sien, c'est très important, parce qu'il fallait que l'auteur dise effectivement tout ce que je lui faisais dire." *Pourparlers: 1972–1990* (Paris: Les éditions de minuit, 2003), 15.

7. "Not from me, but from the *logos* hearing, it is wise to say-the-same [*homologein*] that all is one." Heraclitus, frag. 50 Diels-Kranz, translated by me based upon recommendation of Peter Manchester.

8. See Rudyard Kipling's *The Jungle Book* where Mowgli says "We be of one blood, ye and I."

9. Gilles Deleuze, *The Logic of Sense*, trans. Mark Lester, Charles Stivale and Constantin V. Boundas (New York: Columbia University Press, 1990), 106, translation adjusted by me (translating *indifférencié* as undifferenciated).

10. Gilles Deleuze, *Difference and Repetition*, trans. Paul Patton (New York: Columbia University Press, 1994), 66.

11. I return to this point in what follows and elaborate it in the manuscript *Originary Metaphysics: Why Philosophy has not Reached its End*, under review with Northwestern University Press.

12. Badiou, *Deleuze: The Clamor of Being*, 5.

13. Deleuze, *Negotiations*, 88, and "Responses to a Series of Questions," 42.

14. Deleuze, *Difference and Repetition*, 141. Even though, according to Deleuze, eventually Plato falls short of his intuition (see Deleuze, *Difference and Repetition*, 142).

15. See Plato's *Phaedo* 61b and ff.

16. See Parmenides, frag. 8.34 Diels-Kranz.

17. Heraclitus, frag. 93 Diels-Kranz, trans. Charles Kahn, *The Art and Thought of Heraclitus* (Cambridge: Cambridge University Press, 1999), 43.

18. I explore this idea in "On the Non-Rivalry Between Poetry and Philosophy: Plato's *Republic*, Reconsidered," *Mosaic* 45, no.1 (March 2012): 55–70.

19. Deleuze, *The Logic of Sense*, 74.

20. Deleuze, *The Logic of Sense*, 74.

21. Deleuze, *The Logic of Sense*, 1.

22. Cf. Hesiod, *Theogony* 748–57, ed. and trans. Glenn W. Most, Loeb Classical Library 57 (Cambridge, MA: Harvard University Press, 2006), 64–65.

23. Heraclitus, frag. 57 Diels-Kranz. Translation adapted from Kahn's *The Art and Thought of Heraclitus*, 37.

24. Kahn, *The Art and Thought of Heraclitus*, 109.

25. Kahn, *The Art and Thought of Heraclitus*, 37 and Richard McKirahan, *A Presocratic Reader* (Indianapolis: Hackett, 2011), 41, emphasis added in both quotations.

26. Deleuze, *The Logic of Sense*, 172.

27. See Deleuze, *The Logic of Sense*, 3.

28. Deleuze, *The Logic of Sense*, 78.

29. Deleuze, *Difference and Repetition*, 68, emphasis added.

30. See Badiou, *Deleuze: The Clamor of Being*, 68–70. Villani writes that Deleuze "permits us to take into account what is positive in Plato: one of Deleuze's fundamentals is the Idea as a problematic complex." Arnaud Villani, "Why Am I Deleuzian?," *Deleuze and Philosophy*, ed. Constantin V. Boundas (Edinburgh: Edinburgh University Press, 2006), 230.

31. See Jacques Derrida, *Of Hospitality*, trans. Rachel Bowlby (Stanford: Stanford University Press, 2000), 79.

32. Deleuze, *The Logic of Sense*, 179.

33. This is not a matter of inadequate translation: "L'univocité de l'être ne veut pas dire qu'il y ait un seul et même être: au contraire, les étants sont multiples et différents, toujours produits par une synthèse disjonctive, eux-mêmes disjoints et divergents." Gilles Deleuze, *Logique du sens* (Paris: Les éditions de minuit, 1969), 210.

Unlike Deleuze I am not capitalizing the word "being," and I use "oneness" instead of "the One" because even though both notions are creatively re-appropriated by Deleuze they can be easily confused with their homonyms—traditionally understood Being and the One of the One-Many dichotomy.

34. "I can say with truth that the chief rule I have always observed in my studies, which I think has been the most useful to me in acquiring what knowledge I have, has been never to spend more than a few hours a day in the thoughts which occupy the imagination and a few hours a year on those which occupy understanding alone [*l'entendement seul*]. I have given all the rest of my time to the relaxation of the senses and the repose of the mind. And I include among the exercise of the imagination all serious conversations and anything which needs to be done with attention." To Elizabeth, June 28, 1643. René Descartes, *Philosophical Letters*, tr. Anthony Kenny (London: Oxford University Press, 1970), 141–142, translation adjusted by me.

35. Gilles Deleuze and Félix Guattari, *A Thousand Plateaus: Capitalism and Schizophrenia*, trans. Brian Massumi (Minneapolis: University of Minnesota Press, 2002), 21.

36. Deleuze and Guattari, *A Thousand Plateaus*, 5.

37. Deleuze and Guattari, *A Thousand Plateaus*, 20.

38. Deleuze and Guattari, *A Thousand Plateaus*, 20.

39. Deleuze and Guattari, *A Thousand Plateaus*, 20.

40. Deleuze and Guattari, *A Thousand Plateaus*, 20.

41. Deleuze and Guattari, *A Thousand Plateaus*, 37.

42. Deleuze and Guattari, *A Thousand Plateaus*, 21.

43. Deleuze, *Difference and Repetition*, 36, emphasis added.

44. Neal Ascherson, "Memories of Amikejo: Europe's Pasts and Possible Future," *London Review of Books* 34, no. 6 (March 2012): 18.

45. As Deleuze points out, to bring out nonsense—this unconscious of language Lewis Carroll needs "a very strict grammar." Deleuze, *The Logic of Sense*, 91.

46. Deleuze, *Difference and Repetition*, 37.

47. Deleuze, *Difference and Repetition*, 39.

48. Deleuze, *Difference and Repetition*, 36, emphasis added (translating *les plus différenciés* as the most differenciated).

49. Parmenides, frag. 8.38–41, trans. Peter Manchester, *The Syntax of Time* (Leiden: Brill, 2005), 171–173.

50. Deleuze, *Difference and Repetition*, 36.

51. Gilles Deleuze and Claire Parnet, *Dialogues* (New York: Columbia University Press, 1987), 3.

52. Deleuze, *The Logic of Sense*, 179.

53. Deleuze, *Difference and Repetition*, 303. Here I disagree with Badiou, and even with Deleuze himself who suggest in *Difference and Repetition* that Aristotle's understanding of being is entirely incompatible with his own. Instead, Deleuze's claim of univocity converges with a certain, even if unconventional, understanding of the idea that "being is said in many ways." Presently I will leave this as a suggestion.

54. Heraclitus, frag. 50 Diels-Kranz, translated by me based upon recommendation of Peter Manchester.

55. The earliest example of *logos* being used to mean "rationality," that is, being able to stand on its own not connected to any specific context or consideration is found in Democritus. Even so, this particular meaning is only one of the numerous meanings of *logos* in Plato's and Aristotle's work. Moreover, it is not until Stoicism that *logos* becomes localized in an individual human being. See Roman Dilcher, *Studies in Heraclitus* (Hildeshein: Georg Olms AG, 1995), 39–40.

56. D. C. Schindler, "The Community of the One and the Many: Heraclitus on Reason," *Inquiry* 46 (2003): 425.

57. Heraclitus, frag. 2 Diels-Kranz: "Although *logos* is shared, the many live as though thinking were private." Translated by me.

58. For a most illuminating analysis of oral culture see Walter J. Ong, *Orality and Literacy: The Technologizing of the Word* (London: Routledge, 1997).

59. Deleuze, *The Logic of Sense*, 182.

60. Deleuze, *Difference and Repetition*, 304.

61. Deleuze, *The Logic of Sense*, 180.

62. See Deleuze, *The Logic of Sense*, 181.

63. Badiou, *Deleuze: The Clamor of Being*, 15.

64. Deleuze, *Difference and Repetition*, 35, emphasis added.

65. Badiou, *Deleuze: The Clamor of Being*, 11.

66. Parmenides, frag. 8,16 Diels-Kranz.

67. A recent study by Jon Roffe confirms my claim: Roffe writes that Badiou in The Clamor of Being "misunderstands and misrepresents" Deleuze's philosophy. He argues that "Badiou's thesis, according to which Deleuze mounts and defends a metaphysics of the One, functions not as a conclusion drawn on the basis of a careful study of the latter's texts, but as an initial axiom, a filter or lens through which the material under consideration is examined. It is principally this mode of approach that leads Badiou astray from the very beginning." John Roffe, *Badiou's Deleuze* (Montreal: McGill-Queen's University Press, 2012), 5. Yet, defending Deleuze Roffe appears to miss the crucial point that oneness is not opposed to difference; it is not different from difference. He writes: "It is difference that is superior, interior and supereminent (in a certain genetic if not ontological respect) to the One." Roffe, *Badiou's Deleuze*, 18.

68. Badiou, *Deleuze: The Clamor of Being*, 51.

69. Badiou, *Deleuze: The Clamor of Being*, 52. Badiou's misunderstanding of Deleuze's project is traceable to his misconstruction of the arguments about names in Plato's *Sophist*. The Visitor's arguments for the impossibility of oneness that Badiou embraces do not hold up to a closer scrutiny, and are intended by Plato to be sophistical, that is, aim to disrupt our habitual ways of thinking.

70. Badiou, *Deleuze: The Clamor of Being*, 92.

71. Badiou, *Deleuze: The Clamor of Being*, 32.

72. Badiou, *Deleuze: The Clamor of Being*, 33.

73. Badiou, *Deleuze: The Clamor of Being*, 49. In elucidating Deleuze's concept of univocity Badiou identifies a distinction between the formal and the real he finds in Deleuze: "The multiple acceptations of being must be understood as a multiple that is

formal, while the One alone is real, and only the real supports the distribution of sense (which is unique)." Badiou, *Deleuze: The Clamor of Being*, 25. Such a formulation can easily lead to a misunderstanding, which is exactly what happens in Badiou's case.

74. "Bergson never gives up the idea that duration, that is to say time, is essentially multiplicity." Gilles Deleuze, *Bergsonism*, trans. Hugh Tomlinson and Barbara Habberjam (New York: Zone Books, 1991), p. 79.

75. Deleuze, *Bergsonism*, 81.

76. Deleuze, *Difference and Repetition*, 238.

77. Cf. Deleuze, *Difference and Repetition*, 239.

78. Deleuze, *Bergsonism*, 85.

79. Deleuze, *Difference and Repetition*, 238.

80. Deleuze, *Bergsonism*, 93.

81. Deleuze, *Bergsonism*, 92, emphasis added.

82. Deleuze, *Difference and Repetition*, 239.

83. Deleuze, *Difference and Repetition*, 239.

84. Deleuze, *Difference and Repetition*, 228.

85. Deleuze, *Difference and Repetition*, 239.

86. Deleuze, *Bergsonism*, 94, translation adjusted by me (translating *se différencie* as differenciated).

87. Deleuze, *Bergsonism*, translation adjusted by me.

88. See Deleuze, *Bergsonism*, 95.

89. Deleuze, *Bergsonism*, 95, translation adjusted by me (translating *différenciation* as differenciation).

90. Oneness is potentially countable, but it does not have a potential that is waiting to be actualized.

91. Deleuze and Parnet, *Dialogues*, 14.

92. Deleuze and Parnet, *Dialogues*, 6.

93. Deleuze and Parnet, *Dialogues*, 15.

94. See Plato *Parmenides* 130c.

95. Deleuze, *Pourparlers*, 186, translation adjusted by me.

References

Aristotle. *Metaphysics*. Translated by Richard Hope. Ann Arbor: University of Michigan Press, 1960.

Ascherson, Neal. "Memories of Amikejo: Europe's Pasts and Possible Future." *London Review of Books* 34, no. 6 (March 2012): 17–22.

Badiou, Alain. *Deleuze: The Clamor of Being*. Translated by Louise Burchill. Minnesota: Minnesota University Press, 1999.

Deleuze, Gilles. *Bergsonism*. Translated by Hugh Tomlinson and Barbara Habberjam. New York: Zone Books, 1991.

———. *Difference and Repetition*. Translated by Paul Patton. New York: Columbia University Press, 1994.

———. *The Logic of Sense*. Translated by Mark Lester, Charles Stivale and Constantin V. Boundas. New York: Columbia University Press, 1990.

———. *Negotiations*. Translated by Martin Joughlin. New York: Columbia University Press, 1995.

———. *A Thousand Plateaus*. Translated by Brian Massumi. Minneapolis: University of Minnesota Press, 1987.

Deleuze, Gilles and Arnaud Villani. "Responses to a Series of Questions." *Collapse: Philosophical Research and Development* III (2007): 39–43.

Deleuze, Gilles and Claire Parnet. *Dialogues*. New York: Columbia University Press, 1987.

Derrida, Jacques. *Of Hospitality*. Translated by Rachel Bowlby. Stanford: Stanford University Press, 2000.

Descartes, René. *Philosophical Letters*. Translated by Anthony Kenny. London: Oxford University Press, 1970.

Dilcher, Roman. *Studies in Heraclitus*. Hildeshein: Georg Olms AG, 1995.

Hesiod. *Theogony*. Edited and translated by Glenn W. Most. Loeb Classical Library 57. Cambridge, MA: Harvard University Press, 2006.

Kahn, Charles. *The Art and Thought of Heraclitus*. Cambridge: Cambridge University Press, 1999.

Manchester, Peter. *The Syntax of Time*. Leiden: Brill, 2005.

McKirahan, Richard. *A Presocratic Reader*. Indianapolis: Hackett, 2011.

Roffe, John. *Badiou's Deleuze*. Montreal: McGill-Queen's University Press, 2012.

Schindler, D. C. "The Community of the One and the Many: Heraclitus on Reason." *Inquiry* 46 (2003): 413–448.

Sushytska, Julia. "On the Non-Rivalry Between Poetry and Philosophy: Plato's *Republic*, Reconsidered." *Mosaic* 45, no.1 (March 2012): 55–70.

Villani, Arnaud. "Why Am I Deleuzian?" *Deleuze and Philosophy*. Edited by Constantin V. Boundas. Edinburgh: Edinburgh University Press, 2006.

CHAPTER SIX

Deleuze and Badiou on Being and the Event

Alain Beaulieu

Context

In the mid-1970s, Badiou turns in mockery to the philosophy of "Saint Gilles and Saint Félix," which he qualified as "egoist" and "anti-militantist."[1] The "ideology of desire" that Deleuze and Guattari develop in *Anti-Oedipus* is unfit for supporting real struggles. It defends nothing more, argues Badiou, than a "anarcho-desiring" and "bourgeois" conception of political struggles.[2] It is in this context that Badiou sends his "brigades" into Deleuze's classes with the mission of denouncing Deleuzian politics insensitive to workers' concerns.[3] These attacks launched against the "micro-political" model of the "molecular revolutions" multiplied until the mid-1980s.[4]

Badiou then reassessed his positions. He remained uninterested in Deleuze and Guattari's joint texts, yet nuanced his assertion regarding the goal of freeing Deleuze's solo works from the anarchic philosophy of desire. In his 1997 book devoted to Deleuze, Badiou argues that Deleuzian thought has nothing of the anarcho-desiring expressionism with which it is often associated. This thought remains, on the contrary, "resolutely *classical*."[5] From the very first chapter of Badiou's work, we learn that the two thinkers exchanged an intense correspondence between 1991 and 1994 (for obscure reasons, Deleuze seems to have destroyed these letters) and that Badiou considers Deleuze his primary philosophical rival in the development of an "ontology of the multiple"; the two form "a sort of paradoxical tandem." In perusing this work, the reader quickly understands that Badiou considers Deleuze's vitalist attempt at thinking the pure multiple to be a failure. The most polemic part of his interpretation argues that—unlike what is generally believed—Deleuze's thought is not a philosophy of difference and of infinite differentiation. Rather, it was rigorously and platonically oriented to the question of the univocity of being. This argument has numerous and sometimes counter-intuitive implications. With the failure of Deleuzian vitalism, which operates on an ascetic thinking of the transcendence of One,

137

Badiou believes it necessary to oppose a true ontology of the pure multiple, founded on the axiomatic. Paradoxically, Deleuze and Guattari formulated a similar grievance against Badiou's thought. In *What is Philosophy?*, they describe Badiou's work as a "particularly interesting undertaking," but Deleuze and Guattari also reproached Badiou's thought for "reintroducing the transcendent" into immanence and thus reactivating "an old conception of the higher philosophy."[6]

In the early 1990s, Badiou had already publically discussed his litigious rapport with Deleuze by devoting four of his lectures to *What is Philosophy?*.[7] These lectures were subsequent to the writing, several years earlier, of a long critical review[8] of Deleuze's book on Leibniz in which Badiou exposed his re-evaluation of Deleuzian philosophy for the first time. This is the primary argument expressed in this literature review: Deleuze's organicist ontology, which does not resort to the mathematical theory of ensembles, remains incapable of thinking the "multiple without one," which would be picked up and deepened in *Deleuze: The Clamor of Being*. As we might easily imagine, this presentation provoked lively reactions from supporters and defenders of Deleuzism.[9] Badiou faced many accusations of misrepresenting Deleuzian thought. He made the effort to respond, this time insisting on the opposition that separates the Deleuzian ontology, which is turned towards the One-Whole-Organic, and his own conception of the axiomatized multiple.[10] At the heart of this metaphysical quarrel is the ability to articulate immanence without injecting it with transcendence.

To better situate this debate, let us review several points of convergence and divergence that feed these two thinkers' unique rapport. In terms of points in common, let us mention that:

- Badiou and Deleuze practice a radical philosophy and categorically refuse to endorse the ambient liberal democratism, contemporary parliamentarism and the consensualist ideal that know nothing of singular claims;
- They are uninterested in the hermeneutic tradition, which they associate with scholasticism;
- They both renounce assimilation, by the analytical philosophy, of philosophy into a cognitive logic and a generalized grammar;
- They unconditionally reject the pathos of finitude associated with dominant historicism;
- They refuse to compromise with humanist ideology and with all forms of moralism by reconnecting with the Socratic model of philosophy as an undertaking of moral corruption;
- They both admit unlimited admiration for Beckett;
- They are indifferent to the end of metaphysics, considering the undertakings of destruction, overcoming, and deconstruction as artificial;

- They rehabilitate the value of eternity and the rapport with the infinite in favour of redefining the philosophical status of the idea and in conserving the spirit of the system;
- They evacuate all teleological principles that camouflages a desire to rally lost believers to the resorption of a pretended civilizational crisis;
- And, finally, they both declare their atheism.

Their divergences are just as numerous, and perhaps even more fundamental:

- Badiou maintains the categories of the subject and the truth while Deleuze argues for de-subjectivation and is indifferent to the notion of truth;
- The first is interested in Lacanian psycho-analysis, while the second comes to vigorously denounce the psychoanalytic interpretation of the unconscious;
- Badiou is Sartrian in that he renews the heroism of a non-conformist subject, while Deleuze considers the Sartrian model of liberation to be outdated;
- Badiou fights in the Maoist spirit, while Deleuze is distrustful of all political organizations;
- The author of *Being and Event* identifies with the Platonism that sets philosophy's horizons (via politics, art, science, love, and its mathematized doctrine of ideas) while the author of *Difference and Repetition* seeks an alternative to Platonism in Nietzsche and the Stoics;
- The Badiou's philosophy discredits the reference to the powers of the virtual and takes interest in the "actualized" phenomena, while the Deleuze's thought considers reality as both actual and virtual;
- Badiou proposes a de-continuist model of history, punctuated by nothingness, while Deleuze's naturalist philosophy sees the incessant and on-going effects of forces.

Being

Badiou sketches an original topography of the fields of thought. Mathematics does not just provide ontological background, it is ontology; only mathematics is able to produce declarations on being. The four "generic procedures" (science, politics, art, love) make up as many possible sites from which arise rare and localized truths. Procedures are also the conditions of philosophy. There is no such thing as "pure philosophy" since thought is essentially conditioned by the truths it does not produce. Philosophy is neither the sovereign "queen of sciences," nor the guardian of the "being-qua-being" rhetoric (which comes down to mathematics); rather, it remains in the service of the truths issued from political revolutions, scientific inventions, artistic creations and love experiences. More modestly, philosophy must resolve to conceptually determine the compossibility of its conditions of truth that remain exterior to its powers.

Cantor's set theory shows us that there is not a "set of all sets," and therefore no truth that universally and definitively establishes the consistency of the One. Badiou presents this ontology, which seeks to radically break with univocity, as a Platonism of the pure multiple or of the "multiple without one" that no longer depends on a unique truth. Badiou undertakes the vast work of *desuturation* to bring an end to the prejudices considered to be the toughest questions of our time, characterized by a generalized oversight of the ontological value of mathematics. The task, therefore, is to "desuture" philosophy from ontology, as well as from each pretention to truth. In this context—where only mathematics are depositories of adequate language for being (they are ontology) and where philosophy welcomes the truths produced independently from it—there is no such thing as philosophical politics (social movements create truth without philosophy dictating their future); science is not the only condition of philosophy (epistemology becomes a secondary philosophical question); the Age of Poets where philosophy connects with the poetic arts has expired (Heidegger is representative of this ultimate wandering); and, the love experience is not the last possibility of philosophy (Romanticism belongs to the past).

Badiou develops his critique of Deleuzian ontology—provocative, at the least—on these theoretical bases. Somewhat like Heidegger who pointed out, about Nietzsche, the insufficiencies of overturning Platonism to better ensure his overcoming, Badiou argues, about Deleuze, that it is not enough to think the univocity of being via simulacra to overcome the philosophy of the One. Therein lies the failure of Deleuzian thought which, ignorant of the ontological theory of ensembles, is not able to develop an adequate philosophy of the multiple. According to Badiou, Deleuze thinks the multiple in terms of "impurity" by invariably submitting the ensembles to the law of the univocity of being. The diversity of Deleuze's theoretical approaches regarding the multiplicity of the cases he examines would invariably be to return the multiple to the univocity of being, which goes by many names (virtual, eternal return, fold, outside, disjunctive synthesis, etc.). Against this "monotony" of the vitalist variations that secondarizes the multiple *vis-à-vis* the One, Badiou offers to submit this thought to Cantor's set theory, which is presented as an ontological basis of the "multiple without one."

With good reason, Badiou points out just how much Deleuzian commentators have tended to neglect the question of Being, which is nevertheless very present in the Deleuzian corpus. We see in Deleuze's work an admiration for Being taken as univocal by Duns Scotus and Spinoza (*Expressionism in Philosophy: Spinoza, Difference and Repetition*), an affirmation of the univocal Being thought as the future and desire for power (*Nietzsche and Philosophy*), and the idea of an ontological communication between all Events (*The Logic of Sense*). The "clamour of being"[11] fascinates Deleuze. Not only must we assimilate part of Deleuze's work into an ontological examination, we must admit along with Badiou that the Deleuzian ontology clings to Being as it is thought in its univocal acceptation. This ontological position, and Badiou's interpretation of it, provoke two remarks.

First, it is difficult to affirm with certitude that Deleuze, in the 1960s, established a hierarchy between Being and the play of differences. What interested Deleuze in these years was not so much the fact that Being can be said each time in the same way or that the perspective according to which the way of saying it differs each time. Deleuze does not value the univocity of Being more or less than the differentiation of the simulacra. He seeks to go beyond representation by thinking Being as difference, and difference according to its ontologically univocal value. This attempt to degrade difference between the univocal and the multiple simulacra seems clearly expressed in the two excerpts, entitled "*The Univocity of Being (I)*" and "*The Univocity of Being (II)*," respectively, which Badiou quotes in the Appendix to his work on Deleuze. The first is taken from *Difference and Repetition*, in which Deleuze writes: "The essential in univocity is not that Being is said in a single and same sense, but that it is said, in a single and same sense, *of* all its individuating differences or intrinsic modalities. [. . .] Being is said in a single and same sense of everything of which it is said, but that of which it is said differs: it is said of difference itself."[12] The second excerpt, taken from *The Logic of Sense*, reformulates the same idea: "The univocity of Being does not mean that there is one and the same Being; on the contrary, beings are multiple and different, they are always produced by a disjunctive synthesis, and they themselves are disjointed and divergent, *membra disjoncta*."[13] Deleuze tries to dissolve the ontico-ontological difference in favour of a "world of simulacra" located beyond the field of representation; in other words, across or below the strict univocity of Being and the difference between beings. Badiou underestimates the radicalism of this progressive destruction of representation, putting emphasis on a supposed Deleuzian desire to present the univocal being. This abuse is strategic in that it allows Badiou to reveal in Deleuzian ontology a fundamental inability to formulate a real thought of the multiple. It would appear preferable to consider that the "clamour of being" paradoxically escapes all desire for "presentification" (to transpose Heideggerian language to Deleuzian vitalism).

Our second remark is more incriminating. If it is true that all Deleuzian ontology perceives Being in its univocity, it is false to reduce all of Deleuze's philosophy to ontology. That on which we can agree is summarized in the following statements, taken from Badiou's interpretation: "From beginning to end, and under the constraint of innumerable and fortuitous cases, his work is concerned with thinking thought (its act, its movement) on the basis of an ontological precomprehension of Being as One. [. . .] Deleuze purely and simply identifies philosophy with ontology"[14]; "The profound motivation that this doctrine [of the simulacra] covers is integrally maintained through the very last works" (*Le motif profond que cette doctrine* [des simulacres] *recouvre se maintient intégralement jusqu'aux toutes dernières œuvres*).[15]

An interest in Being does not penetrate Deleuze's work "from beginning to end." This is why we suggest distinguishing "Deleuze-I" and "Deleuze-II" by using a turning point in Deleuzian thought or a least a significative shift that goes from the theoretical study of the univocity of being to what we call a "pragmatic of the disjunctive singularities." The "first Deleuze" is attached to ontology while the "second Deleuze" distances himself with the ontological way to face problems. This turning point is easily dated: it corresponds with the beginning of Deleuze's collaboration with Guattari. In fact, Deleuze definitively stops referring to the vocables of "being,"[16] "One," and "simulacrum" starting in *Anti-Oedipus* (1972); this is several years after *The Logic of Sense* (1969), which already announced him turning towards a de-ontologization. Though definitive, it is not, however, a radical change since the pragmatic of the disjunctive singularities leads Deleuze to commemorate his first infatuation with Empiricism (*Empiricism and Subjectivity* was published in 1953) by experimenting this time with the unfounded contradictions of which he explains the different modes of functioning. After 1972, the most determining element in Deleuzian thought is no longer the theoretical attempt—aimed at making the multiplicities and univocity of being coincide—but rather becomes the ontologically sceptical experimentation of various figures (schizophrenic desire, *faux raccords* and other audio-visual anomalies in modern cinema, series of non-human becomings of man, anorganic life, Bacon's figures, Beckett's triple language, Luca's poetic stuttering, the Outside more distant than any external world, etc.). The explanations of all these "cases" are in no way monotonous (except perhaps, dare we say, when we have not experienced the intensity of Deleuzian life). Rather, they contribute to illustrating the dynamic of a life that is no longer founded on totally harmonious, unifying and coherent laws. This does not mean that the rupture with the question of the univocity of being leads the experimenter into the whirlwind of universal disorder. Quite the opposite: The impersonal forces that condition experience have a chaosmic value, and they produce a semi-ordered or partially coherent universe, although order remains localized and randomly composed.

Contrary to Badiou's affirmation, Deleuze's thinking after the shift is no longer oriented on the science of being. It does not defend a federating univocal being, but rather bears witness to the presence of singularities unconnected to any unifying ontological enterprise. Therefore, we observe a crumbling of the founding and superior discourse that tradition assimilated into ontology. The philosophical creation of concepts, following the examples of art (music, painting, literature, etc.) and science (embryology, metallurgy, ethology, etc.), provides tools that explain how to experiment the localized and particular states of intensive life. In this context, where theory is second to experience, Deleuze was led to think the lack of utility and even the destructive character of his old ontological attempt, which sought to gather all arguments into one (ontology). He now argues that such a theoretical search may annihilate the experience of evenemental singularities. As such, even Deleuze's most "theoretical" books after the shift (*Foucault*, *The Fold*, *What is Philosophy?*) actually push for a de-ontologized experimentation of an impersonal life. It is worth recalling one of later Deleuze's suggestions: "putting the element of Having in place of that of

Being"[17] and to replace the ontological theme with the disjunctive conjunction (the verb "to be" by the conjunction "and").[18] These mutations lead one to abandon concerns for Being (a simulated being, pre-existing essence, meaning, power, etc.) in favour of a creative experiment in "manners of being" (styles, postures, gestures, capacities, powers, speeds, syntaxical creations, etc.). The question is no longer: "What is it?," "What does it mean?," or "What is the being common to all simulacra?." Rather, the question becomes: "How does it work?" Elsewhere, in *What is Philosophy?*, the argument stays in this vein, explicitly taking a position against the Universals (contemplation, reflection, communication): "The first principle of philosophy is that Universals explain nothing but must themselves be explained."[19] The univocal/universal being that so interested the first Deleuze falls under this self-criticism that had, among other things, found a first formulation in a "text of youth" in which Deleuze wrote: "Being, the One and the Whole are the myth of a false philosophy totally impregnated by theology."[20]

Badiou underestimates the scope and radical nature of this self-criticism by Deleuze-II, who distances himself not only from his former interests for the univocity of being, but also frees himself from the reference to the big "Whole." By interpreting the texts of the second Deleuze like a work of "*totalization*,"[21] and setting up a strict equivalency in Deleuze between the "One" and the "Whole,"[22] Badiou implies that Deleuze accepts (the "One-Whole") what he rejects (the Universals). Again, what was true for Deleuze-I is not for Deleuze-II. Of course, the first Deleuze explicitly articulated the coherence of the Whole with the universal being and unique becoming. However, after the turning point, this totality is relieved of its duties and expulsed from the Deleuzian system in favor of deontologized becoming and partial actions. Deleuze-II breaks with the notion of the rational and interiorized ontological whole. Similar to the Being and the One, the Whole disappears from Deleuzian investigation, thus making room for an indetermination of the ensemble: "Not even a puzzle, whose pieces when fitted together would constitute a whole, but rather a wall of loose, uncemented stones, where every element has a value in itself but also in relation to others."[23] The network of unconnected singularities is incompatible with the conception of a gigantesque exteriority, unified by the idea of a huge intellectual and rational entity.

Thus, we must take Badiou's interpretation with a "grain of salt," as it founds the entire Deleuzian philosophy on the quest of the supreme One, univocal Being and great Whole. This reduction overrules the orientation of Deleuzian thought after 1972 and, as a consequence, it is false to pretend that Deleuze is, "from beginning to end," the far-off perpetrator of the Platonism of the One. But it is not enough for Badiou to affirm that Deleuze's uninterrupted Platonism is incompatible with an ontology of the multiple. He must also argue that the Deleuzian model of a "nonorganic vitality" is in opposition to his doctrine of the "pure multiple." It is curious, and somewhat contradictory, that Badiou makes Deleuze into a Platonist when it is time to deconstruct his ontology, and into an Aristotelian when presenting the "organicist" aspect of his thought.[24] The mathematical paradigm of the Number must protect philosophy against transcendence while the defence of the vitalist paradigm of the Animal, Aristotelian obedience, would lead to it.[25] This analysis again neglects to consider the scope of the turning point in Deleuzian thought. Because although, influenced by his reading of Bergson, the first Deleuze could be seduced by the omnipresence of a creative Life, in the second Deleuze this seduction was dissipated. The signs of this rupture with "animalism" are clearly perceptible when Deleuze affirms: "Thus the universe is neither a great living being, nor is in itself an Animal."[26] And elsewhere: "We can dispense with Fechner's or Conan Doyle's splendid hypothesis of a nervous system of the earth."[27] It is the very essence of Deleuze's late hypothesis of a "nonorganic life"[28] to find its effectiveness in immanence; to affect singularities specifically and not globally by partly destabilizing the unity of organisms; to not constitute a perfectly organized unit; to be fragmented; to produce random laws; and, to create effects that are both partial and unpredictable. Badiou comes to synthesize the nature of a certain "nonrapport" with Deleuze, but he neglects to consider that Deleuzian vitalism takes two forms: On the one hand, it is associated with a doctrine of the univocity of being (Deleuze-I), and on the other, it is characterized by a network of nontotalizable singularities (Deleuze-II). Therefore, a de-hierarchized vitalism of the second Deleuze does not correspond with a philosophy of transcendence.

The primary issue, as we mentioned above, is that of determining who of these two people best conquers immanence. It may very well be that Badiou formalizes the pure multiple, whereas the second Deleuze produces the vitalist version. Deleuze disagreed with this formalization, as his correspondence shows, in which he indicated that Badiou's thought falls "back into transcendence and into the equivocity of analogy."[29] If this is the case, the bone of contention between the two thinkers is perhaps less about Badiou's ontology than it is about his conception of the Event.

Event

It is remarkable that the primary work Badiou devotes to Deleuze essentially focuses the discussion on the Being, while it would be just as expedient to centre the debate on the Event. Badiou trues his aim in *Logiques des mondes* by devoting a section to "L'événement selon Deleuze."[30] In this section, he reiterates his criticism of univocity and vitalism that contaminates, in his opinion, all Deleuzian philosophy, including his thought on the Event. Again, this interpretation which may apply to "Deleuze-I" no longer applies to "Deleuze-II"—a distinction to which Badiou makes no reference.

Badiou finalized his theory of the event in *Being and Event*. The unpredictable event arises "at the edge of the void" with a capacity to radically change the aspect of a situation. Badiou is careful to distinguish the Event from the catastrophe of human tragedies, such as murderous natural disasters or the Shoah.

The Event corresponds to a positive transformation or to a moment of collective emancipation without depending on a grand outer order that prescribes the laws of this "happening." Among other things, nothing dictates how one reacts to the Event. Among the events that occupied Badiou's thought over the course of his work, let us mention October 1917, the popular movements of May '68, the Iranian Revolution, China's Cultural Revolution, the storming of the Bastille, Solidarity in Poland, the Vienna school's serialism, set theory, and the resurrection of Christ. As we can see, for Badiou the Event is of "macroscopic" order and fully visible. Badiou argues that the Event does not belong to transcendence as long as it is located on a site, he professes more interest in the consequences of the Event than in its occurrence, and the fact that the Event is apparently subtracted from the laws of presentation changes nothing since the Event is not on the margins of universal history or "beyond chronological time": it is historically incarnated and its designation is generally agreed upon.

For Badiou, the Event as not alone or isolated; rather, it belongs to an ensemble of events that arise in art, science, politics and love. It is the task of philosophy to declare the local truth or the conceptual compossibility—for any given time—of this "fourfold" formed by the procedures of the evenemental truths and it is the task of the subject to retrospectively intervening to witness its loyalty to the Event. Another original feature of this theory of the Event lies in its disconnection from ontology. Badiou's vast undertaking of desuturation (philosophy/ontology, philosophy/politics, philosophy/art, philosophy/love, philosophy/science) also touches on Being's relationship with the Event. Despite what we have just mentioned regarding the Event's macroscopic character, which attributes to the Event a certain value of presence (although this presence is made fragile by the fact that the Event is also confused with unpredictable consequences), Badiou presents the Event as "excessive" (*surnuméraire*) regarding ontology. Thus, if mathematics shows the royal avenue to Being, the Event corresponds to "what-is-not-being-qua-being." In other words, axiomatized ontology has nothing to say about the Event.[31]

As for Deleuze, he wants to revive the Stoics in *The Logic of Sense* by placing the Event in the time of Aion, in a temporality that is strangely similar to eternity without immortalizing a permanent presence, as per onto-theology. Deleuze proposes the following definition: "Unlimited Aion, the becoming which divides itself infinitely in past and future and always eludes the present."[32] The Aion defies not only the "beyond time," but also Chronos without, however, coming back to the Husserlian "living present" of a transcendental subjectivity and without calling on the "ekstatic" character of temporal dimensions that orient the Heideggerian meaning of being. The Aion is the time of the Event, and the Event is an impersonal fragment of destiny that autonomously affects a singularity *vis-à-vis* "good will." In Deleuze's work, this destiny is, however, no longer attached to a "large cosmic order" by rather has the look of a "chaosmos" with paradoxical effects. Whether it belongs to a perfectly ordered universe (the Stoics) or to a partially ordered universe (Deleuze), the Event is irreducible to the present of its spatial-temporal effectuation in a state-of-affairs.

More precisely, the effectuation of the Event is doubled by an expressive counter-effectuation as its reality is "incorporeal" and independent from that in which
it is incarnated.[33] The Event needs matter in order to manifest, but it also possesses an expressive, extra-physical and virtual dimension.

Deleuze rediscovers with the Stoics the singularly language-based nature of
the Event. He gives an example of the Event with the injury of Joë Bousquet
who was paralyzed during World War I, until his death more than thirty years
later. "My wound," writes Bousquet, "existed before me; I was born to embody
it."[34] This event-wound is not simply a state-of-affairs that took place in a
chronologically determinable present. It is stripped of beginning and end, while
offering itself up as a particular fatality to which the person or thing that is affected demonstrates himself or itself to be worthy of, as if it were an "eternal
truth."[35] Further, incorporeal events exceed the simple regime of apparitions and
disappearances to maintain among them on-going relationships by linking the
"quasi-causalities" stripped of all depth or meaning. They disturb common
sense, *sensus communis*. In keeping with the specific logic at work in Lewis
Caroll's *Alice in Wonderland*, quasi-causality is paradoxical. It engenders the
opposite effects and irrational connections; an Event can be the simultaneous
source or the quasi-causality of two other anti-nomic and unpredictable effects.[36]

Deleuze comes back to the question of the Event in *The Fold. Leibniz and
the Baroque*. In keeping with the turning point he gave to his thought, he re-
nounces the idea he defended in *The Logic of Sense* that: "Being is the unique
event in which all events communicate with one another."[37] It is no longer the
"simulated being" of the first Deleuze that is theorized, but rather the evenemental "manner of being" of a singularity and its languages-based expression that
are experienced. The rupture with the old ontology is complete and the capital
letter is shifted from Being to "Mannerism."[38] In *The Logic of Sense*, Deleuze
(along with Bréhier) used the expression "manner (or way) of being"[39] without,
however, taking away from the de-ontologization of "Mannerism." This is what
he accomplishes in *The Fold* where the Stoics, the Baroque that leads the fold to
infinity, and Whitehead's process metaphysics are presented as offering the
three major answers to the question of the Event.[40]

Like all good and respectable theories of the Event, Badiou's and Deleuze's
theories distinguish the Event from the arena of the accident, current events,
opinion, the predictable, daily life, natural disasters, and catastrophes. Repudiat-
ing this distinction would be a contradiction of terms. The two philosophers
agree on the basics: the Event escapes all determined law of apparition while
also being a determinant part of reality. But in terms of form, they seem to be
opposed.

From Badiou's point of view:

- The Event is the result of randomness or a historical contingency;
- There is a void or a discontinuity between evenemental sequences;

- Ontology is silent in regard to the Event;
- A subject arises from the experience of loyalty to the evenemental truth;
- Events belong in a problematic way to current events; and,
- A discredit is thrown on all the philosophies of language.

From Deleuze's point of view:

- The Event is accompanied by *fatum*;
- There is a full production and a continual series of events;
- Being ensures communication between all events (for the first Deleuze);
- The Event is an indication of a process of de-subjectivation;
- The expressivist counter-effectuation of the Event bears witness to its virtual aspect; and,
- The Event maintains an essential rapport with grammar and syntax.

But there is an even more fundamental divergence that we brought up and would like to come back to briefly. Although always surprising in their operations of transformation of historical sequences, the events Badiou studied are obviously visible and universally known. There is a consensus surrounding these Events (a consensual aspect is, however, criticized on other occasions by this militant anti-democrat). Who would dare to deny that the great revolutions took place? Of course, most frequently, it is difficult to be loyal to the implications of the grand plans for emancipation, to measure their scope or to position oneself at the grandeur of the novelties they promise. Nonetheless, this macroscopic conception of the event re-injects some transcendence into immanence. Deleuze considered the events to be not only singular, but also to manifest in an imperceptible manner. The great historical movements may orient Deleuze's thought (the three ages of the Savages, the Barbarians, and the Civilized Men in *Anti-Oedipus*, World War II, that conditions the appearance of the time-image and societies of control, etc.), but these elements of rupture correspond more with a "state of affairs" rather than Events. On this point, Deleuze is closer to Nietzsche, for whom the "noisy revolutions" and all that belongs to the public domain do no enter into the definition of the Event. Badiou's likening of his conception of the Event to Nietzsche's is not very convincing.[41] On the contrary, Badiou's manifestation of the event always has a historical (political revolution, scientific invention, artistic movement) or meta-corporal (love experience) character that gives it a kind of universal veracity. For this reason, the concept of the event Badiou develops seems to come under transcendence. Deleuze avoids this trap since the event as he sees it is a singular "surface effect" incarnated not by universal history, but by a body that is intensive, speaking, living and affected by the chaosmic forces.

Conclusion

Badiou's interpretation has many merits. We must point out his admirable capacity to destroy the common image of Deleuze as a thinker of anarchic desire; his rightful evocation of Deleuze's ascetic and creative Stoicism as one key to his work; his respect of Deleuze as a "pure metaphysician"; and, his exemplary comparison between Deleuzian ontology and the Heideggerian question of being. These points of analysis indicate just as many future avenues for the exegesis of Deleuzian work. But one of the strangest things in Badiou's interpretation of Deleuze is his persistence to demonstrate the Deleuzian ontology, illustrate its insufficiency and "monotony," to liberate the pure multiple when Deleuze himself had seen the limitations to his ontological undertaking, which was at risk for being confused with totalization. Deleuze took haste to neutralize this ambiguity with a decisive gesture; he thought a plane of immanence intensified with pure events or haecceities without essence or substance (an hour of the day, the blue of the sky, a bird song, a life, a walk, etc.). No longer a being confused with his simulacra, but a "Mannerism," "manners of being" that are clearly distinct to experience.

It is legitimate to insist, as Badiou does, on certain excesses of ontological univocity in Deleuze; the affirmation of being as a unique event can lead to a certain onto-theological confusion. However, we have attempted to show that Badiou's interpretation also presents two fundamental blind spots: its ignorance of the Deleuzian turning point that works on the rupture with the molar Being-One-Whole in favor of the molecular Having-Mannerism and its inability to remain loyal to Deleuze's immanent conception of the Event. In sum, Deleuze neutralizes the risks associated with the thought of ontological univocity by re-centering his philosophy on the singularity of the Event. Badiou attempts to think the pure multiple in terms of ontology, but his philosophy would appear unable, from a Deleuzean standpoint, to satisfy the real conditions of the immanence of the Event.[42]

Notes

1. Alain Badiou, *Théorie de la contradiction* (Paris: François Maspero, 1975), 72.

2. Badiou, *Théorie de la contradiction*, 75.

3. François Dosse, *Gilles Deleuze et Félix Guattari: Biographie croisée* (Paris: La Découverte, 2007), 433–434.

4. Alain Badiou, *De l'idéologie* (Paris: François Maspero, 1976), 8; Alain Badiou, "Le flux et le parti (dans les marges de *L'Anti-Œdipe*)," in *La Situation actuelle sur le front de la philosophie*, ed. Alain Badiou and Sylvain Lazarus (Paris: François Maspero, 1977), 24–41; Alain Badiou, *Théorie du sujet* (Paris: Seuil, 1982), 236; Alain Badiou, *Peut-on penser la politique?* (Paris: Seuil, 1985), 16.

5. Alain Badiou, *Deleuze: The Clamor of Being*, trans. Louise Burchill (Minnesota: Minnesota University Press, 1999), 44.

6. Gilles Deleuze and Félix Guattari, *What is Philosophy?*, trans. Hugh Tomlinson and Graham Burchell (New York: Columbia University Press, 1994), 151–152.

7. Later, Badiou mentions his "lesser interest" (*moindre intérêt*) in the collaborative works between Deleuze and Guattari. See Alain Badiou, "Un, multiple, multiplicité(s)," *Multitudes* 1 (2000): 210, note.

8. Alain Badiou, "Gilles Deleuze: Le Pli. Leibniz et le baroque," *Annuaire philosophique* (1989): 161–184.

9. See for instance Éric Alliez, Arnaud Villani and José Gil, "Dossier Badiou/Deleuze," *Futur antérieur* 43 (April 1998): 49–84.

10. Alain Badiou, "Une lettre à Gilles (juillet 1994)," *Libération* (November 7, 1995): 36; "L'ontologie vitaliste de Deleuze," in Alain Badiou, *Court traité d'ontologie transitoire* (Paris: Seuil, 1998), 61–72 (this text, with a new introduction, was published as "De la vie comme nom de l'être" included in the special issue on "Gilles Deleuze. Immanence et vie," in *Rue Descartes* 20 (1998): 27–34); "Un, multiple, multiplicité(s)," *Multitudes* 1 (2000), 195–211; "Deleuze, sur la ligne de front," *Magazine littéraire* 406 (February 2002): 19–20 ; "L'événement selon Deleuze," in Alain Badiou, *Logiques des mondes* (Paris: Seuil, 1988), 403–410. In 2002, Deleuze's book *Francis Bacon: Logique de la sensation* was re-edited in a collection directed by Alain Badiou and Barbara Cassin called "L'Ordre philosophique" (Seuil). An enthusiastic preface by Alain Badiou and Barbara Cassin was added to this new edition.

11. Gilles Deleuze, *Difference and Repetition*, trans. Paul Patton (New York: Columbia University Press, 1994), 35 and 304.

12. Deleuze, *Difference and Repetition*, 36.

13. Gilles Deleuze, *The Logic of Sense*, trans. Mark Lester, Charles Stivale and Constantin V. Boundas (New York: Columbia University Press, 1990), 179.

14. Badiou, *Deleuze: The Clamor of Being*, 19.

15. Badiou, "Un, multiple, multiplicité(s)," 209, note (my translation).

16. Alain Badiou quotes a passage taken from one of Deleuze' later texts where Deleuze seems to agree with Heidegger's surpassing of the Husserlian intentionality towards being. See Gilles Deleuze, *Foucault*, trans. Sean Hand and Paul Bove (London: The Athlone Press, 1988), 110; quoted in Badiou, *Deleuze: The Clamor of Being*, 22. However, this reference deals less with the movement towards being than the movement (made by Heidegger, Foucault and Deleuze) that goes from the intentional subjectivity to desubjectivation.

17. Gilles Deleuze, *The Fold: Leibniz and the Baroque*, trans. Tom Conley (Minneapolis: University of Minnesota Press, 1993), 109. See also the topic "having a body" disseminated in *Anti-Oedipus* and *A Thousand Plateaus*.

18. Gilles Deleuze and Félix Guattari, *A Thousand Plateaus*, trans. Brian Massumi (Minneapolis: University of Minnesota Press, 1987), 25 and 98; Gilles Deleuze, *Negotiations*, trans. Martin Joughlin (New York: Columbia University Press, 1995), 44–45 and elsewhere.

19. Deleuze and Guattari, *What is Philosophy?*, 7.

20. Deleuze, *The Logic of Sense*, 279. This passage is sometimes presented, incorrectly, as a counter-argument to Badiou's interpretation. The quotation is taken from a 1961 article included in *The Logic of Sense* and it remains partly exterior to the content of

the book. In *The Logic of Sense*, Deleuze changed his mind (although not in a definitive way) and he clearly defended an ontological position. If one views *The Logic of Sense* as a work of transition, it is not because it defends some ontological and non-ontological positions (*The Logic of Sense* clearly stands on the side of ontology), but rather because it combines an ontology and a disjunctology. After the ontological episode of the 1960s (*Difference and Repetition, The Logic of Sense*), the later Deleuze recast his very first critique of the "Being-One-Whole" made in 1961.

21. See for instance Badiou, *Deleuze: The Clamor of Being*, 58.

22. Badiou, *Deleuze: The Clamor of Being*, 62 and 97.

23. Gilles Deleuze, *Essays Critical and Clinical*, trans. Daniel W. Smith (Minneapolis: University of Minnesota Press, 1997), 86.

24. Deleuze is presented by Badiou as an Aristotelian in "Gilles Deleuze: Le Pli. Leibniz et le baroque," 166; and as a Platonician in *Deleuze: The Clamor of Being*, 19, 25, 45 and 60.

25. Alain Badiou, *Being and Event*, trans. Oliver Feltham (London: Continuum, 2007), last note of the introduction (the only reference to Deleuze in this book); "Gilles Deleuze: Le Pli. Leibniz et le baroque," 166; *Deleuze: The Clamor of Being*, 2; *Court traité d'ontologie transitoire* (Paris: Seuil, 1998), 72.

26. Deleuze, *The Fold. Leibniz and the Baroque*, 9.

27. Deleuze and Guattari, *What is Philosophy?*, 213.

28. Deleuze and Guattari, *A Thousand Plateaus*, 411 and 498–503; Deleuze and Guattari, *What is Philosophy?*, 182; Deleuze, *Essays Critical and Clinical*, 131; Gilles Deleuze, *Francis Bacon: The Logic of Sensation*, trans. Daniel W. Smith (Minneapolis: University of Minnesota Press, 2004), 39–41 and 104; and elsewhere.

29. Badiou, *Deleuze: The Clamor of Being*, 90.

30. Badiou, *Logiques des mondes*, 403–410.

31. Badiou, *Being and Event*, chap. 17 and 18.

32. Deleuze, *The Logic of Sense*, 5.

33. Deleuze, *The Logic of Sense*, 151.

34. Deleuze, *The Logic of Sense*, 148.

35. Deleuze, *The Logic of Sense*, 146 and 149.

36. Deleuze, *The Logic of Sense*, fourteenth series, 82–93.

37. Deleuze, *The Logic of Sense*, 180.

38. Deleuze, *The Fold. Leibniz and the Baroque*, 53. Deleuze writes "Maniérisme" with a capital "M" in the original French version.

39. Deleuze, *The Logic of Sense*, 5.

40. Deleuze, *The Logic of Sense*, sixth series.

41. Alain Badiou, *Saint Paul: The Foundation of Universalism*, trans. Ray Brassier (Palo Alto: Stanford University Press, 2003), last paragraph of the conclusion.

42. A first version of this article was presented at the annual meeting of *The Canadian Society for Continental Philosophy*, York University (Toronto, Canada), May 31, 2006. This article was supported by a grant from Social Sciences and Humanities Council of Canada.

References

Alliez, Éric, Arnaud Villani and José Gil. "Dossier Badiou/Deleuze." *Futur antérieur* 43 (April 1998): 49–84.

Badiou, Alain. *Being and Event.* Translated by Oliver Feltham. London: Continuum, 2007.

———. *Court traité d'ontologie transitoire.* Paris: Seuil, 1998.

———. *De l'idéologie.* Paris: François Maspero, 1976.

———. "De la vie comme nom de l'être." *Rue Descartes* 20 (1998): 27–34.

———. "Deleuze, sur la ligne de front." *Magazine littéraire* 406 (February 2002): 19–20.

———. *Deleuze: The Clamor of Being.* Translated by Louise Burchill. Minnesota: Minnesota University Press, 1999.

———. "Gilles Deleuze: Le Pli. Leibniz et le baroque." *Annuaire philosophique* (1989): 161–184.

———. "L'événement selon Deleuze." In *Logiques des mondes,* 403–410. Paris: Seuil, 1988.

———. "Le flux et le parti (dans les marges de *L'Anti-Œdipe*)." In *La Situation actuelle sur le front de la philosophie,* ed. Alain Badiou and Sylvain Lazarus, 24–41. Paris: François Maspero, 1977.

———. *Peut-on penser la politique?* Paris: Seuil, 1985.

———. *Saint Paul: The Foundation of Universalism.* Translated by Ray Brassier. Palo Alto: Stanford University Press, 2003.

———. *Théorie de la contradiction.* Paris: François Maspero, 1975.

———. *Théorie du sujet.* Paris: Seuil, 1982

———. "Un, multiple, multiplicité(s)." *Multitudes* 1 (2000): 195–211.

———. "Une lettre à Gilles (juillet 1994)." *Libération* (November 7, 1995): 36.

Deleuze, Gilles. *Difference and Repetition.* Translated by Paul Patton. New York: Columbia University Press, 1994.

———. *Empiricism and Subjectivity.* Translated by Constantin V. Boundas. New York: Columbia University Press, 2001.

———. *Essays Critical and Clinical.* Translated by Daniel W. Smith. Minneapolis: University of Minnesota Press, 1997.

———. *Expressionism in Philosophy: Spinoza.* Translated by Martin Joughlin. New York: Zone Books, 1992.

———. *Foucault.* Translated by Sean Hand and Paul Bove. London: The Athlone Press, 1988.

———. *Francis Bacon: The Logic of Sensation.* Translated by Daniel W. Smith. Minneapolis: University of Minnesota Press, 2004.

———. *Negotiations.* Translated by Martin Joughlin. New York: Columbia University Press, 1995.

———. *Nietzsche and Philosophy.* Translated by Michael Hardt. New York: Columbia University Press, 2006.

———. *The Fold: Leibniz and the Baroque.* Translated by Tom Conley. Minneapolis: University of Minnesota Press, 1993.

———. *The Logic of Sense.* Translated by Mark Lester, Charles Stivale and Constantin V. Boundas. New York: Columbia University Press, 1990.

Deleuze, Gilles, and Félix Guattari. *Anti-Oedipus.* Translated by Robert Hurley and Mark Seem. New York: Penguin Classics, 2009.

————. *A Thousand Plateaus.* Translated by Brian Massumi. Minneapolis: University of Minnesota Press, 1987.

————. *What is Philosophy?* Translated by Hugh Tomlinson and Graham Burchell. New York: Columbia University Press, 1994.

Dosse, François. *Gilles Deleuze et Félix Guattari: Biographie croisée.* Paris: La Découverte, 2007.

CHAPTER SEVEN

Disanalogous Being: Deleuze, Spinoza, and Univocal Metaphysics

Adrian Switzer

"Spinoza's philosophy remains in part unintelligible if one does not see in it a constant struggle against [. . .] equivocation [. . .] and analogy."

—Gilles Deleuze, *Expressionism in Philosophy: Spinoza*, 48–49

1. Metaphysics as Activity, Affirmation, and Historical Critique

For Deleuze, philosophy is always a matter of *doing* philosophy; in this way, a philosophical ontology is always active. As familiar as this idea sounds—it seems to say nothing more than that *how* one thinks informs *what* one thinks, that is, that a methodology determines a philosophy—it is the seeming familiarity of Deleuze's idea of philosophy that allows him to remake metaphysics along different lines. It is, in short, the seeming coincidence between a Deleuzian active ontology and a methodologically reflective philosophy that makes of the former a *critical* metaphysics; though not, as we will see, in the same sense in which Kant's critical philosophy is a correction of the metaphysical tradition.

In *Difference and Repetition* (1968), and without any indication of diverging from the history of metaphysics as he here describes it, Deleuze writes, "[t]here has only ever been one ontological proposition; Being is univocal [*l'Être est univoque*]."[1] Whether it is in the saying of univocal being by Duns Scotus, or in the various sayings of the same, "from Parmenides to Heidegger," Deleuze discerns "[a] single voice" that raises "the clamor of being."[2] Deleuze nowhere announces his intention of interrupting this unbroken, univocal saying of being; he intends, instead, to add his voice to such univocity in order to say the same, differently.

Continuing, Deleuze explains univocal being as a matter of, "individuating differences or intrinsic modalities" being included in "[t]he essence of univocal being [*l'essence de l'être univoque*]."[3]

There are no two "paths of being," as Parmenides claims in his ancient metaphysical poem: there is no "equivocity" to being. Rather, there is a single path along which "individuating differences" are said in a univocal voice. Through repetition over the course of the history of metaphysics, such univocity becomes individually differentiated.[4] To put this last point in the Spinozistic language Deleuze uses in the above quote, the repetition of the univocal saying of being restates substance monism in its "intrinsic modalities." The latter, as Deleuze argues, "express" the former while the former is "implicated" in its modes.

What emerges from the repeated saying of being is a univocal saying of *difference*: "Being is said in a single and same sense of everything of which it is said, but that of which it is said differs: it is said of difference itself."[5] No other metaphysics is needed apart from what the philosophical tradition has offered, univocally, since its beginning; an "other" metaphysics would be merely equivocal, and, as such, inactive and non-affirmative. Rather, what is needed, and what Deleuze realizes by joining voices with Spinoza, is an accenting of the univocal saying of being toward "difference itself [*différence elle-même*]"; what is needed is an ensemble of discordant voices within the otherwise tonal chorus of western metaphysics.

Before considering its Spinozistic details, it is helpful to begin by enumerating some of the general characteristics of a Deleuzian univocal metaphysics of difference. In this way, we are able to recognize what Deleuze borrows from Spinoza; we can also appreciate the ways Deleuze departs from Spinoza's philosophy. In order, we will consider the following aspects of Deleuze's metaphysics: activity; immanence; affective positivity (or, more simply, affirmativeness); actuality; critical historicity; and specificity (or, particularity). The remainder of section one is given to defining these features of Deleuze's thought.

Recalling the language with which we began, namely, that for Deleuze philosophy is always a matter of *doing* philosophy, another way to describe a univocal metaphysics of difference is as an *active* ontology. This idea of "activity" is variously articulated in Deleuze's corpus, and it goes by different names relative to the philosopher with whom Deleuze is presently engaged. In the context of Deleuze's reading of Spinoza, "activity" is said in terms of "expression." It was also claimed, to begin, that an active philosophical ontology in the Deleuzian sense is something other than a methodologically reflective philosophy. Deleuze's idea of philosophy as a form of activity—in *What is Philosophy?* (1994), Deleuze and Guattari describe philosophy as a "[l]aying out, inventing, and creating" of concepts[6]—is not a matter of a thinking that reflects upon *how* it thinks. Equally, we misread Deleuze's description of the power of Spinoza's philosophy, which is "measured by the concepts it creates, or whose meaning it alters, concepts that impose a new set of divisions on things and actions,"[7] when we treat the creation of concepts as a "methodologically" separate matter apart from the philosophical thought conducted through those concepts.

What is needed is a methodological principle, or, better, an idea of philosophy, that is immediately self-reflective. In reference to Spinoza's method, Deleuze writes of such a self-reflective idea, "[a] true idea [in Spinoza's sense] is, from the viewpoint of its form, an idea of an idea; from the viewpoint of its matter, it is an adequate idea." The "idea of an idea" by which Spinoza proceeds philosophically is a "reflexive idea"; or, in Deleuze's reformulation of Spinoza, a self-reflexive idea is "expressive." Philosophy, then, is a principled practice guided by self-reflexive "adequate" or "expressive" ideas; further, it is an active, immanent practice when it proceeds by such ideas since it is then undivided in its idea (of itself) and its thought (of itself). Without such a principle or idea, philosophy becomes divided from itself and falls into inactive non-immanence.

As noted, the correlate, in Spinoza, of an "immediately reflective idea" is what is called an "adequate idea." Spinoza defines this term in Part II of the *Ethics*: "Every idea which in us is absolute, that is, adequate and perfect, is true."[8] An "adequate idea" is immediately reflective—and this is what Spinoza signals with the language of "absolute," "perfect," and "true"—as the thought in God of what constitutes the essence of the human mind.[9] The content of an adequate idea is thought, and thought "perfectly" and "truly" defines the being and activity of the human mind.

If thought conducted through adequate ideas is immanent and active, it follows that the thought of inadequate ideas is non-immanent and inactive. Active, adequate knowledge, and passive, inadequate knowledge give rise, in Spinoza, to positive affectivity and negative affectivity, respectively; or, more simply, to pleasure and sadness.[10] Deleuze, in turn, translates this Spinozistic pair into the language of "joyful and sad" passions.[11] All told, an immanent active philosophy is one that is affirmative and joyous; and, it is a philosophy practiced through an idea, whether called "adequate" or "expressive," that is self-reflexive in being both thought *by* and that is the thought *of* such a philosophy. Spinoza stands out from the history of metaphysics, then, not by equivocally departing from its univocity, but by orienting such univocity toward positivity and affirmation. All told, according to Deleuze, Spinoza makes philosophical thought a "truly expressive and affirmative proposition."[12]

Consider, in this regard, the following two Propositions from Part III of Spinoza's *Ethics*: "The active states of the mind arise only from adequate ideas; its passive states depend solely on inadequate ideas,"[13] and, "[a]mong all the emotions that are related to the mind insofar as it is active, there are none that are not related to pleasure or desire."[14] Together, these two propositions link the adequacy of ideas to the activity of thought to the positivity of affect. In this way, as Deleuze writes in his letter on Spinoza to Reda Bensmaïa, Spinoza covers each part of the "philosophical trinity": "concepts, or new ways of thinking; percepts, or new ways of seeing and construing; and affects, or new ways of feeling."[15] Together, these three elements, "*get things moving*," that is, they activate philosophy. Spinoza's tripartite philosophy is also "philosophy as opera";[16] though, as we have suggested, it is philosophical opera sung in a distinctly minor key.

Still, we must extend these Spinozistic claims and situate them at the level of metaphysics. Or, to state the same in terms of philosophical methodology, we must translate the language of "adequate ideas" and "positive affectivity" into methodological principles to guide philosophy in its thinking of the highest and fullest order of being. If an expressive *idea*, in Deleuze, is an idea the thought of which coincides with the act of thinking it, the question to be asked, now, is what constitutes an expressive *philosophy*?

In the above language of "creating concepts" from *What is Philosophy?*, an expressive philosophy employs concepts whose creation is inseparable from their use in thought. It is possible to engage in "both" practices, namely, the creation and thought of philosophical concepts, because "both" occur on the same "plane of immanence." As Cliff Stagoll explains this notion, a "plane of immanence" is the surface-like context of a concept that contains every one of its permutations; the same plane also holds every force that shapes and (re)defines the concept: "The plane [of immanence] can only be defined in terms of the concepts operating upon it, and the concept can only have meaning relative to the forces at work on the plane."[17] The coincidence between a concept and the milieu that contains all of its manifestations means that the creation of a concept provides a whole context for further thought of the same: all thought of a concept is already present in the context of its creation.

It is through a plane of immanence that the philosophical creation of a concept is equated with the thought of that concept: creation (of concepts) and thought (of concepts) are actively immanent to one another on the same plane. An expressive *philosophy* is, then, the thinking of the creation and of the thought of concepts, which is to say, it is the thinking of the plane of immanence as the milieu on which "both" activities occur as one. In the philosophical thought of the plane of immanence, univocal metaphysics is the thought of difference—the activities of creation and thought are, after all, distinguishable even if they are not actually distinct—and sameness. There is sameness, or, univocity, in thinking the plane of immanence because, as equal activities on the same plane, concept-creation and concept-thought coincide. In section three, below, we will match these Deleuzian claims to Spinoza's idea of a divine attribute as it relates in the so-called 'third kind of knowledge' to the idea of God. The latter is an adequate or expressive idea at the level of a philosophical metaphysics; and, the affirmative, positive affect that stems from thinking the idea of God is the joyful passion of beatitude.

The immanent, active character of Deleuzian metaphysics can also be shown by way of its difference from Kantian critical philosophy. To turn to Kant at this point is not without rationale: Deleuze refers to his own philosophy in Kantian terms as a "transcendental empiricism," that is, one in which the conditions of the possibility of the empirical determination of intuitions are transcendentally equivalent to intuitions as thereby determined.[18] By "empiricizing" Kant's "transcendental idealism," Deleuze makes concepts, which Kant treats as the conditions of the *possibility* of empirical determination, into conditions of the *actuality* of the empirical.[19] Note that this last idea re-expresses, in Kantian terms, the above point concerning a plane of immanence containing all *actual*, and not merely possible, articulations of a created concept.

Deleuze's transcendental empiricism also draws Kant's critical philosophy close to its Hegelian successor;[20] sharpening, as it were, the critique of the latter by the former. Speculative thought, which in Hegel constitutes its object in the act of thinking it, becomes for Deleuze an affirmation of affectivity. There is receptivity in Deleuze's active philosophy: it is a matter of the body being affected by the myriad sensations of experience (or, in Spinozistic terms, the human mind affectively "receives" a God-granted succession of ideas).[21] Active philosophical thought, then, does not create its object as in Hegelian speculation, but affirms its object through the sensations it affects in the body. In this regard, note that the highest joy in Spinoza's philosophy is beatitude: the pleasure of blessedness, and thankfulness at receiving God's gift of life and nature.

Once Kantian sensible receptivity is transformed in this way by Deleuze into a logic of affect and sensation, the concepts that otherwise determine the (mere) possibility of experience become the actual ideas of active philosophical thought. The following, while critical of Kantian transcendentalism, nevertheless points toward a reclamation of Kant to Deleuze's own project of philosophical immanence: "When the subject and the object [. . .] are taken as universal subject or object in general to which immanence itself is attributed, then the transcendental is completely denatured and merely reduplicates the empirical (as in Kant) while immanence is deformed and ends up being contained in the transcendent."[22]

If Kantian critical philosophy is to be made affirmative and active, then the transcendental must not be conceptualized in terms of the transcendent;[23] further, the empirical must be treated as metaphysically equivalent with the transcendental. This last task is accomplished, as Deleuze here suggests, by way of a non-general conception of subjectivity—Levi Bryant, following Deleuze, argues that this as a matter of "temporalizing," and thereby specifying, the Kantian transcendental subject.[24] In turn, immanence is not to be identified with the "conditionless determination" of transcendental ideas and made an attribute of the human being *qua* general subject. In the same vein, "immanence" is not to be treated as an attribute of a philosophical concept, that is, as one possible "mode" in which such a concept can be treated. Rather, and, here again the Spinozism of Deleuze's thought is evident, immanence must be treated as the actuality of an active philosophy as it expresses itself through its thinking of its created concepts.

In still further Spinozistic fashion, Deleuze argues that the immanent self-expression of the activity of philosophy must be "individuated" along the lines of the specific, modal expression of substance monism. Above, we saw this same idea cast in terms of "individuating differences" or "intrinsic modalities" being said of difference itself. Relative to Kant (or Descartes), this same point can be made in terms of the rational subject in general being replaced in Deleuze by the specific, or "molecular,"[25] subject with its range of specific sensations.[26]

Kant lacks an active idea of philosophy. It is from such a lack that Kant is led to a merely critical, rather than to a critico-expressive, philosophy. An active *idea* of philosophy, in Kant, would be one in which the highest employments of thought—those to which we are impelled by reason—are transcendentally determinative on the same order, though not in the same way, as are the conditions of possible experience. Transcendental ideas of reason as regulative principles of speculative thought remain bound, in the logic of the "*als ob* [as if]," to the difference between what is conditionally possible and what is determinately real: "Reason is therefore the faculty which says: 'Everything happens as if. . . ,'" from which it follows, according to Deleuze, that transcendental ideas do not determine that the "totality of conditions" are *actually* given in the object.[27]

Kant rests assured in the "*als ob*" status of the ideas of reason by securing them through analogy with the pure concepts of the understanding: as the transcendental ideas of the highest employments of reason are to philosophical systematicity, so are the pure concepts of the understanding to the complete conditions of a pure, empirical intuition.[28] Yet, the figure of analogy, while seemingly uniting the disparate matters of rational ideas and discursive concepts, in fact equivocates on their difference in the name of a univocal metaphysics. Without pursuing this point at length, since the inadequacies of an analogical philosophy will occupy us in section two, below, here it will suffice to note that the specification of transcendental ideas through analogy with concepts of the understanding leaves the former indeterminate. Just as the latter provide merely the conditions of the *possibility* rather than of the *actuality* of empirical determination, so transcendental ideas only regulate the highest employments of reason. A philosophy practiced through indeterminate ideas, as Kant's is as guided by transcendental ideas, is non-specific, and to that extent inactive and non-affirmative.

Kant's lack of a specific, immanent idea of philosophy, that is, one that is thought in particular *by* and that is the particular thought *of* philosophy, follows from his merely critical attitude toward the history of metaphysics. In order to assess critically the validity of traditional metaphysical claims, Kant insists that we must first interrupt the metaphysician; here is Kant's programmatic announcement from the *Prolegomena*, "My intention is to convince all of those who find it worthwhile to occupy themselves with metaphysics that it is unavoidably necessary to suspend their work for the present [. . .] and [. . .] to ask the question, 'whether such a thing as metaphysics is even possible at all.'"[29] Whatever findings follow from Kant's critical philosophy, and whatever answer is given to this last question concerning the possibility of metaphysics, it will be extrinsic to the activity of thought since it will have been extracted from metaphysics whilst suspended.

Though it is Deleuze's engagement with Spinoza that ultimately concerns us, it is useful to consider Kantian critique at some length, as we have, because it is indicative of the critical character of Deleuze's own engagement with the history of metaphysics. Further, it is not Spinoza's metaphysics *per se* that interests

Deleuze in *Expressionism in Philosophy: Spinoza* (1968), but how such metaphysics relates to and informs the practice of philosophy. As the original French title of the book indicates—"*Spinoza et le problème de l'expression* [Spinoza and the problem of expression]"—Spinoza's metaphysics of infinite substance and modes reformulates the univocal saying of being, and, in so doing, problematizes traditional philosophy. Kant, for all of his critical modernism, belongs unproblematically to this tradition in his merely analogical thinking of difference within his own philosophical practice. Spinoza, by contrast, does not equivocate on the topic of difference; Spinoza thinks difference univocally by absorbing the *figure* of analogy into the immediacy of the self-reflexive adequate idea.

To begin, we described Deleuze's active philosophical ontology as a "critical metaphysics": a moniker with clear affinities to Kant's critical philosophy. We also noted, above, that Deleuzian critique differs from its Kantian predecessor. The proximity and distance between Kant's philosophy and Deleuze's lends the latter its actively historical character. Critique as an historicized activity follows from Deleuze's idea of philosophy as a creation of concepts, which, contrary to its name, is not a free contrivance. As John Rajchman explains the limits imposed upon an active philosophy, "[the philosophical "fabrication" of concepts] comes in response to problems that [. . .] are constantly being recast, reformulated, or 'dissolved' from new perspectives."[30]

The history of metaphysics is the record of these reformulations. Each philosopher presents a new perspective on certain basic problems that s/he inherits from the tradition; and, the philosophical activity of creating concepts, in Deleuze's sense, is practiced always in the context of these successive reformulations. Each created philosophical concept is formed in relation to the history of philosophy, but it is formed in relation to an *active* form of that history, that is, the ongoing history of actively formulating and reformulating basic philosophical problems.

Deleuze forges the concept of "expression" in Spinoza in the historico-active context of Descartes and Leibniz.[31] By such means, Deleuze follows both Spinoza and Leibniz who "rediscovered" the concept of expression from a "rather hidden, and rather forbidden" philosophical history.[32] Creating the concept of "expression" in this way, Deleuze succeeds in practicing philosophy both actively and critico-historically. An active ontology is at the same time a critical metaphysics insofar as it is conducted through created, yet also historically situated, concepts, that is, concepts created on the plane of immanence formed around a particular philosopher: for example, Spinoza in relation to early modern rationalism. Such "planar" or "situated" philosophical activity endows the created concept (of expression) with the character of the formulations and reformulations of the problems that define Spinoza's philosophy. Thus, the concept functions as a critique of the various solutions to those problems; recall, again, that the French title of Deleuze's book is, Spinoza et *la problème* de l'expression.

The foregoing clarifies how Deleuze's (Spinozistic) metaphysics is histori-cally critical of the philosophical tradition; further, it shows how Deleuze cri-tiques traditional metaphysics without succumbing to Kant's historicism and falling into inactivity and non-immanence. Yet, and despite our brief discussion of Deleuze's idea of a "plane of immanence," what is missing is an explanation of how philosophy might be a general practice conducted in an immanent fash-ion on its own created concepts. A concept, like "expression," which is formed in the context of the problems that define Spinozistic metaphysics, risks being extrinsic to any other practice of philosophy once it is applied in a different mi-lieu. How can a created philosophical concept be actively critical, and thus par-ticular, while also being immanent to the very practice of philosophy, and, as such, generally applicable? More pointedly, how can a Spinozistic concept cre-ated in the specific context of Leibniz and Descartes inform the highest em-ployment of philosophy in its thinking of being?

In going back over the history of metaphysics, what Deleuze is looking for is a concept of problematic status, which thus reflects the ongoing process of formulating and reformulating basic philosophical problems; a concept that is affirmative in its mode, and, as such, demonstrative of the creative impulse in the activity of philosophy. "Expression," as Deleuze derives it from Spinoza's philosophy, is just such a critico-historical and creative concept. "Expression" is problematic, and thus critico-historical, precisely because it does not appear, as such, in Spinoza's philosophy;[33] and, it is creative in occupying an articulated plane of immanence. An expressive *philosophy*, then, is one in which the meta-physical concept of "expression" is placed in non-figurative relation to the activ-ity that thinks it: thinking metaphysically, and what is thought in such thinking, are in Spinoza different *expressions* of the same concept and activity.[34] Again, to realize such an expressive philosophy, the long-standing tradition of analogical-ly figuring the relationship between different orders of thought must be trans-formed into a single, univocal practice.

This last point returns us to the claim that Deleuze's active, critical meta-physics is something different than a methodologically reflective philosophy. Above, we noted that methodological reflections introduce into philosophy a degree of inactivity and de-intensification—they make philosophy joyless and sad. Section two, below, argues that a dispassionate philosophy is one that fig-ures the relationship between what is thought in metaphysics and the act of met-aphysical thinking analogically. The first chapter of *Difference and Repetition* explores the link between metaphysical analogy and an inactive, non-immanent philosophy through a careful study of analogy in Aristotelian metaphysics. Fol-lowing Deleuze, we will trace a critical path through Aristotle's equivocal use of analogy in order to arrive, finally, at the disanalogous univocity of Spinoza's "different" metaphysics.

2. The Equivocal Logic of Analogical Difference

Aristotelian metaphysics is premised on the doctrine that "being [*to on*]" is "said in many ways"; this idea is stated and defined at a number of spots in the *Metaphysics*. Initially, in Book Delta, Chapter 7, Aristotle writes, "Being, too, means either an accidental or an essential being [*to on legetai to men kata sumbebēkos, to de kath' auto*]";[35] and, the "essential [*kath' auto*]" meanings of "being" are said according to the "categories [*katēgorias*]": whatness [*ti estin*]; quality [*to poion*]; quantity [*to poson*]; relation [*pros ti*], etc.[36] Subsequently, Aristotle begins Book Zeta, Chapter 1, with a direct restatement of the plural saying-of-being: "Being is said in many ways [*to on legetai pollachōs*]"; and, continuing, he reiterates the earlier point that the multiple sayings of being are arrayed according to a "categorical" structure, that is, whatness, quality, quantity, etc.[37]

In restating the categorical structure of the saying-of-being, Aristotle adds that there is a primary sense in which it is said, namely, "whatness [*ti estin*]," which denotes, "substance [*ousia*]."[38] Aristotle also explains that while "primary" has several meanings, "substance" is primary in all senses of the term. Aristotle's reason for this is two-fold: first, no categorical saying-of-being can occur without reference to substance, that is, the categories are metaphysically dependent upon substance. Second, substance is primary in the sense of being metaphysically independent: substance subsists on its own, without metaphysical dependence on any of the categories.[39] Ever since G. E. L. Owen introduced the terminology into the secondary literature, this relation between substance and the categories has been referred to as a "focal" relation.[40] What Owen's phrase is meant to capture is the way the categories all "focus" in on substance as the primary way in which being is said. In turn, being, said as "substance," is "focally" projected through the categories as if through a multi-sided lens.

Questions of methodology enter Aristotelian metaphysics at the point where its order is specified, that is, at the point where Aristotle indicates that the categorical sayings of being are "focally" arrayed around substance. A designation of the structure of being is of a different status than being as it is thereby described: the focal character of the order of being is not, itself, part of its own metaphysical order. Though the language of "focal relation" is not native to his philosophy, Aristotle writes in an extra-metaphysical vein whenever he reflects and comments on the arrangement of categories relative to substance.

What logic informs Aristotle's philosophical reflections on the order of being? What is the principle of his philosophical description of being as categorically and "focally" arranged around substance? Since being is ordered according to the "logos" of an identical, unified "saying [*legein*]" of being (as substance), and a plural saying-of-being (as categories), we would initially think to answer such questions by citing this very same "logos" as the basis for Aristotle's philosophical reflection on the order of being. The logic of Aristotelian metaphysics would then be identical to the logos of being itself.

Yet, it is not by a logic of identity that we arrive at this conclusion. The form of the preceding argument is not an *identification* of being with the philosophical thought of being; rather, it is an *analogy*: as the logos of the many ways in which being is said is to the order of substance and the categories, so, the logos of the "focal order" of those sayings is to Aristotle's philosophy of being. The need to employ an analogous argument to move from the structure of being to a philosophy of being suggests that analogy is metaphysically basic; or, at least, that analogy is more basic than identity since the identification of the order of being with metaphysics *follows from* an analogical argument that proceeds from the former to the latter. What this implicit appeal to analogy suggests is that the logic of Aristotle's metaphysics might differ from the one that governs the "one-and-many" order of being.

By reading Aristotle's metaphysics according to a logic of identity, we tend to emphasize substance and sameness to the difference and plurality of the categories. We are also led to a particular conception of the "scientific" character of Aristotle's philosophy. The presumption is that a science must adhere to certain systematic requirements, even when it proceeds "endoxically," as Aristotle tends to do, by collecting and collating various opinions on the topic of study.[41] The requirements Aristotle stipulates for a science, which include unity, the possession of its own first principles, and its having a unique subject matter,[42] are granted priority over the plural, diverse findings of the empirical method.

Finally, the presentation of Aristotle's metaphysics is assumed to be dictated by the requirements of a scientific philosophy. *Metaphysics* Book Gamma becomes the starting-point and textual basis for the rest of the book; and, it is here, at the beginning of chapter three, that Aristotle argues for the unity of the "science [*epistēmē*]" of being on the grounds that "being [*to on*]" is "one [*to hen*]."[43] It is only subsequently, and three books later, that the manifold saying-of-being "in many ways" is introduced.[44]

Reading the order of Aristotle's science back into its content, the bi-directionality of the focal relation—from substance to the categories, and from the categories to substance—is effectively decided in favor of unity and substance; the plural saying-of-being is made secondary and derivative. Thus, the (methodological) idea we hold of *how* a philosophy is to be conducted shapes *what* we understand to be thought by such a philosophy: a scientific philosophy governed by a logic of identity thinks substance and sameness before it thinks, if at all, the categories and difference.

By contrast, once we recognize that the logic of the philosophy of being is not identical with the order of being, and this is what Deleuze argues for in the first chapter of *Difference and Repetition*, then the plural, categorical saying of being emerges from the sameness and unity of the scientific saying of being as one and substance. Deleuze, in short, detects in Aristotle a saying-of-being that is both univocal and differentiated; a saying-of-being that is both same and different. In order to reveal this univocal metaphysics of difference, the identical logic that has, so far, guided our reading of Aristotelian metaphysics must give way to a logic of analogy.

As the "focal-point" of the categorical ways of saying being, substance is always restated in however many ways being is said. Here is Deleuze, commenting on the consequences of such focal arrangement for Aristotelian metaphysics: "[G]eneric or categorical difference remains a difference [. . .] and does not collapse into simple diversity or otherness. [And] [a]n identical or common concept [. . .] still subsists."[45] The question to ask is how persistent the "common concept" of genus and species is in Aristotle; and, accordingly, whether there is a way to retrieve categorical difference from substantial sameness.

The focal order of being can be treated in one of two ways. Either we begin from the idea of a philosophical metaphysics as a science and accent univocity and substance; or, we proceed "endoxically"—linking individual instances to one another analogically—so that difference is given equal voice to sameness. The following signals Deleuze's intention to read Aristotle in the second of these two ways according to the logic of analogy: "The two characteristics of the concept of being—having no more than a distributive common sense and having a hierarchical primary sense [. . .] also show that the equivocity of being is quite particular: it is a matter of analogy."[46]

With the figure of analogy, equivocity intrudes into univocal metaphysics. The "two characteristics" of the concept of being—categorical difference and substantial sameness—are analogically, equivocally related. Such intra-metaphysical equivocation occurs, in Aristotle, because of the higher order equivocity in his efforts to compose a philosophical system.

Though it discards the principle of identity that assumes philosophy and its object are correlated one-to-one, an analogical metaphysics nevertheless leaves philosophy non-immanent by introducing into it distinct levels of thought. The analogy on which Aristotelian metaphysics is founded—and, on which it founders—is that the scientific unity of metaphysics as the thought of being *qua* being is like the thought of the focal arrangement of the categories around unitary substance. To put the same point simply, the analogy that motivates Aristotelian metaphysics equivocates on the genitive in "the thought *of* being": the thought *of* being is the being *of* thought.

While closer to univocity in operating fully within the domain of thought or the "saying" of being, Aristotle's analogical metaphysics remains equivocal in comparing different ways of thinking the same topic, for example, the idea of metaphysics as a science and what is thought under this designation is mediated through an implicit reference to the common thought of being. Nevertheless, Deleuze finds in Aristotle "a new chance for the philosophy of difference";[47] and, he discerns this "new chance" in Aristotelian analogy despite its equivocal comparison of two different orders of thought. What sense can be made of this claim, given Deleuze's otherwise critical remarks on analogy in *Difference and Repetition*?

To answer this last question, we must return to the issue, raised above, of the prevalence of the genus-species structure in Aristotle's philosophy. The following, from Deleuze, suggests an exception to this order, and it does so in the form of an "immanent" relation between plural difference and single substance:

"These terms (categories) need not have an equal relation to being: it is enough
that each has an *internal* relation to being."[48] There is an internal order to Aristotelian metaphysics, and Deleuze here raises the possibility of displacing the
"equal relation" of the generic categories with this other, immanent relation.
Given the context within which Deleuze raises this possibility, such an immanent metaphysical relation is somehow figured in the form of the analogy.

***

As Mary Hesse points out, "analogy [*to analogon*]" is usually used by Aristotle
in reference to intra-generic relations. In its normal usage, the specific differences of individuals or species within a genus are said to be "analogically" related to one another, as in the analogical physiologies of different organisms within
the genus "animal," for example, "nail to hoof, hand to claw, and scale to feath-
er."[49] Still, there are moments in the Aristotelian corpus where the logic of analogy applies across different genera. Hesse's example of an inter-generic analogy
comes from the *Posterior Analytics* where Aristotle gives the mathematical axiom "take equals from equals and equals remain," and shows how it applies, analogically, to the separate mathematical sciences of arithmetic and geometry.[50]
The problem with an analogy applied across genera, or, as in the case of relations of numerical and geometric equality, between different mathematical sciences, is that a shared context for the related terms seems to be missing; or, as
Hesse puts the point, "there is no property in common" between a number and a
line segment.[51]

There are a few exceptional passages in Aristotle's texts that complicate this
last claim; these passages suggest a "common property" that holds between inter-generically, analogically related terms. Given the rarity with which Aristotle
refers to such a relation, and, given its divergence from the commonality that
underlies related terms within a single genus, this analogical relation is easily
overlooked. In the example of the relation between numbers, on the one hand,
and line segments, on the other, the arithmetical character of the former does not
rule out its analogical comparison to the geometry of the latter. Here is Hesse,
writing in reference to this example from the *Posterior Analytics*: "Nothing is
said about the individual terms other than that they are relata of a common relation."[52] An inter-mathematical "common relation" replaces the generic common
bond that holds together different species: a number, analogically related to a
geometrical figure, becomes a relata of a relation that extends between two genera.

An inter-generic analogy is of metaphysical consequence because it disturbs
the regular two-fold way in which individuals, for Aristotle, are identified. Typically, individuals are identified by the specific differences that define them as
what they are relative to the other members of their genus; individual identity is
further constituted through the quality, quantity, etc. that determines the being's
substantial "whatness." Terms or individuals whose metaphysical identity is
normally constituted by intra-generic specific differences are in certain rare instances differentiated from themselves when they are related, analogically, to

individuals of another genus. A different difference is introduced into the being of specific individuals; it is a difference that is not specific to the genus under which they fall; nor is such a difference structured according to the focal logic of substance and categories.

The logic of analogy, at least in those cases in which it is operative between one genus and another, alters the standard Aristotelian notion of sameness and difference. The generic basis for sameness is replaced by the common relationality of two analogical terms: the specific basis for difference is replaced by the inexactitude of the analogy, that is, number as number is still something other, and is non-identical with, number as a relata of a particular ratio or increment. Thus, in analogical relations between inter-generic terms, we seem to find an Aristotelian metaphysics of difference and sameness where the latter is in no way given priority over the former. The following, which Hesse quotes from the *Posterior Analytics*, signals this alternate metaphysical relation: "The cause is different for lines and for numbers, and yet it is the same; different if the lines are considered as lines, and the same if they are considered as exhibiting a given increment [*allo gar aition hen grammais kai arithmois kai to auto ge, he men gramme, allo, he d'echon auxēsin toiandi, to auto*]."[53]

Unsurprisingly, Deleuze is interested in these same rare "relational" instances of Aristotelian analogy, that is, analogy not as a feature of intra-generic specific differences, but as the inter-generic form of common relations. In a footnote added to the above-cited passage from *Difference and Repetition* that explains the equivocity in terms of analogy, Deleuze uses "*pros hen* [in relation to one]" to describe an "analogy" between generically different terms: "The *pros hen* are said in relation to a unique term. This is like a common sense [. . .] [that] forms only a distributive unity [. . .] not a collective, explicit and unique unity such as we find in genera."[54] Concluding the passage, Deleuze agrees, on these grounds, with the scholastic terminology of "analogy of proportionality [*analogie de proportionnalité*]" to name the commonality between relata that are otherwise different (as existing in different genera, or as the objects of different scientific study).[55]

Whereas Aristotle, at least in the *Posterior Analytics*, and Hesse in her interpretation of Aristotelian analogy, restrict the "relational" analogical structure to mathematics, Deleuze argues that "this analogy must not be understood in the strict mathematical sense."[56] Rather, Deleuze states that this relational, analogical structure runs through Aristotelian metaphysics as an unacknowledged undercurrent; and this, despite the fact, as Deleuze reminds us, that "[w]e know that Aristotle himself did not speak of analogy with regard to being."[57]

The key to realizing the wide metaphysical significance of inter-generic analogy in Aristotle is given in an *active* conception of being: "Being is first, *in act*, analogy of proportionality"[58]—and all thinking, whether *of* metaphysics as a science or *within* the science of metaphysics, is an activity. This recalls the above point that for Deleuze a philosophical metaphysics is and must be an *active* metaphysics practiced on immanent concepts. In more familiar Aristotelian terms: if there is equivocity when being is *said* as the focal relation between quantity, quality, etc., and substance, then it is only in the *saying* of being in terms of analogical relationality that metaphysics is univocal. What is said in the univocal *saying* of being is the relation of analogy on which traditional metaphysics equivocates.

Ultimately, though, the thinking of analogical relationality proves unfit to serve as the methodological principle by which an immanent, active metaphysics is practicable. After reviewing Aristotle's metaphysics, Deleuze claims that analogy, "rests essentially upon a certain complicity between generic and specific differences";[59] and this, despite the fact, as we have seen, that analogical relations of sameness and difference are not bound to the genus-species order. Now, of such inter-generic, analogical "common relations," Deleuze argues that they are no more than "the middle regions of genus and species in terms of mediation and generality—identity of the concept in general and analogy of the most general concepts."[60] The genus-species structure, then, is absolutely pervasive in Aristotle's metaphysics; it informs even the "other" metaphysical relation of inter-generic proportionate analogy; in so doing, it leaves the thought of this other relation inactive.

In the above example of the analogical relation between numbers and line segments, the specific differences of the relata within an analogical relation still depends upon the generic identification of the terms: it is only against the backdrop of number *as number* that number *as analogical relata* of a line segment gains its different identity. Hence, the "common relations" forged between inter-generically terms depend upon the very order of genus and species from which they seem to depart: this is the implication of Deleuze's point that such relations are "complicitous" with generic and specific difference. Once more, then, Aristotle equivocates on relations of difference in thinking them by a distinct, separate logic.

Analogical identity and difference is borrowed from generic (and specific) identity and difference. What Aristotle's metaphysics does not admit of is the active thinking of analogical relationality itself, and this because the common form of such relationality is not immanent to the relation. Above, we anticipated this same conclusion by showing how a thinking through analogies, while seemingly immanent and univocal in overcoming the logic of identity, is actually non-immanent and equivocal in maintaining different levels of thought. Now, this conclusion has been specified by way of the equivocal difference between intra-generic relations and the "common relations" of inter-generic analogy.

Translating this conclusion into Deleuze's language from *Difference and Repetition*: the "individuating differences" of specific, analogically related terms, for instance, the specific difference of a number from itself in the above mathematical example from the *Posterior Analytics*, must be said univocally of being without "mediation."[61] The result of such unmediated, non-figurative saying of specific difference is the univocal saying of being as difference itself: "With univocity, however, it is not the differences which are and must be. It is being which is Difference, in the sense that it is said of difference."[62] Insofar as the specific saying of difference is mediated in the figure of analogy, difference cannot thereby be said univocally of difference itself.

In failing to say individuating difference univocally, and thus as difference itself, a metaphysics conducted through analogy is to that extent equivocal and inactive. Arguably, the same conclusion would follow for *any* mediated or figurative metaphysics. There is, however, a preponderance of analogy in the history of metaphysics; as such, it is the key figuration for Deleuze to overcome in realizing a Spinozistic affirmative univocity. So, for instance, in criticizing Leibniz's symbolic figuration of expression in *Expressionism in Philosophy*, Deleuze focuses on Leibniz's use of the logic of analogy to "expres[s] different types of unity relative to the multiplicities they involve." The result, in Leibniz, of this appeal to analogy is that "[s]uch a symbolic philosophy is necessarily a philosophy of equivocal expressions."[63] What is needed if the long history of metaphysical equivocity from Aristotle to Leibniz is to be corrected is a non-figurative means of thinking difference. Deleuze finds just such a means by creating the concept of "expression" on the plane of immanence called "Spinoza."

3. Spinoza's Two-fold, Immanent *Ethics*

Concluding his discussion of analogy in Aristotle in the first chapter of *Difference and Repetition*, Deleuze offers a brief history of metaphysics as comprised of three moments; it is the second of these three moments that interest us in the present context: "With the second moment, Spinoza marks a considerable progress."[64] Part of this "progress," as already noted, is that Spinoza's metaphysics is affirmative; in this way, it marks an advance over past metaphysics, which have tended to treat univocal being as "neutral or indifferent."[65] Such "affirmativeness," Deleuze now explains, is a matter of Spinoza working against "the Cartesian theory substance thoroughly imbued with analogy."[66]

In place of Descartes' analogical theory of substance, Spinoza "organizes a remarkable division [of ontology] into substance, attributes and modes."[67] What makes this ontology noteworthy is that it treats attributes as "absolutely common to substance and the modes" without thereby undermining the essential difference between the two.[68] Commonality, or sameness, and difference are both present in Spinoza's ontology; they are neither identified with one another, nor are they set in analogical relation to one another.

The non-figurative and non-identical result of Spinoza's idea of attributive commonality is that the attributes, "behave like real qualitatively different senses which relate to substance as if to a single and same designated," while substance "behaves like an ontologically unique sense in relation to the modes that express it."[69] The attributes themselves are for Spinoza different and the same: they are different insofar as they are aspects of the infinitely plural modes; they are the same insofar as attributes are all expressions of single substance. The "commonality" between the modal and substantial attributes is, further, non-analogical. Ontologically, all attributes are different expressions of God; and, God, as Spinoza understand Him, does not stand in analogical relation to world-ly phenomena nor to the characteristics of such phenomena.[70] As expressions of the being of God, then, modal attributes, on the one hand, and substantial attrib-utes, on the other, are not related to one another according to a logic of analogy.

Finally, modal and substantial attributes are non-identical. While attributes are "common" to substance and modes, Deleuze insists that "substance and modes do not have the same essence."[71] The "essential" difference between (at-tributes of) modes and (attributes of) substance is simply a restatement of the expressive difference in God Himself: God is different from Himself in express-ing himself modally (as he is the same as Himself in expressing himself substan-tially).

Spinoza's non-analogous, three-fold ontology occupies Deleuze throughout *Expressionism in Philosophy*. Here, too, Deleuze explores Spinoza's metaphys-ics relative to the question of how philosophy might be practiced affirmatively and actively. In this regard, Deleuze's interest in Spinoza in the *Expressionism* book departs both from *Difference and Repetition*, where Deleuze's concern is to compose a different philosophical ontology, and from the *Ethics*, where Spi-noza never directly raises the question of how to practice philosophy.

In other respects, *Expressionism in Philosophy* and *Difference and Repeti-tion*, which both appeared the same year in the French press, are companion texts: just as Spinoza is credited in the latter with inaugurating an advanced, "second moment" in the history of metaphysics, so in the former Deleuze high-lights Spinoza's difference from Aquinas, who represents the "first moment" in that history. Further, just as in *Difference and Repetition* where Spinoza's "pro-gress" in metaphysics is measured in terms of his overcoming an analogical fig-uration of substance, so in the *Expressionism* book, Spinoza is distanced from Aquinas and Aristotle for his non-analogical metaphysics.

Given the Aristotelianism of his metaphysics, and thus the tradition of using analogy to argue from one order of being to another, Aquinas treats divine at-tributes as analogously related to creaturely life: as omnibenevolence as a divine attribute is to the being of God, so goodness is to the worldly order created by God. The issue with Thomistic analogy is not that it diminishes divinity; nor, is the problem that it confuses creator with creation. Rather, as Deleuze presents Aquinas' "analogical" method for thinking of divine attributes, "qualities at-tributed to God imply no community of form between divine substance and creatures, but only an analogy, a 'congruence' of proportion or proportionali-ty."[72] Above, in the context of the history of metaphysics Deleuze offers in the first chapter of *Difference and Repetition*, we noted the association of (Aristote-lian) "analogy of proportionality" with the medieval tradition; here, in the *Ex-pressionism* book, Deleuze identifies this notion with Thomistic metaphysics and specifies the analogical, proportional relation as one that obtains between divine attributes and the defining *differentiae* of creaturely beings.

While appropriately non-identical—Aquinas does not use the characteristics common between them to equate God as creator with His creation—

nevertheless, an "analogical proportionality" leads to sameness being granted priority over difference. Spinoza, according to Deleuze, overcomes this problem in Aquinas by altering analogy: "The significance of Spinozism may here be judged by the way in which it inverts the problem";[73] and this, in order to avoid conflating the very matters analogy is introduced to distinguish, namely, the essence—and essential difference—between God's expressive presence in all of creation, and God's substantial essence as singularly creative or expressive.

To avoid this confusion of essences, which is really a misunderstanding of the essence of God, Spinoza abandons a figurative conception of relation; and, he does so by denying the Scholastic wont to conceive the relative difference between creation and creator quantitatively. Divine attributes are not simply quantitatively greater instances of characteristics that creatures possess in lesser form, e.g., divine omnipotence is not creaturely power cast on a mass scale. Accordingly, there is no way to move by proportionate analogy from the smallness of the mundane to the grandeur of the divine. Rather, there is a qualitative difference between aspects of creation and attributes of the creator, and this because there is an essential, expressive difference within God. Spinoza, then, effectively reverses the order of analogical thought; or, as Deleuze puts the point, Spinoza "insists on the identity of form between creatures and God, while permitting no confusion of essence."[74]

By reversing the direction in which analogical relations have been thought, Spinoza corrects the metaphysical tradition's tendency to conflate the essences of creator and creation. Rather than treat divine attributes and features of creaturely life as given identities, which are subsequently compared by way of analogy, Spinoza, according to Deleuze, begins from the traditional assumption that attributes, "constitute the essence of substance," and adds the novel insight that they are "forms common to both" substance and modes. Spinoza is able to take this last step by claiming that modes, in Deleuze's language, "imply" or "express" divine attributes.[75] What this makes of an "attribute" is a common form underlying both divine and creaturely being, where the former is essentially defined by its attributes, and the latter implies that essence: "Attributes are thus forms common to God, whose essence they constitute, and to modes or creatures, which imply them essentially."[76] Divine substance, in turn, "explicates" itself through modes; it is does so in the form of attributes, which are common between substance and modes.

The creaturely "implication" of divine substance, and the divine "explication" of itself through creatures, are two forms of the same expressiveness that runs between modes and substance through their shared common attributes. Deleuze is right, then, to credit Spinoza with great "originality"; especially once the two-fold logic of expression is recognized as a correction of the pervasive logic of analogy that runs through the history of metaphysics.[77] Yet, the originality of Spinoza, on this point, is still greater than we might first appreciate.

To do so, it is helpful to recall the above discussion of inter-generic analogy in Aristotle. Unlike analogies within a single genus, inter-generic analogies involve forging a common context through which generically different, specific individuals can be compared. The problem with such analogies, despite their departure from the standard way in which identity and difference is constituted, is that the specific identities of the related terms still rely upon the genus-species structure. Spinoza employs the form of the (Aristotelian) inter-generic analogy while overcoming the problem of specific identity and difference being borrowed from a different relational order; and, he does so by making the inter-generic form of analogy into a divine attribute. As a feature of the infinite, substantial being of God, an attribute is an absolutely common form of relation; as a characteristic of modes, an attribute is specified to each individual being.

What Spinoza strikes upon in the idea of a divine attribute is not just a form of the common relation that subsists between beings that exist in different orders, but *the form of all relations of difference whatsoever*. Further, by subjecting the attribute to the logic of expression—at least on Deleuze's reading of the different forms of "causation" in the *Ethics*—Spinoza enables the thinking of analogical relationality in a way that Aristotle and the Scholastic tradition could not. "Expression" renders the attribute insubstantial; it allows the attribute to take on the expressive character of whatever relation it is presently mediating; thus, the attribute can be thought in the immanent context of each of its specific relations. Deleuze, concluding this line of argumentation, writes, "Spinoza's [non-analogical] method [. . .] work[s] with common notions. And the whole of Spinoza's theory of common notions finds its principle precisely in this status of the attribute."[78]

If we appeal to the above language of "reversing" the traditional logic of metaphysical analogy, we might put this last point as a matter of Spinoza dissolving analogy *as a figure* and incorporating its sameness-difference structure into the expressive thinking of all metaphysical relations as common notions. Here, then, is where the idea of philosophy becomes reflexive; here, too, the practice of philosophy becomes immanent and affirmative: to think an attribute, in Spinoza, is to think the relational form of (traditional metaphysical) analogy. Deleuze makes just this point in concluding the *Expressionism* book. Unlike Leibniz, who, "multiplies the types of distinction" in order to secure the "resources of [. . .] analogy," Spinoza argues for "univocity of being, univocity of production, [and] univocity of knowing," that is, "the three figures of the Univocal that combine absolutely in an idea of the third kind."[79]

Deleuze's reference to an "idea of the third kind" refers to what Spinoza calls the "third kind of knowledge: "[T]here is [. . .] a third kind of knowledge, which I shall refer to as 'intuition.' This kind of knowledge proceeds from an adequate idea of the formal essence of certain attributes of God to an adequate knowledge of the essence of things."[80] Unlike the first and second kinds of knowledge, which continue to think nature and God separately, in the third kind of knowledge, all essences are thought together in the essence of God—in Deleuze's language, Spinoza's "third kind of knowledge" is a fully immanent form of thought.

If, as we have argued above, the idea of divine attribute is the idea of sameness and difference, and thus, the idea of relationality *per se*, then in thinking the adequate idea of God in the third kind of knowledge one also thinks all similar and all different relata in that idea. Here is Spinoza in Part Two of the *Ethics*, arguing the same point: "Now, since all things are in God and are conceived through God, it follows that from this [third kind of] knowledge, we can deduce a great many things so as to know them adequately."[81] That Spinoza uses the language of "deduction" in this last quote should not mislead: the "deduction" of all things from the third, adequate knowledge of God is immediate, or, what Spinoza calls, "intuitive"; and, in continuing the passage, Spinoza makes this clear in the example of an intuitive grasp of a whole mathematical proof.[82]

With Deleuze, we can read Spinoza's "third kind of knowledge" as the name for an immanent, expressive philosophy—and this, again, despite Spinoza nowhere linking such knowledge to the practice of philosophy. Further, as a thinking of the essence of all things through the essential grasp of the highest order of being, Spinoza's "third kind of knowledge" is an immanent, expressive *metaphysics*. In *Expressionism in Philosophy*, Deleuze enumerates the characteristics of Spinoza's metaphysics as follows: through the immediate thought of God as an adequate idea, we think the "particular" essence of all things; we think, "the greatest number of all things"; and, finally, we think the producing and comprising of all things fulfills.[83] Point for point, this enumeration of Spinoza's metaphysics coincides with the characteristics of an immanent, active philosophy that we laid out in section one of the present essay. As previously noted, an immanent metaphysics is also affirmative and joyous; so, too, does the third kind of knowledge in Spinoza correspond to the positive passion of "beatitude": "Beatitude designates the possession not only of an active joy as it is in God, but of an active love as it is in God also."[84]

Where the whole metaphysical tradition before him failed, Spinoza, according to Deleuze, succeeds. In the adequate idea of divine attribute, Spinoza creates an immanent, active concept; and, in the thinking of such an idea in the "third kind of knowledge," Spinoza creates an immanent philosophy of positive affect and joy. Remarkably, what enabled Spinoza to advance so far beyond the metaphysical tradition is his hermeneutical principle for textual interpretation.

Spinoza is able to think difference metaphysically because he reclaims divine essence from the theological mistake of thinking it in terms of what are mere "*propria*" of God. Theologians have tended to treat such "properties" as "goodness, being, reason, life, intelligence, etc." as if they are essentially determinative of the being of God; for this reason, theology has never actually thought the essence of God. Traditionally, metaphysics has followed suit and thought metaphysical concepts in terms of their *propria*; thus, it, too, has failed to think difference because it could not think in non-figurative, disanalogous manner the expressive difference within the essence of the highest form of being.

We can be still more specific in identifying the error of theology and metaphysics that Spinoza corrects. Here is Deleuze, succinctly explaining the single failing of the theological and metaphysical tradition: "Spinoza's answer [to the question of why metaphysicians and theologians have never thought the essence of divine substance] is simple: they lacked a historical, critical and internal method capable of interpreting Scripture."[85]

The hermeneutical error made by traditional theology is to read Scripture as a series of analogical expressions of the word of God; and, in "running through the whole of theology," this error further, "compromises philosophy as a whole."[86] To put this last point in more familiar philosophical language, the hermeneutical error made with respect to the idea of expression is to treat it as a figure like analogy, that is, to fix it as a structure or model of interpretation for passing between different orders of thought and being. Spinoza's non-figurative, active practice of metaphysics consists in his folding the figure of analogy back onto itself so that the thinking of being becomes, instead, the immanent thought of expression itself; or, what is the same, Spinoza's philosophy is an immanent, active metaphysics that thinks relational difference itself.

***

The argument of this chapter, in sum, is that analogy does not so much disappear in Spinoza's metaphysics, as that it is made fully self-reflexive, and so becomes immanently thinkable by that metaphysics. Given our concluding reflections on Spinoza's method as an "expressive" hermeneutics of Scripture, we might read a metaphysics of immanent analogy as a basically textual matter. In fact, there is, on Deleuze's reading of Spinoza, good reason to do so. Here, for instance, is how Deleuze ends the "Appendix" to *Expressionism in Philosophy*: "There are thus as it were two *Ethics* existing side by side, one constituted by the continuous line or tide of propositions, proofs and corollaries, and the other, discontinuous, constituted by the broken line or volcanic chain of the *scholia*."[87] Continuing, Deleuze associates the first "continuous line" of the *Ethics* with a kind of logical "terrorism of the head" without practical implication; the second "discontinuous [. . .] line" of *scholia* are all about "the joys of the heart," and "the practical struggle against sadness."[88] If "[t]he *Ethics*," as Deleuze concludes, "is in this sense a double book,"[89] then to practice an active philosophy through such a "double book" is to read the first, main line of the text, and its secondary, scholastic subtext, as univocally differentiated, that is, as immanent analogies for one another.

In the Preface to *Difference and Repetition*, Deleuze offers an example of what such a text looks like; in so doing, Deleuze gives us a model on which to practice our immanently active and analogical way of reading the thought of being. The example Deleuze chooses comes from a story by Jorge Luis Borges: "Pierre Menard: Author of the Quixote." What the author Pierre Menard sets out to accomplish in Borges' story is to rewrite Cervantes' *Don Quixote*. Menard aims to do so, not by copying the original, but, rather, by writing the novel again for the first time. The result, as Deleuze describes it, is *Don Quixote* as a "most exact, [and] strict repetition," which, by its very strictness of repetition "has as its correlate the maximum of difference."[90]

As in the case of the "two" texts of Spinoza's *Ethics*, so Borges envisions "two" *Don Quixote*'s that are the same in being precisely different from one another. By appealing to Borges in this way, and at the beginning of his own work on a metaphysics of difference, what Deleuze seems to announce is that our task, as practitioners of an active philosophy, is to read all works on metaphysics differently: there are "two" *Ethics* by Spinoza; *Difference and Repetition* is a double book—or, perhaps, we must read, as we have here, *Expressionism in Philosophy* as a kind of second *Difference and Repetition*. Reading in this fashion, we engage in the practice of philosophy actively; we affirm difference in itself, that is, immanently and analogically; and, just as we laugh at Borges' absurdist idea of two *Don Quixote*'s, so we are affectively joyful in actively thinking the univocal difference of being.

Notes

1. Gilles Deleuze, *Difference and Repetition*, trans. P. Patton (New York: Columbia University Press, 1994), 35.

2. Deleuze, *Difference and Repetition*, 35.

3. Deleuze, *Difference and Repetition*, 36.

4. Deleuze, *Difference and Repetition*, 24.

5. Deleuze, *Difference and Repetition*, 36.

6. Gilles Deleuze and Félix Guattari, *What Is Philosophy?*, trans. H. Tomlinson (New York: Columbia University Press, 1996), 77.

7. Gilles Deleuze, *Expressionism in Philosophy: Spinoza*, trans. M. Joughin (New York: Zone Books, 1992), 321.

8. Baruch Spinoza, *Ethics*, in *The Essential Spinoza: Ethics and Related Writings*, trans. S. Shirley (Indianapolis: Hackett, 2006), II, P34, 48.

9. Spinoza, *Ethics*, II, P34, 48.

10. Spinoza, *Ethics*, IV, P23, 114.

11. Deleuze, *Expressionism in Philosophy*, 242–243.

12. Deleuze, *Difference and Repetition*, 40.

13. Spinoza, *Ethics*, III, P3, 65.

14. Spinoza, *Ethics*, III, P59, 92.

15. Gilles Deleuze, "Letter to Reda Bensmaïa, On Spinoza," *Negotiations: 1972–1990*, trans. M. Joughin (New York: Columbia University Press, 1995), 165.

16. Deleuze, "Letter to Reda Bensmaïa," 165.

17. Cliff Stagoll, "Plane," *The Deleuze Dictionary*, ed. A. Paar (New York: Columbia University Press, 2005), 205.

18. Gilles Deleuze, "Immanence: A Life," *Pure Immanence: Essays on a Life*, trans. A. Boyman (New York: Zone Books, 2001), 25.

19. Levi Bryant, *Difference and Givenness: Deleuze's Transcendental Empiricism and the Ontology of Immanence* (Evanston: Northwestern University Press, 2008), 3.

20. Bryant makes this same point, in reference to Deleuze's "Hegelian" speculative reworking of Kant's critical philosophy, as follows: "It is precisely at this point [where the Kantian subject is found to be situated within time] that critical philosophy becomes indiscernible from speculative philosophy" (Bryant, *Difference and Givenness*, 184).

21. Gilles Deleuze, "Lecture Transcripts on Spinoza's Concept of Affect," *Le Cours de Gilles Deleuze, Cours Vincennes–24/01/1978*, trans. T. S. Murphy, accessed 15 June 2012, http://www.webdeleuze.com/php/texte.php?cle=14&groupe=Spinoza&langue=2/.

22. Deleuze, "Immanence: A Life," 26–27.

23. There is an implicit criticism of Heidegger's "transcendent" reading of Kantian transcendentalism in Deleuze's insistence on the immanence of the transcendental to the empirical. For Heidegger's reading, see: Martin Heidegger, *Kant and the Problem of Metaphysics*, trans. R. Taft (Bloomington: Indiana University Press, 1997), 61–62.

24. Bryant, *Difference and Givenness*, 184.

25. Tom Conley, "Molecular," *The Deleuze Dictionary*, ed. A. Parr (New York: Columbia University Press, 2005), 172–174.

26. On the relationship between the body and the plural specificity of sensations, see Gilles Deleuze, *Francis Bacon: The Logic of Sensation*, trans. D. W. Smith (Minneapolis: University of Minnesota Press, 2005).

27. Gilles Deleuze, *Kant's Critical Philosophy: The Doctrine of the Faculties*, trans. H. Tomlinson and B. Habberjam (London: The Athlone Press, 1984), 19.

28. Deleuze, *Kant's Critical Philosophy*, 21.

29. Immanuel Kant, *Prolegomena to Any Future Metaphysics*, trans. G. Hatfield (New York: Cambridge University Press, 1997), 5.

30. John Rajchman, *The Deleuze Connections* (Cambridge: The MIT Press, 2000), 33.

31. Deleuze, *Expressionism in Philosophy*, 17ff.

32. Deleuze, *Expressionism in Philosophy*, 322.

33. Pierre Macherey, "The Encounter with Spinoza," *Deleuze: A Critical Reader*, ed. P. Patton (New York: Blackwell, 1996), 143–144.

34. Simon Duffy, who claims that "explication of th[e] logic" of expression is the "defining problematic of [Deleuze's] *Expressionism in Philosophy*," articulates the structure of expression as follows: "[A]n immanence of expression of what is expressed [. . .] both in what expresses itself [. . .] and in its expression [. . .] such that what expresses itself [. . .] implicates what is expressed [. . .] in itself, while the expression [. . .] implicates what is expressed [. . .] in other things." Simon Duffy, "The Logic of Expression in Deleuze's *Expressionism in Philosophy*: A Strategy of Engagement," *International Journal of Philosophical Studies* 12, no. 1 (2004): 57.

35. Aristotle, *Metaphysics*, trans. H. Tredennick, Loeb Classical Library, Vol. 271 (Cambridge, MA: Harvard University Press, 1933), 5.7.1017a7–8.

36. Aristotle, *Metaphysics* 5.7.1017a23–2.

37. Aristotle, *Metaphysics* 7.1.1028a10–12.

38. Aristotle, *Metaphysics* 7.1.1028a15.

39. Aristotle, *Metaphysics* 7.1.1028a30–35.

40. G.E.L. Owen, "Logic and Metaphysics in Some Earlier Works of Aristotle," in *Logic, Science, and Dialectic: Collected Papers in Greek Philosophy*, ed. M. Nussbaum (Ithaca, NY: Cornell University Press, 1986), 184.

41. Terence Irwin, *Aristotle's First Principles* (Oxford: Oxford University Press, 1988), 8ff.

42. Michael Ferejohn, "Aristotle on Focal Meaning and the Unity of Science," *Phronesis* 25, no. 2 (1980): 117–118.

43. Aristotle, *Metaphysics* 4.2.1003b23.

44. Aristotle, *Metaphysics* 7.1.1028a10–12.

45. Deleuze, *Difference and Repetition*, 33.

46. Deleuze, *Difference and Repetition*, 33.

47. Deleuze, *Difference and Repetition*, 33.

48. Deleuze, *Difference and Repetition*, 33.

49. Mary Hesse, "Aristotle's Logic of Analogy," *The Philosophical Quarterly* 15, no. 61 (October 1965): 330.

50. Aristotle, *Posterior Analytics*, trans. E.S. Forster, Loeb Classical Library, Vol. 391 (Cambridge, MA: Harvard University Press, 1960), 1.10.76a40–42.

51. Hesse, "Aristotle's Logic of Analogy," 331.

52. Hesse, "Aristotle's Logic of Analogy," 331.

53. Aristotle, *Posterior Analytics*, 2.12.99a9–11.

54. Deleuze, *Difference and Repetition*, 308fn.5.

55. Deleuze, *Difference and Repetition*, 308–309fn.5.

56. Deleuze, *Difference and Repetition*, 309fn.5.

57. Deleuze, *Difference and Repetition*, 308fn.5.

58. Deleuze, *Difference and Repetition*, 309fn5, emphasis added.

59. Deleuze, *Difference and Repetition*, 38.

60. Deleuze, *Difference and Repetition*, 38.

61. Deleuze, *Difference and Repetition*, 39.

62. Deleuze, *Difference and Repetition*, 39.

63. Deleuze, *Expressionism in Philosophy*, 329.

64. Deleuze, *Difference and Repetition*, 40.

65. Deleuze, *Difference and Repetition*, 40.

66. Deleuze, *Difference and Repetition*, 40.

67. Deleuze, *Difference and Repetition*, 40.

68. Deleuze, *Difference and Repetition*, 40.

69. Deleuze, *Difference and Repetition*, 40.

70. Spinoza appeals to the Scholastic terminology of "formal causation" to describe the non-analogical relation between God as creator and nature as His creation; see Baruch Spinoza, "Short Treatise on God, Man, and His Well-Being," *Spinoza: Complete Works*, ed. M. L. Morgan (Indianapolis: Hackett Publishing Company, 2002), 42

71. Deleuze, *Difference and Repetition*, 40.

72. Deleuze, *Expressionism in Philosophy*, 46.

73. Deleuze, *Expressionism in Philosophy*, 47.

74. Deleuze, *Expressionism in Philosophy*, 47.

75. Deleuze, *Expressionism in Philosophy*, 47.

76. Deleuze, *Expressionism in Philosophy*, 47.

77. Tad Schmaltz, "The Disappearance of Analogy in Descartes, Spinoza and Regis," *Canadian Journal of Philosophy* 30, no. 1 (March 2000): 96.

78. Deleuze, *Expressionism in Philosophy*, 48.

79. Deleuze, *Expressionism in Philosophy*, 332.

80. Spinoza, *Ethics*, II, P40 schol. 2, 51.

81. Spinoza, *Ethics*, II, P47, schol. 1, 55.

82. Spinoza, *Ethics*, II, P47, schol. 1, 55.

83. Deleuze, *Expressionism in Philosophy*, 304.

84. Deleuze, *Expressionism in Philosophy*, 309.

85. Deleuze, *Expressionism in Philosophy*, 56.

86. Deleuze, *Expressionism in Philosophy*, 56.

87. Deleuze, *Expressionism in Philosophy*, 345.

88. Deleuze, *Expressionism in Philosophy*, 345.

89. Deleuze, *Expressionism in Philosophy*, 345.

90. Deleuze, *Difference and Repetition*, xxii.

References

Aristotle. *Metaphysics*. Trans. H. Tredennick, Loeb Classical Library, Vols. 271 and 287. Cambridge, MA: Harvard University Press, 1933.

———. *Posterior Analytics*. Trans. E.S. Forster, Loeb Classical Library, Vol. 391. Cambridge, MA: Harvard University Press, 1960.

Bryant, Levi. *Difference and Givenness: Deleuze's Transcendental Empiricism and the Ontology of Immanence*. Evanston: Northwestern University Press, 2008.

Conly, Tom. "Molecular." In *The Deleuze Dictionary*. Edited by A. Parr, 172–174. New York: Columbia University Press, 2005.

Deleuze, Gilles. *Difference and Repetition*. Trans. P. Patton. New York: Columbia University Press, 1994.

———. *Expressionism in Philosophy: Spinoza*. Trans. M. Joughin. New York: Zone Books, 1992.

———. "Immanence: A Life." In *Pure Immanence: Essays on a Life*. Translated by A. Boyman, 25–34. New York: Zone Books, 2001.

———. *Kant's Critical Philosophy: The Doctrine of the Faculties*. Translated by H. Tomlinson and B. Habberjam. London: The Athlone Press, 1984.

———. "Lecture Transcripts on Spinoza's Concept of Affect." In *Le Cours de Gilles Deleuze: Cours Vincennes 24/01/1978*. Translated by T. S. Murphy. Accessed 15 June 2012, http://www.webdeleuze.com/php/texte.php?cle=14&groupe=Spinoza&langue=2/.

———. "Letter to Reda Bensmaïa, On Spinoza." *Negotiations: 1972–1990*. Trans. M. Joughin. New York: Columbia University Press, 1995. 164–166.

———. *Francis Bacon: The Logic of Sensation*. Trans. D. W. Smith. Minneapolis, MN: University of Minnesota Press, 2005.

Deleuze, Gilles and Félix Guattari. *What is Philosophy?* Translated by H. Tomlinson. New York: Columbia University Press, 1996.

Duffy, Simon. "The Logic of Expression in Deleuze's *Expressionism in Philosophy*: A Strategy of Engagement." *International Journal of Philosophical Studies* 12, no. 1 (2004): 47–60.

Ferejohn, Michael. "Aristotle on Focal Meaning and the Unity of Science." *Phronesis*, 25, no. 2 (1980): 117–118.

Heidegger, Martin. *Kant and the Problem of Metaphysics*. Translated by R. Taft. Bloomington: Indiana University Press, 1997.

Hesse, Mary. "Aristotle's Logic of Analogy." *The Philosophical Quarterly* 15, no. 61 (October 1965): 328–340.

Irwin, Terence. *Aristotle's First Principles*. Oxford: Oxford University Press, 1988.

Kant, Immanuel. *Prolegomena to Any Future Metaphysics*. Translated by G. Hatfield. New York: Cambridge University Press, 1997.

Macherey, Pierre. "The Encounter with Spinoza." In *Deleuze: A Critical Reader*. Edited by P. Patton, 139–161. New York: Blackwell, 1996.

Owen, G.E.L. "Logic and Metaphysics in Some Earlier Works of Aristotle." In *Logic, Science, and Dialectic: Collected Papers in Greek Philosophy*. Edited by M. Nussbaum. Ithaca, NY: Cornell University Press, 1986. 180–199.

Rajchman, John. *The Deleuze Connections*. Cambridge, MA: The MIT Press, 2000.

Schmaltz, Tad. "The Disappearance of Analogy in Descartes, Spinoza and Regis." *Canadian Journal of Philosophy* 30, no. 1 (March 2000): 85–113.

Spinoza, Baruch. *The Essential Spinoza: Ethics and Related Writings.* Translated by S. Shirley. Indianapolis: Hackett Publishing Company, 2006.

———. "Short Treatise on God, Man, and His Well-Being." In *Spinoza: Complete Works.* Translated by S. Shirley. Edited by M. L. Morgan, 31–107. Indianapolis: Hackett Publishing Company, 2002.

Stagoll, Cliff. "Plane." *The Deleuze Dictionary.* Ed. A. Paar. New York: Columbia University Press, 2005. 204–206.

CHAPTER EIGHT

Crowned Anarchies, Substantial Attributes, and the Transcendental Problem of Stupidity

Gregory Kalyniuk

By means of what process are the powers of the mind constituted, and what role does the primordial chaos out of which we are borne play in this process? Do we simply overcome this chaos once and for all at the beginning of life, as though it were only an accidental feature of our coming into the world, or is it rather an integral component of the mind that must be understood, in Spinoza's terms, *sub specie aeternitatis*, and which must be perpetually relived in order for thought to realize its full creative capacity? For Spinoza, reason is opposed to the passions in principle. Reason destroys the passions by forming adequate ideas of their causes, leading to an increase in our power of acting. But if thought surpasses the consciousness that we have of it, then perhaps reason and thought, insofar as we are conscious of them, are borne out of their confrontation with impulses and passions in the primordial chaos that exceeds our consciousness. For Deleuze, this primordial chaos must be perpetually relived, and starting with Nietzsche, he passes through a series of exemplars in order to dramatize this. Not least amongst these exemplars is Antonin Artaud, who along with Nietzsche plays an important if not understated role in Deleuze's (and Guattari's) subversion of the rationalist presuppositions in Spinoza's philosophy. This subversion forms the subject of the following discussion, which will stage an imaginary encounter between Artaud and Spinoza. Artaud's influence on Deleuze and Guattari often gets overlooked, if not simply because his schizophrenia can make it difficult to fully appreciate the philosophical and metaphysical (and not merely aesthetical and polemical) value of his writing. We will take as our point of departure two of Deleuze's (and Guattari's) most ambitious claims about Artaud, which will be shown to cast complementary light on one another: first, the claim that Artaud inaugurates a transcendental empiricism by presenting the question of stupidity and the violence necessary to engender thought as specifically metaphysical problems; and second, the claim that Artaud's work is interchangeable with Spinoza's *Ethics*. In the *Ethics*, a substance is what exists in and is conceived through itself and not another; an attribute is what the intellect perceives of sub-

179

stance as constituting its essence; and a mode is what exists in or is conceived through something other than itself, or the substance of which it is a modification.[1] Spinoza begins the *Ethics* by proposing that there may be many attributes, each with its own substance, before coming to equate Nature with one Substance that possesses all of the attributes.[2] This initial reduction of substance to attribute seems to give priority to the perspective of modes in the confused world of passions. For substance to be said of modes instead of modes being said of substance seems to contradict their very definitions, yet making substance turn on its modes is Deleuze's very aim in his interpretation of Spinoza. In *A Thousand Plateaus*, the substance that is said of modes is reworked as the substantial attribute alluded to at the beginning of the *Ethics*, and is equated with Artaud's Body without Organs (BwO). The following discussion will aim to show how the world of crowned anarchy that the BwO desires to reach is a world where it is the animality peculiar to thought that allows for passions to be overcome, rather than reason *per se*.

In *Difference and Repetition*, Deleuze credits Artaud for inaugurating a transcendental empiricism that opposes the *genitality* of a fractured thought to the assumed innateness of a common sense incapable of escaping its subjective or implicit presuppositions.[3] For Artaud, "innateness" does not consist of common sense and its presuppositions, but of a genitality that violently forces thought to think its own central collapse, and discover that its natural "powerlessness" is indistinguishable from its greatest power. In order to even be able to begin to think, one must first be liberated from all that *everybody knows* and *no one can deny*, or the postulates of the system of non-philosophical knowledge constitutive of what Deleuze calls the dogmatic Image of thought. Painfully dramatizing the work of managing to think something at all in his exchange of letters with Jacques Rivière, Artaud insists upon the fundamental obscurity and discordance of thought, while Rivière defends the image of an autonomous thinking function with pre-given possibilities. On 6 June 1924, Artaud writes to Rivière:

> Dear Mr. Rivière
>   My mental life is all shot through with petty doubts and unalterable certainties expressed in clear, coherent language. My weaknesses are more tremulous in texture, themselves larval and ill-formed. They bear living, anguished roots reaching down into the heart of life. But they do not bear life's turmoil, since in them we do not feel the cosmic afflatus of a soul shaken to its foundations. . . .
>   Now supposing I felt this will sweep through me. . . . Tell me if any literary work is in keeping with such states? . . . If only I had the strength, I would sometimes indulge in the luxury of mentally subjecting any prominent mind, any writer young or old who produces material, whose new-born ideas are listened to, to the mortification of such cruel pain and see what would be left of him. We should never be too hasty in judging men. We should give them credit *ad absurdum*, right down to the last dregs. . . .[4]

To which Rivière responds on 8 June 1924:

Dear Mr. Artaud,
. . . You say, "a man is only in possession of his faculties at intervals, and even when he is, he never fully achieves self-knowledge." That man is you. But I can also tell you it is me. . . .
In order to explain the alterations I go through, like you, I set aside the convenient symbol of inspiration. We are dealing with something deeper, more "substantial," if I may be allowed to distort the meaning of the word, than a happy inspiration which might or might not spring from the depths of the mind. We are dealing with the stages I pass through in my own reality. Unfortunately, not willingly! But in a purely accidental way. . . .
In any case, I believe it is a fact that men of a certain type are prone to fluctuations in their mental level. When we often adopt an habitual psychological attitude, how often have we abruptly discovered it transcends us, or rather have we grown surreptitiously unequal to it! How often has our most normal character suddenly seemed false, or even fictitious, through lack of the mental or "basic" resources which should nourish it![5]

While Rivière assumes the givenness of "basic" mental resources of habit and judges the false and fictitious on this basis, for Artaud the cruel pain of life's turmoil is the most basic mental resource, and for this reason he claims that men should not be judged but be given credit *ad absurdum*. Rivière's and Artaud's respective positions inform the distinction that Deleuze draws between a notion of error derived from the structure of common sense, and a stupidity [*bêtise*] or groundlessness that is the animality peculiar to thought, without being animality *per se*.[6] Against the notion that error, conceived of as the failure of good sense within the form of an intact common sense, comprises the sole "negative" of thought, Deleuze claims that stupidity, malevolence, and madness must be understood as properly transcendental problems in their own right.[7] Stupidity must be irreducible to error, since error is incapable of accounting for what stupidity is in relation to the individual who thinks, the ground of their thought, and the process of individuation through which the thinking individual and the ground are linked by virtue of the question of stupidity. "Crowned anarchy," echoing the subtitle of Artaud's *Heliogabalus*, is the name Deleuze gives to the mode of thinking which is able to give birth to its own ground, and of which stupidity functions as the transcendental limit.

In order to escape the subjective presuppositions of thought that trace the transcendental from the empirical and that limit it to the empirical forms that appear under the determination of common sense, Deleuze claims that the transcendental form of each faculty must be shown to be indistinguishable from its disjointed, superior, or transcendent exercise.[8] Appropriating the genetic procedure undertaken by Kant to account for the relations between faculties in the *Critique of Judgment*, in which the experience of the sublime results from the imagination being forced beyond its limits by reason, Deleuze is able to surpass the psychologistic deduction of the faculties found in the *Critique of Pure Rea-*

son, according to which the transcendental structures are said to be surreptitiously derived from the empirical acts of a psychological consciousness.[9] Rather than deducing the necessity and universality of synthetic *a priori* judgements from common sense, the genetic procedure involves reason pushing the imagination beyond the sensible while denying it access to the rational Idea. Freed from the constraints of the understanding and entering into a discordant agreement with reason, the imagination discovers its suprasensible destination in passion, and together with reason, their transcendental origin in the suprasensible unity of the faculties.[10] Deleuze claims that this procedure establishes the model of a properly transcendental empiricism, capable of destroying the dogmatic Image of thought along with the pre-given common sense upon which it is founded. It then becomes a question not of a habitual psychological attitude that either transcends us or that we grow unequal to, as Rivière would have it in his misunderstanding of Artaud, but of the faculties that take this attitude as their object being shown to be indistinguishable from their transcendent exercise. Everything is then reconceived as beginning with misosophy, forcing philosophy to commence without presuppositions on the basis of an individual full of ill will who does not manage to think, and not on the basis of an individual endowed with good will and a natural capacity for thought.[11] It is in this same sense that Artaud, unable to presuppose the possibility of simply recognizing the object of his thought, instead seeks out the violent encounter that will force him to think. He states this clearly in the opening lines of *Nerve Scales*:

> I really felt you break down the environment around me, I felt you create a void to allow me to progress, making room for an impossible space, for what was then only potentially within me. For an entire, virtual germination yet to come, drawn into the spot that presented itself.
> I have often gotten myself into this impossible, absurd state, so as to try to create thought within me. There are a few of us in these times, who want to cut things down and so create areas of life within us, areas which did not exist and did not seem to belong in space.[12]

The transcendent exercise of reason reveals stupidity to be a transcendental problem that surpasses the empirical determinations of reason, to the extent that the equal distribution of good sense can no longer be presupposed in the "impossible space" within which the fortuitousness of the bad encounter now becomes the greatest risk in the creation of thought. The notion of error is incapable of accounting for how this risk can lead to either the tyrant who institutionalises stupidity, such as the young Roman emperor Heliogabalus, or the private thinker who overcomes stupidity and is able to create poetry, such as the young Artaud. This is because stupidity cannot be reduced to simple corporeal capacities or traits of character or society, but is a structure of thought as such. Stupidity demands, as intimated by Artaud, a space of its own, or a transcendental landscape in which places for the tyrant, the slave, and the imbecile must be found, but whose empirical determinations must never be confused with this transcendental landscape.[13] For this would be to reduce the absurdity of the superstitions from which they suffer to their kernel of error as Rivière would have, something that Spinoza, as we will see, would have rejected no less forcefully than Artaud. The crowned anarchy capable of engendering thought will find its counterpart in the mysterious substantial attribute, one of the most puzzling and contentious features of Spinoza's *Ethics*.

In order to cast light on the substantial attribute, let us consider what Deleuze has to say about it in his article on Martial Gueroult's *Spinoza, I,— Dieu, Ethique I*, which Deleuze had written the year following the appearance of his own exegesis of Spinoza, *Expressionism in Philosophy*. For Deleuze, the novelty of Gueroult's general method for the study of Spinoza rests, first of all, in its structural distinction between two orders of reason: simple reasons of knowledge, which form an order of regressive analysis destined to lead *as quickly as possible* from any true idea whatsoever, which can nonetheless still be impregnated with fiction, to the determination of God's constitutive elements as reasons of being; and genuine reasons of being, which form a synthetic order of production that determines the constitutive elements as objects of a genetic construction, integrating the regressive analysis with its *self-suppression*.[14] In order to avoid the confusions of according the first eight propositions of the *Ethics* a hypothetical rather than categorical sense, Gueroult places special emphasis on each qualified substance enjoying the properties of being unique in its kind, self-caused, and infinite. On the one hand, there is only one substance per attribute and therefore just as many qualified substances as there are attributes, and on the other hand, only a real and by no means numerical distinction can be drawn between the attributes.[15] This insistence upon the logic of real distinction is what allows Gueroult to reconcile the qualified substances, which are each affirmed in their difference without negation, with the single, absolute substance that they are together constitutive of. The intrinsic difference and reciprocal heterogeneity implied by the concrete plurality of attributes is thus better understood to be a formal or qualitative multiplicity of the type that Bergson would have attributed to lived duration, than as an abstract multitude of parts reducible to number. The integration of these attributes or substantial forms *qua* differential, constitutive elements into the idea of God reflects what Deleuze calls, echoing his own conception of Nietzsche's will to power, *a genealogy of the substance itself*, which while not the same as the genesis of modes from the substance, can nonetheless be spoken of univocally *in one and the same sense*.[16] The substantial attribute is therefore not the object of the genetic construction, but rather the object of a *demonstration from absurdity* that seeks to overcome the fiction of a separately existing substance resulting from the reduction of a mode's extrinsic determinations to its intrinsic determinations. This possibility, as the supposition of the regressive analytic process, is overcome as quickly as possible by affirming the difference between the logical constitution of the single, absolute substance out of really distinct attributes, and the physical constitution of its numerically distinct modes.[17] Yet this overcoming only comes about at the *nexus* between the series represented by the first eight propositions, which posit the substantial at-

tribute, and the series represented by the three propositions immediately following these first eight, which posit the genealogy of the substance that integrates
the substantial attributes.[18] At the juncture of this *nexus*, the notion of *causa sui*
plays a central, if not on first glance paradoxical role: besides being a property
of each qualified substance, it derives itself from the infinite insofar as it is the
full perfection of *essence*, as expressed through the difference of the attributes,
while grounding the infinite insofar as it is the absolute affirmation of *existence*,
as expressed through the identity of the attributes.[19]

   The role that Gueroult gives to the *causa sui* of the substantial attribute
seems to be paralleled by the role that Deleuze gives to the hubris of crowned
anarchy in *Difference and Repetition*, and this bears consideration of Artaud as
well as Nietzsche. Like Artaud's larval and ill-formed weaknesses, whose an-
guished roots reach down into the heart of life and express its essence without
bearing the turmoil of its existence, the essential aspect of *causa sui* expressed
by the difference of the attributes is derived from the same infinite that is
grounded by the existential aspect of *causa sui*, which is expressed by the identity of the attributes. Artaud's wish to submit other minds to the experience of
anguish and cruelty would affirm the existence of a single, absolute substance
grounded in this experience, and not simply the essence derived from his own
qualified substance. Unlike the deeper, more "substantial" stages that Rivière
passes through in his own hypothetical reality as if by accident, the substantial
attribute of the regressive analysis categorically gives credit to men *ad absurdum*, and rather than hastily judging the truth or falsity of their beliefs, reveals
the share of truth or falsity that they deserve on the basis of the sense that they
conceive. This share of truth or falsity expresses the ontological hierarchy of
active and reactive forces. Nietzsche calls its inseparability from genealogy the
problem of free spirits, or the problem of the will to power as the spirit of interpretation that judges forces on the basis of their origin and quality.[20] Reactive
forces hubristically declare the "fact" of their triumph over active forces, and
separate them from what they can do on the basis of an artificial hierarchy of
law and virtue; or on the basis of a fiction that must be overcome according to
the test of the eternal return, which puts hubris to a different sort of use.[21] Subordinating the identical to the different, being to becoming, and substance to its
modes, the eternal return becomes the highest power of the genealogy of the
substance, or the synthetic order of production formed out of the regressive
analysis integrated with its self-suppression. This synthetic order of production
is univocal with the synthesis of affirmation that integrates the reactive forces
with their active self-destruction by the will to power. It is here where the *causa
sui* of the substantial attribute transcends the limit that is the basis of its initial
deployment, and encounters what is both its suprasensible destination and its
transcendental origin, or the single, absolute substance that integrates the substantial attributes. The reversed hierarchy of the slave is overturned, giving way
to a crowned anarchy closer to the identity of difference and origin in Nietzsche's ontological hierarchy. Its unequal distribution of sense paradoxically
forms the basis of the enveloping measure that is the same for all things.[22] The

causa sui of Artaud's larval and ill-formed weaknesses, expressed by the difference of the attributes and the inequality of sense that Rivière obscures with his
artificial hierarchy, is thus derived from the same infinity that is grounded by the
causa sui expressed by the identity of the attributes and the equality of being,
which redeems hubris in the active self-destruction of reactive forces according
to the existential test of the eternal return.

The ontological priority of ill will and hubris comes into play in relation to
the BwO in *The Logic of Sense*, where Deleuze first appropriates Artaud's idea
into a psychoanalytic context. Basing his discussion around a reworking of
Melanie Klein's theories of early childhood development,[23] Deleuze posits the
BwO as one of two schizoid poles, along with partial objects, facing the good
object. For Klein, the emotional life of the infant is characterised by persecutory
anxieties and a fear of annihilation stemming from the working of the death instinct, which is only overcome through the formation of object-relations according to processes of introjection and projection. Because the infant is only capable of perceiving partial objects such as the mother's breast, however, its anxieties are further exacerbated by the initial uncertainty of these relations with the
external world. The infant's mouth and the mother's breast are perceived as bot-
tomless depths, and the mother's entire body is split apart into a good and a bad
object: Klein describes this as the paranoid-schizoid position of the child.[24] For
every introjection it makes of the bad, poisoning breast, the infant projects its
anxiety back on to the mother in the form of a sadistic aggression aiming to fill
her body with poisonous excrements. But while for Klein, good objects are introjected in the same way that bad objects are, Deleuze thinks that every object
is bad in principle according to the paranoid-schizoid position, since it is only in
the subsequent depressive position that the child strives to reconstitute a complete good object with which to identify itself.[25] What the schizoid position
opposes to the anal-sadistic partial objects, according to Deleuze, is rather the
urethral-sadistic BwO, "with neither mouth nor anus, having given up all introjection and projection, and being complete, at this price."[26] The bad objects,
being hard and solid substances that change like simulacra, are imagined as excrements whirling and exploding in a hollow depth, or within the id as a reser-
voir from which the good object extracts its force. Meanwhile, the perfection
and completeness of the BwO is fluid and liquid and is imagined as urine, melt-
ing and welding together all of the toxic excrements that people its full depth
like a den of introjected savage beasts, from which the good object extracts its
complete and integrated form as an ego.[27] With the onset of the depressive position, however, the good object is elevated into the heights and idealised as a
transcendent principle. It extracts a Voice out of the disjunctive communication
of bodies in depth and replaces the liquid principle of the BwO, giving way to
the dynamic genesis of language on a metaphysical surface fashioned out of
eating and shitting.[28] But while this subversion of the BwO gives birth to language, the recovery of the death instinct within it dissolves the ego, desexualises
the libido, and engenders thought out of the displaceable energy.[29] Therefore it
is not the BwO itself that is the object of the regressive analysis, so much as the

form of the individual ego that is extracted from the BwO by the good object, and which must be integrated with its self-suppression by the death instinct before it can be possible to think. The univocity of language is "sculpted out of shit"[30] on the metaphysical surface of thought by the death instinct, whose disjunctive rather than negative force reaches nonsense as the degree zero of the surface, upon which the full depth of the BwO and the height of the good object communicate in order to produce language. The death instinct and the partial objects are therefore not overcome during normal childhood development but rather persist through the formation of inclusive disjunctions, and the schizoid position returns with every instance of creative thought over the course of adult life. In his work with Guattari, however, Deleuze will replace the death instinct with the BwO.

In *Anti-Oedipus*, Deleuze and Guattari reconceive the BwO in the context of capitalist production as the disjunctive synthesis of anti-production, and partial objects as the component desiring-machines of the connective synthesis, or the production of production. While in *The Logic of Sense*, the metaphysical surface is the site of the inclusive disjunction between the full depth of the BwO and the height of the good object, in *Anti-Oedipus* the BwO falls back on all of production and constitutes a surface over which it distributes the productive forces of desiring-machines, appropriating their surplus-production so that it appears to emanate from the full BwO as a *quasi-cause*.[31] Yet this appropriation succeeds an initial repulsion towards the desiring-machines from the empty BwO, echoing its opposition to the persecuting bad objects before it had assimilated them into its full depth. The genesis of the machine and its undifferentiated surface lies in this repulsive "primary repression," which takes the form of a paranoiac machine before being succeeded by a miraculating machine that appropriates surplus-production and produces the full BwO. Paralleling this coupling of the BwO with the process of desiring-production is its coupling with the process of social production. Historically, the full BwO functions as a *socius* in the name of the earth, the tyrant, and finally capital, at which point it increasingly comes to play the role of a recording surface that produces the objectification characteristic of Marx's commodity fetishism.[32] Judge Schreber mirrors the disjunctions performed on this recording surface when he divides himself up into parts that correspond to earlier and later empires, or superior or inferior Gods, leading Deleuze and Guattari to ask whether the genealogy of the schizo-paranoiac recording process is Oedipal, or whether it simply lends this appearance due to its re-appropriation of attempts to domesticate it according to the Oedipal code.[33] Naturally, they reject the priority of the Oedipus complex and try to show how Schreber puts its avatars to his own anti-oedipal use. Denying that his parents had produced him, or that his own intrinsic determinations could be reduced to his parents as extrinsic determinations, Schreber appears to undertake a regressive analysis in order to purge the fiction of the Oedipal triangle and succeed it with a synthetic order of production. Its delirious, seemingly Oedipal expressions are simply the nonsensical result of integrating the regressive analysis with its self-suppression. The genealogical series constitutive of the recording process would therefore not aim at a retelling of the story of Oedipus, but rather a genealogy of the substance whose retelling of the story of *causa sui* would take on cosmic rather than Oedipal proportions. But while Deleuze and Guattari may invoke Spinoza when they orient the BwO as the immanent substance where intensity equals zero, with the partial objects as its ultimate attributes or intensive degrees,[34] the substantial attribute does not yet figure into their account in *Anti-Oedipus*. Instead, Schreber's passage through these intensive degrees is conceived in terms of Nietzsche's eternal return. Succeeding the simultaneously attractive and repulsive interdependence between desiring-machines and the BwO, part of the libidinal energy that was transformed by the first two syntheses is drawn off by a third synthesis of conjunction, which consummates their alliance with a celibate machine and the residual formation of a nomadic subject. While the celibate machine produces intensive quantities as lived states, the nomadic subject is perpetually reborn out of them and lives through each of them as an individual other than the one it believes itself to be, in the same sense as when Nietzsche says, *"Every name in history is I . . . ."*[35]

In *A Thousand Plateaus*, Deleuze and Guattari return to the BwO in the plateau entitled "November 28, 1947: How Do You Make Yourself a Body without Organs?," where the concept receives its most sustained account. Heliogabalus' crowned anarchy is equated with Spinoza's *Ethics*,[36] and the empty (suicidal) and cancerous (fascist) BwO's are posited as the limits of a program of experimental decomposition, whose aim is to construct a full BwO capable of obtaining the totality of BwO's. Returning to themes first introduced in *Anti-Oedipus*, Deleuze and Guattari describe the BwO as "*the field of immanence* of desire, the *plane of consistency* specific to desire (with desire defined as a process of production without reference to any exterior agency, whether it be a lack that hollows it out or a pleasure that fills it)."[37] They claim that "the attributes are types or genuses of BwO's, substances, powers, zero intensities as matrices of production,"[38] but without elaborating very much on the implications of this alternative reading of Spinoza. The real is produced as an intensive quantity starting from these non-stratified and unformed zero intensities of matter, which are oriented differently for each BwO. As the substantial attribute Pain, the sewn-up body of the masochist is the degree zero of intensity that allows *pain-waves* to circulate, and as the substantial attribute Cold, the drugged body of the addict is the degree zero of intensity that allows *refrigerator-waves* to circulate.[39] The relation of partial objects to the BwO initially posited in *Anti-Oedipus*, where they are likened to the ultimate attributes or intensive degrees of the BwO *qua* immanent substance, is further complicated by the introduction of substantial attributes. The organs, as partial objects, are no longer understood to be the enemies of the BwO. Instead, the BwO and its "true organs" are opposed to the artificial hierarchy of the organism *qua* organic organisation of the organs.[40] Each of the BwO's is made up of plateaus of intensity, and each BwO is itself a plateau of intensity in communication with other plateaus, forming components of passage whose totality is obtained on the plane of consistency by an abstract machine that constructs it.[41] The totality of BwO's, however, excludes the cancerous (fascist) and empty (suicidal) bodies, and it is not clear whether this totality is solely logical. If it were solely logical, then the intuitive knowledge of God that Spinoza calls *beatitude* would be sufficient to obtain it. But if the passage of substances were real, then something closer to Nietzsche's perspectival knowledge would be required. The BwO's would produce a series of states in the celibate machine while the nomadic subject would consume and consummate these states, passing through the circle of the eternal return that would finally select the full BwO's. The connective and conjunctive syntheses of *Anti-Oedipus* would be effectively integrated into the BwO and its operation of the disjunctive synthesis. Nonetheless, the relation of the BwO to Spinoza's philosophy remains problematic for many different reasons, the greatest of which are the use of the substantial attributes, and the importance given to abstraction in attaining what would seem to be a form of adequate knowledge that bypasses the path of common notions.

How to make sense of Deleuze and Guattari's claim that Spinoza's *Ethics*, with its imperative of cultivating a joyful art of wisdom according to a triple denunciation of consciousness, values, and sad passions, is the great book of Artaud's BwO? The immanent rules and procedures of experimentation of the BwO would appear to make consciousness, values, and sad passions into the very means of approaching the degree zero of intensity, where the art of caution as opposed to wisdom prevails in the strange program of dismantling and shutting down the organism. To what end does this experimental program of approaching degree zero serve, and does it not entail a diminishing of the powers of acting and being affected, effectively contradicting the very nature of Spinoza's ethical project? All those who judge things confusedly, according to Spinoza, are unable to know things through their first causes, because they do not distinguish between the modifications of substances and the substances themselves.[42] The path toward realizing one Substance made possible by the BwO would seem to pass through similar confusions, such as the stupidity, malevolence, and madness that must be exorcised in order for the BwO to be discovered as the continuum of all substances in intensity and all intensities in substance. The problem, however, would pass from one of confused judgement to one of cautious experimentation: instead of distinguishing substances from their modifications, their continuity would be deliberately posited in order to uncover the substance of all substances. What if rather than being overcome as quickly as possible, the fictitious abstractions of the regressive analysis were instead prolonged according to the experimental program of the BwO? The absolute affirmation of the existence of a single, absolute substance would be delayed, allowing desire to approach the turmoil of life just long enough for the substantial attribute to produce *pain-waves* and *refrigerator-waves* that would sustain its imaginary separate existence. Would the qualitative multiplicity of attributes then have to be experienced in lived duration before the superstitions of a separate existence could be overcome, leaving the substantial attributes in the position of having been the objects of a genetic construction after all?

Perhaps a mode whose existence is not yet enveloped by its essence reflects the choice that Man had, according to Artaud in his radio play *To Have Done with the Judgement of God*, to have kept his anus closed in order to avoid shitting, paradoxically choosing to live by consenting to not exist in duration, but instead as a BwO or substantial attribute whose fabrication would have delivered him from his faecal automatisms and restored him to his true liberty.[43] The peopling of such a BwO with innumerable, infinitesimal beasts, whose development as partial objects would risk the hubristic stupidity of the human unconscious, would render these smallest of animalcules equivalent to the largest of universal attributes. The developed diversity of all of their degrees would touch the equality of an enveloping measure that would be the same for all things, or a univocal Being that Artaud would conceive of as shit.[44] But Artaud's scatological claim about God in this regard would risk confusing the full BwO with its empty (suicidal) or cancerous (fascist) doubles. By means of a cautious procedure that would render their circulation across the BwO, these beasts, as intensities or individuating factors, would overturn the analogical judgement of God that had overseen their division according to a hierarchical distribution, and redistribute themselves into a formal-real multiplicity, in which they would fuse back together and engender thought in lived duration. After ripping apart the organic organization of the organism, the despotic illusion of God's judgement would be vanquished, and the *asylum ignorantiae*, that refuge for those seeking the reason of final causes behind all things,[45] would be destroyed.

But while the *asylum ignorantiae* may in this sense be a refuge for sad passions seeking purpose and intelligibility, it is the continual variations of existence by duration, according to Deleuze in *Spinoza: Practical Philosophy*, that are truly the last refuge of the bad.[46] In other words, not simply the illusion of final causes, but the efficient cause of the *conatus* as the *right* of the existing mode, or the appetite of the mode to persevere after having passed into existence that counsels struggles, hatreds, angers, and trickery before becoming a possessed and active power of the mode.[47] As intoxication, poisoning, or indigestion, that which is bad for the body only comes to be imagined as *evil* in itself according to the superstitions of the *asylum ignorantiae*, which simultaneously separates the body from its *conatus* while pushing it to imagine the death that lies beyond its limits in mythical terms. But the interlocking of relations of motion and rest between smaller bodies, such as the chyle and lymph, compose the blood according to a third, dominant relation constitutive of the organic body. The destruction of this dominant relation, rather than being caused by evil, simply comes about when its parts are so disposed that they acquire a *different relation* of motion and rest.[48] Whether an act is associated with an image of something it either decomposes or to which it joins its own relation is what determines whether it will appear as being either good or evil, and whether the idea associated with it will be either adequate or inadequate.[49] But while Spinoza may expel evil from the order of individual relations constitutive of bodies, does he also manage to expel evil from the order of singular modal essences that lie deeper than the individual relations constitutive of bodies? In *The Peyote Dance*,

Artaud provides us with a hint as to how what Spinoza calls *asylum ignorantiae* may not simply be a refuge for the imaginary abstractions of a consciousness that mistakes effects for causes, but alternatively a technique of awareness capable of saving consciousness from sad passions. The Tarahumara Indians of Mexico apply such a technique to prepare their consciousness against the risks of falling into abstraction after consuming peyote, such as the evil that results from a loss of consciousness.[50] Artaud mentions the usefulness of having *the obsession of counting* when intoxicated by peyote, ostensibly because it preserves conscious control over the power of abstraction, and saves one from a loss of consciousness.[51] When the bad finds its final refuge in the formal-real multiplicity of qualitative duration, the illusion of numerical distinction becomes an essential feature in the art of caution, aiding the *conatus* in its attempt to ward off the perceived threat of evil. As objects of the genetic construction itself, the substantial attributes make use of the imaginary abstractions of consciousness, such as number and evil, as artificial constraints meant to protect its constitutive relations from decomposing too quickly.

Ciguri is the divine name for the Infinite, the God of Peyote, the peyote plant itself, and the concoction that the Tarahumara consume when practicing the sacred Rite of *Ciguri*. *Ciguri* is also the God of equilibrium and self-control, since to consume too much of the concoction will result in the immediate disappearance of *Ciguri* and the coming of the Evil Spirit in his place.[52] *Ciguri* allows the Tarahumara to abandon the illusions of normal consciousness and the body, and reach a higher plane of consciousness or immanence upon which they transcend the world of things and bear witness to truth as the play of masculine and feminine principles animating reality,[53] which is simply *Ciguri*:

> . . . MAN as SELF-CREATED, HIMSELF in the space HE *was constructing* FOR HIMSELF, when God murdered him. . . . these principles were not in the body, never reached the body, but obstinately remained like two immaterial ideas suspended outside of Being, eternally opposed to HIM, and which moreover made *their own bodies*, bodies in which the idea of matter is volatilised by CIGURI.[54]

And yet, the experience of good and evil can never be traced back to the source that distributes the nameless impulses that cause one to judge according to this experience.[55] As a crowned anarchy or substantial attribute, *Ciguri* can only be apprehended through cautious experimentation with physical-chemical states, and not through the false perception of God's judgment over good and evil. While still an object of real experience for Artaud, evil is ultimately untruth, or that which does not actually exist in the bad encounter.[56] He would thus remain in agreement with Spinoza against Blyenbergh in denying that there could be any singular modal essences to which it *pertains* to poison,[57] even though his opposition to the Western rationalist tradition would lead him to seek out something redeeming in what might otherwise be dismissed as superstition:

The infinite emulsion of the heart is what Evil has tried to kill in the worlds, but in this emulsion there are many folds, thicknesses, substances, and textures, and each thickness is an idea, and the idea a state of the heart, and a creature with its own soul, and each state of the sensible a substance that has come out of God, and the Source of all Substance this Giving Heart, Distributor of substances of being who gives its substance to Being in the Multiformity of the Infinite.[58]

Evil is not error but untruth, perhaps an expression of the hubristic stupidity of the human unconscious, that natural "powerlessness" that is indistinguishable from the greatest power of thought, which in this case would be the excess of *Ciguri* that brings about the Evil Spirit in his place. It is in Artaud's divergence from Spinoza in this regard that Deleuze and Guattari can be seen to be taking their cue with the subverted Spinozism of the BwO, as well as Deleuze by himself perhaps, when he claims that the transcendental form of each faculty must be shown to be indistinguishable from its disjointed, superior, or transcendent exercise. If the transcendent exercise of thought should lead it into the *asylum ignorantiae*, it would not at all be in the same sense as when Badiou condemns the virtual for being no better than finality in *The Clamor of Being*,[59] but rather as a cautious test intended to purge the virtual of its illusions by means of those illusions, according to the efficient cause of the *conatus*. Beginning with one excessive equivocation, it puts an end to equivocity and constructs all of univocity.[60]

Normally it would be assumed that according to Spinoza, the second kind of knowledge and the adequate ideas corresponding to it could only be obtained by means of an increase in our powers of acting and being affected. The imagination, as the condition under which common notions are formed and ideas are made adequate, is the same as the condition under which the *asylum ignorantiae* substitutes for rationality. The only ideas that we have under the natural conditions of our perception are the ideas that represent *what happens* to our body through its mixture with other bodies, but these ideas are necessarily inadequate.[61] The common notions are physico-chemical or biological Ideas, since the very first common notions that we form express a kind of organic continuity between bodies in agreement, relative to the natural conditions of our perception, through which our ideas come into agreement.[62] Deleuze suggests that it is through these least universal common notions that substantial attributes are grasped by way of hypothesis, before the sufficient synthetic explanation of a single, absolute substance is reached.[63] The most universal common notions, on the other hand, are mathematical, but still biological in that they both articulate and further enable the disjunction of bodies or ideas in necessary disagreement, allowing them to develop through more productive arrangements. An increase in our understanding of something as being necessary would seem to correspond to a common notion of increased universality, while the intensity of our feeling towards something imaginary would surpass the certainty of necessity. But the procedure of the BwO seems to bypass the path of common notions[64] and go in the opposite direction, by way of a decrease in our powers of acting and being affected, in their approach toward the degree zero of intensity. Not only are the common notions bypassed (the BwO "is not at all a notion"),[65] but adequate ideas must be attained according to a procedure able to circumvent the impossibility of forming them through bad encounters. According to Deleuze, the passage to lesser states of perfection that results from a diminution of the powers of acting and being affected only pertains to existence or duration, and not to essence.[66] Duration is the last refuge of the bad, precisely because the sadness expressed through this passage only has reality according to the right of the *conatus* that drives the mode to persevere in its existence, if even at the cost of qualifying itself as a substance. Would this leave the essence to which the corresponding state or affection pertains instantaneous? Deleuze hesitates before explaining why it would not. While existence constitutes a "physical-chemical test" of experimentation and not of judgment, such as Artaud's experience with peyote amongst the Tarahumara, essence is eternal and not instantaneous because it forms the state of intensive quantity contemporaneous with qualitative duration in existence. Essence expresses itself relationally as an eternal truth, even if it is the untruth of evil that reveals itself to Artaud when he consumes too much peyote. The degree zero of intensity therefore expresses the eternal truth of a singular modal essence. Like Klein's infant, it expresses the smallest possible number of affections coming from itself, and for this reason, perhaps, can only apprehend itself in duration as a separately existing and self-causing substantial attribute. But this still leaves us at a loss to explain how such an entity could even begin to form adequate ideas, when the single attribute that expresses its essence is not Thought, but Pain or Cold. By what means would it gain the power to moderate and restrain its affects, and avoid falling into what Spinoza calls bondage?[67] If Thought would truly be absent for the substantial attributes Pain and Cold, would they even be capable of forming inadequate ideas, let alone adequate ones? And does the power of imagining belong to Thought exclusively, if at all? Perhaps Pain and Cold are grasped hypothetically through common notions of the least universal type, before the formation of adequate ideas categorically affirms them as the differential elements of a single, absolute substance.

On inadequate ideas, Spinoza states that they "are adequate in the mind of God not insofar as he contains only the essence of the mind that thinks them, but insofar as he also contains in himself, at the same time, the minds of other things."[68] It is not the essences of other minds, but rather the minds of other things themselves that God contains in relation to the essence of the mind that thinks inadequate ideas. What could these other minds possibly be? Between the mind thinking the inadequate idea and God containing the same idea in adequate form, the presence of other minds somehow interferes in the passage from inadequate to adequate, finite to infinite. Because there can be no adequate ideas of bodies that disagree or of affections that are not present, the existence of these other minds is perhaps posited *in abstracto*, in the guise of qualified substances that can only be conceived through themselves and not through another, enjoying the imagined properties of being unique in their own kind, self-caused, and infinite. In this sense, they would be like the substances that Artaud finds in the infinite emulsion of his heart. The poisonous excess of peyote decomposes Artaud's dominant organic relation while Evil tries to kill it in the supernatural worlds of *Ciguri*, or the unknown attributes that express the qualified substances. Or alternatively, perhaps these other minds belong to the poison itself. "The War of Principles" in Artaud's *Heliogabalus* shows how qualified substances are perceived in Paganism when they appear to transcend a consciousness blocked by the depth of its fall: they are gods existing as veritably separate entities or cosmic faculties, that can only be conceived of as a numerical multiplicity of divine names by an individual consciousness only capable of thinking in images and forms.[69] As separate principles existing behind things, these gods, Artaud tells us, borne from the separation of forces, will die of their reunion like crabs that devour one another in a basket,[70] in what seems like a mystical version of the transcendent exercise of the faculties. Following a path through classical esotericism, Artaud discovers the underlying realities of numerically distinct principles in the notion of divinities that divide their energies and fuse back together. In much the same way, according to Pythagoras, Number does not regress back to the cardinality of quantity but rather suppresses this logical regression, by affirming the absence of quantity in ordinal degrees of vibration where the principles are reduced to nothing.[71] These degrees of vibration are like the formal-real multiplicity of innumerable beasts that circulate between BwO's and establish their continuity in duration. Meanwhile, the principles are the minds contained in God together with the inadequate ideas, of which the mind that thinks inadequate ideas is the partial cause. The principles accounting for God's will in the *asylum ignorantiae*, or the wills of the pagan gods, cancel themselves on the intensive continuum upon which the totality of BwO's is obtained by means of this war of principles. The genealogy of the substance and its synthetic order of production are thus realized through a genealogy of divine names,[72] whose identification with the series of lived states of intensity in the eternal return dramatizes Nietzsche's claim that "*Every name in history is I . . . .*"

Yet how do the substantial attributes or BwO's pass from separately existing yet really distinct singular modal essences, reduced as they are to the degree zero of intensity, to an existence that takes the form of duration as a qualitative multiplicity, and proceeds to reunite them on the plane of immanence? It becomes a question of making intensities pass between the BwO's, and the challenge of increasing the powers of acting and being affected from degree zero upwards. In the absence of ideas or modes of thought, Artaud's innumerable beasts, in expressing the reality of sad passions, are experienced as *pain-waves* or *refrigerator-waves*. But as a "physical-chemical test" by means of which the composition of the body is deliberately but cautiously decomposed, how does experimentation with such states reflect the process of genetic construction that integrates the regressive analysis with its self-suppression? Between these physical and logical variations of what Deleuze and Guattari present as essentially the same problem, we can perhaps see the intoxicated imagination enacting the

regressive analysis by transforming modes of infinite substance into really separated substances, or breaking it into as many substances as it perceives modes. It
would thereby undertake an analysis of its own chemical composition, not unlike Artaud contemplating over the substances folded within the infinite emulsion of his heart. Artaud's war of principles, on the other hand, would enact the
self-suppression of this process by means of the passage from numerically distinct principles to the fusion of their denoted intensities, in the formal-real multiplicity of innumerable beasts vibrating and circulating between BwO's. Unlike
the event of poisoning, in which the power of being affected is absolutely fulfilled while the power of acting tends towards degree zero of intensity, linking
up the totality of BwO's on the plane of immanence absolutely fulfills both the
powers of acting and of being affected, affirming the convergence of substantial
attributes upon a single, absolute substance. Meanwhile, the genetic construction
of the BwO that determines whether it will become either full, empty (suicidal),
or cancerous (fascist) is determined by those same careful doses of caution that
inform Artaud's consciousness when he experiments with peyote amongst the
Tarahumara, or the power to moderate and restrain the affects that informs Spinoza's avoidance of human bondage.

What further light could the concept of becoming-animal help to cast on the
relationship between stupidity and the BwO? In *Difference and Repetition*,
Deleuze states clearly that stupidity [*bêtise*], in the sense in which he means it,
has nothing to do with animality, since the animal is protected by specific forms
that prevent it from being "stupid."[73] But this would not seem to preclude that in
the programmatic transmission of forces between man and animal, stupidity
could play no role, since as groundlessness stupidity is, like Artaud's innumerable beasts, the animality peculiar to thought. In his essay "The Transcendental
'Stupidity' ('Bêtise') of Man and the Becoming-Animal According to Deleuze,"
Derrida claims that the single appearance of *bêtise* in *A Thousand Plateaus*, in
which it refers to the stupidities of psychoanalysis when confronted with the
becoming-animal of masochism, has nothing to do with what Deleuze may have
intended in *Difference and Repetition*.[74] However, this would perhaps be to
overlook the difference between the stupidity that is indistinguishable from the
greatest power of thought and the stupidity that is institutionalized by the tyrant.
For the masochist who is constructing himself a BwO, becoming-animal is an
essential step in making intensities pass across it. Seeking to destroy his instinc-
tive forces in order to replace them with transmitted forces, the masochist effects
an inversion of signs whose purpose is to tame the animality innate to his power
of thinking.[75] Between the horse's series (innate force, force transmitted by the
human being) and the masochist's series (force transmitted by the horse, innate
force of the human being), the powers of acting and being affected are increased
through a circuit of intensities that fills the plane of immanence of desire without determining its aim according to pleasure as its extrinsic measure.[76] It is
therefore an exercise in self-mastery that renders animality thinkable and trans-
ferable, rather than an act of voluntary servitude in which thought is blindly
dominated by the animality peculiar to it. Between the becoming-animal leading

to the masochist's psychic individuation as a horse and the BwO as ground, stupidity would appear to be the occasion or quasi-cause that allows the BwO to
rise to the surface and form adequate ideas, by virtue of the increase in the powers of acting and being affected given to thought through this encounter.

But in the case of the psychoanalytic misapprehension of becoming-animal,
the animal is understood as a representative of drives or a representation of the
parents, without any feeling for the unnatural participations that a child might be
capable of in attempting to come to terms with the senseless cruelty of animal
domestication.[77] This same type of misapprehension is echoed in *Difference and
Repetition*:

> All determinations become bad or cruel when they are grasped only by a
> thought which invents and contemplates them, flayed and separated from their
> living form, adrift upon this barren ground. Everything becomes violence on
> this passive ground. Everything becomes attack on this digestive ground. Here
> the Sabbath of stupidity and malevolence take place.[78]

And again, the single appearance of *bêtise* in *A Thousand Plateaus*, which Derrida claims has nothing to do with *bêtise* in *Difference and Repetition*:

> Similarly, fewer stupidities would be uttered on the topic of pain, humiliation,
> and anxiety in masochism if it were understood that it is the becomings-animal
> that lead to masochism, not the other way around.[79]

It seems apparent that the stupidities of psychoanalysis, with all of its forced
oedipalizations and emptied BwO's, are of the same type as the stupidity that is
institutionalized by the tyrant. Meanwhile, Deleuze distinguishes a positive role
for stupidity in *Difference and Repetition* that does not seem much different
from the full BwO:

> It is true that this most pitiful faculty also becomes the royal faculty when it an-
> imates philosophy as a philosophy of mind—in other words, when it leads all
> the other faculties to that transcendent exercise which renders possible a violent
> reconciliation between the individual, the ground and thought.[80]

While in *Coldness and Cruelty*, Deleuze may have initially seen an affinity between Spinoza and Sade for their commonly naturalistic and mechanistic approaches,[81] this was before the appearance of Guéroult's as well as Deleuze's
own studies of Spinoza. Having later perhaps realized the understated role of the
imagination in forming adequate ideas, he re-evaluated this affinity, and in collaboration with Guattari, established masochism as one of the two most perplex-
ing exemplars of the full BwO. Against the sadistic stupidity that is institutionalized by the tyrant in the form of the "sadomasochism" that renders BwO's either
empty (suicidal) or cancerous (fascist), we have the masochistic stupidity that is
indistinguishable from the greatest power of thought, capable of desiring with-

out recourse to lack, and of constructing the plane of immanence upon which the totality of full BwO's can be realized.

Spinoza asks what Deleuze and Guattari take to be the fundamental question of political philosophy in *Anti-Oedipus*: "Why do men fight *for* their servitude as stubbornly as though it were their salvation?"[82] Neither ignorance nor illusion is sufficient to explain the phenomenon of fascism when desire is not taken into account, and the psychoanalytic reduction of desire to the triangulation of Oedipus as its sole measure merely serves to proliferate its repressive mechanisms and prepare desire for its fight for servitude. The tyrant who institutionalizes stupidity depends upon such an Oedipal Image of thought, in the same sense that the fascist or cancerous BwO belongs to a stratum of the organism, signifiance, or subjectification that has begun to proliferate.[83] But according to what rations must one keep enough of the organism, signifiance, and subjectification in order to ensure the success of the full BwO,[84] and avoid a fate even worse than that of Oedipus? In light of this question, Deleuze and Guattari's attitude towards the strata in *A Thousand Plateaus* seems like a cautious rejoinder to the schizophrenic destruction of the dogmatic Image of thought celebrated by Deleuze in *Difference and Repetition*.[85] It also seems to anticipate the identification made between the plane of immanence and the Image of thought in *What Is Philosophy?*, where they assume their most moderate position after appearing to abandon the anti-oedipal BwO while opposing two forms of idiocy as conceptual personae: the old idiot, who like Descartes searches for indubitable truths following from the subjective presuppositions of his Image of thought, and the new idiot, who like Dostoevsky or Artaud wants to turn the absurd into the highest power of thought.[86] Are the hallucinations, erroneous perceptions, and bad feelings engendered by *Ciguri* simply illusions that fog up the plane of immanence,[87] or as the objects of a disjointed, superior, and transcendent exercise, can they still impart the project of transcendental empiricism with sense?

For a being to go to the limit of what it can do, claims Deleuze in *Difference and Repetition*, still presupposes a limit that refers to that upon the basis of which the being is deployed and deploys all of its power.[88] This basis has less to do with what is best distributed according to univocal principles of division and hierarchy, than it does with how the equality of univocal being is borne out of the hubris and anarchy of beings, and comes to act as the enveloping measure for the nomadic distribution of individuating factors.[89] This crowned anarchy that makes substance turn on its modes finds expression in what Deleuze calls the leitmotiv of Darwin's *The Origin of the Species*: we do not know what individual difference is capable of.[90] By connecting free-floating differences and making them diverge as fixed differences, natural selection plays the role of a differenciator of difference. But the status of individual difference remains unclear so long as it cannot be distinguished from the indeterminate variability of free-floating differences. Weismann's discovery of sexed reproduction as the principle of varied individual difference, in which the germ plasma was believed to program the somatic development of the parts of the organism in advance of and without the intervention of any external factors,[91] effected a Copernican

Revolution in Darwinism that recast the egg as the primary site of natural selection.[92] The differenciation of germ plasma in the egg according to the mechanism of sexed reproduction allowed for a clearer distinction to be drawn between individual difference and the free-floating differences out of which it was formed. But the consequences of recasting the egg as the primary site of natural selection were to be even more far reaching. According to Deleuze, von Baër's conclusion that epigenesis proceeded from the more to the less general points these highest generalities of life beyond species and genus in the direction of individual and pre-individual singularities.[93] Embryonic individuation therefore precedes the actualization of species, parts, and sexes, which are consequently understood to turn on its individual difference. According to Deleuze and Guattari, this condition continues to apply to the fully developed adult organism with differenciated species, parts, and sex. The conditions of embryonic life remain adjacent (and not simply prior) to it as its BwO, or as the intense germen that defies the numerical distinction between parents and children accorded by organic representation.[94] Instead, the BwO incorporates the natural cause of its individual difference, or sexed reproduction, into itself. This explains how the child can be the germinal contemporary of its parents. When Artaud claims that "I, Antonin Artaud, am my son, my father, my mother, and myself,"[95] he means that the conditions of embryonic life do not simply mark the beginning of his organic existence, but that they constitute thought itself, which is neither innate nor acquired, but *engendered.* And it is perhaps for this same reason that Deleuze claims that dreams are our eggs and that the world itself is an egg:[96] in addition to the production of the varied individual differences of mortal embryos (and not of the potentially immortal amoebae that reproduce with minimal variance according to cell division), the play of masculine and feminine principles, as incarnated by *Ciguri,* also animates oneiric and worldly realities.

While Deleuze and Guattari reject the death instinct in *A Thousand Plateaus,* Deleuze's appropriation of it in his earlier account of the genitality of thought bears further consideration in relation to our understanding of the BwO. As an intrinsic determination of psychic life, the death instinct is constituted (rather than served) by the desexualized energy of the libido, whose reflux upon the ego makes it narcissistic while emptying time of its mnemic content.[97] This leaves behind a fractured I that acts upon the narcissistic ego as an Other, together forming an aborted cogito that engenders thought out of the resulting displaceable libidinal energy. As the prototype of the death instinct, empty time loses its circular shape and assumes a straight form that unites past, present, and future, while causing them to be played out according to its abstract and impersonal nature. In the sense that it undoes the too well centered natural or physical circle of the organism, this empty form of time seems to parallel the empty (suicidal) BwO that is fabricated by means of a descent toward the degree zero of intensity. But the straight line of time forms a circle once again following the destruction of the past as Id and the present as ego. Nietzsche's eternal return reveals itself as the other face of the death instinct that is oriented toward the future, affirming everything of chance except for what subordinates it to the

One, the Same, and the Necessary.[98] Closer as it is to the hubris and anarchy of beings than it is to the division and hierarchy of being, this face of death acts as the extrinsic enveloping measure that forms a single maximum the same for all things. It has nothing to do with the limitation imposed by matter on mortal life, or the opposition between matter and immortal life. What it affirms of chance are the fortuitous second-degree differences that allow series of first-degree differences to communicate through inclusive disjunctions, or the intensities whose violence can only be endured under the conditions of embryonic life, be it in the womb of the mother or in the perpetually aborted thought of the larval subject or BwO.[99] The eternally decentered circle of time is reflected in these intensities, which people the BwO as though they were *a priori* Others whose expression of possible worlds[100] were to force it to think. In raising each event to the power of the eternal return, the BwO, as a fortuitous case, affirms its distance with respect to every other event, before passing through all of the other BwO's implied by them and extracting the unique Event of its universal freedom.[101] Through this act of counter-actualization, the full BwO performs a disjunctive synthesis that makes each individual series resonate inside all of the others *a priori*. In Bergsonian terms, each duration has the power to disclose and encompass other durations, which are only simultaneous insofar as they subsume each other in a single, universal and impersonal Time,[102] or the eternal return as the intensive continuum of all BwO's.

On first appearance, the respective conceptions of death in Spinoza and Freud could not possibly appear to be more antithetical to one another. For Spinoza, the *conatus* is only limited by death, which affects the extensive parts constituted under it in an externally occurring empirical event, while not affecting the singular modal essence itself. Freud's death instinct, on the other hand, expresses every organism's wish to die in its own way. Deleuze suggests that this will-to-die is undermined by Freud's idea that every organism also wishes to return to the state of inanimate matter, and that every psyche wishes to regress to an amoeboid state of neuronic inertia.[103] But Freud and Spinoza are each in their own way right: Freud with regard to the internal will-to-die and Spinoza with regard to the event of death that can never be willed as our own. Deleuze emphasizes the necessary non-correspondence of the objects of their claims, despite the attempt to make them coincide in the case of suicide.[104] Even in suicide, the ultimate cause of death remains external to the *conatus*. For Spinoza, death does not take the form of a will-to-die internal to the existing mode, but always comes from outside accidentally. Rather than finding its ultimate aim in a return to inanimate matter, the *conatus* aims to increase its powers of acting and being affected and preserve its existence in duration. With help from the imagination, it finds the cause of joy and that which destroys the cause of sadness.[105] To be obsessed by the fear of death is slavery for Spinoza, for whom the free man thinks of nothing less than death. But in relation to the other face of death, or the eternal return, the *conatus* must assume the method of extracting its true thoughts according to the rule of chance.[106] By risking encounters with forces of various unknown quantities that could bring death, it would receive the quality corresponding to the quantity of its own force.[107] Out of these encounters, the *conatus* would find its genealogical element in the guise of Nietzsche's will to power with its *affirmative* and *negative* primordial qualities, or to return to Spinoza, in the guise of the substantial attribute that would discriminate the limits of self-causation according to a genealogy of the substance while following the same principle of interpretation and evaluation. As the differential and genetic element added to force, the substantial attribute would then be the internal principle of both the qualitative and the quantitative determination of relations between forces.[108]

Throughout our discussion, we have attempted to show how the animality peculiar to thought is integral to the genetic constitution of thought, and how Spinoza's *Ethics*, by way of Artaud as well as Nietzsche, can be seen to support the priority of this animality. Yet the monstrosity that such thought engenders in the absence of judgement and rational presuppositions leaves us faced with the problem of discerning joy from sadness and desire from death, and the challenge of making such discernments according to Spinoza's initial criteria. The biggest challenge facing the BwO is undoubtedly the test that is posed to the consciously desiring *conatus*: how to distinguish within desire between that which pertains to the proliferation of strata or too-violent destratification on the one hand, and what pertains to the construction of the plane of consistency on the other.[109] According to what criteria is it able to make the right selections for the construction of the plane from amongst BwO's that, like the good and bad objects, all too often pose difficulties in being able to be told apart? And most importantly, what does it take to overcome the fascist desire for servitude? Will the world of crowned anarchy that the BwO desires to reach be a world of tyranny ruled by a crowned anarchist like Heliogabalus, in which the substance that is said of modes only stands for the self-annihilating aspect of reactive forces? Or will it be a utopian anarchist world in which individuals mutually seek out each other's advantages, and in which the substance that is said of modes stands for the singularity of each individual in relation to all others, that nonetheless forces each individual to pass through all others?[110] The eternal return, in forcing us to pass through the *a priori* Others folded within the names of history, must operate its selection of forces without destroying us in the process. The transcendent exercise of the faculties must engender thought without irretrievably plunging us into stupidity, whether by means of a dogmatic Image of thought that would help to institutionalize it, or by means of the absence of any Image of thought that would make experimentation all the more fortuitous for us to undergo in light of its unforeseeable dangers. Quite simply, the absence of the stratifying tendency characteristic of the Image of thought must be compensated for through the linking together of full BwO's on the intensive continuum. While their formal-real distinction precludes them from having anything like a greater strength in numbers, it is through the reduction of number to vibrations of intensity that allows for qualitatively dissonant and harmonic effects to spontaneously coalesce between them, and it is through these effects alone that they must realize their beatitude.

Notes

1. Benedict de Spinoza, *Ethics*, in *The Collected Works of Spinoza*, vol. 1, ed. and trans. Edwin Curley (Princeton: Princeton University Press, 1985), I, def. 3–5.

2. Spinoza, *Ethics*, I, P1–8.

3. Gilles Deleuze, *Difference and Repetition*, trans. Paul Patton (New York: Columbia University Press, 1994), 147.

4. Antonin Artaud, *Collected Works*, vol. 1, trans. Victor Corti (London: John Calder, 1999), 41–42.

5. Artaud, *Collected Works*, vol. 1, 42–44.

6. Deleuze, *Difference and Repetition*, 275, 150.

7. Deleuze, *Difference and Repetition*, 148–51.

8. Deleuze, *Difference and Repetition*, 143.

9. Deleuze, *Difference and Repetition*, 143.

10. Gilles Deleuze, *Desert Islands and Other Texts, 1953–1974*, ed. David Lapoujade, trans. Michael Taormina (New York: Semiotext(e), 2004), 62–63.

11. Deleuze, *Difference and Repetition*, 130, 139. With regards to ill will and what Deleuze calls misosophy, Shestov claims that Nietzsche had hidden the disgust he had for his own egoism and poverty behind aristocratic manners, and that for this reason was closer to being an "underground man" in Dostoevsky's sense than an aristocrat: "Nietzsche's great merit lies in his ability to defend before the eyes of the whole world the 'egoism' of poverty—not the poverty that is fought by social reform, but the kind for which, even in the best organised state of the future, there will be found nothing but pity, virtues, and ideals. . . . But Nietzsche did not want virtues and asceticism, and he did not believe in the morality of abnegation. . . . He already knew that all the pompous words of abnegation in the mouths of moralists and philosophers were sham. 'What,' he asked, 'do such people have in common with virtue?' By virtue, they usually understand those principles of life that guarantee them the greatest success in their cause. 'What then,' Nietzsche asks, 'does the ascetic ideal betoken in a philosopher? Asceticism provides him with the condition most favorable to the exercise of his intelligence. Far from denying 'existence,' he affirms *his* existence, and his alone, perhaps even to the point of *hubris: pereat mundus, fiat philosophia, fiat philosophus, fiam!*' The last words are an almost literal translation of the famous statement of the poor hero from the underground: 'Is the world to go to pot, or am I to have my tea? I say that the world can go to pot, as long as I get my tea.' Could he ever believe that the phrase he hurled in a fit of blindness and anger at the unhappy prostitute would be translated by a famous philosopher into the language of Cicero and Horace and offered as a formula defining the essence of the *highest* of human aspirations?" Lev Shestov, *Dostoevsky and Nietzsche: The Philosophy of Tragedy*, trans. Spencer Roberts, in *Dostoevsky, Tolstoy and Nietzsche: The Good in the Teaching of Tolstoy and Nietzsche: Philosophy and Preaching & Dostoevsky and Nietzsche: The Philosophy of Tragedy*, trans. Bernard Martin and Spencer Roberts (Athens: Ohio University Press, 1969), 313–14.

12. Artaud, *Collected Works*, vol. 1, 69.

13. Deleuze, *Difference and Repetition*, 151.

14. Deleuze, *Desert Islands*, 146–51.

15. Deleuze, *Desert Islands*, 150.

16. Deleuze, *Desert Islands*, 150–51.

17. Deleuze, *Desert Islands*, 151.

18. Deleuze, *Desert Islands*, 152.

19. Deleuze, *Desert Islands*, 152–53.

20. Gilles Deleuze. *Nietzsche and Philosophy*, trans. Hugh Tomlinson (New York: Columbia University, 1983), 8, 60–61.

21. Deleuze claims that Nietzsche understood Heraclitus to have opposed the instinct of the game, or the play and innocence of the dice-throw, to hubris, but also that the real problem of every Heraclitean was how hubris could allow everyone to find the being that makes him return. Hubris is the weapon of both the artificial hierarchy and of the eternal return that brings about the overturning of this hierarchy. What makes it so dangerous is therefore its ambiguous characterization of both active and reactive forces. Deleuze, *Nietzsche and Philosophy*, 25. Deleuze, *Difference and Repetition*, 41.

22. Deleuze, *Difference and Repetition*, 37.

23. For a useful discussion of Klein's influence on Deleuze in *The Logic of Sense*, see Nathan Widder, "From Negation to Disjunction in a World of Simulacra: Deleuze and Melanie Klein," *Deleuze Studies* 3, no. 2 (2009): 207–30.

24. Gilles Deleuze, *The Logic of Sense*, trans. Mark Lester with Charles Stivale, ed. Constantin V. Boundas (New York: Columbia University Press, 1990), 187.

25. Deleuze, *The Logic of Sense*, 187–88.

26. Deleuze, *The Logic of Sense*, 188.

27. Deleuze, *The Logic of Sense*, 188–90. Deleuze relates this distinction to two characteristic features of schizophrenic language: words-passions as splintered, excremental bits, and words-actions as blocks fused together by a principle of water or fire.

28. Deleuze, *The Logic of Sense*, 193.

29. Deleuze, *The Logic of Sense*, 199.

30. Deleuze, *The Logic of Sense*, 193.

31. Gilles Deleuze and Félix Guattari, *Anti-Oedipus: Capitalism and Schizophrenia*, trans. Robert Hurley, Mark Seem, and Helen R. Lane (Minneapolis: University of Minnesota Press, 1983), 10. In some of the secondary literature on Malebranche and Leibniz, the term *quasi-cause* is used interchangeably with *occasional cause*. This seems to be in keeping with Deleuze and Guattari's claim that the BwO is Numen, or a cause that is perceived mentally but not through the senses.

32. Deleuze and Guattari, *Anti-Oedipus*, 10–11.

33. Deleuze and Guattari, *Anti-Oedipus*, 13–14.

34. Deleuze and Guattari, *Anti-Oedipus*, 327.

35. Deleuze and Guattari, *Anti-Oedipus*, 21.

36. Gilles Deleuze and Félix Guattari, *A Thousand Plateaus: Capitalism and Schizophrenia*, trans. Brian Massumi (Minneapolis: University of Minnesota Press, 1987), 158.

37. Deleuze and Guattari, *A Thousand Plateaus*, 154.

38. Deleuze and Guattari, *A Thousand Plateaus*, 153.

39. Deleuze and Guattari, *A Thousand Plateaus*, 152–53, 157. The Cold that names the substantial attribute of the drugged body is a reference from William S. Burroughs' novel *Naked Lunch*, which covers the subject of heroin addiction in a series of hallucinatory vignettes (intensive quantities) that Burroughs produced over a period of severe withdrawal from the drug (degree zero of intensity). His experimental cut-up writing and theories surrounding it may also be of interest in further explaining how the BwO constitutes a recording surface for the inscription of disjunctions. Burroughs began his experiments by randomly splicing together different tape recordings before moving on to texts, and incorporating the results as well as his theories about them into his novels. In *Nova Express*, he offers the following thought experiment: "Postulate a biologic film running from the beginning to the end, from zero to zero as all biologic film run in any universe—

Call this film X1 and postulate further that there can only be one film with the quality X1 in any given time universe. X1 is the film and performers—X2 is the audience who are all trying to get into the film—Nobody is permitted to leave the biologic theater which in this case is the human body—Because if anybody did leave the theater he would be looking at a different film Y and Film X1 and audience X2 would then cease to exist by mathematical definition—In 1960 with the publication of *Minutes To Go*, Martin's stale movie was greeted by an unprecedented chorus of boos and a concerted walkout—'We seen this five times already and not standing still for another twilight of your tired Gods.'" In the same sense that the junkie wants the Cold inside and not outside, the biologic theatre is the human body that no one is permitted to leave, while biologic film X1 is the attribute that qualifies the body as an enclosed substance. But whereas the junkie experiments with the full body, the biologic film is a recording surface that seeks to appropriate the desires of the audience by imposing the will of the tyrannical Nova Mob. By walking out of the theatre, the audience enters film Y and passes through a different BwO. Burroughs further explains how the recording surface is constituted: "Since junk *is* image the effects of junk can easily be produced and concentrated in a sound and image track—Like this: Take a sick junky—Throw blue light on his so-called face or dye it blue or dye the junk blue it don't make no difference and now give him a shot and photograph the blue miracle as life pours back into that walking corpse—That will give you the image track of junk—Now project the blue change onto your own face if you want The Big Fix. The sound track is even easier—I quote from *Newsweek*, March 4, 1963 Science section: 'Every substance has a characteristic set of resonant frequencies at which it vibrates or oscillates.'—So you record the frequency of junk as it hits the junk-sick brain cells –" The resonant frequencies of the junk substance are recorded in order to appropriate the surplus-production of non-junkie desiring-machines, and turn them on to junk by means of projection as inclusive disjunction (and not projection in the psychoanalytic sense). Burroughs' rejection of the One God Universe in favor of a Magical Universe also seems to agree with Deleuze and Guattari's reading of Spinoza. William S. Burroughs, *Nova Express* (New York: Grove Press, 1964), 8–9.

40. Deleuze and Guattari, *A Thousand Plateaus: Capitalism and Schizophrenia*, 158. In *Francis Bacon: The Logic of Sensation*, Deleuze reconceives the "true organs" of the BwO as being *indeterminate and polyvalent*. Meanwhile, the BwO is defined according to the *temporary and provisional presence* of determinate organs, echoing the self-suppression of the regressive analysis that defines the substantial attribute for Gueroult. In relation to the hysterical body that Deleuze finds in Bacon's paintings, the reality of sensation is neither qualitative nor qualified but intensive. Gilles Deleuze, *Francis Bacon: The Logic of Sensation*, trans. Daniel W. Smith (London: Continuum, 2003), 45–48.

41. Deleuze and Guattari, *A Thousand Plateaus*, 158.

42. Spinoza, *Ethics*, I, P8, schol. 2.

43. Antonin Artaud, *Watchfiends & Rack Screams: Works from the Final Period*, ed. trans. Clayton Eshleman with Bernard Bador (Boston: Exact Change, 1995), 291–307.

44. Artaud, *Watchfiends & Rack Screams*, 294.

45. Spinoza, *Ethics*, I, Appendix.

46. Gilles Deleuze, *Spinoza: Practical Philosophy*, trans. Robert Hurley (San Francisco: City Lights Books, 1988), 39.

47. Deleuze, *Spinoza: Practical Philosophy*, 98, 102–3.

48. Deleuze, *Spinoza: Practical Philosophy*, 32. The interlocking of relations of motion and rest of chyle and lymph can be related to Deleuze's claim in *Difference and Repetition* that humor is the implicated art of intensive quantities, since chyle and lymph are bodily humors [*humeurs*] according to the pre-modern etymology, from which comic

humor [*humour*] also derives. As individuating factors that acquire a different relation of motion and rest in relation to the dominant relation constitutive of the organic body that has become decomposed through poisoning, the humors would evoke Simondon's theory of the individual as de-phased and multi-phased being, which Deleuze appropriates into his own account of individuation. Deleuze, *Difference and Repetition*, 245–46.

49. Deleuze, *Spinoza: Practical Philosophy*, 36.

50. Antonin Artaud, *The Peyote Dance*, trans. Helen Weaver (New York: Farrar, Straus and Giroux, 1976), 10.

51. Artaud, *The Peyote Dance*, 14.

52. Artaud, *The Peyote Dance*, 28.

53. In *Electronic Revolution*, Burroughs writes: ". . . I advance the theory that the virus is a very small unit of word and image. I have suggested how such units can be biologically activated to act as communicable virus strains. Let us start with three tape recorders in the Garden of Eden. Tape recorder 1 is Adam. Tape recorder 2 is Eve. Tape recorder 3 is God, who deteriorated after Hiroshima into the Ugly American. Or to return to our primeval scene: Tape recorder 1 is the male ape in a helpless sexual frenzy as the virus strangles him. Tape recorder 2 is a cooing female ape who straddles him. Tape recorder 3 is DEATH." In light of Burroughs' theory of the three tape recorders, the play of masculine and feminine principles animating reality may be understood in relation to how the attraction of the miraculating machine succeeds the repulsion of the paranoiac machine in *Anti-Oedipus*. Burroughs claims that tape recorder 3 can be used to orchestrate political scandals by splicing together disapproval tapes from tape recorder 1 with sex tapes from tape recorder 2, similarly to how the recording surface of the BwO is able to appropriate surplus-production. The question would be whether part of the libidinal energy that is transformed by tape recorder 3 can consummate the alliance of the first two syntheses with a celibate machine and the residual formation of a nomadic subject. William S. Burroughs, *Electronic Revolution* (Bonn: Expanded Media Editions, 1998), 10 ff.

54. Artaud, *The Peyote Dance*, 31.

55. Artaud, *The Peyote Dance*, 74.

56. Artaud, *The Peyote Dance*, 75.

57. Deleuze, *Spinoza: Practical Philosophy*, 37–38.

58. Artaud, *The Peyote Dance*, 80.

59. Alain Badiou, *Deleuze: The Clamor of Being*, trans. Louise Burchill (Minneapolis: University of Minnesota Press, 2000), 52.

60. Deleuze, *The Logic of Sense*, 248. The Stoic univocity of infinitive verbs discussed in *The Logic of Sense* could perhaps in this regard help to cast further light on how the symbolic, as the essence of the process of repetition, might be capable of reconciling the *asylum ignorantiae* with Spinozist univocity, if only as a fiction to be exorcised after serving its use.

61. Deleuze, *Spinoza: Practical Philosophy*, 73.

62. Gilles Deleuze, *Expressionism in Philosophy: Spinoza*, trans. Martin Joughin (New York: Zone Books, 1992), 278. Deleuze, *Spinoza: Practical Philosophy*, 115.

63. Deleuze, *Spinoza: Practical Philosophy*, 113–14. Deleuze would seem to be diverging from Gueroult in this regard, for whom the first eight propositions of the *Ethics* have a perfectly categorical rather than hypothetical sense.

64. Or alternatively, the BwO does not seem to move beyond the very least universal common notions.

65. Deleuze and Guattari, *A Thousand Plateaus*, 149.

66. Deleuze, *Spinoza: Practical Philosophy*, 39–40.

67. Spinoza, *Ethics*, IV, Preface.

68. Spinoza, *Ethics*, III, P1, Dem.

69. Antonin Artaud, *Heliogabalus, or, The Crowned Anarchist*, trans. Alexis Lykiard (Washington, D.C.: Solar Books, 2006), 55–58, 61.

70. Artaud, *Heliogabalus, or, The Crowned Anarchist*, 62.

71. Artaud, *Heliogabalus, or, The Crowned Anarchist*, 63–67.

72. For a useful discussion of Spinoza on the *asylum ignorantiae* and divine names in relation to Badiou's critique of Deleuze, see Mogens Laerke, "The Voice and the Name: Spinoza in the Badioudian Critique of Deleuze," *Pli: The Warwick Journal of Philosophy* 8 (1999): 86–99.

73. Deleuze, *Difference and Repetition*, 150.

74. Jacques Derrida, "The Transcendental 'Stupidity' ('Bêtise') of Man and the Becoming-Animal According to Deleuze," ed. Erin Ferris, in *Derrida, Deleuze, Psychoanalysis*, ed. Gabriele Schwab (New York: Columbia University Press, 2007), 38–41.

75. Deleuze and Guattari, *A Thousand Plateaus*, 155–56. Freud as well as the early Deleuze would have understood this movement in terms of a process of desexualization, which Deleuze and Guattari reconceive of in the broader terms of deterritorialization, reflecting their rejection of the death instinct.

76. Deleuze and Guattari, *A Thousand Plateaus*, 156.

77. Deleuze and Guattari, *A Thousand Plateaus*, 259–60.

78. Deleuze, *Difference and Repetition*, 152.

79. Deleuze and Guattari, *A Thousand Plateaus*, 260.

80. Deleuze, *Difference and Repetition*, 152.

81. Gilles Deleuze, *Coldness and Cruelty*, in Deleuze and Leopold von Sacher-Masoch, *Masochism*, trans. Jean McNeil (New York: Zone Books, 1991), 20.

82. Deleuze and Guattari, *Anti-Oedipus*, 29.

83. Deleuze and Guattari, *A Thousand Plateaus*, 163.

84. Deleuze and Guattari, *A Thousand Plateaus*, 160.

85. Deleuze, *Difference and Repetition*, 148.

86. Gilles Deleuze and Félix Guattari, *What Is Philosophy?*, trans. Hugh Tomlinson and Graham Burchell (New York: Columbia University Press, 1994), 37, 61–63.

87. Deleuze and Guattari, *What Is Philosophy?*, 49–50.

88. Deleuze, *Difference and Repetition*, 37.

89. Deleuze, *Difference and Repetition*, 36–37.

90. Deleuze, *Difference and Repetition*, 248.

91. Keith Ansell Pearson, *Germinal Life: The difference and repetition of Deleuze* (New York: Routledge, 1999), 5.

92. Deleuze, *Difference and Repetition*, 248–49.

93. Deleuze, *Difference and Repetition*, 249. This disengagement of generality from the particular in favor of the singular suggests that these highest of generalities may be akin to the least universal common notions through which substantial attributes are grasped by way of hypothesis. Deleuze, *Spinoza: Practical Philosophy*, 113–15.

94. Deleuze and Guattari, *A Thousand Plateaus*, 164.

95. Artaud, *Watchfiends & Rack Screams: Works from the Final Period*, 192–93.

96. Deleuze, *Difference and Repetition*, 250–51.

97. Deleuze, *Difference and Repetition*, 110–13.

98. Deleuze, *Difference and Repetition*, 115.

99. Deleuze, *Difference and Repetition*, 117–18. As a principle of natural selection, the eternal return would ostensibly determine the survival of individual differences prior to the differenciations of species, parts, and sexes, on the unique basis of their individuation into adult organisms, as well as specific instances of de-differenciation in which cells

revert back to an earlier developmental stage. Deleuze does not seem to be citing de-differenciation as an instance of regression, but rather as an instance of the death instinct being manifested at the organic level, such as cancer (249).

100. Deleuze, *Difference and Repetition*, 260–61.

101. Deleuze, *The Logic of Sense*, 178.

102. Gilles Deleuze, *Bergsonism*, trans. Hugh Tomlinson and Barbara Habberjam (New York: Zone Books, 1991), 80.

103. Deleuze, *Difference and Repetition*, 259.

104. Deleuze, *Difference and Repetition*, 259.

105. Deleuze, *Spinoza: Practical Philosophy*, 101.

106. Deleuze, *Expressionism in Philosophy: Spinoza*, 134.

107. Deleuze, *Nietzsche and Philosophy*, 44.

108. Deleuze, *Nietzsche and Philosophy*, 51.

109. Deleuze and Guattari, *A Thousand Plateaus*, 165.

110. Daniel Colson attempts a political interpretation of Deleuze's work on Spinoza that would parallel the anarchist philosophies of Proudhon, Bakunin, and the Makhnovists. Critical of the Marxist interpretations of Spinoza by Matheron, Negri, and Balibar for being anthropocentric and despotic, he aims to reunite nature with second nature, the human with the non-human, and the natural with the artificial by way of Deleuze's account of force, multitude, the physico-chemical model of composition and decomposition (common notions), and the plane of immanence. Surprisingly, Colson does not discuss Artaud, crowned anarchy, or the BwO in relation to these concerns. Daniel Colson, "Anarchist Readings of Spinoza," trans. Jesse Cohn and Nathan Jun, *Journal of French Philosophy* 17, no. 2 (2007): 90–129.

References

Ansell Pearson, Keith. *Germinal Life: The difference and repetition of Deleuze*. New York: Routledge, 1999.

Artaud, Antonin. *Collected Works*. Vol. 1. Translated by Victor Corti. London: John Calder, 1999.

———. *Heliogabalus, or, The Crowned Anarchist*. Translated by Alexis Lykiard. Washington, D.C.: Solar Books, 2006.

———. *The Peyote Dance*. Translated by Helen Weaver. New York: Farrar, Straus and Giroux, 1976.

———. *Watchfiends & Rack Screams: Works from the Final Period*. Edited and translated by Clayton Eshleman with Bernard Bador. Boston: Exact Change, 1995.

Badiou, Alain. *Deleuze: The Clamor of Being*. Translated by Louise Burchill. Minneapolis: University of Minnesota Press, 2000.

Burroughs, William S. *Nova Express*. New York: Grove Press, 1964.

———. *Electronic Revolution*. Bonn: Expanded Media Editions, 1998.

Colson, Daniel. "Anarchist Readings of Spinoza." Translated by Jesse Cohn and Nathan Jun. *Journal of French Philosophy* 17, no. 2 (2007): 90–129.

Deleuze, Gilles. *Nietzsche and Philosophy*. Translated by Hugh Tomlinson. New York: Columbia University Press, 1983.

———. *Bergsonism*. Translated by Hugh Tomlinson and Barbara Habberjam. New York: Zone Books, 1991.

————. *Coldness and Cruelty*. In Gilles Deleuze and Leopold von Sacher-Masoch. *Masochism*. Translated by Jean McNeil. New York: Zone Books, 1991.

————. *Difference and Repetition*. Translated by Paul Patton. New York: Columbia University Press, 1994.

————. *Expressionism in Philosophy: Spinoza*. Translated by Martin Joughin. New York: Zone Books, 1992.

————. *The Logic of Sense*. Translated by Mark Lester with Charles Stivale. Edited by Constantin V. Boundas. New York: Columbia University Press, 1990.

————. *Spinoza: Practical Philosophy*. Translated by Robert Hurley. San Francisco: City Lights Books, 1988.

————. *Francis Bacon: The Logic of Sensation*. Translated by Daniel W. Smith. London: Continuum, 2003.

————. *Desert Islands and Other Texts, 1953–1974*. Edited by David Lapoujade. Translated by Michael Taormina. New York: Semiotext(e), 2004.

Deleuze, Gilles, and Félix Guattari. *Anti-Oedipus: Capitalism and Schizophrenia*. Translated by Robert Hurley, Mark Seem, and Helen R. Lane. Minneapolis: University of Minnesota Press, 1983.

————. *A Thousand Plateaus: Capitalism and Schizophrenia*. Translated by Brian Massumi. Minneapolis: University of Minnesota Press, 1987.

————. *What Is Philosophy?*. Translated by Hugh Tomlinson and Graham Burchell. New York: Columbia University Press, 1994.

Derrida, Jacques. "The Transcendental 'Stupidity' ('Bêtise') of Man and the Becoming-Animal According to Deleuze." Edited by Erin Ferris. In *Derrida, Deleuze, Psychoanalysis*. Edited by Gabriele Schwab, 35–60. New York: Columbia University Press, 2007.

Gueroult, Martial. *Spinoza, I. Dieu, Éthique I*. Paris: Aubier-Montaigne, 1968.

Laerke, Mogens. "The Voice and the Name: Spinoza in the Badioudian Critique of Deleuze." *Pli: The Warwick Journal of Philosophy* 8 (1999): 86–99.

Spinoza, Benedict de. *The Collected Works of Spinoza: Volume I*. Edited and translated by Edwin Curley. Princeton: Princeton University Press, 1985.

Shestov, Lev. *Dostoevsky and Nietzsche: The Philosophy of Tragedy*. Translated by Spencer Roberts. In *Dostoevsky, Tolstoy and Nietzsche: The Good in the Teaching of Tolstoy and Nietzsche: Philosophy and Preaching & Dostoevsky and Nietzsche: The Philosophy of Tragedy*. Translated by Bernard Martin and Spencer Roberts. Athens: Ohio University Press, 1969.

Widder, Nathan. "From Negation to Disjunction in a World of Simulacra: Deleuze and Melanie Klein." *Deleuze Studies* 3, no. 2 (2009): 207–230.

CHAPTER NINE

Revolution and the Return of Metaphysics

Thomas Nail

What is the relationship between metaphysics and political revolution? Despite being two of the most widely discredited concepts in contemporary European philosophy, this chapter argues that we are witnessing the return of both in the work of French philosophers Gilles Deleuze and Alain Badiou.[1] Their return, however, is no mere repetition of the previous forms of classical metaphysics and modern revolution—defined by totality and the state. Rather, it is a differential return: a return that changes something fundamental about these concepts and breathes into them a desperately needed new life. Many contemporary European philosophers have announced the "end of metaphysics" and the "death of philosophy." They have buried the ideas of metaphysics and revolution many years ago, but continue to pursue the endless task of vilifying them—lest their specters return from the grave.

Contemporary philosophy is thus pulled in two post-metaphysical directions: a positive post-Kantian direction and a more negative critical direction. In the first direction, philosophy's access to the real is relativist or "correlationist," as Quentin Meillassoux argues. In this direction, philosophy's access to the real is mediated through and limited by its cultural-historical context, its language, or its body-consciousness. The world only appears "for us" and never "in itself." In the second direction, philosophy is the watchdog of the real, vigilant, and critical against every metaphysical pretender that dares to usurp the kingless throne of the true and the real. These two post-metaphysical traditions can be mapped on to the two dominant traditions in continental philosophy: phenomenology and deconstruction.

In the political domain the concept of revolution confronts a similar fate. Not only is there no single sovereign with direct access to political truth, it is argued, but there is no representable will of the people that can access this truth either. After the failure of the communist experiment, it is no longer philosophically tenable to believe in the power of people to determine the truth of political life. Like metaphysics, revolutionary politics is pulled in two directions—each of which denies the existence of a contemporary political truth distinct from the present situation of parliamentary capitalism. In one direction, revolutionary politics has become merely relative or correlative to some form of the state or party: state-socialism, national liberation movements, etc. Even the recent Icelandic and Egyptian "revolutions," have all fallen back on a mediating body of revolutionary truth: the state. In the other direction revolutionary politics has busied itself with the endless critique of all revolutionary struggles whose implications claim to be universal, egalitarian, or true in any way. The real revolution, it is argued, is in an eternally future politics "to come," beyond the party, state, and market. The revolution is always potential, but never actual. Metaphysics and revolution thus share a similar disrepute: it is no longer possible to believe in the real without the mediating forces of language, culture, party, and state.

Against this disrepute, this chapter argues that we are witnessing the return of metaphysics and revolution without mediation and political representation. But if this return is not a mere repetition of classical metaphysics and revolutionary statism, what is it? The return of metaphysics and revolution is a bold claim and requires some unpacking. To help me unpack this claim I will draw on the work of two contemporary philosophers who, throughout the later twentieth century, have rejected the so-called 'end of metaphysics,' the 'death of philosophy,' and the 'exhaustion of revolution': Gilles Deleuze and Alain Badiou. Ultimately, my argument is that whatever differences may exist between these two thinkers, we can find a very specific and common formulation of the return to metaphysics that I believe also offers us a promising new direction toward a non-representational theory of political revolution. More specifically, I argue that despite (or precisely because of) their important disagreements over ontology and the relationship between philosophy and politics, Deleuze and Badiou both share a commitment to what I call a "metaphysics of the event." By a metaphysics of the event, what I mean is that their realism is based on two philosophical commitments: (1) the necessary condition of ontological contingency (or multiplicity), and (2) the sufficient condition of the existence of events and their consequences. While for Badiou events may be relatively rare, and for Deleuze they are more numerous, what is important here is that for both thinkers events are what make possible the return of metaphysics and revolution.

But before developing this thesis any further, the first part of this chapter will respond to what is likely the most immediate objection to my thesis: that Deleuze and Badiou's philosophies are not only different but that they are incompatible. In particular, there is a significant recent literature from both Badiou and Badiouians critiquing Deleuze's philosophy and politics (or supposed lack thereof). In the face of such overt criticisms, how is it possible to argue that both share a revolutionary metaphysics of the event? But these criticisms are not just an exercise in polemics, they are the key to understanding the political dangers posed by a return of metaphysics based on a philosophy of the multiple—as it is in both Deleuze and Badiou. Additionally, understanding these criticisms will allow us to clarify, as appropriate, a certain vision of evental metaphysics worth pursing beyond the work of Deleuze and Badiou.

The remainder of this chapter is thus broken up into two sections. In the first section I highlight two important political dangers of a return to metaphysics based on multiplicity in the form of a Badiouian critique of Deleuze: political ambivalence and virtual hierarchy. Ultimately, I argue that, as criticisms, they fail, but as dangers they can help us clarify a realist position common to both Deleuze and Badiou. In the second section I argue that we can distinguish a metaphysics and revolutionary politics of the event common to both thinkers.

I. The Political Dangers of Multiplicity

The return of revolutionary realism, however, is not simply a politicization of multiplicity and contingency. In fact, the politicization of multiplicity poses two dangers to the return of revolutionary realism: political ambivalence and virtual hierarchy. Since 1997, three full-length books have been devoted to outlining these dangers in the form of a sustained critique against Deleuze: Alain Badiou's *Deleuze: the Clamor of Being* (1997); Slavoj Žižek's *Organs Without Bodies* (2003); and Peter Hallward's *Out of This World: Deleuze and the Philosophy of Creation* (2006). The following section is a synthesis of these works and the dangers they identify in the politicization of multiplicity.

Political Ambivalence

The valorization of pure, contingent, ontological multiplicity poses the danger of political ambivalence. Deleuze and Badiou are both thinkers of multiplicity in the following sense, concisely formulated by Quentin Meillassoux: "Being is multiple to the strict exclusion of its opposite—namely, the One. Being is not therefore a multiplicity composed of stable and ultimate unities, but a multiplicity that is in turn composed of multiplicities. Indeed, mathematical sets have for their elements not unities but other sets, and so on indefinitely."[2]

The perceived advantage of affirming the multiplicity of being, in contrast to its unity, is that such a multiplicity would overflow any limits or political forms like the party or state that would aim to organize the multiples once and for all. Being *qua* multiplicity would always allow for a difference within itself that could offer the possibility of something new. Thus, the political affirmation of ontological multiplicity is the affirmation that something new is always possible—that political life is never totalizable under any form of political representation: the party, the state, the market, etc. The ambivalence of this political position is that being *qua* multiplicity *may* result in a new non-representational space of freedom and equality, *or* it may result in a new space of increasing militarization and capitalist expansion. Not only is there no way to know or fully control what the results will be, but either result is equally indifferent to being *qua* multiplicity.

Slavoj Žižek, in particular, frequently attributes this political ambivalence to Deleuze and Guattari's politics, when he (accurately) notes that deterritorialization is both the condition for capitalist expansion and revolution. Thus, for Žižek, "there are, effectively, features that justify calling Deleuze the ideologist of late capitalism."[3] But to say, as Alain Badiou does, that affirming multiplicity as such is to affirm a "purely ideological radicality" that "inevitably changes over into its opposite: once the mass festivals of democracy and discourse are over, things make way for the modernist restoration of order among workers and bosses," would be to overstate the problem.[4] Rather, it would be much more appropriate to say, with Paolo Virno, that "[t]he multitude is a form of being that can give birth to one thing but also to the other: ambivalence."[5] Bruno Bosteels offers a similar criticism of what he calls the "politico-ontological optimism and unapologetic vitalism" that can be found in the work of Michael Hardt and Antonio Negri.[6] For Hardt and Negri, "The Multitude" is both the condition for the successful function of Empire, which is constantly setting up new barriers only to overthrow or deterritorialize them—thus allowing it to create even more expansive barriers further along. The politico-ontological affirmation of the multitude is, according to Bosteels, ambivalent and speculative.

Opposed to merely pointing out the ontological contingency of all political life and hoping for a positive outcome, Bosteels argues that we need something more politically constructive. "A subject's intervention," Bosteels says, "cannot consist merely in showing or recognizing the traumatic impossibility, void, or antagonism around which the situation as a whole is structured."[7] Rather, a "political organization," according to Badiou, "is necessary in order for the intervention, as wager, to make a process out of the trajectory that goes from an interruption to a fidelity. In this sense, organization is nothing but the consistency of politics."[8]

Insofar as Deleuze, Hardt, Negri, and others merely affirm the political potentiality of being's pure multiplicity, without theorizing the militant consequences of its consistency and organization in political struggle, their political philosophy remains fundamentally ambivalent. To be fair, this is not what I believe to be happening in Deleuze's political philosophy. However, a full defense of these criticisms would take us too far afield and duplicate what I have already defended elsewhere.[9] For our present purposes, it is important simply to understand that the political affirmation of being *qua* pure multiplicity is fundamentally ambivalent. By affirming it, we affirm only the vague potentiality that something *might* be real and revolutionary, not that something *is* truly revolutionary. This is a danger for a realist revolutionary politics and not a position held by either Deleuze or Badiou. But there is one more danger of politicizing multiplicity: virtual hierarchy.

Virtual Hierarchy

In addition to the danger of ambivalence, politicizing multiplicity also poses the danger of forming a hierarchy of the virtual over the actual. This danger of multiplicity is spelled out most explicitly in Badiou's political criticism of Deleuze, in his book, *The Clamor of Being:*

> contrary to all egalitarian or "communitarian" norms, Deleuze's conception of thought is profoundly aristocratic. Thought only exists in a hierarchized space. This is because, for individuals to attain the point where they are seized by their preindividual determination and, thus, by the power of the One-All—of which they are, at the start, only meager local configurations—they have to go beyond their limits and endure the transfixion and disintegration of their actuality by infinite virtuality, which is actuality's veritable being. And individuals are not equally capable of this. Admittedly, Being is itself neutral, equal, outside all evaluation . . . . But 'things reside unequally in this equal being.' And, as a result, it is essential to think according to 'a hierarchy which considers things and beings from the point of view of power.'[10]

The political thrust of this argument is that, if we understand revolutionary realism as the virtual or potential for change as such, and not merely change for or against certain pre-existing powers, then, contrary to any kind of egalitarianism, there will instead be a hierarchy of actual political beings that more or less participate in a *degree* of pure potential transformation. The more actual political beings renounce their specific and local determinations and affirm their participation in the larger processes of pure multiplicity, the more valorized they are. If the task of political philosophy is to analyze local political interventions and in every case show to what degree these struggles renounce all their concrete determinations and affirm their capacity to become something else (*qua* multiplicities), then Badiou thinks there seems to be a new form of ontological "asceticism" and hierarchy in such an analysis.[11] If multiplicity were a normative category, its pure form would be at the top and its lesser degrees of actualization would be at the bottom.

Peter Hallward makes a similar criticism of Deleuze in his book, *Out of This World.* Hallward argues that, for Deleuze, the pure becoming of multiplicity is a superior form of life and that all others forms strive for this. Beings must reject their concrete life to affirm the life of the virtual. As such, Deleuze's political philosophy, according to Hallward, is absolutely "indifferent to the politics of this world."[12] Hallward claims that "once a social field is defined less by its conflicts and contradictions than by the lines of flight running through it," any distinctive space for political action can only be subsumed within the more general dynamics of creation, life, and potential transformation.[13] And since these dynamics are "themselves anti-dialectical if not anti-relational, there can be little room in Deleuze's philosophy for relations of conflict and solidarity."[14] If each concrete, localized, actual political being *is* only in so far as its actual being is subtracted from the situation into a virtual event, "and every mortal event in a single Event,"[15] the processional "telos" of absolute political deterritorialization is completely indifferent to the actual politics of this world.[16]

By holding all actual political struggles up to the standard of pure multiplicity, Hallward argues that Deleuze is guilty of affirming an impossible utopianism. "By posing the question of politics in the starkly dualistic terms of war machine or state," Hallward argues, "—by posing it, in the end, in the apocalyptic terms of a new people and a new earth or else no people and no earth—the political aspect of Deleuze's philosophy amounts to little more than utopian distraction."[17]

Again, to be fair, this is not what I believe to be happening in Deleuze's political philosophy. A full book-length rebuttal of the accusation of virtual hierarchy is available elsewhere.[18] For my argument here, it is important simply to understand that if the task of political philosophy is to valorize only those political struggles that affirm their pure multiplicity over their concrete determinations then we risk creating a virtual hierarchy which devalues actual struggles. Further, this sort of political philosophy reaches the same unhelpful conclusion at the end of every analysis: being is multiplicity.

Revolutionary Realism

The upshot of these two dangers is that politicizing multiplicity is insufficient for returning to a revolutionary realism. Luckily, Deleuze's later work does not fall prey these dangers. Not only do these critics almost exclusively cite Deleuze's earlier works, but beginning at least with *A Thousand Plateaus* Deleuze and Guattari explicitly reject the politicization of multiplicity. "Politics," they say "precedes being" [*avant l'être, il y a la politique*].[19] In fact, they say that such an "absolute negative deterritorialization" is politically the "worst thing that can happen."[20] Instead, in *A Thousand Plateaus,* Deleuze and Guattari, claim to overthrow ontology altogether and create a practical political typology of assemblages toward the aim of real revolutionary political transformation.

Revolution is real for Deleuze and Guattari, not because it is the realization of an independently determined correct mode of action, nor because it is against all normative modes of action altogether. Revolution is real, for Deleuze and Guattari, insofar as it is an event that creates new modes of existence that are not mediated by the pre-existing structures of parties, states, or capitalism. Revolutionary realism is the direct and participatory rule of the people over themselves without rulers, representatives, or markets. There is no single person or group who can speak for the others—there is no political totality. But the aim of this chapter is not to provide a detailed account of Deleuze and Guattari's theory of revolution, which I have done elsewhere in book-length.[21] The goal of this chapter is simply to uncover the minimal philosophical conditions required for the *realism* of their philosophy of revolution.

The purpose of identifying the dangers above is not to settle once and for all the differences between Deleuze and Badiou. This is a problem for a different chapter. The present chapter is primarily concerned with their similarities—however few there may be. In what sense can it be argued that Deleuze and Badiou are both realists (i.e., that they are metaphysicians of the event)? In order to answer this question and further clarify exactly what kind of realism Deleuze and Badiou have in common we do, however, need to identify at least two major differences that will help us be more precise about their similarities. This will then put us in a better position to say, in what (most minimal) sense, Deleuze and Badiou are both metaphysical and political realists.

The first difference between Deleuze and Badiou is that, for Badiou, mathematics is the one and only speaking of being *qua* being, which he defines as "inconsistent multiplicity." Insofar as natural language presupposes that it is speaking about or referring to some thing, it assumes existence, or what Badiou calls an "existential quantifier." However, since mathematics, according to Badiou, is purely symbolic and does not refer to or presuppose that it is speaking of any existing thing, it is the properly formal language of being *qua* being—independent of existence. Deleuze and Guattari in *A Thousand Plateaus,* however, not only reject such a mathematical formulation of being, but claim to "overthrow ontology" altogether. They argue that the logic of the "is" (ontology) should be replaced with a "logic of the AND," or what they call a non-substantive, non-totalizable, "multiplicity."[22] Opposed to the formally incomplete system of sets, they propose an expressive theory of assemblages. Accordingly, there is no mathematical bracketing of existence, only politically expressive types of assemblages.

These are very different positions. However, whether multiplicity is purely formal and mathematical or whether it is always expressed and arranged, it is equally necessary that multiplicity be non-substantive and contingent. For both Deleuze and Badiou multiplicity is not a thing or substance, nor is it determined in advance as a totality or whole: it is anti-absolutist. Every multiple composes and is composed of at least one more multiple, and so on indefinitely. Further, if multiplicity were a single substance, there would be no possibility of its becoming otherwise. If it were contingent that multiplicity was contingent (non-whole), then it would be possible that being was necessary and whole (thus contradicting the definition of multiplicity). While Deleuze and Badiou differ on whether multiplicity is formal or expressive, they both agree on the necessity of its non-totality.

The second relevant difference between Deleuze and Badiou is a political difference. For Badiou, politics, like mathematical ontology, is a *condition* for philosophy. Politics like mathematics has its own events that intervene in inconsistent multiplicity and create a consistency, which philosophy thinks. Philosophy, however, does not have its own events. Philosophy is a meta-thinking of its four evental conditions: politics, science, art, and love. For Deleuze, on the other hand, philosophy does have its own conditions and events. But there are also political events. Philosophy, for Deleuze, is not a meta-politics, nor does it claim

to speak for or think politics in any way. Rather, philosophy supports or combines with political events without representing or being conditioned by them at
all. The relationship between philosophy and politics, for Deleuze, is not one of
conditions and conditioned, but one of heterogeneity and "aparallel evolution."[23]
In a conversation with Michel Foucault, published as "Intellectuals and Power,"
Deleuze describes the relationship between philosophy and politics as a parallel
"system of relays."[24] Philosophy, politics, and other events are heterogeneous to
one another but can also transform each other—not directly through "conditioning," but indirectly through influence, inspiration, and contagion. When philosophy seems to have slowed down or hit a wall in its thinking, politics is able to
push forward and offer new modes of action, which can in turn inspire new
philosophical modes of thought. For example, Deleuze and Foucault both site
the *Groupe d'Information sur les Prisons* (Prison Information Group), and May
1968 as instances of political novelties that rejuvenated philosophical thinking.[25]
One is not the condition for the other, but the parallel inspiration for the other.

These are very different positions, but they also help us more precisely
identify the minimal commitments that both Deleuze and Badiou have in common, and ultimately in what sense they are both realists. But their return to realism it is not a return to a classical realism defined by an objective set of stable
objects. It is a differential return that changes something about the definition of
the real itself. In fact, Deleuze and Badiou's philosophical commitment to non-
totality, that is, multiplicity, almost sound closer to anti-realism insofar as they
deny an objective totality of the real. If, as they argue, the real is not a totality,
then access to it is only partial and thus incomplete: illusory.[26] But Deleuze and
Badiou are not anti-realists. They both reject the binary premise between the
"for us" and the "in itself," by which anti-realism and realism are defined. By
these definitions, Deleuze and Badiou are neither realists nor anti-realists. "Appearance," as Badiou says, "does not depend on the presupposition of a constituting subject. Being-multiple does not appear for a subject. Rather, it is of the
essence of being to appear."[27] Reality, for Deleuze and Badiou, is thus neither
defined by a constitutive subject nor a fixed state of constituted objects. Rather,
reality is the immanent process by which objects become constituted and identifiable in the first place: as events.

Accordingly, the philosophical position of multiplicity *on its own* is neither
a classical realism (autonomous totality of constituted objects) nor an anti-
realism (the illusion of constituted objects), but rather an "anti-absolutism."[28]
Multiplicity is simply the philosophical position that there is no totality of constituted objects: being is non-whole.[29] It makes no claims about the reality or
illusion of objects. What makes Deleuze and Badiou both realists is that there
are events: *processes*, immanent to being, which give it appearance and order.
Events should not be confused with pre-constituted subjects or objects themselves. Events are neither subjects nor objects; they are the processes that constitute both subjects and objects. Thus, if being were already wholly constituted,
there could be no events. As Badiou says, it is precisely because "being as a
whole does not exist," that "the being of entities [can] appear."[30] Deleuze and

Badiou are realists not insofar as they are theorists of multiplicity, but insofar as they are metaphysicians of the event.

Events are real insofar as they are the processes that constitute the appearance of being itself without the mediation of pre-constituted structures: subjects, objects, states, and parties. How many events there are or what they are called by Deleuze and Badiou are important differences. But these differences also reveal to us a common philosophical commitment: that Deleuze and Badiou are both philosophers of the event and its unmediated reality. If events are the immanent distribution of being itself, irreducible to pre-constituted subjects and objects, then the philosophical analysis of events can be defined precisely as a realist metaphysics of the event.

To conclude this section: it is precisely because there are so many differences between Deleuze and Badiou that we are able to locate the most minimal terms of their agreement and thus the basic requirements for a return to metaphysics and revolution. Firstly, whether multiplicity is formal/mathematical or expressive/constructive, it requires a philosophical commitment to non-totality and the necessity of absolute contingency. Secondly, whether philosophy has events or not, or how rare these events are is an important point of contention, but this should not cause us to overlook their common philosophical commitment to the reality of events. But we have yet to define precisely in what sense these two philosophical commitments to multiplicity and events constitute a return to metaphysical and revolutionary realism. Now that we have discovered the most minimally shared commitments of both philosophers we are finally ready to explore each of these commitments in more detail.

II. The Metaphysics of the Event

In a letter reproduced by Arnaud Villani in *La Guêpe et l'orchidée*, Deleuze says, "I feel I am a pure metaphysician."[31] Later, Badiou, in the *Clamor of Being* will say that "Deleuze's philosophy, like my own, is classical in nature (a metaphysics of Being and of the ground). . . . Accordingly, [Deleuze] readily declared that he had no problem of the 'end of philosophy' kind, which I take to mean (agreeing with him without reserve on this point) that the construction of a metaphysics remains the philosopher's ideal, with the question being not 'Is it still possible?' but 'Are we capable of it?'"[32] These are perhaps the two strongest statements of philosophical agreement between Deleuze and Badiou work to date. It seems that if Deleuze and Badiou agreed on nothing else, they agreed upon a return to metaphysics. As Foucault importantly argues in his review of *Difference and Repetition* and *Logic of Sense:* "to consider a pure event, it must first be given a metaphysical basis. But, we must be agreed that it cannot be the metaphysics of substances, which can serve as a foundation for accidents; nor can it be a metaphysics of coherence, which situates these accidents in the entangled nexus of causes and effects."[33] Rather, Foucault claims, "[Deleuze] leads us joyously to metaphysics—a metaphysics freed from its original profundity as well as from a supreme being . . . a metaphysics where it is no longer a question of the One Good but of the absence of God and the epidermic play of perversity. A dead God and sodomy are the thresholds of the new metaphysical ellipse."[34]

If Deleuze and Badiou share no other significant philosophical commitments, or such other commitments can be derived from their commitments to multiplicity and events, then it seems likely that there is no other basis for their mutual self-identification as metaphysicians then precisely these two commitments.[35] Let's test this hypothesis philosophically. In order to prove that multiplicity and events are the two minimal philosophical requirements for metaphysical realism in the next two sections I will draw on three arguments offered by Meillassoux, Deleuze, and Badiou, in support of precisely this logical conclusion. In particular, Meillassoux offers a very concise formulation of the first necessity of metaphysical realism: "if contingency is necessary, then existence is possible outside thought."

Multiplicity

Let's unpack this a bit. Is being necessary or is it contingent? If all being is necessary being, then it is impossible that a being not be. And if becoming or change is defined as a being's capacity-to-be-other, to come into being or perish from being, then, according to Meillassoux, change is impossible. Meillassoux calls this dogmatic realism. If on the other hand being is contingent, or as Meillassoux paraphrases the position of the correlationist, "it is unthinkable that the unthinkable be impossible," then it is not only possible that being may become-other, it is also possible that being may be necessary [il est impensable que l'impensable soit impossible].[36] But if being is necessary then again change would be impossible. However, if being is necessarily contingent, then it must be possible for beings to become other, or perish, and it is necessary that there be no absolute necessity or totality—except the necessity of contingency.

If being is necessarily contingent then this necessity also cannot be contingent on human thought insofar as humans themselves have the capacity-to-be-other. If this necessity were contingent then it might be possible that being was necessary and thus it would be impossible for being not to be. Thus, change would be impossible. Accordingly, being's contingency must be a necessity that is not determined by human thought. No matter what or if we think, there must be an absolute necessity of beings contingency or there would be no becoming. Thus, if we can discover an absolute necessity independent of human thought, as we just did regarding the necessity of being's contingency, we have access to a mind independent truth: beings necessary contingency. Thus, according to Meillassoux, we have shown (here in brief) that knowledge is possible outside of human thought and the correlational circles of language, culture, party, and state.

This is precisely the philosophical commitment made by both Deleuze and Badiou in their respective, although different, commitments to multiplicity, that is, non-totality. For Deleuze, Badiou, and Meillassoux, all philosophical positions that deny the non-totality of being are logically inconsistent and contradictory. According to Badiou, there is a "logical inconsistency of any concept of an absolute totality or reference," because "it gives rise to a formal contradiction."[37] In fact, it is still Russell's paradox that remains the "mainspring of the logical demonstration of the inconsistency of the absolute totality."[38] Badiou recounts this paradox of totality in his own terminology: If there is a Whole of all multiples, this totality is divisible into two types of multiples: reflexive multiples (there is at least one which includes itself in itself, the Whole) and non-reflexive multiples (those that are included in the Whole, but which do not include themselves). But if the Whole is "all non-reflexive multiples," than it is nothing other than non-reflexive multiples. But this is impossible since we just presumed it was a reflexive multiple. The Whole is by definition the multiple *of* all non-reflexive multiples, that is, a reflexive multiple. However, if the Whole is a reflexive multiple, then it cannot be "all non-reflexive multiples," since it is not a non-reflexive multiple. Finally, Badiou concludes: "If the universe is conceived as the totality of beings, there is no universe."[39] In other words, if the universe is not included as a being within the totality of beings, which it cannot be, than it is not a being: it is not.

Similarly, according to Deleuze, it is Russell and Gödel that demonstrate the inconsistency of a formal logic of the Whole. "According to the two aspects of Godel's theorem," Deleuze says, "proof of the consistency of arithmetic cannot be represented within the system (there is no endoconsistency), and the system necessarily comes up against true statements that are nevertheless not demonstrable, are undecidable (there is no exoconsistency, or the consistent system cannot be complete)."[40] "Consequently," Deleuze concludes, "we can and must presuppose a multiplicity of planes, since no one plane could encompass all of chaos without collapsing back into it."[41] If there were One plane that was "the totality of all planes," this One plane would be nothing other than all planes, and thus, no longer a One plane, but the many planes themselves. As soon as the One plane becomes "all planes" it would thus "collapse back into" being multiple planes and no longer One plane.

Thus, the necessity of contingency, that is, multiplicity, is not simply a naïve presupposition for Meillassoux, Deleuze, and Badiou; it is a philosophical and logical argument, which they all accept. However, it is not yet a sufficient argument for realism, only one for the necessity of anti-absolutism. Multiplicity only guarantees the logical possibility of events, not their existence.

The Event

This brings us to the final and most important point of convergence between Deleuze and Badiou's metaphysics: the event. Although well-argued and persuasive in many ways, Meillassoux's argument is ultimately insufficient for the return of metaphysics and revolution. His argument that "if contingency is necessary, then existence is possible outside thought," only affirms the *possibility* of existence outside thought. Just as correlationism is, according to Meillassoux, not "an anti-realism but an anti-absolutism," so Meillassoux is not a realist, but an absolutist insofar as he affirms the absolute necessity of contingency.[42] The purpose of the event is to *actually* demonstrate the existence and consequences of an event constitutive of reality and subjectivity itself. This is the fundamental difference between Meillassoux and Deleuze and Badiou. Meillassoux has no theory of the event. Thus, one cannot locate a revolutionary realism or any identifiable politics at all in Meillassoux's thought.

This is a significant shortcoming identified by Nick Srnicek in the first edited collection of essays on speculative realism, *The Speculative Turn*. It is clear that speculative realism has demonstrated "a notable absence so far when it comes to issues of subjectivity and politics," Srnicek says.[43] However, Srnicek's contribution to the book attempts to locate the implications of speculative realism for politics and concludes that realism "constitute[s] the necessary, but not yet sufficient, conditions for constructing new empirico-transcendental spaces incommensurable with the capitalist socius."[44] In other words, speculative realism is *insufficient* for thinking politics. This insufficiency is further supported by other realists. For example Ray Brassier is quite clear when he says, "there can be no ethics of radical immanence."[45] Peter Hallward, too, argues that speculative realism even fails to account for any "actual process of transformation or development."[46] Thus, the return of metaphysics, following Meillassoux's work, only gets us the necessary conditions for possible reality: necessary contingency (i.e., multiplicity). For metaphysics and politics, or what I have been calling in this chapter, revolutionary realism, we need the event to determine the real consequences of worldly becoming. *The Speculative Turn* opens with an interview with Badiou saying exactly this:

> There is a detachment from the present in SR, a kind of stoicism of the present. There is no clear presentation or vision of the present. This is very different from me. There is no theory of the event in SR. They need a vision of the becoming of the world which is lacking but it can be realist in a sense but as of yet they do not say what we need to do. For Meillassoux the future decides, the future and perhaps the dead will make the final judgment. This is a political weakness. The question is how is the Real of the present deployed for the future?[47]

In other words, the political affirmation of necessarily contingent multiplicity confronts the danger of ambivalence. Meillassoux's realism is both the condition for real parliamentary-capitalism as well as the necessary condition for a real revolutionary struggle against it. Thus, as mere ontological possibility, revolution is only a matter of optimism. One must have multiplicity to have becoming, as Meillassoux argues, but becoming as such, tells us nothing about what is in the present, or what should be, or what the consequences of a real event are: "This is a political weakness."

Without the consistency and order that the event gives to being, there is only contingency, potentially, and pure multiplicity. That is, the necessity of contingency risks falling prey to the twin dangers of virtual hierarchy and political ambivalence previously outlined in section two. Opposed to the mere possibility of the real, Deleuze and Badiou both develop complex logics of the event that are both diagnostic and imperative. These logics are far too complex to summarize here. In short, however, the goal of the event is to create a consistency of the real defined by immanent processes of connection that do not presuppose the product they produce (opposed to representation which is transcendent and presupposes the operation of a prior production, i.e. consciousness, the state, the market, etc.). While Badiou calls this the point by point connection of a subjective fidelity to a reflexive multiple, or transcendental index of a world and Deleuze calls this the construction of positively deterritorialized elements into an abstract machine and concrete assemblage; both insist on the importance, contra Meillassoux, of creating a sustained and real evental consistency.

It is thus precisely in this sense that both thinkers propose a return to metaphysics and revolution. Insofar as they remain philosophically committed to the necessary contingency of being's multiplicity, they allow for the possibility of real change independent of human thought. Insofar as they remain philosophically committed to the actual and non-representational reality of events which immanently order being, they are able to conceptualize concrete revolutionary events independent of the party, state, or market.

Conclusion: A New Philosophical Tradition?

If we want to understand the meaning of the contemporary return of metaphysics and revolution, we need to be clear what differences are meaningfully outside this return and what the minimal criteria for inclusion in it are. Thus, this chapter is not intended to be an exhaustive comparison of Deleuze and Badiou's theory of metaphysics or revolution. That is a much larger project. Nor is this chapter intended to create a typology of positions within the return to metaphysics. Again, this is beyond the scope of a single chapter. The aim of this chapter is merely to establish the most minimal conditions and philosophical features of what constitutes a meaningful return to political and philosophical realism.

The courage and boldness of the return to metaphysics to announce a break with the last 150 years of continental anti-realism is impressive and even exciting. However, when the editors of *The Speculative Turn* compare this sort of return with the traditions of phenomenology, structuralism, post-structuralism, post-modernism, and deconstruction, one cannot help but feel an inadequacy compared to these other traditions. What constitutes a new philosophical tradition? There are too many characteristics to list here, but at least one of them is that it bears directly on the actual world in some fashion. Every philosophical tradition has been able to rethink not only "what is," but also how being is specifically distributed in art, love, ethics, and politics. In short, a new philosophical tradition requires a theory of the event.

A meaningful aim of the return to metaphysics is not only to argue for the position of realism against that of correlationism, but for a politically, aesthetically, and scientifically robust realism. There are several such interesting projects already underway that are making the return to metaphysics and speculative realism into more than an "interesting, but ultimately useless theoretical venture."[48] If speculative realism is defined only by its ontological commitment to some variety of realism, but remains too radically divided in its methodology and theory of actuality, it will not be intelligible as a new tradition. This is a particularly unfortunate dilemma given that we are witnessing today the largest world-wide revolutionary movements since the 1960s! It is also possible however, that the return to metaphysics and revolution is an untimely announcement: something which, at the moment, sounds absurd and insufficient, but which in time *will have been true*. Philosophical realism may be the necessary condition forward for contemporary philosophy, but it is definitely not yet the sufficient condition, that is, without events.

Notes

1. I thank my anonymous peer reviewers for their helpful comments and direction with this chapter. I also thank the organizers of the conference, "The Return of Metaphysics" hosted at Villanova University on April 8–9, 2011—at which a draft of this chapter was originally presented. And I finally thank the editors of this collection for their kindness and receptivity to my work, despite its late submission.

2. Quentin Meillassoux, "History and Event in Alain Badiou," trans. Thomas Nail, *Parrhesia: A Journal of Critical Philosophy* 12 (2011): 2.

3. Slavoj Žižek, *Organs Without Bodies: Deleuze and Consequences* (New York: Routledge, 2004), 184.

4. Alain Badiou and François Balmès, *De l'idéologie* (Paris: F. Maspero, 1976), 83.

5. Paolo Virno, *A Grammar of the Multitude: For an Analysis of Contemporary Forms of Life* (Cambridge: Semiotext(e), 2003), 131.

6. Bruno Bosteels, "Logics of Antagonism: In the Margins of Alain Badiou's 'The Flux and the Party,'" *Polygraph: An International Journal of Culture & Politics* 15, no. 16 (2004): 95.

7. Bosteels, "Logics of Antagonism," 104.

8. Alain Badiou, *Peut-on penser la politique?* (Paris: Seuil, 1985), 12.

9. For full defense see: Thomas Nail, *Returning to Revolution: Deleuze, Guattari, and Zapatismo* (Edinburgh: Edinburgh University Press, 2012).

10. Alain Badiou, *Deleuze: The Clamor of Being*, trans. Louise Burchill (Minneapolis: University of Minnesota Press, 2000), 12–13. Badiou is citing here from: Gilles Deleuze, *Difference and Repetition* (New York: Columbia University Press, 1994), 37.

11. Badiou, *Deleuze*, 13.

12. Peter Hallward, *Out of This World: Deleuze and the Philosophy of Creation* (London: Verso, 2006), 162.

13. Hallward, *Out of This World*, 62n16.

14. Hallward, *Out of This World*, 162.

15. Gilles Deleuze, *The Logic of Sense*, trans. M. Lester with C. Stivale (New York: Columbia University Press, 1990), 152.

16. Hallward, *Out of This World*, 97.

17. Hallward, *Out of This World*, 162.

18. For a full defense see: Joshua Ramey, *The Hermetic Deleuze: Philosophy and Spiritual Ordeal* (Durham: Duke University Press, 2012).

19. Gilles Deleuze et Félix Guattari, *Capitalisme et schizophrénie. Tome 2: Mille Plateaux* (Paris: Les Éditions de Minuit, 1980), 249.

20. Deleuze and Guattari, *A Thousand Plateaus*, 161.

21. Thomas Nail, *Returning to Revolution: Deleuze, Guattari, and Zapatismo* (Edinburgh: Edinburgh University Press, 2012).

22. Deleuze and Guattari, *A Thousand Plateaus*, 25.

23. Deleuze and Guattari, *A Thousand Plateaus*, 10.

24. Michel Foucault, *Language, Counter-Memory, Practice: Selected Essays and Interviews*, ed. Donald F. Bouchard, trans. Donald F. Bouchard and Sherry Simon (Ithaca: Cornell University Press, 1977), 207.

25. For a historical account of Deleuze and Foucault's participation in the GIP see: François Dosse, *Gilles Deleuze & Félix Guattari: Intersecting Lives*, trans. Deborah Glassman (New York: Columbia University Press, 2012), 309–13.

26. For a discussion of realism and anti-realism in Deleuze see: Jeffery Bell, "Between Realism and Anti-realism: Deleuze and the Spinozist Tradition in Philosophy," *Deleuze Studies* 5.1 (2011): 1–17.

27. Alain Badiou, *Theoretical Writings*, trans. Ray Brassier and Alberto Toscano (London: Continuum, 2004), 170.

28. Quentin Meillassoux, *After Finitude: An Essay on the Necessity of Contingency*, trans. Ray Brassier (London: Continuum, 2008), 11.

29. Badiou, *Theoretical Writings*, 170.

30. Badiou, *Theoretical Writings*, 170.

31. Arnaud Villani, *La Guêpe et l'orchidée* (Paris: Belin, 1999), 130.

32. Badiou, *Deleuze*, 101.

33. Foucault, *Language, Counter-Memory, Practice*, 172–73.

34. Foucault, *Language, Counter-Memory, Practice*, 171.

35. I have not proved in this chapter these are the only two agreements between Deleuze and Badiou, nor I have I demonstrated that all other possible agreements are derived from these two agreements. This is only a hypothesis. It would lend additional support for my argument, but such support is not necessary for the success of my argument. What I have demonstrated *philosophically*, by thematizing arguments from Deleuze and Badiou, is that the minimum logical conditions for metaphysical realism are multiplicity and events.

36. If on the other hand being is contingent, or as Meillassoux paraphrases the position of the correlationist, "it is unthinkable that the unthinkable be impossible," [*il est impensable que l'impensable soit impossible*] then it is not only possible that being may

become-other, it is also possible that being may be necessary. (Meillassoux, *After finitude*, 41).

37. Badiou, *Theoretical Writings*, 177.
38. Badiou, *Theoretical Writings*, 178.
39. Badiou, *Theoretical Writings*, 178.
40. Gilles Deleuze and Félix Guattari, *What Is Philosophy?*, trans. G. Burchell and H. Tomlinson (New York: Columbia University Press, 1994), 137, *Qu'est-ce que la philosophie?* (Paris: Les Éditions de Minuit 1991).
41. Deleuze and Guattari, *What Is Philosophy?*, 50.
42. Meillassoux, *After Finitude*, 11.
43. Levi Bryant, Nick Srnicek, and Graham Harman, eds., *The Speculative Turn: Continental Materialism and Realism* (Melbourne: re.press, 2011), 165.
44. Bryant et. al., *The Speculative Turn*, 181.
45. Bryant et. al., *The Speculative Turn*, 178.
46. Bryant et. al., *The Speculative Turn*, 139.
47. Bryant et. al., *The Speculative Turn*, 20.
48. Bryant et. al., *The Speculative Turn*, 165.

References

Badiou, Alain and François Balmès. *De l'idéologie*. Paris: F. Maspero, 1976.
———: *Peut-on penser la politique?*. Paris: Seuil, 1985.
———. *Deleuze: The Clamor of Being*. Translated by Louise Burchill. Minneapolis: University of Minnesota Press, 2000.
———. *Theoretical Writings*. Translated by Ray Brassier and Alberto Toscano. London: Continuum, 2004.
Bell, Jeffery. "Between Realism and Anti-realism: Deleuze and the Spinozist Tradition in Philosophy." *Deleuze Studies* 5. no. 1 (2011): 1–17.
Bosteels, Bruno. "Logics of Antagonism: In the Margins of Alain Badiou's 'The Flux and the Party.'" *Polygraph: An International Journal of Culture & Politics* 15, no. 16 (2004).
Bryant, Levi, Nick Srnicek, and Graham Harman, eds. *The Speculative Turn: Continental Materialism and Realism*. Melbourne: re.press, 2011.
Deleuze, Gilles and Félix Guattari. *A Thousand Plateaus: Capitalism and Schizophrenia*. Translated by Brian Massumi. Minneapolis: University of Minnesota Press, 1987.
———. *What Is Philosophy?* Translated by G. Burchell and H. Tomlinson. New York: Columbia University Press, 1994.
Deleuze, Gilles. *The Logic of Sense*. Edited by Constantin V. Boundas. Translated by Mark Lester with Charles Stivale. New York: Columbia University Press, 1990.
———. *Difference and Repetition*. New York: Columbia University Press, 1994.
Dosse, François. *Gilles Deleuze & Félix Guattari: Intersecting Lives*. Translated by Deborah Glassman. New York: Columbia University Press, 2012.
Foucault, Michel. *Language, Counter-Memory, Practice: Selected Essays and Interviews*. Edited by Donald F. Bouchard. Translated by Donald F. Bouchard and Sherry Simon. Ithaca: Cornell University Press, 1977.
Hallward, Peter. *Out of This World: Deleuze and the Philosophy of Creation*. London: Verso, 2006.

Meillassoux, Quentin. *After Finitude: An Essay on the Necessity of Contingency*. Translated by Ray Brassier. London: Continuum, 2008.

————. "History and Event in Alain Badiou." Translated by Thomas Nail. *Parrhesia: A Journal of Critical Philosophy* 12 (2011): 1–11.

Nail, Thomas. *Returning to Revolution: Deleuze, Guattari, and Zapatismo*. Edinburgh: Edinburgh University Press, 2012.

Ramey, Joshua. *The Hermetic Deleuze: Philosophy and Spiritual Ordeal*. Durham: Duke University Press, 2012.

Villani, Arnaud. *La Guêpe et l'orchidée*. Paris: Belin, 1999.

Virno, Paolo. *A Grammar of the Multitude: For an Analysis of Contemporary Forms of Life*. Cambridge: Semiotext(e), 2003.

Žižek, Slavoj. *Organs Without Bodies: Deleuze and Consequences*. New York: Routledge, 2004.

CHAPTER TEN

Whence Intensity? Deleuze and the Revival of a Concept

Mary Beth Mader

Intensities or intensive magnitudes, such as temperatures and speeds, are part of the physical descriptions of the world offered by the natural sciences. Scientific accounts of intensity have their roots in philosophical accounts, specifically in the ontologies developed in the philosophies of medieval Europe. In Western philosophy since that period, there developed a minor tradition of philosophical thought about intensity, generally in the context of ontologies of quality and quantity. In *Difference and Repetition* and several other texts, Gilles Deleuze implicitly revives, enriches, and centralizes this lesser tradition of ontological thought on the nature of intensity in Western philosophy. However, Deleuze rejects what he takes to be neutralizing accounts of intensity found in its treatment in much of Western philosophy. On his view, philosophical accounts of intensity that understand it as quality, or as extended quantity, fail to capture the specific character of intensity and its necessarily ineliminable structuring difference.

In the context of the debates on the concept of intensity, that concept refers to the intensification or remission of a quality, in medieval terms, that is, to its becoming more or less of itself. The term 'intensity' in Deleuze's writings generally refers to this intensive change in a quality. Moreover, for Deleuze, although intensity is the intensification (or remission) of a quality, it is important to note that for this very reason intensity and quality ought not to be identified. A quality's becoming more or less of itself should not be confused with that quality itself. For example, the quality sweet is not identical to a sweetness becoming more or less sweet. Thus, any ontology of intensity that confused it with quality *per se*, instead of providing an account of the intensive change in a quality, would be fundamentally misleading, on Deleuze's view.

This emphasis upon the intensification or remission of a quality accords both with the history of the concept and with Deleuze's general interest, stressed throughout his corpus, in the ontology of becoming. The intensive change in a quality is a central concern of the tradition of medieval philosophy, and hence a resource for Deleuze's reflections upon many sorts of becoming. Thought on intensity has a long history and one to which Deleuze refers at several points in his work. Although its complete history with respect to Deleuze's philosophy is yet to be recounted, some of its chapters already have been told admirably.[1] This is so especially for the philosophy of intensity found in the works of Spinoza, Kant, Hegel, and Bergson. This chapter's aim is to sketch some of the earlier episodes in a history of the concept of intensity that are less studied or known by philosophers interested in Deleuze's metaphysics. These episodes concern, first, the source of the concept of intensity in Aristotle's metaphysical philosophy and, second, several notable medieval receptions of this Aristotelian heritage and their ontologies of intensity devised in response to Aristotle. Although the chief aim of this essay is thus to begin to supply a missing chapter in the scholarship on Deleuze's ontology, namely his relation to medieval thought on the ontology of intensity, it neither exhaustively investigates the complete relation of Deleuze to medieval accounts of intensity nor provides a definitive analysis of Deleuze's renewal of the concept of intensity. It tackles the more restricted goal of presenting some of the hitherto obscure but genuine sources of Deleuze's thought on intensity, in the hopes that this will serve the larger project of situating Deleuze's philosophy more amply within that version of the history of Western philosophy to which he refers.

At stake in the question of the ontology of intensity is the fundamental priority granted it by Deleuze—and presumably by Guattari, as well, in the co-authored books. Scholars have disagreed about the question of the centrality or fundamental nature of intensity in Deleuze's ontology. For instance, in the Anglophone scholarship, John Protevi and Peter Hallward differ on whether the concept of intensity is to be identified with that of the virtual in Deleuze's thought, and on how these two concepts relate to the paramount concept in Deleuze's ontology, that of difference.[2] Other scholars construe Deleuze as a kind of "materialist," partly on the grounds of his frequent apparently valorizing inclusion of language, terms and concepts from the physical and formal sciences in his philosophy.[3] Determining more clearly the senses in which Deleuze employs the notion of intensity, and in what ways his usages retain or relinquish established prior senses from the history of philosophy surely will be pertinent to some of these continuing debates.

Deleuze cites sources and scholarship on this medieval discourse on intensity in a number of works, including in some of his major texts co-authored with Félix Guattari.[4] Although references to the concept of intensity, even central ones, appear in almost all of Deleuze's texts, the chief works to explicitly refer to medieval philosophy of intensity are *A Thousand Plateaus* and *What is Philosophy?* It would be a significant oversight, though, not to include also mention of the capital role of the concept of intensity in *Difference and Repetition* and *Bergsonism*. Accordingly, this chapter takes these four texts as its primary foci among Deleuze's writings.

Deleuze's most cited sources on medieval philosophy of intensity are Pierre Duhem's multi-volume *Le système du monde* (1913–19) and Gilles Chatelet's

Figuring Space: Philosophy, Mathematics, and Physics (*L'Enjeux du mobile* (1993)), particularly "Chapter II: The Screen, the Spectrum and the Pendulum: Horizons of Acceleration and Deceleration" ("*La toile, le spectre et le pendule: Horizons d'accélération et de ralentissement.*") Nicolas Oresme (1320–1382), one of the chief philosophical figures in France in the second half of the fourteenth century,[5] is cited by name in *A Thousand Plateaus* and *What is Philosophy?* Oresme's text, *Tractatus de configurationibus qualitatum et motuum* (*Treatise on the Uniformity and Difformity of Intensities*), is one important locus for the medieval treatment of the concept of intensity. We will not address here the many references to medieval European philosophy in Deleuze's work that do not bear directly upon the question of the ontology of intensity.

But what importance should be granted to the problem of intensity, quite apart from its salience to the task of interpreting and assessing the ontology of Gilles Deleuze? Herman Shapiro astutely notes that our contemporary inclination is to think about the matter in an entirely quantified way. In other words, we take for granted a notion that neither early thinkers on the topic nor Deleuze assume. This is the notion that qualitative intensification is sufficiently and ultimately best understood in thoroughly quantitative terms. The modern reader, Shapiro holds, fails to even discern the problem of the ontology of intensity because qualitative intensities are already translated or transposed into purely quantitative terms. About this general contemporary indiscernibility, he writes that the modern reader tends to understand the qualitative "more" and "less" to be expressed correctly and adequately in quantitative terms. For example, Shapiro claims, presumably referring to the thermometer, that when thinking of heat, we "measure its degree of intensity through the use of an instrument which conveniently translates the quality into a quantity. We have not, that is, *solved* the problem of intension and remission; we have, however, successfully *bypassed* it."[6] Is this the case? In what sense has the problem been skirted, instead of solved? The physical sciences provide us with accounts of temperatures, pressures, altitudes and other intensive quantities expressed in purely quantitative terms. Why should we think that such thoroughly quantitative expressions of phenomena traditionally termed "intensities" have not, in fact, supplied us with the most correct and rigorous account of their nature? What ontological questions remain which have not been solved by the total translation of qualitative intensities into quantities?

One purpose of this chapter is to supply some of the early philosophical history of the concept of intensity as a basis for eventual informed reply to such questions. Revisiting the history of the ontology of intensity can be part of a preliminary effort, then, to assess the state of contemporary philosophical understandings of intensities, as distinct from accounts of intensity as offered in and employed by the contemporary physical sciences. Philosophers of metaphysics and ontology, in other words, may look to the philosophical history of the concept of intensity so as to identify the complexities of the concept that show up in the tale of the triumph of quantitative expression of intensity that today appears so evidently adequate.

1. The Aristotelian Antecedents of the Concept of Intensity

For our purposes, there appears no stronger source of contemporary scholarship on medieval ontologies of intensity, or on the medieval debates over "the latitude of forms," than the highly instructive research of Jean-Luc Solère.[7] His work and the work of Edith D. Sylla, John Murdoch and Marshall Clagett are the main touchstones for the following sketch of some early episodes in the history of the concept of intensity in Western philosophy.[8]

As we have noted, the notion of intensity, and the term itself, stems from medieval European philosophy. But its antecedents are to be found in ancient thought. Specifically, it was Aristotle whose work set out a problem for which the concept of intensity became the main solution in medieval philosophy. Medieval thought saw the flourishing of work on the question of how to understand qualitative change, or cases in which a quality becomes more or less of itself: more or less hot, more or less bright, more or less sweet, more or less loving.

Specifically, the medieval debate on what is termed the 'intensification,' or *intensio* and 'remission,' or *remissio*, of qualities responds to Aristotle's view that "some qualities, as accidental beings, admit of the more and the less."[9] On this point, the pertinent textual source is *Categoriae* 8, where Aristotle writes:

> Qualifications admit of a more and a less: for one thing is called more pale or less pale than another, and more just than another. Moreover, it itself sustains increase (for what is pale can still become paler)—not in all cases though, but in most. It might be questioned whether one justice is called more a justice than another, and similarly for the other conditions. For some people dispute about such cases. They utterly deny that one justice is called more or less a justice than another, or one health more or less a health, though they say that one person has health less than another, justice less than another, and similarly with grammar and the other conditions. At any rate things spoken of in virtue of these unquestionably admit of a more and a less: one man is called more grammatical than another, juster, healthier, and so on.[10]

It should be noted that "sustaining increase" "it itself" is the sort of change at issue, here, as Aristotle specifies elsewhere, as well: "Again, a thing is called more, or less, such-and-such *than itself*; for example, the body that is pale is called more pale now than before . . ."[11] So, the concept of intensity is not devised to solve a problem with respect to comparison of quality or qualitative change between two qualities in two differing beings or subjects, but to craft an account of the ontology of qualitative change within a single being or subject. Moreover, the qualitative change at issue is not the sort of change that brings about the conversion of one quality into its contrary quality. Nor does it cause the subject of the quality to degenerate.[12] As Solère writes: "For Aristotle, intensification is in fact a limited alteration that does not make the species change."[13]

Of course, not all kinds of beings, for Aristotle, admit of "the more and the less." Neither substances nor quantities do.[14] What kinds of beings admit of "the more and the less," according to Aristotle? Some kinds of qualities do. The kinds of qualities that admit of the more and the less are: (i) states and dispositions (e.g., virtue); (ii) affections of bodies (e.g., sweetness, heat); and (iii) affections of the soul (e.g., anger).[15] But not all kinds of qualities admit of the more and the less. For example, geometrical shapes do not.[16] That a quality admits of a more and a less implies that some type of change must be taking place; but how ought this change to be understood, for Aristotle? To grasp his answer to this question, we must return to his well-known classification of types of change or motion: "There are six kinds of change: generation, destruction, increase, diminution, alteration, change of place."[17]

Among other sorts of change or motion, Aristotle here distinguishes between two strictly different kinds. One kind is called 'increase,' along with its contrary, 'decrease' or 'diminution,' and the other kind is called 'alteration.' ('Increase' is sometimes also translated as 'augmentation.') These two different sorts of change apply to two different sorts of categories. The kind of change or motion called 'increase' or 'augmentation' is reserved for quantity. "Motion in respect of Quantity has no name that includes both contraries, but it is called increase or decrease according as one or the other is designated."[18] Increase or augmentation also has several essential requirements. That which increases or augments must have distinct parts, which permit divisibility, and additive parts, which are characteristic of quantity.

The kind of change or motion called 'alteration,' on the other hand, is reserved for quality. "Motion in respect of Quality let us call alteration, a general designation that is used to include both contraries, and by Quality I do not here mean a property of substance (in that sense that which constitutes a specific distinction is a quality) but a passive quality in virtue of which a thing is said to be acted on or to be incapable of being acted upon."[19] As is clear in the continuation of the passage on the six kinds of change or motion, Aristotle explicitly argued that alteration is sort of change distinct from all other five sorts of change. Most importantly, he especially separates analytically alteration from increase and decrease. He writes:

> That the rest are distinct from one another is obvious (for generation is not destruction, not yet is increase or diminution, nor is change of place; and similarly with the others too), but there is a question about alteration—whether it is not perhaps necessary for what is altering to be altering in virtue of one of the other changes. However, this is not true. For in pretty well all the affections, or most of them, we undergo alteration without partaking of any of the other changes. *For what changes as to an affection does not necessarily increase or diminish—and likewise with the others.* Thus alteration would be distinct from the other changes. For if it were the same, a thing altering would, as such, have to be increasing too or diminishing, or one of the other changes would have to follow; but this is not necessary. Equally, a thing increasing—or undergoing some other change—would have to be altering. But there are things that increase

without altering, as a square is increased by the addition of a gnomon but is not thereby altered; similarly, too, with other such cases. Hence the changes are distinct from one another.[20]

That is, although alteration is a kind of change rightly described in terms of "the more and the less," it is *not* a species of increase or decrease, terms that apply only to quantities. Alteration of a quality is rightly described in terms of "the more and the less," but "the more and the less" of a quality are not instances of increase or decrease. A thing can be generated, destroyed, increase, decrease, and change place without altering. Correlatively, a thing can alter without also being generated, destroyed, increased, decreased, or changing place. For Aristotle, the fact that a quality can alter independently of all of these other kinds of changes demonstrates that the alteration of a quality is a distinct sort of change.

What is of special importance here is that, for Aristotle, the alteration that is a quality's change in respect of the more and the less is a kind of change that is not quantitative. It is, rather, to be understood in entirely qualitative terms, and by means of the classical fundamental Aristotelian concepts of act and potency. The account is given in terms of the concepts of contrary qualities, act and potency, and preponderance: "On his purely qualitative account, the more and the less [of a quality] depend only on the preponderance of a quality over its opposite . . . ."[21] This preponderance, or "the more and the less," is explained "in terms of act and potency: " . . . the more its contrary is in potency, the more the quality is actualized."[22]

This conception is supposed to be a rigorously qualitative notion of change, which "results only from the interplay of potential and act, and is totally distinct from the processes implying a more and a less that are quantitative. . . . Alteration is a change that can take place independently of any other movement, in particular without any quantitative modification. This movement thus must be conceived in itself, solely in terms of the actualization [*de passage à l'acte*] of what was already present in potential form, without any extrinsic addition whatsoever of anything new."[23] A white thing may become "more" white and a soul may become "more" charitable but, as alterations, these changes must be "the gradual elimination of the contrary and the actualization of that which of the quality remained potentially."[24] Notably, such changes, on an Aristotelian view, could not be described in terms of the addition of external parts, as such additions would imply quantity, and often a preexisting quantity. On the Aristotelian position, the growth in whiteness of a thing already white cannot be conceived of as the adjunction of supplemental white parts that are added to an initial whiteness. The white thing that whitens cannot be conceived of as having parts of white added to it, as if its growth resembled the growth in extension of a line to which separate and external linear segments are adjoined. Of course, the same holds in the case of qualitative remission and its comparative non-resemblance with the subtraction of extended quantities.

This notion of change of a quality over time that is described in terms of "the more and the less"—but where a "more" and a "less" are understood to be strictly non-quantitative—serves as the basis for ontological puzzles for which the medieval concepts of intensity are proposed solutions. An extremely fertile debate over the ontology of intensity develops in the medieval period, set off by problems with the ontology of Aristotle's purely qualitative notion of "more" and "less" of a quality. However, the medieval solutions that come to prevail actually challenge and abandon this qualitative construal of "the more and the less." In fact, this allegedly purely qualitative version of alteration is treated to increasingly quantitative explanation, ending in the complete quantification of quality and its becoming, according to Solère. As he puts it, "Everything in the Aristotelian bases and treatment of the problem opposed augmentation [or increase] and *intensio*. However, the Medievals brought them as close together as they could."[25]

2. Intensity and the Medieval Tradition of Aristotelian Commentary

Aristotle bequeathed to medieval thought the problem of how qualitative change rightly could be described in terms of 'the more and the less' and yet not be quantitative. The problem was to determine the nature and source of the variation described in the phrase "the more and the less." Proposals for such an explanation struggled to identify the exact seat of the qualitative change under investigation: " . . . does intensification occur in the form itself, or in the subject?"[26] In medieval usage "qualitative form" or, simply, "form", designates a quality that is susceptible to intension and remission. The particular qualitative changes that prompted this question were intensifications of qualities of the first Aristotelian sort, such as charity, justice and health. When such a quality intensifies, does this quality not itself remain unchanged, with the subject of such a quality—namely, the charitable, just or healthy individual—doing the changing, rather than the quality itself? If the variation takes place in the subject alone, then the form or quality itself would remain invariable. If the variation takes place in the form or quality itself, however, some medieval thinkers reasoned, the form itself must be thought to have some 'latitude.' What, exactly, is undergoing change in cases of intensification?

This sort of puzzle had theological implications in the medieval period. The Aristotelian account of changes in states and dispositions in terms of alteration gave rise to a particular Christian theological problem. The problem was whether charity could be increased in the human soul, and how to understand such increase if it is possible.[27] Prevalent theological understandings of human charity conflicted with the Aristotelian schema for conceiving of qualitative change in a human state or disposition such as charity. Two obstacles in particular were of importance. A dominant theological conception of human charity made it identical with the Holy Spirit, one of the three persons of God, itself. But if human charity is identical with the Holy Spirit itself, this yields an untenable result. For the Holy Spirit, being divine and therefore unchanging, should neither be subject to increase nor to alteration. Further, Aristotle's account of alteration bases it upon an ontology of qualities taken in pairs, in which each quality in the pair is the contrary of the other. A strictly Aristotelian account of the intension or re-mission of charity in a human soul, then, should imply that charity grows as its contrary quality diminishes. But this, in turn, would imply that charity has a contrary, a view that must be rejected on theological grounds; for "charity, as a divine gift, has no contrary."[28]

Solère here describes an early step in the gradual abandonment of Aristo-tle's purely qualitative notion of intensive change. This process of departure from Aristotle's theory of alteration turns in part on the question of whether qualities are species in themselves, such that were something to be added to or subtracted from them, those additions or subtractions would change their species or kind. Solère argues that intensification is progressively assimilated to in-crease, namely, to "an adjunction of a preexisting quantity," as Aristotle had understood increase.[29] Some medieval philosophers propose the solution that qualities are not fully determined species, but have an internal "latitude" for additions or subtractions to occur in them. On this view, such qualities could undergo additions and subtractions without changing in kind. In this way, a thoroughly qualitative theory of intensive change begins to be moved in the di-rection of a quantitative explication. For with such theories of qualitative lati-tude, the addition of parts—for Aristotle, a characteristic feature of increase—is employed to understand alteration, a process of change in quality that is alleged-ly independent of quantitative change, as Aristotle had argued in *Categories*.

But, interestingly, at this stage, some partitive theories of the intensification of a quality actually separate the notion of a part from the notion of quantity. For Aristotle, of course, they are joined; as Solère specifies, Aristotle held that in-crease "(or diminution) can only occur where parts can be distinguished and subsequently added (or subtracted)."[30] The innovation here, then, is the idea that a quality itself can have parts, or degrees, which divide it such that a kind of addition of parts or degrees of a quality, rather than parts or degrees of a quanti-ty, is conceivable. Thus, the previously separated concepts of intensity and quantity are joined in the concept of an intensive quantity. But numerous theo-ries of intensive quantity are developed, and elaborate disputes over their vary-ing pictures of the growth and diminution of a quality abound in fourteenth cen-tury Europe, within the context of the emergence of a natural philosophy that began to be critical of Aristotle.[31]

Three Theories of Intensification

Scholars differ on the question of how to classify the many theories of intensity developed in the medieval period. Solère divides medieval theories of intensification into three types: theories of actualization, succession, and addition. Edith Sylla and Herman Shapiro adopt a different tripartite classificatory vocabulary, retaining the types of succession and addition, but using the category of "admixture" instead of actualization.[32] Anneliese Maier considers the two most important theories of intensive alteration to be those of succession and addition.[33] For our purposes, we follow Solère's designations, as the term "actualization" appears to capture well, and to retain, the Aristotelian foundation of theories of intensive alteration that explain it by appeal to an "admixture" of contrary qualities in a subject. A synopsis of the essentials of these theoretic approaches, with emphasis on Aquinas's position, follows.

The Actualization Theory

The chief proponent of the actualization theory is Thomas Aquinas in the thirteenth century.[34] On Aquinas's view, alteration is the actualization of potential, rather than the addition of anything new. As to the question of the seat of change, and whether intensification takes place in the form or quality itself or in the subject it qualifies, Aquinas holds that quality itself does not vary. It is only "qualified things (*qualia*)" that are intensified or remitted.

Aquinas advances explicit objections to the additive theory. Confusing the increase in quality with the increase in a body is one source of error. This species of charge, namely, the claim that rival theories engage in a confusion of radically distinct kinds of growth and diminution, recalls the Aristotelian position. Even considered apart from any intensive change, the *apparent* extension of qualities found in ordinary expressions should not be considered metaphysically accurate. Thus, the white of a white surface and the time interval of an action, although they can be described as "large" or "long," are not properly speaking quantitative realities.

Aquinas's chief objection amounts to questioning how charity could be augmented by addition of charity to charity. Addition requires distinct items to be summed, and distinction must be either by species or by number. But two instances of charity are not different in species, so they cannot be added as distinct species. They are not different in species because Aquinas holds that difference in species "follows diversity of objects," and hence would be a matter of increase as an extension to new objects. But charity is such that its increase cannot be described in terms of its extension to apply to more and more objects; this is because "even the slightest charity extends to all that we have to love by charity."[35] So, there can be no distinct charity to be added to an initial charity to extend its scope; its scope is already essential to its very identity as charity, and cannot be increased. Nor can charity be increased by addition on the basis of numerically distinct instances of charity. By contrast to specific distinction, determined in reference to objects, Aquinas holds that numeric distinction is a matter of the distinction of subjects. Thus, in order for two instances of charity to differ numerically, they must inhere in different subjects, as their accidents. But in that case, their addition would require two subjects to be added, which is not possible since the subjects in question are souls. Moreover, the issue at hand was how to understand the increase in charity in a single soul. Even if souls could be summed, Aquinas notes, "the result would be a greater lover, but not a more loving one."[36]

How ought variation in quality to be understood, then? According to Solère, Aquinas's view Platonizes the Aristotelian position. Although a quality itself is immutable, variation occurs only in the participation of a subject in a quality. Intensive variation, then, is variation in the degree to which a subject participates in a quality. But the position still retains an Aristotelian aspect, since Aquinas conceives of participation itself in terms of potency and act. Moreover, a subject can participate in a quality across a range of degrees; that is, a quality can be actualized to varying degrees depending on the degree to which the subject participates in it. The intensification of a quality, then, is a function of the progressive participation of a subject in a quality, that is, of the actualization of the quality through the subject's participation in it. Intensification also takes place along a range and has an endpoint or maximum. The limit to the actualization of a quality is to be located in the potency of the subject. Thus, Aquinas preserves the Aristotelian view that "a thing's possessing a quality in a greater or lesser degree means the presence or absence in it of more or less of the opposite quality."[37] At the same time, actualization is lent a Platonic meaning since the change in the presence or absence of a contrary quality is understood ultimately to be a matter of the participation of the subject in a quality.

In the *Summa Theologica*, the positive analysis is carried out with specific reference to the question of whether charity can increase. Here, Aquinas argues that the quality of charity can increase in a soul, but it can "by no means increase by addition of charity to charity."[38] In the case of charity, as an accidental form whose being is to adhere to its subject, it increases "solely by being intensified," that is, by being "more in its subject." Increase in charity is for charity "to have a greater hold on the soul."[39] Aquinas compares this to kinds of increase in knowledge: if knowledge increases by extension to new truths, this is an increase by addition, by "knowing more things." But we can also say that knowledge increases by intensification when someone "knows the same scientific truths with greater certainty now than before."[40] Aquinas also describes intensification, this being "yet more in its subject," as a "greater radication in the subject."[41] He stresses that this radication is an increase in charity essentially, in charity as an accident, and that this increase is not to be explained by anything being "generated anew" or "beginning anew."[42] This latter rejected position, which suggests that intensification in some way would need to be understood in terms of the first two of Aristotle's six types of change, is the theory explicitly adopted by several prominent fourteenth century rivals to Aquinas's account.

The Succession Theory

This rival theory of intensification pursued the notion that variation in intensity should be conceived on the model of replacement or succession, and hence of the destruction and generation of forms of a given degree. Chief proponents of this succession theory of intensification were Geoffroy of Fontaine and Walter Burley in the early fourteenth century. For these thinkers, intensification is never a matter of addition or accumulation, but only of renewal.[43] Intensification is "a succession of more and more perfect realizations of a form that remains the same in species or essence," but does not remain numerically the same. In intensification, each form is entirely destroyed and is replaced by a new form of the same species but in a greater degree than the previous form. Importantly, there is thus no composition of new forms with prior forms, or with their parts, since prior forms are destroyed. Given the prevailing conception of quantity, according to which quantitative growth would require distinct pre-existing and persisting parts so as to permit divisibility and addition, in the succession theory the process of intensification is decidedly not quantitative. As Solère insightfully remarks, "here, addition is not even a metaphor. We may only relate each form to an extrinsic measure."[44]

The Addition Theory

Another rival theory of intensification is the addition theory, developed in the fourteenth century by Franciscans and the later Oxford Calculators. To move towards an account of intensification in terms of addition is to approach a quantitative conception of it and thus to depart from Aristotle's understanding of alteration. According to the addition theory, in the intensification of a quality "[a] distinct reality is added to the quality's pre-existing degree, thereby creating a new unity."[45] Multiple routes away from Aristotle's purely qualitative account of qualitative intensification were adopted. The new additive theories of intensification offered ontologies of quality that began to lend quality the property of being divisible into parts. One common problem confronted in this progressive abandonment was whether there is a conception of quality such that a quality could be subject to the addition or subtraction of parts without its changing in species.[46] As mentioned, the critical innovation in the additive theory was the notion of an inherent variability *within* a quality, such that intensification would be change along an internal range of possible variation of a quality. This is the notion of a latitude, or *latitudo*, numerous conceptions of which were developed in the various additive medieval approaches to the ontology of intensity. Hence, a central Franciscan objection to the actualization theory is that "[v]ariation in actuality (or being, *esse*) requires latitude in essence."[47] It is the additive theory that eventually prevails generally, and is the theoretical source of the thoroughly quantified views of intensity of today. A quality itself comes to be understood as having parts that are susceptible to addition and subtraction and thus are liable to being treated, ultimately, in quantitative terms of some sort. As Solère explains, "No longer regarded as intrinsically immutable and indivisible, qualitative forms will be regarded instead as subject to processes of construction and deconstruction part by part, and to calculation (although not in our modern sense)."[48]

3. Nicolas Oresme and the Geometricization of Quality

A special place in the history of the concept of intensity and Deleuze's reception of it must be reserved for the medieval French theologian, Nicolas Oresme (1320–1382).[49] Oresme was an eminent theologian, "man of science," and cosmologist, as well as being a major translator of Aristotle into French. His contribution to medieval thought on intensity is to be found in *De configurationibus qualitatum et motuum*, most likely written in the 1350s.[50] A. Maier characterizes "Oresme's method of graphical representation" as "undoubtedly the most original achievement of the fourteenth century."[51]

Oresme develops a graphic representation of a quality in two ways so as to show both its extension and its intensity. They are aptly called "configurations," as they figure both of these aspects together. Oresme also retains the terms "longitude" and "latitude" that were used in the debate on intensity that preceded him. He uses a horizontal line to represent the extension, in space or in time, of a quality, and a vertical line to represent the intensity of that same quality. These two lines, which also should vary to represent variation in the quality's extension and intensity, actually form bounded planes or areas. It is these planes that represent intensities composed with extensities. The extension of a subject is represented on the horizontal line; the intensity of a subject is represented on the vertical line. The work of Gilles Châtelet clarifies the difference between Oresmian configuration and Cartesian coordination.[52] Importantly, the longitude in Oresme is extensive, but it does not co-ordinate as the Cartesian abscissa does; in other words, it does not make an intensity correspond fully to an extensity. Oresme's longitude is not an abscissa and not a coordinate; it does not co-order, but composes into a surface area. Qualities are represented along two straight lines, which lines yield an entire area, not points or lines, as would a coordinate system.

The critical difference between the two modes of representation, here, is that the specificity of intensity and extensity are not identified and fused in the Oresmian diagram. The coordinate system, by contrast, reduces the two radically distinct realities of extensity and intensity to the one-dimensional line, that is, to an extension. Oresmian configurations retain the dualism of the two represented realities by composing them into the two dimensional area. Of course, the produced plane is indeed an extended geometrical figure, and in Oresme's hands proves to be additive and manipulable, as was any traditional geometrical figure of the time. But it did preserve the dual features of intensity and extensity in the two dimensions of the surface area used. By joining the two features in a single two-dimensional graphic, instead of in a line, according to Châtelet, "Oresme showed that he had succeeded in grasping intensities and extensions in one common intuition, without going beyond a tradition that carefully distinguished them."[53] He explains that the distinctive value of Oresme's diagrams is "to succeed in articulating these two measures, to dominate their opposition and to bring into play the principle that holds that in the corporeal order ontological degrees and extensive magnitudes *cooperate without confusion.*"[54]

As we will see below, Deleuze approves of this duality, and of preserving—while composing—the distinctive difference between intensity and extension. Deleuze appreciates Oresme's theory of intensity for not forcing intensive ordinates into coordination with extensities, that is, for not being a thoroughly modern mechanician's account. That is, Deleuze endorses the idea that the distinctive features of both intensive and extensive quantities are displayed in relation to each other in Oresme's configurations. But he also appears to count Oresme's theory as a step toward the reduction or neutralization of intensity found in later purely extensive formulations in the historical development of thought on intensity. It is unlikely that Deleuze could favor the equation—implied by the additivity of the surface areas of qualities in Oresme's account—that, as Oresme says, "a uniform speed that lasts for three days is equal to a speed three times as intense that lasts for one day."[55] Of course, Deleuze is not denying the importance of Oresme's (or others') mean speed theorem to physics and to its history. But the extensive equivalences of intensities found in such equations imply a loss of the distinctive *experiences* of intensive variation, and thus work against his aim of a philosophy of sensibility and of the experience of difference as intensive.

4. Medieval Philosophy of Intensity and Deleuze's Thought

At least four main texts by Deleuze, or Deleuze and Guattari, make clear the centrality of his, and their, thought on intensity and suggest its indebtedness to medieval accounts of intensity. Here, we merely sketch some of central points in these four texts that link medieval thought on intensity with Deleuze's ontology of intensity.

In *Bergsonism* (1966), Deleuze presents Bergson's critique of intensity, which critique charges thinking that is based on the concept of intensity with creating a false problem. The falsity in the problem of intensity is alleged to be that the concept of intensity necessarily deals in composites that amount to conceptual confusions. Something that is not ultimately determinable as part of a composite is nonetheless understood only as a component; when so mixed, it cannot be grasped as what it is. The charge finds at least two arguments. One is that intensity is always wrongly conceived as being explicable in extensive terms. The psychophysics of the period famously came in for attack by Bergson in *Time and Free Will* for reducing affective intensities to purportedly complete expression in terms of quantifiable sensations, or in terms of their even more quantifiable external causes. Here, the misleading composite is the explanation of intensity as a measurable quantity of some sort, which entirely obscures the qualitative nature of an intensity. Indeed, it is intensive quantity that is the object of Bergson's critique here. The second argument assumes that the discourse of intensity presupposed a gradational ontology of quantitative degrees, and that the quantitative continuity that this implies means that differences in kind are obscured or indiscernible. Here, the "composite" is the amalgamation or fusion of elements whose distinction ought to imply a trenchant difference in kind rather than a scalar, fused continuity of degrees. Mere differences in degree cover over striking difference in kind. As Deleuze puts it, for Bergson, "the notion of intensity involves an impure mixture between determinations that differ in kind."[56] Bergson holds that these composites thus must always be split up so as to reveal their properly qualitative element, distinguished as it should be from the extensive element to which it has been conceptually joined. This properly qualitative element is fundamentally and non-spatially temporal. Thus, the standard notion of intensity that Bergson critiques is one that in his view already wrongly included a measurable, quantifiable element. To purify such composites of these quantifiable elements is one of Bergson's aims. As Deleuze explains, however, "The critique of intensity in *Time and Free Will* is highly ambiguous."[57] By this Deleuze means that there appear to be three different moments in Bergson's thought on intensity and that they do not offer identical objections to traditional and contemporary conceptions of intensity. We can see that the question of the singularity of quality and qualitative change, so present in the medieval debates over the specificity of alteration proposed by Aristotle, is essential to Bergson's own philosophy. He clearly seeks to establish the uniqueness of qualitative phenomena with the concept of duration, among other such concepts, and to strenuously resist the reduction of such phenomena to extensive, spatial, or quantitative terms. Deleuze's account of Bergson's thought on intensity necessarily employs many of the central concepts set out in medieval discussions of the issue: alteration, quantity, quality, increase, degree, divisibility, extension, number, magnitude, composition, and many others.

As is well known, *Difference and Repetition* (1968) is the essential text for the presentation of Deleuze's philosophy of intensity. Intensity is metaphysically primordial for the ontology of difference developed in that work. We find discussion of it, therefore, in much of the book and in differing philosophical idioms: mathematical, physical, psychoanalytical, aesthetic. The opening to Chapter V: "Asymmetrical Synthesis of the Sensible" includes treatment of many of the most important features of the concept of intensity in this work.[58] Mainly, the account is given in terms of the discourse of physical systems, in particular those treated in terms of energy. Despite the fact that the relevant passages remain fairly generalized, apparently describing physical systems in general, and with few examples, Deleuze does discuss intensity in the explicit context of "energetics." Here, his discussion of physical systems quotes from two 1922 French studies in the philosophy of science, as well as citing Carnot's and Curie's principles, Kant, Novalis, signal-sign systems and entropy. These pages do not explicitly refer either to ancient or to medieval philosophers. But they do employ the expressions developed in medieval natural philosophy's accounts of intensity, many of which are retained in Bergson's language. Deleuze writes: "It turns out that, in experience, *intensio* (intension) is inseparable from an *extensio* (extension) which relates it [i.e., intension] to the *extensum* (extensity)."[59] This is in the context of his effort to argue for the claim that in a system "each intensity is already a coupling. . . , thereby revealing the properly qualitative content of quantity."[60] Although it simplifies matters too much to make as a complete claim, we can say that in *Bergsonism* Deleuze aims chiefly to provide a reading of Bergson's thought, while in *Difference and Repetition* he works out his own philosophical proposals. These include a tripartite philosophy of intensity that seeks to lend it a specifically philosophical sense, I wish to suggest, which is not synonymous with any of the scientific conceptions of intensity that treat it as exhaustively definable in purely quantitative terms. The present essay is but a small part of a larger argument that is required to demonstrate the point that Deleuze's conceptions of intensity depart from the scientific conception of intensity as susceptible to adequate and complete quantitative expression.

The quote about intensity as a coupling makes clear that Deleuze wishes to expose an ineliminable qualitative aspect to the kind of energetic quantities he treats in these important passages on intensity and physical science. Above, we noted one reason for which Deleuze considers the identification of a quality with its intensification to be an ontological fault. In addition to that reason, however, Deleuze advances another reason for which this identification would be mistaken. For in *Difference and Repetition* he argues that qualities are ontologically dependent upon intensities, even though our experience of intensities can only take place through our registration of qualities. That is, in this text, Deleuze holds that intensities, although they are the source of sensations and of experience, are not sensed or experienced as intensities themselves. It is the coupling of an intensifying or remitting quality with an extension that is the way in which intensities are registered. In other words, they are only registered by their impact as extended qualities, or qualities as extended. Thus, to identify quality with intensity would be to deny the ontological dependence of quality upon the allegedly more primordial level of intensities.

In *A Thousand Plateaus* (1980), Deleuze and Guattari clearly adopt the medieval language of intensity, although it is difficult to establish all of their sources solely from that text with any sense of certainty. We can, however, identify two evident references to medieval thought on intensity in the work. In Plateau 10. "1730: Becoming-Intense, Becoming-Animal, Becoming-Imperceptible. . . ," Deleuze and Guattari offer a discussion of the problem of accidental forms that explicitly refers to Nicolas Oresme, directing readers to "Pierre Duhem's classic work *Le système du monde*" (1913–1959) on Oresme and "the problem of intensities in the Middle Ages."[61] The same section, "Memories of a Theologian," makes explicit reference to Duns Scotus's concept of a haecceity.[62] Here, we see repeated the exact terms of the medieval debate on intensive variation: "accidental forms are susceptible to *more and less*: more or less charitable, but also more or less white, more or less warm. A degree of heat is a perfectly individuated warmth distinct from the substance or subject that receives it."[63] The allusion is imprecise and is likely to Scotus's unique ontology of intensity, with scarce care for the immensely complex detail of that ontology. Explicit reference to Oresme seems to endorse the composition of intensities and their charting in terms of "latitudes" and "longitudes." Part of the effort here is to gesture toward an ontology of individuals distinguished or composed of intensities. However, when we compare the hasty discussion in this section with the extremely refined and nuanced theoretical armories developed by medieval philosophers of intensity, Deleuze and Guattari appear to have created their own composite of quite different medieval approaches to conceiving of intensive variation. Here, it seems that the important insights they wish to draw from medieval thought, chiefly via Duhem's work, are the notions that intensities can be individuating and that there is a singular reality in intensity that cannot be explicated in purely quantitative terms.

In *What is Philosophy?* (1991), Deleuze and Guattari return to the work of Nicolas Oresme, in reference to Pierre Duhem and to Gilles Châtelet's "La toile, le spectre, la pendule," in *Figuring Space: Philosophy, Mathematics, and Physics.*[64] Their chief concern here is the Oresmian moment in the history of the concept of intensity in which we find a graphic means for the representational composition of intensities with extensities. These pages in *What is Philosophy?* contain a clear philosophical employment of this idea of the Oresmian composition of intensities and extensities, as well as of the later practice of coordinating intensities and extensities in a properly coordinate system. However, it is critical to notice that this employment is precisely *not* an endorsement of such a coordinative concept of intensity in the field of philosophy. Indeed, the coordination of intensities with extensities is a mark of the *non*-philosophical. For *What is Philosophy?* in fact argues that this coordinative concept of intensity is a characteristic mark of a logical, mathematical or scientific project, and not of a properly philosophical one. It is absolutely clear that in this text Deleuze and Guattari in no way are adopting the fully extensive and quantitative construal of an intensity that we find in our contemporary physical, and other, sciences.[65] Indeed, it appears that Deleuze himself never endorses a contemporary physical notion of intensity for *philosophical* and ontological purposes. As *What is Philosophy?* makes clear, this position does not imply that contemporary scientific conceptions of intensity are illegitimate in their scientific uses. It means, rather, that Deleuze does not adopt any of these conceptions, especially on their own self-understandings, for his own philosophical constructions.

Given this synoptic reconstruction of some high points in the history of the philosophical concept of intensity, one might wonder whether Deleuze would endorse Aristotle's philosophy of qualitative change and in particular whether he would favor Aristotle's non-quantitative account of qualitative change. There are a number of reasons to suppose that Deleuze would not find Aristotle's account acceptable. For present purposes, perhaps the plainest such reason is that Aristotle's account, given in terms of act, actualization and potential, does not conform well to Deleuze's express ontological commitments throughout his works. We know that Deleuze rejects the Aristotelian ontology of potential and actualization as well as a Bergsonian metaphysics of possibility. On this matter, his thinking is much closer to that of Spinoza, Ruyer, and Simondon. For his use of the notion of actualization rejects the ontology of potential in favor of a specific Deleuzian conception of the virtual. Neither Aristotle nor Bergson appears to have supplied Deleuze with satisfactory ontologies of the potential.

5. Conclusion

Deleuze contrasts science, a practice in which a plane or level of reference is constructed by means of functions, to philosophy, a practice for the creation of concepts on a plane or level of immanence, or consistency.[66] To refer, for Deleuze, is to co-order at least two different variables within a limited plane or field or system of reference. Reference is essentially a coordinated location of an ontological mixture. The difference between co-ordinates and co-ordination, on the one hand, and ordinates and ordination, on the other hand, is critical here. The domain of intensity, philosophy and the concept is the domain of the ordinate, not of the co-ordinate. An intensity is essentially a set of ordered differences, not co-ordered differences.

We may return to Shapiro's above quoted question and, in a provisional manner, hypothesize that for Deleuze there is a difference between a given temperature and a given measured temperature. The temperature would be an intensive ordinate; the measured temperature would be the co-ordination of such an intensive ordinate of temperature with the extended substance of, say, the mercury of a mercury thermometer. The extension of the mercury would be the extensive expression of the intensive ordinate of temperature, or its co-ordination with the extended mercury.

Deleuze's position is that science and philosophy are distinguished, and are to be distinguished, in part on the basis of the question of the neutralization of intensities. The modern mechanician, who does not and need not notice that an extensive and an intensive quantity have been rendered in a common extensive quantity, is not taking this distinction to be relevant to his or her intellectual project. Science is a practice of establishing coordinate systems, and working with the functions that they permit. Philosophy will be the intellectual pursuit that attends to intensities, in addition to tending to them: the concept, the chief creation of the practice of philosophy, is essentially intensive. In this way, then, the stakes of the question of the nature of intensity become the stakes of the proper province of philosophy.

A difficult philosophical problem also emerges from this review of the history of the concept of intensity thus far, if we seek to identify the quantitative or qualitative nature of a given historical conception of intensity under examination. This is the problem of which definitions of quality and quantity to employ—from amongst the unfolding and varying theoretical accounts of intensification that we find in the history of philosophy—in order to designate a conception as qualitative or quantitative. For it appears that to answer the question of when, how and to what extent a conception of intensity is qualitative or quantitative will require us to adopt at least a working definition that provisionally relates to the very terms under examination—quantity and quality—although this definition may or may not be identical to any of the definitions catalogued in the history under review. Whenever, then, we want to assert that a conception of intensive change is qualitative or quantitative, we should ideally at least specify as clearly as possible which senses of those terms we are employing. Subsequent work on the problem will need to tie our claim that Deleuze's conception of intensity retains a non-quantitative aspect to the specific definitions of quantity offered in the history of philosophy tributary to Deleuze's thought.

Notes

1. See especially Simon Duffy, *The Logic of Expression: Quality, Quantity and Intensity in Spinoza, Hegel and Deleuze* (Aldershot, UK: Ashgate, 2006); Daniel Smith, *Essays on Deleuze* (Edinburgh: Edinburgh University Press, 2012); Juliette Simont, *Essai sur la quantité, la qualité, la relation chez Kant, Hegel, Deleuze: Les "fleurs noires" de la logique philosophique* (Paris: Éditions L'Harmattan, 1997). Important work on Deleuze's ontology of intensity has been carried out by many others, including: Keith Ansell-Pearson, Alain Beaulieu, Michel de Beistegui, Jeffrey Bell, Véronique Bergen, Levi Bryant, Claire Colebrook, Manuel DeLanda, Peter Gaffney, Peter Hallward, Joe Hughes, Leonard Lawlor, Jean-Clet Martin, Dorothea Olkowski, Paul Patton, John Protevi, Jon Roffe, Anne Sauvagnargues, Judith Wambacq, François Zourabichvili.

2. See Peter Hallward, *Out of This World: Deleuze and the Philosophy of Creation* (London and New York: Verso, 2006); John Protevi, "Review of Hallward, *Out of This World: Deleuze and the Philosophy of Creation*," *Notre Dame Philosophical Reviews: An Electronic Journal*, 2007.08.03. http://ndpr.nd.edu/news/23058-out-of-this-world-deleuze-and-the-philosophy-of-creation.

3. See, for example, Manuel DeLanda, *Intensive Science and Virtual Philosophy* (London: Continuum, 2002).

4. This chapter does not address the content of the individual philosophy of Félix Guattari or seek to distinguish it from that of Gilles Deleuze in their co-authored works.

5. Jeannine Quillet, ed., *Autour de Nicole Oresme* (Paris: Librairie Philosophique J. Vrin, 1990).

6. Herman Shapiro, "Walter Burley and the Intension and Remission of Forms," *Speculum* 34, no. 3 (July 1959): 416–7, n 8.

7. We here rely upon a number of Prof. Solère's essays, but recommend in particular: Jean-Luc Solère, "The Question of Intensive Magnitudes According to Some Jesuits in the Sixteenth and Seventeenth Centuries," *The Monist* 84, no. 4 (2001): 582–616; "Tension et intention. Esquisse de l'histoire d'une notion," in *Questions sur l'Intentionnalité*, eds. L. Couloubaritsis and A. Mazzù (Bruxelles: Ousia, 2007), 59–124; "Plus ou moins: le vocabulaire de la latitude des formes," in *L'Élaboration du vocabu-*

laire philosophique au Moyen Âge, eds. J. Hamesse and C. Steel (Turnhout: Brepols, "Rencontres de Philosophie médiévale" 8, 2000), 437–488.

8. See "Bibliography" for the major works of these scholars of medieval thought that treat the topic of medieval philosophy of intensity.

9. Solère, "The Question of Intensive Magnitudes According to Some Jesuits in the Sixteenth and Seventeenth Centuries," 582.

10. Aristotle, *Categories* 8.10b26–11a4.

11. Aristotle, *Categories* 5.4a 3–4, my emphasis. See also Jean-Luc Solère, "D'un commentaire à l'autre: l'interaction entre philosophie et théologie au Moyen Âge, dans le problème de l'intensification des formes," in *Le Commentaire entre tradition et innovation*, ed. M.-O. Goulet (Paris: Vrin, "Bibliothèque d'histoire de la philosophie" nouvelle série, 2000), 411, n. 1.

12. Jean-Luc Solère, "The Question of Intensive Magnitudes According to Some Jesuits in the Sixteenth and Seventeenth Centuries," 583. Aristotle, *Physics* 5.2.226b1–2, 7.2.244b6–12.

13. Jean-Luc Solère, "Thomas d'Aquin et les variations qualitatives," in *Compléments de Substance (Études sur les Propriétés Accidentelles offertes à Alain de Libera)*, eds. Chr. Erismann and A. Schniewind (Paris: Vrin, 2008), 148. (My translation.) Here the Aristotelian reference is to *Physics* 5. 2.226b1–2.

14. Aristotle, *Categories* 5.3b33: "Substance, it seems, does not admit of a more and a less." *Categories* 6.6a19: "A quantity does not seem to admit of a more and a less."

15. Aristotle, *Categories* 8.8b26; *Categories* 8.9a14; *Categories* 8.9a28.

16. See Aristotle, *Categories* 8.11a5.

17. Aristotle, *Categories* 14.15a13.

18. Aristotle, *Physics* 5.2.226a30.

19. Aristotle, *Physics* 5.2.226a26.

20. Aristotle, *Categories* 14.15a13 ff., my emphasis.

21. Solère, "The Question of Intensive Magnitudes According to Some Jesuits in the Sixteenth and Seventeenth Centuries," 584.

22. Solère, "The Question of Intensive Magnitudes According to Some Jesuits in the Sixteenth and Seventeenth Centuries," 584.

23. Solère, "Plus ou moins: le vocabulaire de la latitude des formes," 460. (My translation.)

24. Solère, "Thomas d'Aquin et les variations qualitatives,"148. (My translation.)

25. Solère, "Plus ou moins: le vocabulaire de la latitude des formes," 460. (My translation.)

26. Solère, "The Question of Intensive Magnitudes According to Some Jesuits in the Sixteenth and Seventeenth Centuries," 583.

27. See Solère, "The Question of Intensive Magnitudes According to Some Jesuits in the Sixteenth and Seventeenth Centuries," 584ff.

28. Solère, "The Question of Intensive Magnitudes According to Some Jesuits in the Sixteenth and Seventeenth Centuries," 584. For a nuanced qualification of this point as a matter of Aristotle interpretation, see "The Question of Intensive Magnitudes According to Some Jesuits in the Sixteenth and Seventeenth Centuries," 609, n. 20.

29. Solère, "The Question of Intensive Magnitudes According to Some Jesuits in the Sixteenth and Seventeenth Centuries," 585. The pertinent reference in Aristotle is *De Generatione et Corruptione* 1.5.320b30–31.

30. Solère, "The Question of Intensive Magnitudes According to Some Jesuits in the Sixteenth and Seventeenth Centuries," 584. The pertinent reference in Aristotle is *De Generatione et Corruptione* 1.5.321a4–5, 1.5.321a20–21, 1.5.321b13.

31. The chief centers for this late medieval natural philosophy were Paris and Oxford, according to Anneliese Maier. See Anneliese Maier, *On the Threshold of Exact Science: Selected Writings of Anneliese Maier on Late Medieval Natural Philosophy*, ed. and trans. Steven D. Sargent (Philadelphia: University of Pennsylvania Press, 1982), 145.

32. Edith Dudley Sylla, "The Oxford Calculators," in *The Cambridge History of Later Medieval Philosophy*, eds. Norman Kretzman, Anthony Kenny, and Jan Pinborg (Cambridge: Cambridge University Press, 1980), 555. Herman Shapiro, "Walter Burley and the Intension and Remission of Forms," *Speculum* 34, no. 3 (July 1959): 414ff.

33. Maier, *On the Threshold of Exact Science: Selected Writings of Anneliese Maier on Late Medieval Natural Philosophy*, 160.

34. See Solère, "The Question of Intensive Magnitudes According to Some Jesuits in the Sixteenth and Seventeenth Centuries," 586ff.

35. Aquinas, *Summa Theologica* IIa, IIae q. 24, a. 5: "Whether charity increases by addition?"

36. Aquinas, *Summa Theologica* IIa, IIae q. 24, a. 5: "Whether charity increases by addition?"

37. Aristotle, *Physics* 5.2.226b ff. *The Complete Works of Aristotle. The Revised Oxford Translation*, ed. Jonathan Barnes. Vol. 1 (Princeton: Princeton University Press, 1984), 383.

38. Aquinas, *Summa Theologica* IIa, IIae q. 24, a. 5: "Whether charity increases by addition?"

39. Aquinas, *Summa Theologica* IIa, IIae q. 24, a. 5: "Whether charity increases by addition?"

40. Aquinas, *Summa Theologica* IIa, IIae q. 24, a. 5: "Whether charity increases by addition?"

41. Aquinas, *Summa Theologica* IIa, IIae q. 24, a. 4: "Whether charity can increase?"

42. Aquinas, *Summa Theologica* IIa, IIae q. 24, a. 4: "Whether charity can increase?"

43. Solère, "The Question of Intensive Magnitudes According to Some Jesuits in the Sixteenth and Seventeenth Centuries," 587. For Burley's arguments against addition theories, see especially Herman Shapiro, "Walter Burley and the Intension and Remission of Forms," *Speculum* Vol. 34, No. 3 (Jul., 1959), pp. 413–427. On identification of the addition theory's origin, and its attribution to Scotus by A. Maier, see Shapiro, 415, n. 5.

44. Solère, "The Question of Intensive Magnitudes According to Some Jesuits in the Sixteenth and Seventeenth Centuries," 587.

45. Solère, "The Question of Intensive Magnitudes According to Some Jesuits in the Sixteenth and Seventeenth Centuries," 585. Also, see this essay for a fascinating account of some prominent 16th century addition theorists' arguments against succession theory.

46. The property of changing in species by means of addition or subtraction finds a related thesis in the view espoused by both Bergson and Deleuze that intensive phenomena are characterized by a kind of divisibility that produces change in species or change in measure.

47. Solère, "The Question of Intensive Magnitudes According to Some Jesuits in the Sixteenth and Seventeenth Centuries," 587.

48. Solère, "The Question of Intensive Magnitudes According to Some Jesuits in the Sixteenth and Seventeenth Centuries," 587.

49. Deleuze refers by name to Oresme in Gilles Deleuze and Félix Guattari, *A Thousand Plateaus: Capitalism and Schizophrenia* (Minneapolis: Minnesota University Press, 1987), 253; 540, n. 29; and Gilles Deleuze and Félix Guattari, *What is Philosophy?*, trans.

Hugh Tomlinson and Graham Burchell (New York: Columbia University Press, 1994), 121; 226, n. 3.

50. Cf. Marshall Clagett, *Nicole Oresme and the Medieval Geometry of Qualities and Motions: A Treatise on the Uniformity and Difformity of Intensities Known As* Tractatus de configurationibus qualitatum et motuum (Madison: University of Wisconsin Press, 1968), 14.

51. Anneliese Maier, *On the Threshold of Exact Science: Selected Writings of Anneliese Maier on Late Medieval Natural Philosophy,* 39.

52. Gilles Châtelet, *Figuring Space: Philosophy, Mathematics, and Physics,* trans. Robert Shore and Muriel Zagha (Dordrecht, Netherlands: Kluwer Academic Publishers, 2000).

53. Châtelet, *Figuring Space: Philosophy, Mathematics, and Physics,* 39–40.

54. Châtelet, *Figuring Space: Philosophy, Mathematics, and Physics,* 44. (My translation.)

55. Georges Molland, "The Oresmian Style," in *Nicolas Oresme, Tradition et innovation chez un intellectuel du XIVème siècle,* eds. P. Souffrin and A. Ph. Segonds (Paris: Les Belles Lettres, 1988), 23. (My translation.)

56. Gilles Deleuze, *Bergsonism.* Trans. Hugh Tomlinson and Barbara Habberjam. (New York: Zone Books. 1991),19.

57. Deleuze, *Bergsonism,* 91–92.

58. Gilles Deleuze, *Difference and Repetition.* New York: Columbia University Press, 1994), 222–223.

59. Deleuze, *Difference and Repetition,* 223.

60. Deleuze, *Difference and Repetition,* 222.

61. Deleuze and Guattari, *A Thousand Plateaus,* 540, n. 29.

62. Deleuze and Guattari, *A Thousand Plateaus,* 252–3; 540, n. 33.

63. Deleuze and Guattari, *A Thousand Plateaus,* 253.

64. Deleuze and Guattari, *What is Philosophy?,* 121; 226, n. 3.

65. For more on this stark differentiation in conceptions of intensity and their use, see Deleuze and Guattari, *What is Philosophy?,* Chapter 5: "Functives and Concepts," 117–133, especially 121 ff.

66. Deleuze and Guattari, *What is Philosophy?,* 216; Gilles Deleuze and Félix Guattari, *Qu'est-ce que la philosophie?* (Paris: Les Éditions de Minuit, 1991), 204.

References

Aristotle. *Categories* and *De Interpretatione.* Translated by J.K. Ackrill. Oxford: Clarendon Press, 1963.

Aristotle. *The Complete Works of Aristotle. The Revised Oxford Translation.* Edited by Jonathan Barnes. Vol. 1. Princeton: Princeton University Press, 1984.

Châtelet, Gilles. *Figuring Space: Philosophy, Mathematics, and Physics.* Translated by Robert Shore and Muriel Zagha. Dordrecht, Netherlands: Kluwer Academic Publishers, 2000.

———. *Les Enjeux du mobile: Mathématiques, physique, philosophie.* Paris: Éditions du Seuil, 1993.

Clagett, Marshall. *Nicole Oresme and the Medieval Geometry of Qualities and Motions: A Treatise on the Uniformity and Difformity of Intensities Known As* Tractatus de configurationibus qualitatum et motuum. Madison: University of Wisconsin Press, 1968.

―――. *The Science of Mechanics in the Middle Ages.* Madison, WI: University of Wisconsin Press, 1959.

Couloubaritsis, L. and A. Mazzù, eds. *Questions sur l'Intentionnalité.* Bruxelles: Ousia, 2007.

DeLanda, Manuel. *Intensive Science and Virtual Philosophy.* London & New York: Continuum, 2002.

Deleuze, Gilles. *Le Bergsonisme.* Paris: Presses Universitaires de France, 1966.

―――. *Différence et Répétition.* Paris: Presses Universitaires de France, 1968.

―――. *Foucault.* Translated by Sean Hand. Minneapolis: University of Minnesota Press, 1988.

―――. *Bergsonism.* Translated by Hugh Tomlinson and Barbara Habberjam. New York: Zone Books, 1991.

―――. *Difference and Repetition.* Translated by Paul Patton. New York: Columbia University Press, 1994.

―――. *Francis Bacon. Logique de la sensation.* Paris: Éditions du Seuil, 2002.

―――. *L'Île Déserte et autres textes.* Paris: Les Éditions de Minuit, 2002.

―――. *Francis Bacon. The Logic of Sensation.* Translated by Daniel W. Smith. Minneapolis: University of Minnesota Press, 2003.

―――. *Desert Islands and Other Texts: 1953 1974.* Translated by Mike Taormina. New York: Semiotext(e), 2004.

Deleuze, Gilles and Félix Guattari. *Anti-Oedipus: Capitalism and Schizophrenia.* Translated by Robert Hurley, Mark Seem, Helen R. Lane. Minneapolis: Minnesota University Press, 1983.

―――. *A Thousand Plateaus: Capitalism and Schizophrenia.* Translated by Brian Massumi. Minneapolis: Minnesota University Press, 1987.

―――. *Mille Plateaux: Capitalisme et schizophrénie, tome 2.* Paris: Les Éditions de Minuit, 1980.

―――. *Qu'est-ce que la philosophie?* Paris: Les Éditions de Minuit, 1991.

―――. *Expressionism in Philosophy: Spinoza.* Translated by Martin Joughin. New York: Zone Books, 1992.

―――. *What is Philosophy?* Translated by Hugh Tomlinson and Graham Burchell. New York: Columbia University Press, 1994.

Duffy, Simon. *Virtual Mathematics: The Logic of Difference.* Bolton, UK: Clinamen Press, 2006.

―――. *The Logic of Expression: Quality, Quantity and Intensity in Spinoza, Hegel and Deleuze.* Aldershot, UK: Ashgate, 2006.

Duhem, Pierre. *Le système du monde.* Vol. 7, *La physique parisienne au XIVᵉ siècle.* Paris: Hermann, 1913–1959. See esp. chap. 6, "La latitude des formes. Nicole Oresme et ses disciple parisiens."

Hallward, Peter. *Out of This World: Deleuze and the Philosophy of Creation.* London and New York: Verso, 2006.

Hamesse, J. and C. Steel, eds. *L'Élaboration du vocabulaire philosophique au Moyen Âge.* Turnhout: Brepols Publishers. "Rencontres de Philosophie médiévale" no. 8, 2000.

Mader, Mary Beth. *Sleights of Reason: Norm, Bisexuality, Development.* Albany: State University of New York (SUNY) Press, 2011.

Maier, Anneliese. *On the Threshold of Exact Science: Selected Writings of Anneliese Maier on Late Medieval Natural Philosophy*. Edited and translated by Steven D. Sargent. Philadelphia: University of Pennsylvania Press, 1982.

Molland, Georges. "The Oresmian Style: Semi-Mathematical, Semi-Holistic." In *Nicolas Oresme, Tradition et innovation chez un intellectuel du XIVe siècle*. Edited by P. Souffrin and A. Ph. Segonds. 13–30. Paris: Les Belles Lettres, 1988.

Murdoch, John E. and Sylla, Edith D. "The Science of Motion." In *Science in the Middle Ages*. Edited by David C. Lindberg. 206–64. Chicago: University of Chicago Press, 1978.

Quillet, Jeannine, ed. *Autour de Nicole Oresme*. Paris: Librairie Philosophique J. Vrin, 1990.

Protevi, John. "Review of Hallward, *Out of This World: Deleuze and the Philosophy of Creation*." *Notre Dame Philosophical Reviews: An Electronic Journal*, 2007.08.03. http://ndpr.nd.edu/news/23058-out-of-this-world-deleuze-and-the-philosophy-of-creation.

Shapiro, Herman. "Walter Burley and the Intension and Remission of Forms." *Speculum* 34, no. 3 (July 1959): 413–427.

Smith, Daniel. *Essays on Deleuze*. Edinburgh: Edinburgh University Press, 2012.

Solère, Jean-Luc. "Thomas d'Aquin et les variations qualitatives." In *Compléments de Substance (Études sur les Propriétés Accidentelles offertes à Alain de Libera)*. Edited by Chr. Erismann & A. Schniewind. 147–165. Paris: Vrin, "Problèmes & Controverses," 2008.

———. "Tension et intention. Esquisse de l'histoire d'une notion." In *Questions sur l'Intentionnalité*. Edited by L. Couloubaritsis & A. Mazzù. 59–124. Bruxelles: Ousia, 2007.

———. "The Question of Intensive Magnitudes According to Some Jesuits in the Sixteenth and Seventeenth Centuries." *The Monist* 84, no. 4 (2001): 582–616.

———. "Plus ou moins: le vocabulaire de la latitude des forms." In *L'Élaboration du vocabulaire philosophique au Moyen Âge*. Edited by J. Hamesse and C. Steel, 437–488. Turnhout: Brepols, "Rencontres de Philosophie medieval" 8, 2000.

———. "D'un commentaire à l'autre: l'interaction entre philosophie et théologie au Moyen Âge, dans le problème de l'intensification des forms." In *Le Commentaire entre tradition et innovation*. Edited by M.-O. Goulet, 411–424. Paris: Vrin, "Bibliothèque d'histoire de la philosophie" nouvelle série, 2000.

Souffrin, Pierre. "La quantification du movement chez les scolastiques: La vitesse instantanée chez Nicole Oresme." In *Autour de Nicole Oresme*. Edited by Jeannine Quillet, 63–83. Paris: Libraire Philosophique J. Vrin, 1990.

Souffrin, P. and Segonds, A. Ph. *Nicolas Oresme, Tradition et innovation chez un intellectuel du XIVe siècle*. Paris: Les Belles Lettres, 1988.

Souffrin, P. and Weiss, J. P. "Le Traité des configurations des qualités et des mouvements: Remarques sur quelques problèmes d'interprétation et de traduction." *Nicolas Oresme, Tradition et innovation chez un intellectuel du XIVe siècle*. Edited by Souffrin, P. and Segonds, A. Ph., 125–134. Paris: Les Belles Lettres, 1988.

Oresme, Nicole. "Tractatus de Configurationibus Qualitatum et Motuum." Trans. P. Souffrin and J.P Weiss. In *Nicolas Oresme, Tradition et innovation chez un intellectuel du XIVe siècle*. Edited by Souffrin, P. and Segonds, A. Ph., 135–144. Paris: Les Belles Lettres, 1988.

Sylla, Edith Dudley. "The Oxford Calculators." In *The Cambridge History of Later Medieval Philosophy*. Edited by Kretzman, Norman, Kenny, Anthony, and Pinborg, Jan. 540–63. Cambridge: Cambridge University Press, 1980.

ABOUT THE CONTRIBUTORS

ALBERTO ANELLI studied theology in Italy, Germany, and the United States and received his specialized Licentiate in Systematic Theology from the Facoltà Teologica dell'Italia Settentrionale (Milan). He studied philosophy at the University of Freiburg (Germany) from which he received his PhD. His books include *Processualità e definitività. La teologia a confronto con Whitehead* (2004), *Heidegger und die Theologie. Prolegomena zur zukünftigen theologischen Nutzung des Denkens Martin Heideggers* (2008), and *Heidegger e la teologia* (2011). He is editor of *Heidegger. Tra filosofia e teologia* (2013) and is currently working on two books: one on Heidegger and the problem of evil and another on gender in a philosophical and theological perspective. He is also the author of a number of articles, and the editor and translator of several works.

ALAIN BEAULIEU is associate professor of philosophy at Laurentian University (Canada). He has a Doctorat de 3ᵉ cycle in philosophy from the Université de Paris 8 with a thesis on *Gilles Deleuze et la phénoménologie* (Sils Maria/Vrin, 2ⁿᵈ ed. 2006). He has published *Cuerpo y acontecimiento. La estética de Gilles Deleuze* (Buenos Aires, Letra Viva, 2012), *Gilles Deleuze et ses contemporains* (Harmattan, 2011) and (co)edited the following works: *Abécédaire de Martin Heidegger* (Sils Maria/Vrin, 2008), *Michel Foucault and Power Today* (Lexington, 2006), *Gilles Deleuze. Héritage philosophique* (PUF, 2005), as well as *Michel Foucault et le contrôle social* (Presses de l'Université Laval, 2ⁿᵈ ed. 2008). He is also co-editor of *Foucault Studies*.

ROCCO GANGLE is associate professor of philosophy at Endicott College. His articles have appeared in *Philosophy Today*, *Synthese*, *Substance*, *Political Theology*, and the *Logic Journal of IGPL* among other journals and edited collections. He has translated the work of Francois Laruelle and is the author of Francois Laruelle's *Philosophies of Difference: A Critical Introduction and Guide* (Edinburgh University Press, 2013).

GREGORY KALYNIUK is currently completing his PhD in the Cultural Studies Program at Trent University in Peterborough (Ontario, Canada), where he has led seminars on Modern Culture and Science Fiction over the past four years. His previous academic background is in philosophy and social and cultural anthropology. His areas of interest include continental philosophy, psychoanalysis, literature, and the history of medicine. His dissertation, entitled *Individuation, Intensity, and Humour in Deleuze's Philosophy*, elucidates Deleuze's theory of humour by connecting its different instances in his *oeuvre* while extrapolating upon some of its loose ends.

EDWARD KAZARIAN teaches in the Philosophy and Religion Studies Department at Rowan University. He received his PhD in 2009 from Villanova University, with a dissertation entitled *The Science of Events: Deleuze and Psychoanalysis*. His research centers on twentieth and twenty-first century French philosophy and psychoanlaysis, especially Deleuze and Guattari, Foucault, and François Laruelle. He has published articles in *Substance* and *International Studies in Philosophy*, and is co-translating François Laruelle's *Mystique non-philosophique à la usage des contemporains* (with Joshua Ramey).

MARY BETH MADER is professor of philosophy at the University of Memphis, where she specializes in recent and contemporary continental philosophy; feminist philosophy; twentieth Century French philosophy; ontology; and continental philosophy and the life sciences. She is the author of *Sleights of Reason: Norm, Bisexuality, Development* (SUNY Press, 2011), and articles on the work of Luce Irigaray, Michel Foucault and Sarah Kofman. She is the translator of Luce Irigaray's book, *The Forgetting of Air in Martin Heidegger*, Léopold Senghor's "What the Black Man Contributes," and Emmanuel Levinas' "Being Jewish." Her current work focuses on the history of the philosophical concept of intensity in relation to the thought of Gilles Deleuze.

THOMAS NAIL is an assistant professor of philosophy at the University of Denver. He is the author of *Returning to Revolution: Deleuze, Guattari and Zapatismo* (Edinburgh University Press, 2012) and is currently finishing a monograph on the political philosophy of migration entitled, *The Figure of the Migrant* (under contract with Stanford University Press). His work has appeared in *Angelaki*, *Theory & Event*, *Philosophy Today*, *Parrhesia*, *Deleuze Studies*, *Foucault Studies*, and elsewhere. A complete list of his publications can be found at http://du.academia.edu/thomasnail.

JOSHUA RAMEY is the author of *The Hermetic Deleuze: Philosophy and Spiritual Ordeal*, and the editor of *SubStance* 39.2: Spiritual Politics After Deleuze. He is currently co-translating François Laruelle's Mystique non-philosophique à l'usage des contemporains (with Edward Kazarian) and writing a new monograph, *Politics of Divination: Neoliberal Endgame and the Religion of Contingency* (Palgrave Macmillan). He is assistant professor of philosophy at Grinnell College.

JULIA SUSHYTSKA teaches at Pacifica Graduate Institute. Her areas of expertise are ancient Greek and twentieth century continental philosophy. Her research focuses on convergences between ideas of Ancient Greek philosophers—especially of Parmenides, Heraclitus, and Plato—and the work of twentieth century thinkers, in particular Gilles Deleuze, Alain Badiou, and Julia Kristeva. Her essay on Plato's Republic, "On the non-Rivalry between Poetry and Philosophy: Plato's Republic, Reconsidered," appeared in an interdisciplinary journal *Mosaic*, and an article on Tarkovsky's film *Nostalghia* is forthcoming in the *Journal of Aesthetic Education*. Her work on the philosophical notion of Eastern Europe appeared in a special issue of *Angelaki*, as well as in edited volumes published by Routledge and Wehrhahn Verlag. Sushytska is currently working on a manuscript entitled *Internal Strangers and the Transformation of the Polis*, in which she argues that metics, or resident aliens, are indispensable for the existence of political, cultural, and philosophical places.

ADRIAN SWITZER is an assistant professor in the Department of Philosophy at the University of Missouri Kansas City. The co-translator of *Parmenides, Cosmos and Being* (Marquette, 2008), contributor to the *Cambridge Foucault Lexicon* (Cambridge, 2014), and author of articles and book chapters on Kant, Foucault, Deleuze, Merleau-Ponty, Irigaray, Nietzsche and Jean-Luc Nancy, Dr. Switzer is currently completing a manuscript on Nietzsche's political philosophy.

SJOERD VAN TUINEN is assistant professor in philosophy at Erasmus University Rotterdam and Coordinator of the Centre for Art and Philosophy (www.caponline.org). He is editor of several books, including *Deleuze Compendium* (Amsterdam: Boom, 2009), *Deleuze and The Fold. A Critical Reader* (Basingstoke: Palgrave Macmillan, 2010) *De nieuwe Franse filosofie* (Amsterdam: Boom, 2011), and *Giving and Taking. Antidotes to a Culture of Greed* (V2, NAi), and has authored *Sloterdijk. Binnenstebuiten denken* (Kampen: Klement, 2004). Van Tuinen has been awarded a VENI scholarship from the Netherlands Organisation for Scientific Research (2012–2016) for a research project on *ressentiment* and democracy. He is also preparing a book in which he proposes a speculative concept of Mannerism, entitled *Matter, Manner, Idea: Deleuze and Mannerism*. See also www.svtuinen.nl.

ARNAULD VILLANI has taught philosophy for many years at the khâgne level (preparatory course for arts section of the École normale supérieure) at Lycée Masséna in Nice. His first book was on Kafka. He then became interested to Gilles Deleuze, to whom he dedicated two books (*La Guêpe et l'orchidée*, Belin, 1999; *Le Vocabulaire de Gilles Deleuze*, co-ed., CHRI/Vrin, 2002) as well as many articles. He co-translated Alfred North Whitehead's *Process and Reality*

(Gallimard, 1995) and the work of the German poet Peter Huchel (Atelier la Feugraie, 2009 and 2011). He recently published a new translation and a commentary on Parmenides' *Poem* (Hermann, 2011). His publications also include *Petites Méditations métaphysiques sur la vie et la mort* (Hermann, 2008) as well as *Court Traité du rien* (Hermann, 2009). He is currently preparing a book on poetry and another one on the *Logique de Deleuze*.

DANIEL WHISTLER is lecturer in philosophy at the University of Liverpool. He is the author of *Schelling's Theory of Symbolic Language: Forming the System of Identity* (Oxford University Press, 2013) and *The Right to Wear Religious Symbols* (with Daniel J. Hill; Palgrave, 2013). He is also co-editor of *After the Postsecular and the Postmodern: New Essays in Continental Philosophy of Religion* (CSP, 2010) and *Moral Powers, Fragile Beliefs: Essays in Moral and Religious Philosophy* (Continuum, 2011).

INDEX